Parliaments and Legislatures Series

Parliaments and Legislatures Series

Comparing
Post-Soviet Legislatures

A Theory of Institutional Design
and Political Conflict

Joel M. Ostrow

OHIO STATE UNIVERSITY PRESS / *Columbus*

Library of Congress Cataloging-in-Publication Data

Ostrow, Joel M.
    Comparing post-Soviet legislatures : a theory of institutional design and political
conflict / Joel M. Ostrow.
      p.   cm. — (Parliaments and legislatures series)
    Includes bibliographical references and index.
    ISBN 0-8142-0841-X (alk. paper) — ISBN 0-8142-5044-0 (pbk. : alk. paper)
    1. Russia (Federation. Federal'noe Sobranie.   2. Russian (Federation). Federal'noe
Sobranie. Gosudarstvennaia Duma.   3. Legislative bodies — Russia (Federation).
4. Estonia. Riigikogu.   5. Legislative bodies — Estonia.   I. Title.   II. Series.

   JN6697.7 .O85 2000
   328.47'09'049 — dc21   99-059121

Cover design by Gore Studio
Type set in Janson Text by Keystone Typesetting, Inc.
Printed by McNaughton & Gunn

The paper used in this publication meets the minimum requirements of the American
National Standard for Information Sciences — Permanence of Paper for Printed Library
Materials. ANSI Z39.48–1992.

9 8 7 6 5 4 3 2 1

To my parents,

RICHARD D. AND BARBARA R. OSTROW,

for supporting me far too well, far too long for words to suffice

CONTENTS

Foreword   viii

Acknowledgments   x

Introduction   A Theory of Comparative Legislatures: Institutional
Design and Legislative Conflict   1

Part 1   The Russian Supreme Soviet
A Well-Oiled Machine, Out of Control   29

1   The Nonpartisan, Committee-Centered Supreme Soviet   35

2   A Well-Oiled Legislative Machine   46

3   External Activities: A Machine Out of Control   72

Part 2   The Russian State Duma
Complete Chaos, Under Control   93

4   The State Duma: An Unlinked, Dual-Channel Design   99

5   Procedural Breakdown and Deadlock in the Duma   118

6   External Activities: Negotiation and Cooperation   159

Part 3   The Estonian Riigikogu
The Benefits of a Linked, Dual-Channel Design   193

7   How Linkage Promotes Conflict Management   195

Conclusion   Designing Legislatures: Prescriptive Lessons,
for Russia and Beyond   229

Notes   251

Bibliography   289

Index   301

FOREWORD

An important aim of research on parliamentary institutions is to develop a genuinely comparative theoretical framework for such research, a framework that entertains the collection of empirical data about parliamentary institutions and behavior. In this book, Joel M. Ostrow engages in such theorizing and empirical analysis for the Russian Supreme Soviet, the Russian State Duma, and the Estonian parliament. These parliaments are creatures of the 1990s, established in the aftermath of the demise of the Soviet Union (USSR). Observations about their institutional design, their behavior, and their performance could be made as these parliaments emerged and began to develop their institutional personae.

As parliamentary institutions go, these bodies in Russia and Estonia are very new. Although they may draw upon European parliamentary experience, Russian and Estonian legislators have been opening new institutional territory without much experience in the rigors and practices of parliamentary democracy. How do they do it? What is more, scholars have only limited experience in studying parliamentary life in the Russian setting. Ostrow's research breaks new ground and is one of only a few empirical studies of emerging parliamentary government within the old Soviet orbit. Often drawing on the experience of scholars of the U.S. Congress, Ostrow has amassed a rich array of documentary, eyewitness, and interview data to analyze parliamentary operations in Russia and Estonia.

This study focuses upon the institutional design of legislatures, particularly anatomizing parliamentary political parties and legislative committees in the two Russian and the Estonian parliaments. Was the downfall of the Supreme Soviet caused by design failure? How has its successor, the State Duma, functioned under different structural conditions? In contrast, what accounts for the comparatively smooth operation of the Estonian legislature? The author conducts his inquiry into these matters by following the streams of the budgetary process in these systems, for it is there that the crucial conflicts of national politics are played out.

He enjoyed a remarkable opportunity to accumulate observations about budgeting in the Russian State Duma as a "fly on the wall" — attending

1994 Budget Committee meetings and interviewing members. Earlier in the 1990s, the author had observed the operation of the Supreme Soviet firsthand. In addition, he conducted interviews with members of the budget committee of the Estonian parliament, and was able to utilize transcriptions of budget debates. This rich cache of empirical resources, rigorously analyzed, makes this study an important contribution to understanding how the design of parliamentary institutions may mold and shape their performance.

Samuel C. Patterson

ACKNOWLEDGMENTS

If any book was ever the fruit of the efforts of many, this is the book. None has been more influential than George W. Breslauer, my dissertation advisor at Berkeley. No graduate student ever had a more dedicated advisor. George took an active role in this project as the research phase was coming to a close, and it was the greatest stroke of luck in my entire academic career. He provided meticulous comments on lengthy drafts with enthusiasm and mind-boggling rapidity; creative and insightful methodological, theoretical, and organizational suggestions; and untiring efforts to promote my virtues to prospective employers and anyone else who cared to listen. George set a standard I can only dream of approaching in my relations to my own students. I thank him for showing me what advisor-student relations should be like, after having unfortunately experienced what they most certainly should not be like.

Others at Berkeley were extremely influential in the shaping of this project. Nelson W. Polsby always seemed to know just what it was I needed to read. My education on legislatures and on institutions benefited from his sage advice and from his incredible availability and willingness to explain things to this interloper from Soviet Studies. To Chris Ansell I owe deep gratitude for sharing with me his concept of "dual channels." Henry Brady made valuable contributions at both early and late stages of my research and writing and has helped me to think more theoretically about my material.

The Berkeley Program in Soviet and Post-Soviet Studies and the Department of Political Science provided generous financial support for the research and writing of this dissertation. The BSP also introduced me to the Institute of International Economic and Political Studies in Moscow, which graciously provided me with institutional support during my year and a half of research. Also at Berkeley, Ellen Borrowman and Anne Faye deserve medals in recognition of their tremendous service to the political science department. I'd also like to thank the Professional Development Fund at Benedictine University for generously providing funds, on very short notice, that enabled production of an index for the book.

I guaranteed my interview subjects in Russia and Estonia anonymity, so I must issue a collective thanks to the hundreds of legislators, government officials, and staff members who gave of their precious time to answer what must have seemed to many to be truly odd questions! I also thank them for their assistance more generally. However, I have to thank by name the chairs of the Budget Committees of the Russian Supreme Soviet and the Russian State Duma, Aleksandr P. Pochinok and Mikhail M. Zadornov, respectively. Zadornov opened the doors of his Committee to me, providing me not only access to the process but also access to the people and the papers that made this study possible. Pochinok steered me to the people and the documents that survived the destruction of the Supreme Soviet, and he and his assistants never tired of explaining things to me. Without the generosity of these two men, this dissertation could never have happened.

Irina A. Andreyeva of the Parliamentary Library was kind enough to open her doors and make her library's collection available to me for long stretches of time, and her capable staff energetically tracked down additional materials I requested. This library was a joy to work in — while others working in archives and other libraries grumbled, I smiled on my way to Tsvetnoy Bulvar.

The pack of Russian correspondents covering the State Duma helped me to preserve my sanity. Two individuals in particular helped me to understand how Russian legislatures work, how to survive in them, and how to make sense of the budget process. Ivan Rodin and Ivan Trefilov were my educators, my guides, my protectors, and my friends. They and their friends warmly and enthusiastically accepted me into their circle, let me tag along as they followed the scent of a story, and willingly shared information with me that they often kept from each other. There is a community of energetic, enterprising, and bright young Russian journalists that brings true cause for optimism for that country's future. My memories of them are already lifelong, and I look forward to a long future of friendship and collaboration.

Yuriy Satarov and Mikhail Zakhvatkin at INDEM are wonderful research colleagues with a fabulous database and other material on the Russian legislature and politics more generally that is of continuing value. I am also forever in debt to Yuri Baturin for planting a seed long ago that resulted in this study.

In Estonia, Raivo Vetik at the University of Tartu was an invaluable contact and an enthusiastic collaborator. I thank him in particular for introducing me to Andrus Mae and Tarvo Tamm, research assistants who forged contacts for me in the Riigikogu and read and translated stenographic records, newspapers, and other documents. I would never have met Raivo were it not for an earlier friendship with the late Andrus Pork. One of the clearest thinkers I have ever known, his tragic death is a severe blow to Estonian social science and to all of us who had the pleasure of knowing him. I am deeply saddened that he never learned how much he influenced this project.

During long months in Moscow, my friends Brian Taylor and Valerie Sperling turned into soul mates, supporters, and educators in Moscow. They helped me make sense of what was going on and have read (and compelled me to change) much of what I wrote. I apologize for that! Hopefully, I have rendered at least some valuable assistance in their own work. I also thank Donald Blackmer, Timothy Colton, Kim Gross, Eugene Huskey, Robert Moser, Greg Noble, Susan Siena, Brian Silver, and Edward Walker for reading and commenting on some or all of the chapters that follow. If I stand, it is on the shoulders of all these colleagues; if I fall, it is entirely on my own.

Finally, I thank my wife, Mary Pat McVay, for my being able to say just those words. It is my incredible fortune to have someone who not merely tolerates but celebrates this book, which has been such a disruption. Her sacrifices have been immense, and I am deeply grateful.

INTRODUCTION

A Theory of Comparative Legislatures: Institutional Design and Legislative Conflict

The first Chair of the Russian State Duma Budget Committee was plagued by a split personality. For months, he fought vigorously in his Committee for passage of the 1994 Budget, and successfully lobbied for the inclusion of more than 70 percent of the changes that he and his faction demanded. Yet only days after winning passage in his Committee, when he came before the full Duma to lead debate on final adoption of the budget, it was as if a completely different person were speaking. He abandoned his own Committee, and in effect his own budget, as his faction refused to support the law. As a result, neither he nor anyone else had the slightest idea what the result of the final vote would be. The Duma did eventually pass the budget but suffered several failed votes, mind-boggling chaos, and breakdown and unpredictability in doing so. This scenario is regularly repeated in the Duma on other bills from other committees; however, on nonbudget issues, breakdown and deadlock in the legislative process frequently leave the Duma unable to act at all.

Nothing like this could ever have happened in the Duma's predecessor, the Supreme Soviet. When the Supreme Soviet Budget Committee Chair took the podium to lead debate on his Committee's legislation, the final outcome was never in doubt. The Budget Committee Chair, like all committee chairs, had every reason to believe that the full Supreme Soviet would follow his Committee's positive or negative recommendations on the law as a whole and on proposed amendments. Supreme Soviet committee positions routinely carried with near or even absolute unanimity. The legislative process was highly collegial and extraordinarily efficient.

1

Yet Russian President Boris Yeltsin decreed the Supreme Soviet out of existence and, on October 4, 1993, used the firepower of T-72 tanks to enforce that decree. The Supreme Soviet had pursued such an intractable line of conflict that it provoked the Russian President to bomb it out of existence. Although it efficiently managed and overcame internal conflict to pass legislation, the Supreme Soviet was unable to manage its conflict with the executive branch. The Duma is just the opposite: although it is frequently plagued by deadlock internally, with the executive branch it has repeatedly demonstrated a capacity to negotiate and reach compromise.

What explains such dramatic differences between Russia's two post-Soviet legislatures? Why are their experiences so different from Estonia's legislature, which consistently demonstrates an impressive capacity to manage conflict in its internal legislative process and in its relations with the executive branch?

This book is in large part an exercise in theory building. It elaborates a comparative theory for explaining variation in legislative behavior. In so doing, it fills a glaring void in the voluminous literature of comparative legislative studies. It then applies this framework to explain the vast differences in the performance of these three post-Soviet legislatures. Why did the Supreme Soviet get blown up? Why has the Duma been safe from suffering a similar fate? Why is Estonia's legislature more effective than either of its Russian counterparts at managing political conflict? In developing a truly comparative framework, this book goes beyond simple description and single case-study elaboration to develop an explanatory framework with relevance beyond the immediate cases examined here and beyond the postcommunist environment. The findings should help to serve as a guide for legislative designers in new states.

Legislatures are an omnipresent component of any modern democracy.[1] In one form or another they have existed in "virtually every political system known to mankind," as Nelson W. Polsby observes in his classic contribution on the subject.[2] Yet at the same time, they have an often spotty record; one observer even calls legislatures "the least successful institution in contemporary governments."[3] But even where they have failed or have been abolished, they have reemerged.[4] The Russian State Duma is a dramatic and recent example of this truth, emerging only three months after the spectacular and globally televised firefight that marked the demise of the Supreme Soviet.

Democracy presupposes the existence of conflict. Rather than eliminating conflict, democracy requires institutions to provide for its "civilized" expression and resolution.[5] Democracy assumes multiple competing interests, organizations, and ideologies struggling for political predominance.[6] Democratic institutions, including legislatures, "are supposed to be conflict regulators, not conflict generators."[7] They are successful insofar as they are able to manage and channel political conflict to productive ends. Legislatures are a central institutional embodiment of democracy, and this book evaluates three different legislatures according to how they fare in managing various forms of political conflict.[8] Moreover, since the legislatures discussed exist in nascent, aspiring democracies, evaluating their capacity for managing conflict also contributes to an evaluation of the stability and prospects of democracy in those states.

When the Soviet Union disintegrated in 1991, the newly independent states faced choices regarding the nature of their political institutions, particularly given that most of these states explicitly declared themselves to be abandoning Soviet socialism and on a path to modern democracy. The postcommunist states thus constitute an ideal set of cases for studying the effects of institutional design on legislative performance. The Russian Supreme Soviet, the Russian State Duma, and the Estonian Riigikogu reflect three different choices that postcommunist states have made for designing their legislatures. The Supreme Soviet excluded partisan factions from its institutional design; the rules organized the legislature entirely around the issue-oriented committees. Its successor, the Duma, essentially grafted a faction-based organization onto the Supreme Soviet's committee structure, creating an unlinked, dual-channel design. The Estonian legislature also has a dual-channel design, but the parties and the committees are linked throughout the legislature's structures.

This study demonstrates the consequences that the choice for institutional design holds, by explaining the dramatic variation in the capacity of these three legislatures to manage conflict.[9] My institutionalist approach reflects my fundamental agreement with the premise that the fate of a new democracy depends on the design of its political institutions, and not only on economic and social conditions.[10] The obliteration of the Russian Supreme Soviet in a barrage of T-72 tank fire vividly demonstrates "the danger of institutional arrangements that do not provide clear mechanisms for the resolution of conflict."[11] Estonia's dramatic success is in stark contrast to the other newly independent post-Soviet states. How legislatures are designed clearly holds consequences not only for the policy process but also for political stability more generally and for the success of democratization in postcommunist states. This study reveals that some designs may exacerbate conflict, or ameliorate one type while exacerbating another.

The following three sections of this chapter elaborate my comparative institutional framework for studying legislatures. The final sections briefly discuss the research methods I employed and outline the following chapters of the book.

THE INDEPENDENT VARIABLE: INSTITUTIONAL DESIGN

Any comparative study that speaks of "the legislature" in general terms is of questionable value, whether the generalizations refer to its design, behavior, or functions. There are many ways to design legislatures, and the differences affect virtually all aspects of a legislature's behavior. The institutional design of a legislature is determined by the structure of its two primary subunits. Members of a legislature may organize themselves into parties, and they may also organize themselves into committees. Parties and committees constitute two different organizational channels, or subunits; they present different incentives and pose different constraints on the members.

To recognize this is to overcome a longstanding division in the legislative studies literature, whose authors seem divided into two camps. One camp focuses on committees, while the other focuses on parties, as bases for explaining legislative behavior. The division is most dramatically evident in the literature on the U.S. Congress. The prevailing trend has seen committees as the dominant suborganization in the U.S. Congress since Woodrow Wilson described a Congress that met merely "to sanction the conclusions of its Committees."[12] Fenno's classic work on the House Appropriations Committee launched more recent studies of committee power, and a quarter-century later leading students of Congress continue to focus exclusively on committees as "the main organizational features that give structure to the work lives of members."[13] Others have branded the emphasis on committees to the exclusion of parties "unrealistic." They try, in essence, to "bring the parties back in" by highlighting the role political parties play in the organization and operation of Congress. These studies typically focus exclusively on party cohesion, leadership, and control, some going so far as to say it is "not" committees "but" parties that structure Congress and determine its behavior.[14]

For those interested in comparing legislatures, or developing a body of theory on legislatures, this divide in the literature seems unnecessarily dogmatic and misses the point. Most legislatures, including Congress, include both parties and committees, and variations may exist in their relative strength and weakness.[15] However, it is not enough simply to assert that both exist and that their interplay is "essential."[16] Such has been the uniform approach in the comparative legislative studies literature, which renders those studies atheoretical and descriptive and robs them of any ability to explain how different ways of designing legislatures result in different forms of behavior. Even those few authors who consider the roles played by parties and committees in a legislature treat the subjects separately rather than simultaneously.[17] Nor is it enough to state in universal terms that either parties or committees perform certain functions. Parties, for example, may organize the legislature into majorities, may have clear statements of policies, and may be responsible for organizing the chamber.[18] But they may not. Similarly, committees may control agendas, procedures, and promote "equilibrium" in the institution.[19] But they may not. Having numerous committees may be a sign of "institutionalization," but this is far from obvious.[20] It may just as easily be a sign of unresolved conflict, destructive duplication, and lack of internal coherence in the institution. What either channel does or does not do is to a large degree a factor of the overall design of the legislature, of how the two channels stand relative to each other. Variations in the resultant structure affect the rules that follow, and the resultant incentives confronting the members and the strategies they accordingly pursue in their behavior.

How the two channels are integrated and balanced against each other defines the space within which the members of the legislature may exercise individual discretion. The institutional design determines whether the combination of incentives and constraints compels the members to pursue conflict-management strategies or leaves them unconstrained to pursue strategies of conflict and confrontation. It is wrong to say that either parties or committees do this. Some combinations of parties and committees may promote consensus building, while others may fuel confrontation and conflict. The question is, which combinations have which effects?

Parties and committees constitute alternative modes of organization and participation for the members of a legislature. Parties are widely presumed to be central to the establishment and the maintenance of stable legislatures.[21] They aggregate political and ideological interests and pursue those interests in the legislature's activities. The predominant theme in the literature is that the primary goal of a legislative party is to further the future election prospects of its current and aspiring members, although it seems not unreasonable to postulate that the pursuit of a common and wide-ranging ideological agenda uniting its members could also be a central goal.[22] For each of these goals, the basic orientation of parties is the same — competition for political power.

In this competition parties pursue a "political" or "partisan" line rather than an "expert" or "technical" line toward policy issues. But these terms do not necessarily refer to "politics conducted from the standpoint of a coherent, comprehensive set of beliefs."[23] Because of the weak nature of parties in postcommunist states, discussed presently, "partisanship" and "political" are used here much as the terms are used today in general American political discourse, particularly around election time. It is about a "we-they" approach to issues, or even a highly personalized "s/he-I" dichotomy. Ideological politics, as Robert D. Putnam describes it, is characterized by "how politicians talk and think about concrete policy problems" rather than by the substance of the issues.[24] It is a general approach rather than a detailed approach to issues, using deductive rather than inductive reasoning.

It is often suggested in democratic theory that parties represent in the legislature the diversity of political orientations and social cleavages in society at large, and that by encompassing this diversity they lend a degree of popular legitimacy to the legislature.[25] Is this true for states with fragile and highly splintered party systems? Does the absence of a party system and weak parties doom a legislature to failure? What are the consequences of different means of designing a legislature given an unstable partisan environment?[26] The experience of postcommunist legislatures indicates that parties may in fact have paradoxical if not perverse effects, particularly in legislatures in new states where the political landscape is highly fragmented.

In contrast to the political or ideological focus of parties, committees stress professionalism and technical expertise in the writing and in the analysis of legislation. Committees aggregate and promote the development of legislative expertise in specific issue areas. Rather than partisan or ideological interests, legislative committees stress professional and technical work on concrete legislation.[27] For legislatures to actively and independently engage in legislating, they must have issue-oriented, expert committees.[28]

Parties and committees thus constitute different modes of organization and different channels for participation. They represent the often contradictory interests of ideological purity on the one hand and technical expertise and competence on the other. How these two channels of organization are balanced in a legislature's institutional design determines the combination of incentives and constraints facing the legislators, and thereby shapes the prevailing strategies of behavior of the legislators.

For postcommunist states, any issue having to do with political parties is particularly vexing. Referring to the new states that emerged in the wake of decolonization after the Second World War, Gerhard Loewenberg calls legislatures in newly independent states "remarkable" for their lack of "organic roots."[29] Recent studies of the newly independent states that emerged in the wake of the collapse of communism have shown how these states lack such key building blocks of democratic societies as organized political parties.[30] After decades of political repression under totalitarian Communist Party rule, "party" and "party member" are more commonly hurled as epithets than they are embraced or praised by the citizenry. In Russian politics, a party is something to be avoided.[31] Those partisan entities that do exist throughout the region are based more on personality than they are on ideological differences or social cleavage structures. Indeed, they almost entirely lack reliable bases of societal support. They more closely resemble "pre-party elite groups" and "cliques" than they do political parties.[32] This was certainly the case during the collapse of the communist regimes throughout the old Soviet Bloc and has remained so throughout the first decade after communism. Whether it is "political clubs" and "political tourism" in the Czech Republic,[33] "exaggerated" fragmentation in Hungary,[34] "continual turmoil" in Poland,[35] or an "anti-party attitude" in Estonia,[36] the newly independent postcommunist states have highly unstable partisan environments. Nowhere is such instability more evident than it is in Russia, and it is clearly a commonality across the postcommunist space. Rather than parties, these organizations, particularly in the legislatures, are best referred to as political factions — ad hoc, shifting alignments of individuals identified with a particular personalistic leader but lacking a coherent ideology or set of programs.[37]

This fractured and fluid political landscape has posed a dilemma for postcommunist states: how are the multitude of fragile and shifting factions to be accounted for in their new legislatures, if at all? Two "ideal types" of legislatures are immediately evident — those that entirely exclude either legislative parties or committees from their institutional design (see table I.1). The latter case, where committees are excluded and the legislature is entirely organized around its constituent parties, is what Polsby calls an "arena."[38] The Westminster model of the British Parliament is the classic example of such a legislature.[39] Such single-channel, partisan legislatures deny any formal institutional role for committees or lack committees entirely. The parties control the leadership, the agenda, the rules, and all floor activity. Such legislatures engage almost entirely in pure partisan debate over government programs; they do not engage in writing or amending legislation.

Table I.1
Parties, Committees, and Legislative Design

	No Parties	*Parties*
No Committees	—	Single-Channel, Partisan "Arena" (British Parliament)
Committees	Single-Channel, Nonpartisan (Supreme Soviet)	Unlinked, Dual-Channel (State Duma)
		Linked, Dual-Channel (Estonia)

The three post-Soviet legislatures examined in this study fall in the bottom row of table I.1. The diametrical opposite of the single-channel, partisan design is a single-channel, committee-centered design. In a nonpartisan, committee-centered legislature the rules exclude partisan organizations, and committees are the sole organizational entity in the legislature of any salience for the members. Such was the design of the Russian Supreme Soviet. The committees controlled the leadership, the rules, the agenda, and the legislative procedure on the floor. Partisan factions existed in name in the Supreme Soviet, but they lacked institutional privileges of leadership, did not control committee leadership or membership assignments, and did not control the agenda. They existed primarily as social clubs. The Supreme Soviet was a nonpartisan, committee-centered design.

Such categorical exclusion of either channel is today the exception. Both parties and committees are normally present in a dual-channel design. Dual-channel legislatures may be differentiated according to the degree to which the channels are linked. The quality of links between the channels in a dual-channel organization determines whether conflict management and consensus building are the predominant strategies of choice for the members. Linkages facilitate the flow of information and communication essential to negotiation and consensus building. They provide a means for negotiation and cooperation, where actors can gain a shared interest in coordination.[40] Georg Simmel offers a sociological elaboration of the same theme. Competing "dyads" may get mired in the "status quo," while their common relation to a third element can free the system from conflict and deadlock. "The third who benefits" gains either by amassing power and authority, by serving as mediator, or by playing the role of independent power broker.[41] In a legislature, a leadership or coordinating body between committees and partisan factions could coordinate or possibly even control the legislature and free the legislative process from the breakdown threatened by its absence.[42] Internal legislative processes feature acceptance of the rules among competing players, who, though competing, follow strategies of engagement as part of a search for legislative consensus.

In the Duma, the two channels are unlinked. Partisan factions and committees in the Duma exist as autonomous networks of organization. It is as if a layer of partisan factions were grafted onto the committee design of the old Supreme Soviet without integrating those factions with the committees. The Duma leadership consists of all faction leaders, on a principle of one faction one vote. The committees have been excluded from that leadership and given no coordinating body of their own; nor do those faction leaders have committee affiliations. The faction leaders control the agenda, the rules, and the committee assignments, and because of the latter they ensure that all factions control at least one committee chair post. Members are also scattered randomly, from a partisan perspective, across committees. The Duma therefore has partisan organizations but no partisan coherence. The leadership spans the partisan spectrum; there is no partisan majority in the leadership, across committee chairs, or in committee memberships. Nor does a partisan majority exist on the floor. Every member has a faction affiliation and a committee affiliation, but these affiliations are autonomous; one's position in the Duma does not depend on one's partisan orientation.

Contrast the Duma to a linked, dual-channel design, such as that in the Estonian Riigikogu. There the rules compel the multitude of factions to coalesce into a majority, in Estonia's case, to produce a government. The important point for the legislative body is that, once formed, the coalition holds together. The coalition forms the legislature's leadership from among its ranks. Factions not part of the coalition are not represented in the legislature's leadership body. Those leaders select the committee chairs from among their ranks so that the committee chairs and legislative leaders all come from the same coalition of factions. Committee memberships are also assigned to ensure that the coalition preserves a majority on all committees. From the leadership of the legislature, to committee chair posts, to committee memberships, to the floor, one's position in the Estonian Riigikogu is integrally linked to one's partisan affiliation. Either one is a member of the coalition and has access to the leadership, the agenda setting and the rule formation, or one is in the opposition and therefore is denied that access.

Different institutional designs produce radically different incentives for the members and radically different capacities of these legislatures to manage conflict. A comparative institutional approach demonstrates the consequences of making a legislature more or less partisan, and the consequences of different ways of combining parties and committees in a legislature. It is therefore a parsimonious model applicable to all legislatures and, where like cases are chosen to control where possible for external variables, promises to be useful for comparing legislatures according to the effects of their institutional designs on their behavior. Recent studies have identified as many as sixteen variables in several categories, leaving us only able to describe legislatures.[43] Several authors have set for themselves the goal of explaining differences in the behavior of various legislatures and failed for lack of a meaningful comparative framework.[44] The framework employed here represents an effort to fill this void and to enable such comparison.

THE BUDGET PROCESS

My research on the Russian and Estonian legislatures focuses on the annual budget process. How do the legislatures deliberate on the budget? How do they evaluate government proposals, make their own proposals and ultimately go about adopting budgets? How do they resolve conflict, internally and with the executive branch, on the technical and political issues of budget legislation? The budget is perhaps the single most controversial policy in any state. Budgets are made because resources are scarce; were they not scarce all claimants would receive everything they want. Since resources are scarce, there is competition among too many claimants for too few resources. Budgets thus concentrate a diverse range of policy areas into a single document. There are winners and losers in the most tangible sense — some get funded while others do not, and more for one often means less for another, as budget decisions are frequently zero-sum.

Budgets are therefore "a perennial battleground"; conflict is inherent to any budgetary process.[45] Conflict over the budget is high because the legislation is important; the functioning of the state's economy and the prospects for development often depend on the content of the budget's provisions. It is thus an ideal issue for examining a legislature's ability to manage conflict. Because all states have and all legislatures consider a budget, it is an ideal issue for comparing legislatures and legislative processes. The budget also provides an advantage over other potential issues for studying legislatures because it is of direct concern to and a priority for most if not all committees and individual legislators and all partisan groups. It thus provides a window into the operation of the entire institution. Moreover, because budgets have to be made annually, the processes and battles surrounding passage hold continuing importance.[46]

Studying the budget allows one to compare quantifiable results, dynamics of the policy process, and changes over time and across countries. Moreover, for post-Soviet states as for any developing countries, the budget carries even greater importance than for wealthy countries, as the latter "can afford to fail" while the former "must be better than the rich — more disciplined, more determined, more self-sacrificing — to do half as well."[47] One might also note that in such an environment, the design of those institutions that must outperform their wealthier counterparts also carries greater importance.

One important qualifying point must be stated at this point. The same characteristics that make the budget an attractive issue for comparing legislatures also pose a drawback. Every state must have a budget of some sort and the legislature normally must approve it. But unlike other legislative issues, inaction on the budget is not normally seen as an option. Nobody has an interest in grinding one's own economy to a halt and shutting down the government, including one's own branch of government. I therefore must treat the budget as a window into the legislatures I study. The process by which each legislature deliberates and adopts the budget reveals tendencies readily observed in their legislative processes more generally. In other words, the budget process is an example of the broader legislative process and reveals strengths and weaknesses of that process to look for on other issues.

The Dependent Variable: Conflict Management

Students of legislatures have tended to classify legislatures according to their "strength" or "weakness,"[48] the degree to which they are "active,"[49] the functions they play,[50] or their "efficiency."[51] But strong or weak at what? Efficient at what? Why are some active and others inactive, whatever those terms mean? What causes a legislature to perform some functions better than others, or to perform them better or worse than other legislatures? The existing literature is inadequate in helping to provide answers to such questions. To develop comparative theories of legislatures we must strive for explanation, including answers to these questions. We must also identify meaningful dependent variables. Recent studies continue to conclude, weakly, that legislatures are "important for democracy"[52] or that "legislatures now merit attention."[53] With more systematic comparison and rigor, we can do better.

A capacity to manage conflict is essential if a legislature is to contribute to the development of a stable democracy, whether or not that legislature is "strong" relative to other institutions of government in a particular state. For democracy to be "civilized," institutions must create the conditions for constraining conflict and the incentives for promoting conflict management and negotiation.[54]

Some legislatures succeed in this while others fail. The interesting question is, what contributes to such success or failure? It is wrong to flatly state that legislatures "offer an institutional framework for the mediation of social conflict."[55] A legislature's design and rules may either foster or inhibit such constraints and incentives and thus may either foster or inhibit a capacity to manage conflict. Far from being "ephemeral" and "unimportant," a focus on design, rules, and procedures is the key to understanding whether conflict management or confrontation will predominate in the legislature.[56] Particularly where parties are weak and fragmented, the design and rules of the legislature may be crucial for creating an environment conducive to consensus building rather than to confrontation.[57]

A legislature's conflict-management capacity refers to its ability to manage conflict between competing actors, to coordinate their activities, and to compel negotiation and consensus building. However, even conflict-management capacity is too vague a concept to be useful. Legislatures face different types of conflict in different settings, from internal and external sources, and may vary in their performance across different settings.

Internal conflict refers to conflict between the members, the committees, the parties or factions, and across these entities. Committees seek technical solutions to legislative issues, but different committees may see different interests or different ideal solutions. Parties and factions pursue political or ideological agendas and compete with each other for political power. Their agendas on any given issue may be contradictory, and may contradict the legislative solution offered by one or more committees. Have they developed rules and procedures that members, parties, and committees accept as constraints on the uninhibited pursuit of individual self-interest? Do rules and procedures enable the legislature to avoid the unpredictability and the instability of ad hoc arrangements, or do they provide incentives for members to ignore, to challenge, and to undermine the rules at every turn in the competitive pursuit of their individual interests or those of their factions or committees? In short, is the internal legislative process about the search for consensus, or is it dominated by unconstrained competition and deadlock?[58]

Legislatures also face conflict with external actors. This study focuses on conflict with the executive branch as the most significant for these states, although conflict with the judicial branch or regional government entities is also possible. Do constraints exist that limit the ability of individual actors to pursue uninhibited competition? Are these constraints effective? Does the legislature have the means to negotiate and to reach consensus with the executive branch, and are those relations characterized by the search for consensus or by the pursuit of confrontation?

In the internal and the external settings, legislatures and their members encounter conflict on a variety of issues. In examining either arena, it is useful to distinguish between legislative and extra-legislative issues. Legislative issues, as the label implies, concern the technical content of legislation. On the budget, for example, conflict may arise over the method of calculating inflation indices, the amount of revenues that can be collected from a particular source, or the amount of spending required in a particular area or for a particular program. Whether looking at internal or external conflict on legislative issues, the subject matter is similar. The question is the extent to which legislators are constrained to cooperate internally to reach consensus on the content of legislation and to adopt that legislation, and to cooperate with the executive branch to achieve agreement on those legislative outputs. Do lines of communication and coordination constrain competing actors to pursue consensus, and are there incentives for members to engage in consensus-building behavior in the legislative process? Or are those actors unconstrained to pursue competitive positions and confrontation? Are there leaders on issues whose authority is accepted by all actors, or are multiple claimants for authority free to battle for the right to run the legislative process?

Extra-legislative issues are those matters beyond the narrow legislative agenda or the content of legislation on which the members expect and are expected to be involved. Most commonly, these have to do with political power and the role of various actors in the political process. On the budget, internal examples would be whether to consider or vote on the budget at all, the processes used to hold those votes, and the power and authority of the Budget Committee versus other committees or partisan factions over the process. More generally, such issues include the filling of leadership posts and responding to various political crises beyond the scope of legislation.

Conflict with the executive branch on extra-legislative budget issues may involve the right of the legislature to act on the budget at all, reflected in government resistance to submitting the law, or the scope of supporting materials the government provides to assist the legislature in its analysis. More generally, such conflict swirls around issues of power and politics, ranging from the balance of power between the branches of government and the role of the legislature with respect to government agencies, to appointments to government and cabinet posts and the issue of confidence in the government itself, to presidential and government decrees, to a range of military, political, or economic crises that plague the new, postcommunist states. Such issues often demand a legislature's attention and are a source of conflict between it and the executive branch, yet have nothing to do with the more narrowly defined lawmaking process. Again, what is measured is the capacity of the legislature to manage conflict on these issues, based on the degree to which it provides the incentives and the means for partisan factions, committees, and individual members to negotiate and reach consensus internally and with the executive branch.

Legislatures, depending on how they are designed, may enjoy a high capacity for managing some types of conflict while being unable to manage other types. Table I.2 summarizes this book's findings regarding the conflict-management capacity of the post-Soviet Russian and Estonian legislatures.

As Richard L. Hall suggests, making a committee representative politically, as opposed to basing membership on expertise or interest in the subject matter, may bring greater partisan conflict and weaken a committee's ability to reach consensual decisions.[59] By including partisan interests in a legislative committee, the expert, technical aspects of writing legislation are brought into direct confrontation with the normative concerns of those partisan interests. Other hypotheses logically emerge from these observations. For example, one may expect that any consensus such partisan committees are able to reach would carry greater political legitimacy by virtue of the inclusion of various partisan interests in the process of achieving that consensus. The executive branch may therefore more readily accept such policy outputs. Conversely, while nonpartisan committees may find it much easier to reach internal consensus on technical legislative issues and be stronger on the floor in carrying their consensual positions, by ignoring or excluding competing partisan interests those decisions may turn out to be less acceptable to other branches of government. The lack of partisan organization in general may leave individual members unconstrained in their pursuit of individual political agendas.

Table I.2
Legislative Design and Conflict-Management Capacity

	Internal Conflict Management		Legislative-Executive Conflict Management	
	Legislative Issues	*Extra-legislative Issues*	*Legislative Issues*	*Extra-legislative Issues*
Single-channel, nonpartisan Russian Supreme Soviet (1991–93)	High	Low	Low	Low
Unlinked, dual-channel Russian State Duma (1994–)	Low	Medium	Medium	Medium
Linked dual-channel Estonian Riigikogu (1993–)	High	High	High	High

The findings in the chapters that follow demonstrate these somewhat paradoxical effects. The Supreme Soviet, with its nonpartisan, committee-centered design, reached extraordinary internal consensus on technical legislative issues, resulting in a highly consensual legislative process. The committees acted as a constraint on each other in their shared goal of adopting legislation. However, by denying an institutional role for partisan interests, the Supreme Soviet lacked mechanisms for managing political conflict with the executive branch. The absence of organized partisan structures enabled individual Supreme Soviet members and, most notably, the Chairman to pursue an unconstrained line of confrontation with the executive branch. The conflict and extended deadlock that ensued culminated in the President's abolishing that legislature by decree and destroying it in a hail of artillery fire.

However, simply including factions without linking them to the committees has left Duma deputies unconstrained in their exercise of individual discretion in the internal legislative process. The absence of links enables or even provides incentives for legislators to shift back and forth between the two channels in their allegiances, to play one channel against the other for personal gain.[60] Where dual channels of organization and power exist without links between them, a "dual power" situation of high instability and continuing conflict results.[61] In the Duma, lines of communication and coordination between the factions and the committees are weak, and rather than a legislative process based on negotiation and consensus building, the process is instead dominated by jealous competition between antagonistic players. Members abandon rules and sabotage each other's initiatives rather than seeking to reconcile differences. Committees fight against committees, factions fight against factions, and committees and factions fight each other. The breakdown and deadlock frequently render the Duma unable to take any action at all on legislation. One theorist describes the problem of unlinked dual channels as follows: "Each hierarchy will attempt to enhance its own credibility. . . . The competition may generate sufficient conflict to distract attention and energy from the overall goals of the organization, so that more careful attention to conflict resolution is required."[62] For a legislature, the lack of a linking mechanism between committees and partisan factions means that the two channels become mired in competition and gridlock, rather than negotiating and searching for consensus to produce legislation in spite of inherent conflict between different interests. Such has been the fate of the Russian State Duma.

However, because all of the partisan faction leaders sit in the Duma leadership body, the Duma has a standing forum for negotiation and conflict management with the executive branch. The leaders constrain each other so that all cooperate. Some support the executive branch and will meet with it to discuss policy issues, legislative and extra-legislative alike. Their partisan opponents, driven by suspicion that deals will be cut behind their backs and motivated by political ambition that requires that their faces and positions appear in the media no less than do those of their political enemies, also appear at the bargaining table. Unlike the single-channel, nonpartisan Supreme Soviet, in the multipartisan Duma no single leader has the space to act and control the political line of the legislature on any issue. The new Russian legislature has a mechanism its predecessor lacked enabling it to negotiate on extra-legislative political issues with the executive branch. Political disputes over the balance of power, government personnel, or government crises no longer degenerate into deadlock and conflict, as lines of communication and negotiation are constantly open between the partisan leaders in the legislature and the executive branch. The Duma's unlinked, dual-channel design has, therefore, exacerbated one type of conflict while easing the other.

When the two channels are linked, the point at which they are connected may have the authority and the means to manage conflict between disputing actors. In Estonia's legislature, a linked, dual-channel design, the coalition majority constitutes that point of linkage. It is the "third who benefits," the glue between the two channels. The majority coalition, produced by the need to form a government, centralizes procedures in the legislature around itself as a coordinating body. The coalition works with the government and the committees to ensure ratification of its political and legislative agenda, embodied by the government's policies. In its legislative activities and in its extra-legislative activities, therefore, Estonia's legislative body consistently produces a high degree of consensus.

How parties and committees are combined in a legislature in large part determines that legislature's ability to perform the important task of managing political and legislative conflict. For new legislatures in new states it may ultimately determine the fate of their long-term development and stability. These findings are generalizable to legislatures beyond the postcommunist environment. Parties and committees may be combined in many different ways, and the cases I explore exhaust neither the types of design nor the potential consequences. But their experiences are suggestive of the effects various institutional designs may have for legislative behavior and for the management of political conflict.

I would hardly argue, however, that institutional design can explain everything about politics in the former Soviet states or even about why their legislatures function as they do. It cannot. In states where the rule of law was unknown during decades of communist rule and where turmoil and breakdown following communism's collapse encompassed virtually all aspects of society, new political institutions and processes would be shaky regardless of how they were designed. As James G. March and Johan P. Olsen put it, "In some societies, people obey traffic laws, pay taxes, and abandon public office gracefully after political defeat. In others, they do not."[63] Most postcommunist states are among the "others." But it is in just such "other" states that institutional design is important to study and in which its effects can be discerned. Institutions either succeed or fail in providing a means for managing conflict. Humans can design, change, and manipulate them. But humans cannot readily control political culture. Given the unstable environment in postcommunist states, the choice of institutional design for a legislature holds important and often overlooked consequences for the ability of that essential democratic institution to manage, to channel, and to overcome conflict. Moreover, an institutionalist approach is particularly fruitful for comparing such legislatures and the policy process in them.

Because inaction on the budget is normally not an option, failure to pass a budget is not an indicator of breakdown. But the budget process does reveal trends to look for regarding conflict management within the legislature and between the legislature and the executive branch on legislative and extra-legislative issues. For example, where a legislature has developed for the budget means for factions and committees to collaborate to work out their differences, procedures accepted by all of the important players, these procedures are likely to hold and be visible on other issues. Conversely, where the budget process is marked by procedural breakdown, by unmanaged competition, by unpredictability and instability of procedures and outcomes, these problems are also likely to be visible on nonbudget issues. On those other issues, deadlock and inaction are likely results.

Most important for this study, therefore, is how each legislature passes the annual budget. It is in the how, in the process, that one can gain an understanding as to the overall ability of a legislature to manage conflict. The budget serves as an indicator of tendencies in each case and may indicate problems with the process even where conflict over the budget is resolved in a given instance. Even if a legislature does adopt a budget in a particular year, if the process surrounding debate and passage indicates severe problems that are already evident on other issues, this could portend similar problems for future incarnations of the budget process and for the stability of that legislature more generally.[64] This is of great importance, especially if one keeps in mind that the legislatures examined here are new legislatures. One must focus on the process, and keep an eye to other issues beyond the budget.

It is also important to keep in mind that the legislatures in this study are new institutions, new legislatures, in new states. As Putnam warns, "Creating a new political institution is neither quick nor easy. Ultimately, success must be measured not in years, but in decades."[65] Any conclusions reached regarding the development of post-Soviet legislatures are necessarily only speculative. This book provides a framework for continuing study of these institutions. Only time will tell whether these legislatures will develop successfully or not, and only time and further study of these and other legislatures will tell whether the framework itself merits further development.

Two final points regard my personal outlook on conflict and legislatures more generally. Absence of conflict is not necessarily good. In a legislature's internal processes, a certain degree of conflict may be necessary to produce the most effective legislation. Conflict can be good, but only where mechanisms exist to manage and channel it in ways that can ultimately enable action. Without such mechanisms, conflict degenerates into deadlock, breakdown, and inaction. But even this result may not be undesirable under certain circumstances. Taking the broader view to long-term political and economic development in post-Soviet states, I am not (and it may be foolish for one to be) a cheerleader for legislatures. If my study finds some forms to be weaker than others, such forms may indeed be the most desirable for new legislatures in new states. Robert A. Packenham eloquently stated the point a quarter-century ago, and it is worth quoting him at length today.

> Strengthening legislatures in developing countries would, in most cases, probably impede the capacity for change which is often crucial for "modernization" and economic development. . . . Legislatures tend to represent, all over the world, more conservative and parochial interests than executives, even in democratic polities. . . . In societies that need and want change, and where political development may be defined as the will and capacity to cope with and to generate continuing transformation, it may not make much sense to strengthen the decision-making function of an institution that is likely to resist change.[66]

I profess no normative desire to see the legislatures I study become stronger or weaker. If pressed, I may even tend toward the latter, but my objective is to evaluate the legislatures as they have been designed and to suggest how different ways of designing legislatures lead to different types of performance. Those wishing to create legislatures immobilized by internal deadlock, for example, should gain as many insights from this study as those wishing to create legislatures free from such problems. The Russian State Duma may be functioning exactly as its creators intended, as the inverse of its unfortunate predecessor. It has mechanisms to manage conflict with the executive branch on extra-legislative, political crises, but it is plagued by internal deadlock and less able to legislate on major economic and political issues. Its greater internal difficulties may not be a bad thing. The Russian government of 1994–95 certainly did not think so. But whether its creators intended this result or not, it is, I argue, a consequence of the Duma's institutional design.

The Promise of Comparative Institutionalism

A concluding chapter in a recent volume on post-Soviet legislatures urges the development and use of "theories and explanations that help us to understand legislatures in general."[67] It is telling, however, that this long-time contributor to the comparative legislative studies literature is unable to point to any comparative theory of legislatures to use or to emulate.

Despite a vast literature on legislatures, surprisingly little is explicitly comparative, and even less is theoretically oriented. Most works in the field of comparative legislative studies either develop descriptive typologies of legislatures based on their characteristics and functions or elaborate single case studies.[68] Little effort has been made to develop and apply criteria for explaining legislative behavior or why some perform better than others.[69]

A comparative institutionalist approach facilitates the identification of variables that are at least potentially manipulatable — rules and procedures. It also facilitates the identification of more substantive and medium-range dependent variables.[70] It entails an emphasis on the conditions that contribute to stable democracy. If democratic institutions are supposed to manage conflict, a focus in institutional design helps us to understand what promotes such behavior and what may inhibit it. Comparative institutionalism helps us to answer the questions, what works and what doesn't work?[71]

The comparative aspect is equally important. This book meets the call to systematize the comparative examination of legislatures and to enable examination and comparison of these and other legislatures.[72] The vast majority of the work on legislatures may claim to offer theories of legislatures but in fact does nothing of the kind.[73] Rather, most studies develop theories of one legislature, the U.S. Congress, and even more narrowly, of the House of Representatives.[74] These studies are hardly generalizable, for if the descriptive works of the comparative legislative studies literature of the 1970s and 1980s offer one lesson, it is that Congress is atypical among the legislatures of the world. Critics of the political science literature on institutions note this well.[75] Anyone studying legislatures from a comparative perspective, let alone new legislatures such as those examined here, would find puzzling the frequent categorical proclamations in these studies, such as "structures induce equilibria," or that the foundation of committee power is "the sequence of proposing, amending and especially of vetoing in the legislative process."[76] Such "laws" are presented as if true for all legislatures, when they seem to have little relevance beyond the U.S. House.[77]

Similarly, there are virtually no in-depth studies explicitly concerned with institution building and the development of new legislatures in new states.[78] However, understanding what factors may inhibit or contribute to a legislature's ability to manage conflict in both its internal and its external activities is, or in any event should be, important for those designing new legislatures. For that matter, it should be of concern to existing states on those rare occasions when they find it necessary to reconfigure their legislatures. This study therefore constitutes a first step toward filling these voids in the literature.

Having leveled this critique of the existing literature, let me now back off a bit. The lack of comparativism in the institutionalist literature is hardly the fault of Americanists who have adopted the approach. At fault are comparativists who have not adopted it. Institutionalism is an approach, not a field.[79] To date, the field of comparative politics has barely considered, much less embraced, institutionalism as an approach. The possible exceptions relevant to this study are works comparing the merits of presidential systems with those of parliamentary systems.[80] But this debate has a much longer history than does institutionalism, and in any case most of these works are neither institutionalist approaches nor explicit comparisons of the legislatures themselves.

The absence of institutionalist comparisons of legislatures per se is curious, for it is hard to argue with the assertion that "democracy depends not only on economic and social conditions but also on the design of political institutions."[81] For those studying the processes and the complexities of democratization, one of the most promising approaches is comparative analysis of the institutions of democratic government.[82] This study thus makes a contribution by being an explicitly comparative institutionalist approach to studying new legislatures.[83]

A comparative institutionalist approach offers much potential for the broader subfield of comparative politics. It embraces a bottom-up approach to theory building that I believe is a refreshing departure from attempts at grand theory and all of the accompanying limitations demonstrated by past and recent "modernization" to "transitions to democracy" approaches. While some may be tempted to brand my approach "narrow," we need to understand "the immediately observable implications of theories" at the middle range before moving to higher levels.[84] It is a matter of starting with simple mechanics before ascending to unified field theory. In any event, if it is possible to call narrow a study that says something general about the consequences of different ways of designing legislatures, an institution that exists in every state in every political system, then this author embraces narrowness! Comparing institutions is one way to begin to compare states, political systems, and politics across regions. An institutionalist approach thus offers much promise for comparativists, provided they are willing to step back from grand theory.

My focus on the budget process when examining conflict in internal legislative activities will also make this study of interest to students of the

U.S. congressional budget process. Recent studies have described the in-creasingly centralized nature of that process over the last two decades, in contrast to an increasingly decentralized Congress.[85] They have also dis-cussed the consequences of these changes. My comparative approach en-ables me to examine the effects of various degrees of centralization in the institutional design on the ability of a legislature to reach internal con-sensus to pass budgets and to reach external consensus with the executive branch on the content of those budgets.

It will also test, albeit indirectly, whether some of the propositions in the literature on the congressional budget process are applicable to budget processes in other legislatures. The general view that emerges from the literature chronicling changes in the U.S. budget process is that the 1974 Congressional Budget Act, by forcing Congress for the first time to make macrolevel decisions on spending, revenues, and deficits, increased conflict by forcing decisions on principles and political goals.[86] Previously, there was no true budget; spending was legislated in more than a dozen separate appropriations bills. Conflict was minimized by virtue of the overwhelming power of the Appropriations Committee and its subcommittees, a univer-sally accepted principle of incremental spending growth, and an intricate process of logrolling, the legislative version of "you scratch my back, and I'll scratch yours."[87] By concentrating all fiscal matters into a single bud-get, dissensus resulted as explicit policy and ideological trade-offs had to be made.[88]

Students of other legislatures can only respond that the United States began doing what others had already long been doing. The difficulties that Congress began facing in its budget process in the late 1970s cannot simply be attributed to trying to pass a budget. Other legislatures succeed in the endeavor year after year. Rather, as Allen Schick recognizes but only in-completely explores, the problem stemmed from the decentralized nature of the House and from the unstable relationships among the players in that process.[89] The decentralization that he describes was manifest in decreased autonomy for the committees, increased authority for congressional par-ties, and unclear relations between them.[90]

This book explores the applicability of these observations of the U.S. congressional budget process to other legislatures. In particular, it explores the consequences of the increased importance of partisan organizations in the Russian State Duma, as compared with the former Supreme Soviet, manifested in the shift from centralization around committees to a dual-channel organization of committees and parties. My findings confirm and generalize those found by John W. Ellwood, Allen Schick, Aaron Wildavsky, and others who have written on the U.S. Congress, that such changes lead to breakdown in internal processes and decrease the legislature's "capacity to cope with conflict."[91] My study of the Estonian legislature suggests alternate ways of combining legislative committees and partisan factions that could be adopted in Russia to ease the Duma's difficulties managing internal legislative conflict.

NOTE ON RESEARCH METHODS

I gained extraordinary access in the Russian State Duma. My research methods mirrored Richard F. Fenno's "soaking and poking — or just hanging around" in his pioneering research on the U.S. Congress.[92] The Budget Committee Chair allowed me to attend Committee meetings, and from February through December 1994, I sat in on all that directly pertained to the budget and on the vast majority of other Committee meetings. Through a combination of participant observation and interviews with more than half of the Committee's members, I gained firsthand knowledge of how the Committee and the legislature worked on the budget. In particular, I was able to distinguish between the formal and the actual roles of factions, committees, and individual members. This access also enabled me to freely attend the plenary sessions, where I interviewed a wide range of Duma members. I thus gained a firsthand feel for the workings of the new legislature as it gained its sea legs. Over the course of a year in the Russian State Duma I viewed it from all perspectives — the deputy's office, the floor, the cafeterias, the hallways, the bars. I was present long enough and consistently enough to in some ways become a part of the Committee and its staff.[93]

As Fenno notes, it is impossible to standardize the research methods of participant observation. Unlike Fenno, I frequently used a Dictaphone.[94] However, the choice demanded a feel for the personality of the deputy being interviewed. With one older Committee member, I never used a Dictaphone or even took notes in his presence, unless the situation was one in which he was surrounded by hungry Russian parliamentary correspondents. In such cases, I followed the pack with my Dictaphone. However, in other respects, such as being a good and genuine listener; in constantly expanding contacts; in casting the net of contacts across partisan affiliation, committee representation, regional background, age, and gender; in guaranteeing anonymity for all respondents; in sometimes assisting friends among members and staff; and in building a real and lasting rapport, my techniques were indistinguishable from Fenno's.[95]

My data on the Duma thus consist of the fruits of this hanging around and listening. They consist of my notes from committee and plenary session proceedings, from informal interviews, and my transcriptions of more formal taped interviews. In all of my observations and discussions, my goal was to learn how the legislature goes about deliberating, debating, and ultimately adopting the annual budget and other legislation. I tried to understand the differences in the influence and roles of the individual deputies, the committees, and the factions in this process.

This access in the Duma put me in an unusual position to compare the two Russian legislatures, for during a previous stay in Moscow, from early 1990 through July 1991, I attended several sessions of the Supreme Soviet. I thus witnessed how both post-Soviet Russian legislatures worked. Most important, I interviewed members and staff who served in both legislatures, including several who served on both Budget Committees, and thus have the benefit of their own comparative perspectives and experience. These interviews proved by far the most informative of my research, as these individuals personally saw and experienced the changes in the roles of partisan factions and the associated changes in the legislative process. Many were personally involved in relations with the executive branch. As with the Duma, in these discussions I tried to gain an understanding of the relative influence and roles of the individual deputies, the committees, the factions, and the leadership in the budget process and in the legislative process more generally.

In all, I conducted more than seventy formal interviews of at least thirty minutes in length and hundreds of briefer exchanges with roughly 150 current and former Russian deputies, staff, and government officials.[96] I also gained virtually unlimited access to the library holdings that survived the October bombing, and to some archive access as well.[97] This enabled me to gain access to the complete stenographic record from the Supreme Soviet's sessions, and I read through this entire record from the 1991 coup until the legislature's demise in October 1993. As a supplement to the recollections of Supreme Soviet members and staff, this record proved an invaluable resource and a window into the workings of the budget process.

Finally, I have substantial database material on both legislatures, including their entire voting records. While not all votes are officially roll call votes, every time a deputy pushes the *za* (aye) or *protiv* (no) button, a computer registers the result. I have helped put together a versatile database that enables complex analysis of these votes along a variety of parameters.[98] In short, I have a composite of data on the Supreme Soviet and the Duma, based on personal observations, interviews, documents, and statistics, which I believe is second to none.

My research on the Estonian Parliament was necessarily of a different nature. As I was based in Moscow, I conducted my research on several visits to Estonia of a few days to three weeks in length. Through a contact at Tartu University, I gained access to Parliament, where I interviewed more than half of the Budget Committee membership, all of its staff, and assorted members of parliament (MPs) and staff from every major party. I conducted more than forty interviews including more than 20 percent of the MPs, several staff members, two government ministers, and three deputy ministers. I also hired a research assistant to read the stenographic records of budget debates and Estonian-language secondary-source accounts of the budget process. As a result, I have sufficient data on which to base my conclusions about the institutional design of and the policy process in the Estonian Parliament.

OUTLINE OF THE BOOK

The following chapters present the results of this research on Russia's and Estonia's post-Soviet legislatures. Part 1 examines the Russian Supreme Soviet. Chapter 1 elaborates the Supreme Soviet's nonpartisan, committee-centered institutional design. Chapter 2 explores how the exclusion of parties and factions reduced conflict in the Supreme Soviet's internal activities, while chapter 3 shows how this same design exacerbated conflict with the executive branch without providing any means for managing that conflict. Part 2 compares the case of the Russian State Duma to its unfortunate predecessor. Chapter 4 elaborates the Duma's unlinked, dual-channel institutional design. Unlike the Supreme Soviet's highly consensual internal legislative process, the Duma frequently finds its legislative process immobilized by deadlock and breakdown between committees and factions, as chapter 5 demonstrates. However, as chapter 6 shows, the Duma's design does constrain the members to pursue strategies of consensus building and negotiation with the executive branch. The heads of the Duma factions meet in the legislature's leadership body, and in this context may also meet with representatives of the president and government to discuss such broad political issues and crises beyond the Duma's legislative calendar. The Duma is far more successful than was the Supreme Soviet in managing political conflict with the executive branch.

Chapter 7 discusses the case of the Estonian Riigikogu, a legislative body in a parliamentary system. The need to form a government compels the factions to coalesce into majority and opposition coalitions, which in turn creates links between the two channels in the legislature. This linkage gives Estonia's legislature a much more bipolar form than its Russian counterpart, with stable legislative majority and minority party coalitions. These coalitions constrain members to pursue collaborative and consensus-building strategies with internal and external actors, on legislative and extra-legislative issues alike.

Although Estonia has a parliamentary constitutional system, its legislature does indicate the benefits for legislative efficiency and consensus building of a linked, dual-channel design. It suggests lessons that may be applicable for nonparliamentary systems. In the final chapter, I consider several options for strengthening the links between the Duma's factions and committees, with an eye toward improving the Duma's internal consensus-building and conflict-management capabilities without jeopardizing its capacity to negotiate with the executive branch. The suggestions are equally applicable to any multipartisan legislature in a presidential system. Among the alternatives I consider is, first, including committee representatives on the Duma's leadership body, alongside faction leaders, to facilitate coordination between the two channels. Second, a committee on committees could be created to coordinate work among the committees, and thereby reduce conflict and duplication of effort between them. Third, the Duma's factions could be linked more closely and more formally to the government, thereby forcing greater consistency and coordination between them and the formation of legislative majority and minority coalitions. Fourth, the number of committees in the Duma could be reduced to ten or so, while increasing the range of topics covered by each individual committee. This action would have the effect of increasing the size of each committee and of increasing the representation of each faction on each committee, in essence turning the committees into "mini-Dumas." Each of these could reduce tension and facilitate consensus building between committees and factions in the Duma's internal legislative activities while maintaining or even enhancing conflict management and consensus building in relations with the executive branch.

More broadly, this study should be of interest and use to practitioners and scholars alike. For the former, it suggests several alternatives for the design of legislatures, and the corresponding implications of each for internal legislative efficiency and broader political conflict management. For the student of legislatures, it points out characteristics of institutional design to look for in other legislatures, particularly in new legislatures, to test and refine the hypotheses that arise from my framework. For students of post-communist transformations, it presents an analytical framework for evaluating the potential and the performance of one institution critical to any state's progress toward democratic stability.

PART 1

The Russian Supreme Soviet:
A Well-Oiled Machine,
Out of Control

The conventional wisdom about the Russian Federation Supreme Soviet is at best a gross exaggeration, at worst simply wrong.[1] Western and Russian observers alike paint the Supreme Soviet as a traditional, totalitarian, Soviet institution, whose omnipotent and malevolent Chair single-handedly dominated policy outputs and controlled the membership.[2] They also commonly blame its continual, budget-busting spending increases for the conflict that provoked its banishment, because President Yeltsin's Decree No. 1400, which culminated in the Supreme Soviet's fiery demise, closely followed its passage of a revised 1993 Budget.

Attempts to explain how and why the Supreme Soviet allowed its Chair to balloon budget deficits out of control reveal only evidence demonstrating the fallacy of both impressions of the Supreme Soviet. In fact, the Supreme Soviet's nonpartisan, committee-centered institutional design gave the Budget Committee[3] wide authority over legislation under its purview, as it did to all committees and their chairs in their respective issue areas. The committees controlled the legislative process and consistently reached broad consensus on the content of legislation, including the budget, which the Supreme Soviet overwhelmingly approved. The committees and their chairs dominated a legislative process that virtually excluded partisan conflict, and they produced legislation that enjoyed overwhelming approval from the entire membership.

Still, the only possible evaluation of Russia's first democratically elected legislature is that it was a spectacular failure. Why was it such a failure? A comparative institutional approach demonstrates that the Supreme Soviet's design undermined that legislature's ability to manage conflict with the executive branch, particularly on extra-legislative issues. A single-channel, committee-centered design enjoys a high capacity for managing conflict on technical legislative issues such as the budget. However, on extra-legislative issues, particularly in relations with the executive branch, a legislature so designed lacks a capacity to manage conflict. This design paved the way to the Supreme Soviet's demise. The exclusion of partisan entities — parties or partisan factions — from the Supreme Soviet's design denied that legislature an ability to negotiate to resolve extra-legislative, political conflict with the executive branch. It lacked any means of constraining the actions of its one politicized deputy, the Supreme Soviet Chair. He was unconstrained in pursuing his personal political agenda. The same nonpartisan design that facilitated internal conflict management and consensus building on legislative issues precipitated unregulated conflict with the executive branch on extra-legislative, political issues. The result was an extended period of political breakdown and deadlock culminating in the president's abolishing the legislature by decree and destroying it in a hail of tank fire.

While several articles and volumes have been published about those dramatic "October Events," as they are known in Moscow, those works fall short of explaining why the Supreme Soviet failed while other legislatures in the former Soviet Union proved more successful at conflict management. They are uniformly limited to descriptive accounts of what occurred in that single case and, lacking a comparative framework, they have limited value for theory building. Of the two most prominent published volumes, one is simply a historical account of the Supreme Soviet from several perspectives; it lacks a comparative context or explanatory framework to examine the conditions that produced the Supreme Soviet's problems.[4] The other presents a "political autopsy" that does not even attempt to answer why the Supreme Soviet in particular met this fate, or what it was about that legislature that made it so different from other legislatures.[5] Approaches that take as a goal to "shed light on" and "illustrate the dynamics of" what happened to the Supreme Soviet are valuable for historical description, but they do not explain why it behaved differently from other legislatures; nor do they predict how different legislatures are likely to behave in the face of existing conflict.[6] Existing works on the Supreme Soviet have not contributed to theory building in the field of legislative studies.

The following three chapters on the Supreme Soviet demonstrate the power of comparative institutional theory for explaining what happened to the Supreme Soviet and for understanding its significance. The theory grounds the Supreme Soviet's demise in the features of its institutional design. By doing so, it also explains and perhaps predicts the behavior of other legislatures that may be similarly designed and carries an implicit warning for those designing new legislatures regarding the consequences of excluding partisan entities from a legislature, no matter how fragmented the partisan environment may be. In this sense, the case contributes to theory building, while the theory helps illuminate the significance of the case.[7] In both respects, this approach meets Michael L. Mezey's timely call for students of postcommunist legislatures to contribute to comparative legislative theory.[8]

Chapter 1 elaborates the essential features of the Supreme Soviet's institutional design. Chapter 2 examines how this nonpartisan, committee-centered design provided for effective management of internal conflict on legislative issues in the Supreme Soviet. It demonstrates that the Budget Committee worked like a machine to resolve conflict and to reach consensus on budget legislation, consensus routinely approved by the full legislature. The same dynamic worked for all committees on their respective legislative issues. Chapter 3 details how this same institutional design provoked conflict with the executive branch on extra-legislative issues, while minimizing the legislature's capacity to manage that political conflict. The result was prolonged deadlock culminating in the legislature's violent destruction.

1

The Nonpartisan, Committee-Centered Supreme Soviet

In its internal legislative activities, the Supreme Soviet operated like a "well-oiled machine," to use the words of several of its members.[1] This fact was not, however, due to one-man rule by the Chair. Rather, it was due to the legislature's nonpartisan, committee-centered institutional design. The legislature was a nonpartisan machine. The Supreme Soviet[2] was centralized and hierarchical, but it was centralized in its twenty-eight committees and committee chairs, not in the single pair of hands of the Supreme Soviet Chair and not in legislative parties.[3] The absence of partisan entities and the organization around committees and their chairs constrained the deputies to cooperate in the internal legislative process. Two factors in particular enhanced the central position of the committees and their chairs. First, as the leaders of the legislature's only significant suborganizations, the committee chairs formed the leadership body of the Supreme Soviet, the Presidium, which became in essence a committee on committees. It was the organizing and coordinating body for the legislative process. Second, although the Supreme Soviet was a permanent, standing legislature, most deputies did not work as full-time legislators. The following sections of this chapter elaborate the single-channel, committee-centered design of the Supreme Soviet.

A Nonpartisan Design

Legislative parties did not exist in the Supreme Soviet because parties did not exist in Russian society. Although the deputies did form partisan factions, the factions were never afforded any formal place in the legislature's organization. Indeed, the basis or role of these factions was never clear.

They were small, numerous, and amoeba-like in form and membership. They formed no partisan majority or opposition in the Supreme Soviet, nor did they form the committees or allocate leadership posts on the basis of partisan affiliation. They had no privileges or role in the legislature's organization. The Supreme Soviet's design left partisan politics to the individual deputy.

Right down to the distribution of information, factions were outsiders, as one exchange on the floor between a faction leader and the Supreme Soviet Chair regarding government documents on inflation illustrates:

> Chair: I should say immediately that *Goskomstat* [State Committee on Statistics] gives us such information.
> Deputy: Ask those in attendance if they know about this!
> Chair: This information exists in every committee.
> Deputy: It should be in every corner of Parliament!
> Chair: Goskomstat gives us exactly the information you request every week. . . . *You, as head of a faction, do not receive such documents but in principle they exist.*[4]

Not surprisingly, it was unclear even to most deputies what the factions were for. Deputies often expressed "the need to determine the role of factions in the work of the Supreme Soviet."[5] One deputy marveled at his view of European legislators: "He doesn't even know the question being discussed, but the party leaders who follow the system of voting simply tell him how to vote. How can we organize this? We are all individualists. We don't have any parties. It means little to tell me: "vote this way.' "[6] Alexander Sobyanin is correct that membership in a faction neither defined nor reflected a deputy's political position on a given issue.[7] Timothy J. Colton finds that less than one-fourth of the deputies consulted with their factions on issues.[8] One can only wonder why not only the media but also knowledgeable scholars referred to factions and their members as either "democrats" or "hard-line conservatives," with the strong implication that these labels served as guides to member behavior.[9]

Some observers have viewed Supreme Soviet factions as having formed simply among groups of friends, as "deputy clubs" that had no obvious ideological or partisan foundation.[10] When it came to partisanship, individuality reigned supreme in the Supreme Soviet. According to one survey, 69 percent of the deputies who claimed a faction affiliation said that they either rarely or never participated in faction activities; of these, 92 percent said that their factions played no role in their positions on issues. More impressive, even for the 31 percent who *did* participate in faction activities, 82 percent said that factions played no role in their positions on issues.[11] Many of the deputies who reported faction affiliation were in fact members of more than one of the fourteen registered factions that existed at the time. That simultaneous membership in more than one faction was not only possible but common is testimony to the factions' tenuous existence.[12]

When the 1990 elections were held, the USSR still existed and the Communist Party was the only party. In the absence of political parties in society, it is no surprise that the legislature also lacked them. However, partisan factions did form among the deputies as legislative experience grew and as the transformation in Russian society accelerated. It is significant that these factions were never afforded a formal place in the Supreme Soviet's organizational design, in spite of the frequent demands for changes to so strengthen them.[13] As a result, they developed even less than did their counterparts across eastern Europe, remaining unstable "political clubs."[14] Factions in the Supreme Soviet could exist or not; deputies could join or not.

Jerry F. Hough suggests that the Supreme Soviet's leaders consciously denied factions a role, fearing that factions would limit their own freedom of action.[15] Whether or not this is so, the exclusion of factions from the legislature's design left the leaders free from the constraints of partisan organization. With factions excluded, individual deputies and, in particular, committee chairs and the Supreme Soviet Chair were unconstrained in their pursuit of individual discretion.

A COMMITTEE-CENTERED DESIGN

Factions may have been marginal, but committees were anything but. The Supreme Soviet was organized around its twenty-eight committees. Committees were the only suborganization in the Supreme Soviet that held any salience for the deputies, and unlike the factions each deputy could belong to only one committee.[16] Also unlike the factions, Supreme Soviet committees had an institutional role that was clear to deputies and observers alike — to carry out detailed preparation and analysis of laws for approval by the full Supreme Soviet.[17] Committees were not formed on a party or partisan basis, just as the Supreme Soviet itself was not so formed. Deputies saw committees not as the place for ideological debate or for partisan competition but as the place where policy "experts" sought technical consensus on legislation.

In this respect and in others, the attitudes of committee members in the Supreme Soviet were remarkably similar to those in more institutionalized legislatures like the U.S. Congress. For example, technical expertise normally was a consequence of legislative experience — prior expertise was irrelevant to committee membership. A bus driver and a physics professor were among the most active members of the Committee on Social Policy and the Budget Committee, respectively. However, these two deputies deservedly gained reputations for expertise on their committees' issues.[18] The idea was that deputies would become expert in their committee's issue areas over the course of time. Their experience was typical of most members and parallels Fenno's findings on the House Appropriations Committee.[19]

Committee chairs, however, were almost always nominated and selected on the basis of expertise — the Chair of the Budget Committee was an accomplished economist; the Chair of the Committee on Social Policy was a legal specialist on labor and social policy; and the successive Chairs of the Committee on Legislation were legal theorists and specialists on constitutional law — to cite just three examples. The committees themselves elected their chairs, and partisan affiliation or orientation played virtually no role in the selection.[20] The consequence of nonpartisan selection was a high degree of partisan inconsistency across committees. With no partisan majority controlling appointments, the ideological orientations of the twenty-eight chairs spanned the entire political spectrum.[21]

The chairs enjoyed wide authority within their committees and within the Supreme Soviet as a whole. Most important in establishing this authority was the fact that they were the leaders of the only suborganizations of any consequence to the members. Two additional factors widely enhanced their prestige and authority, though. First was the curiosity that although the Supreme Soviet was a permanent, standing legislature, being a Supreme Soviet deputy was not necessarily a full-time job. This was a relic of the old Supreme Soviet of the pre-*perestroika* Soviet Union, for which Communist Party elites convened in Moscow for a few days once or twice a year to rubber-stamp Party Central Committee decisions.[22] The new Supreme Soviet was a standing legislature that held long sessions typical of legislatures in most democratic countries, but the members chose whether or not to work full-time there, and many did not. Only ten of the Budget Committee's forty-seven members served full-time; in other committees, about 25 percent worked full-time, and some were not even Supreme Soviet members.[23] Attendance at sessions was so low that proposals to dock absent members' pay were frequent, among other threats.[24] Committees were so understaffed that they repeatedly pleaded for more deputies, any deputies, to participate in their work.[25] But most continued in their old jobs, continued to receive those salaries, and only sporadically participated in the work of the Supreme Soviet. In their committees, they worked on the specific issue or issues that interested them, as they chose.

The most important consequence of this situation was that authority devolved upon the committee chairs. Part-time members treated the full-timers as the experts within a committee, and a committee chair was normally the only one involved in all of the committee's legislation.[26] The fact that the committee chairs were the full-time members doing most of the work greatly enhanced their already impressive prominence and authority.

A second institutional factor cementing the committee chairs' authority was their collective presence in the Supreme Soviet's leadership body, the Presidium. The committee chairs formed the Presidium. It is commonly, though wrongly, thought that the Presidium consisted solely of Supreme Soviet Chair Ruslan Khasbulatov and his cronies, and that it was the mechanism through which Khasbulatov enforced his will upon and dictated to the full Supreme Soviet. In fact, of thirty-two Presidium members, twenty-eight were the committee chairs. The remaining four were the Supreme Soviet Chair and his deputy chairs,[27] but it was the committee chairs who occupied the impressive place in the Supreme Soviet Presidium.

Supreme Soviet deputies of various political stripes, including several Presidium members, admonish observers to "properly understand the role of the Presidium."[28] The Presidium served foremost as a committee of committees, a "coordinating organ" for the committee chairs in the legislative process.[29] The Presidium organized and notified deputies of the schedule of sessions, including special emergency sessions; distributed materials such as drafts of legislation to the members and to committees; and drafted the agenda for plenary sessions "taking into account the opinion of the committees." In other words, it was responsible for ordering the appearance on the daily agenda of items being reported out of committees. It also facilitated joint work between committees and arranged legal and material-technical assistance to them.

The Presidium, in short, coordinated progress on the legislative calendar. Just as the committees focused on the technical substance of drafting legislation, the Presidium focused on the technicalities of the overall legislative process in the Supreme Soviet. That this leadership consisted of the committee chairs is the most important single feature distinguishing the Supreme Soviet's design from that of the new State Duma, where the heads of the partisan factions make up the leadership body. In the Presidium of the Supreme Soviet, committee chairs kept abreast of each other's work and coordinated joint work. As an institutionalized meeting place for committee chairs, the Presidium served as a forum for managing conflict between committees over the responsibility for, the process of producing, and the content of legislation. The committee chairs who gathered weekly in the Presidium accepted each other as equal members of an exclusive legislative "club," as the most authoritative "experts" of the "expert committees," as the "professional" legislators and leaders of the Supreme Soviet.[30]

The committee chairs thus held great authority within their committees, with each other, and in the Supreme Soviet as a whole. This single-channel, nonpartisan design yielded to the committee chairs tremendous space for the exercise of individual discretion. Political constraints on their legislative action were few. In many ways, they served as "little dictators." Deputies, when interviewed, widely referred to committees by the chair's name: "Pochinok's Committee" for the Budget Committee, "Zakharov's Committee" for the Committee on Social Policy, "Piskunov's Committee" for the Defense Committee, and so on.[31] The committee chair set the committee's rules of procedure and determined what subcommittees, if any, were needed. The committee chair determined the committee's political orientation. Committee chairs were the full-time legislators doing most of the work and the ones who decided how that work would get done.

It would be misleading to ignore the ways in which the Presidium and the Chair routinely exceeded their formal powers and violated the formal rules. One need only point to the frequent attempts by the head of Rules Committee to prevent the Chair from violating the rules of procedure or to the less frequent attempts to change the rules to clearly restrict the role of the Chair at plenary sessions.[32] The Chair did at times attempt to "usurp the role" of the Presidium and of the legislature as a whole, but not on legislative matters such as the budget. The Chair's internal functions were codified in the Regulations; his job was to run the plenary sessions, enforce the rules of procedure, and open the floor for speeches. He could determine the time available for such speeches and warn against and sanction violations of etiquette and of the Regulations. But that was the extent of his authority over the internal legislative process.[33]

As demonstrated in chapters 2 and 3, Khasbulatov's excesses pertained almost exclusively to extra-legislative, political issues. He was able to dominate these because the nonpartisan, single-channel design lacked mechanisms for managing such conflict or for controlling the Chair on such issues. The same design that freed committee chairs of constraints on the exercise of individual action on legislative issues gave the Supreme Soviet Chair similarly unconstrained leeway on extra-legislative, political issues.

THE CPD: AN ADDITIONAL CURIOSITY

Russian political life displays myriad contradictions. It has already been pointed out, for example, that although the Supreme Soviet was a permanent, standing legislature, its members were not full-time legislators. Another quirk was that although in 1990 Russia democratically elected its legislature for the first time, that legislature was not elected directly by the people. The 1990 elections were for the larger and constitutionally supreme body, the Congress of People's Deputies (CPD). These 1,068 People's Deputies elected the 250 members of the standing legislature, the Supreme Soviet.[34] While my focus is on the Supreme Soviet, the CPD played an important role in strengthening the Supreme Soviet Chair and thus in the conflict on extra-legislative issues.

The Russian CPD, much like its USSR predecessor, "had little in common with an ordinary parliament." It more closely resembled a "mass rally" or demonstration.[35] With more than 1,000 members, it was not intended to be and never was a working legislative body. Its central function, outside of electing the members of the Supreme Soviet and its leadership, was to gather twice a year for a few days to approve changes to the constitution. In fact, the Supreme Soviet Chair convened it at every hint of political or economic crisis. As such, it was concerned with the broad political issues of the nature of the Russian political system. Given the turmoil associated with the breakdown of communism and the rise of a new state, the CPD became reminiscent of a "political show."[36]

The Presidium for this "political show" or "demonstration" differed from the Presidium of the Supreme Soviet in one telling way — it consisted only of the Chair of the Supreme Soviet and his deputy chairs. It was the Supreme Soviet Chair, not committee chairs and not faction leaders or representatives, who organized and led the congresses.[37] This distinction parallels the distinction between legislative and extra-legislative, political issues. As will be seen, the Supreme Soviet Chair dominated the latter, particularly in the legislature's relations with the executive branch.

A Design Complementing Traditions of Authority and Deference to Leaders

As suggested here, the Supreme Soviet's design gave its leaders wide freedom in the exercise of individual discretion. Such a design probably extended from and fueled traditions of what Richard Pipes calls a "patrimonial" political culture, a feature he sees as an almost permanent aspect of Russian political behavior.[38] The acceptance of inequalities of rank and status were certainly evident in the Supreme Soviet's design, as was the intense "personalization of authority" or "paternalism" that also have equally deep traditional roots in Russian political culture.[39] The Supreme Soviet's design did not create these cultural patterns. But the important point for a comparative institutional theory is that this design did not counter or soften those tendencies. Indeed, the design was entirely compatible with a personalized, authority-based predilection that places enormous value on rank and status. In the Supreme Soviet, the rank and status that had the authority and enjoyed the deference was the rank of *predsetatel'* or Chair. A design lacking any constraints on the political actions of those chairs meant a legislature in trouble.

Before turning to how the Supreme Soviet's nonpartisan, committee-centered institutional design affected its ability to manage legislative and political conflict, the final section of this chapter takes a closer look at that design as manifest in the Supreme Soviet Budget Committee.

The Budget Committee: A Professional Committee

The Supreme Soviet ideal was that committees would be "professional," not "political." The Budget Committee could have served as the prototype for this ideal. The distinction was clear to Committee members. "Our work was on a professional level. We set up a collective, and this was truly hardworking. As we gained more experience we became more professional, and I think that as a collective organ by 1993 we had achieved a professional and responsible level of work." Another member was puzzled by a question regarding the political makeup of the Committee, responding, "The committee is the place for professional decisions, not political decisions."[40]

In the deputies' usage, "professional" meant nonpartisan, nonpolitical. As in the single-channel Supreme Soviet as a whole, partisanship was close to irrelevant on the Budget Committee. From the Committee's conception of its mission to its description of those people who worked in the Committee, a technical approach was the criterion for evaluation of Committee work, not partisan loyalty or political aptitude.[41] The stenographic records reflect that this conception was typical for all committees and was what deputies expected from their own and from other committees.[42] As Colton found in his research, the deputies believed "by far their most important duty" was to be engaged in "making laws as more or less disinterested agents of society."[43] This statement expresses precisely how the members defined a professional approach.

To the outside observer the distinction between "professional" and "political" may not always be so crisp. Because budget decisions involve trade-offs in the allocation of scarce resources, what may seem to be the "technically correct" decision to a Committee member may seem politically or ideologically motivated to an observer. The important point in terms of conflict management in the Supreme Soviet is that the deputies shared an almost universal acceptance of the nonpartisan nature of committee work. This consensus about roles and appropriate behavior facilitated conflict management on internal, legislative issues and contrasted sharply with an absence of consensus regarding political activities.

As if to highlight this principle of nonpartisan committee work, even in the midst of a "political battle between the Supreme Soviet and the President," the Budget Committee Chair maintained that he and the Committee were not engaged in the fight. In reference to his arguments with some of the more radical deputies, he insisted, "I do not like being thrust into politics, instead of economics" and was determined to keep the Committee focused on the latter.[44] His view closely held to the Supreme Soviet norm, that committees should consist of "professionals who care about one thing — to make Russian legislation. Coordinated, technical, and precise legislation. . . . In evaluating committees we should not proceed from political principles, but on the principle of how heavily the committee works."[45]

The Budget Committee's success in achieving this standard is testified to by members and nonmembers alike. Said one member, the Committee "avoided too many political ambitions" in its work. "It knew what needed to be done, and was therefore productive." The Committee "worked professionally. . . . We sat from the beginning and did not leave anywhere," engaging in "professional analysis, independent of any orders or interests." Being "professionally oriented" meant the Committee focused on the technical aspects of "legislative work" and "avoided political motivations" in this process.[46]

Nonmembers generally appreciated the degree to which the Budget

Committee met the ideal that they held for their own committees. One deputy gave typical praise of the Budget Committee, saying before the Supreme Soviet, "Your committee is the only one that truly works beyond politics."[47] This view was a primary basis for the full membership's extraordinary deference to the Budget Committee on the floor, demonstrated in chapter 2.

Perhaps the best testimony to professionalism's being a general characteristic of the committees was unwittingly provided by one deputy, more interested in waging an external battle over power with the government and the President, who told the Budget Committee Chair with more than a hint of scorn, "I get the sense — excuse me if I am mistaken — that your committee like some others does not want to enter into conflict with the Government and the President on principle matters."[48] His mention of "some other" committees indicates his personal frustration with the nonpartisan, professional committee structure of the Supreme Soviet. Confrontational deputies notwithstanding, the more professional a committee was viewed to be, the greater success it had in carrying its positions on the floor.

Government officials likewise appreciated the Budget Committee's professionalism. One Finance Ministry official said, "Purely professionally, for a number of reasons, the Supreme Soviet Deputies in their preparation and their approach to matters tried to defend the interests of the state . . . rather than those of special political interests."[49] Another in the same ministry said that they appreciated above all that, unlike the new State Duma, the Supreme Soviet "followed its own internal decisions. They followed their own process."[50]

But there were not many professionals on the Committee. Like other committees, the Budget Committee had only a few full-time, active members. Of its forty-seven members, only ten worked full-time, and only two or three worked full-time on the budget for a country of 150 million people.[51] As one deputy responsible for budget issues in one of the sectoral committees recalled, "It was not a small committee, formally. But in reality only three or four people actually worked, the Chair and the Deputy Chairs. And each had their own sphere of responsibility — banking, taxation, etc. On the budget there were Deputies A, B, and then it becomes difficult to remember. That was all!"[52]

As will be seen in the following chapter, this curiosity yielded extraordinary authority to the Committee Chair to organize the Committee's work. This nonpartisan, committee-centered design enabled the Supreme Soviet to manage internal conflict and to avoid the breakdown and deadlock in internal legislative processes that plague its successor, even on such an objectively controversial issue as the annual budget. The committees were responsible for centralizing expertise in their clearly defined issue areas and for producing competent legislation in those areas. On the technical aspects of legislation, the Supreme Soviet Chair had no formal role. The committee chairs coordinated their work in the Presidium to ensure passage of legislation.

However, as discussed in chapter 3, this design meant that on extra-legislative issues the Supreme Soviet lacked mechanisms for managing conflict with the executive branch. Neither the nonpartisan committees nor the Presidium offered mechanisms for handling extra-legislative, political matters. What the chairs had in common in the Presidium was their positions as experts on their issue areas, not partisan political affiliation or orientation. The only politicized deputy in a position to act for the legislature on political issues, particularly in its relations with the executive branch, was the Supreme Soviet Chair. The Supreme Soviet's bane was that it lacked any mechanism to check or control the extra-legislative activities of the Chair.

A Well-Oiled Legislative Machine

New states experience a lot of firsts. While Russia may be very old, in late 1991 it attempted to re-create itself as a new state; emerging from seven decades of communist rule, it proclaimed itself to be democratizing. Its legislature, as the chair of one of its committees observed, was in many respects a trailblazer. "Ours was the first democratically elected parliament of Russia [and] the first one to begin to discuss the budget in detail. Never in the Soviet period did a parliament ever influence budget matters. This Supreme Soviet was the first." One staff member described it as "a process of creation . . . and everything was unclear."[1]

The Russian Supreme Soviet is routinely vilified for its actions on budget policy. The attacks are unjust. It instead deserves credit for impressive achievements. Given the inexperience, the general instability, and the totality of the political, social, and economic crises that the country faced, what is surprising is not that there were difficulties. What is surprising is that the Supreme Soviet succeeded in establishing a budget process that worked. Committee members were proud of this achievement. "We worked out a procedure and we worked according to it. Even under such tight conditions . . . we tried all the time to work within that regime, under the law. So the problem was not with the Supreme Soviet—the Supreme Soviet tried to establish a procedure."[2]

According to both western and Russian news accounts and to current and former deputies, during the period 1991–93 Russia "never passed a budget" and "lived three years without a budget."[3] In fact, between August 1991 and September 1993 the Russian Supreme Soviet passed a 1992 Budget, a revised 1992 Budget, a 1993 Budget, and a revised 1993 Budget.[4] It passed budgets every year of its existence and did so with overwhelming internal consensus on their provisions. Perhaps most significant and damning of the conventional wisdom, the government explicitly approved these budgets on the Supreme Soviet floor before their adoption. The Supreme Soviet was highly effective at managing and overcoming conflict on the budget, and its members were proud of their success at preventing conflict from degenerating into deadlock and in reaching consensus on budget policy.[5]

The Supreme Soviet's nonpartisan, committee-centered institutional design facilitated this success. This design provided a high capacity for managing very real conflict within the legislature. It enabled the members to minimize partisan competition on the budget, encouraging them to follow norms of professionalism and reciprocity in forging policy consensus on the technical aspects of legislation, including budget-related legislation. It gave the committees wide authority over legislation in their issue areas while at the same time constraining them to coordinate activities and cooperate to produce consensual outputs.

These findings are consistent with expectations generated by students of the role and behavior of other committee-centered legislatures, most notably the U.S. House of Representatives. The Supreme Soviet enjoyed the "predictable" and "stable patterns of behavior" that a committee structure is purported to provide.[6] That a comparative institutional theory of legislatures can encompass the models and expectations put forth by students of congressional committees, while explaining other types of legislatures and legislative behavior that the congressional literature cannot and that the comparative legislatures literature does not, is extremely promising. This chapter explains why the Supreme Soviet was a legislative machine in its internal legislative activities, confirming the expectations of committee-based models of the U.S. Congress with a non-American case study. The following chapters, however, explain outcomes that models based on Congress cannot account for. They explain why the Supreme Soviet was out of control and ultimately failed and why its successor, the Duma, is unable to manage internal conflict on legislation despite having a committee structure. The models developed by students of Congress shed little light on these other behavior patterns that appear common, if not universal, to legislatures outside the United States. In other words, the findings presented in this chapter demonstrate that my comparative institutional theory encompasses the theoretical observations of Keith Krehbiel, Kenneth A. Shepsle, Barry R. Weingast, and others regarding the role of committees, while also lending theoretical muscle to the descriptive observations of Timothy J. Colton, Jerry F. Hough, Thomas F. Remington, and others that the Supreme Soviet was able to legislative effectively.

The Committee's Procedures

The Supreme Soviet budget process was codified in the special Law on the Budget Process, written by the Budget Committee.[7] The procedures called for strict deadlines. First, they required that the government begin work on a draft budget eighteen months before the beginning of the fiscal year and submit the draft to the legislature by "the beginning of April" preceding the fiscal year, which begins January 1. The Supreme Soviet was therefore to have at least nine months to approve a budget. The Budget Committee had two weeks to conduct an evaluation of the draft budget for the first plenary session reading, to be held within one month of the budget's submission. If the Supreme Soviet rejected the draft on the first reading, the draft was to go back to the government for revision.[8] Once adopted on the first reading, the government had until September 15, or nearly four months, to submit revisions based on the legislature's demands. Each committee (and, presumably, individual deputy) then had one month to make an evaluation and submit amendments to the Budget Committee. By the end of November, the Committee had to submit its recommendations on the draft and its amendments to the Supreme Soviet for approval on the second reading. The President then had two weeks to sign or veto the budget.[9]

The procedural law did not require initial ratification of spending, revenue, and deficit ceilings at the outset. On the contrary, the provisions clearly mandated initial approval of the separate articles with subsequent approval of the totals.[10] Another important feature was that the Committee and the Supreme Soviet were to examine every article and provision at each reading.[11]

This procedure differed from other legislation in various respects. For one, the government submitted the budget. On other issues, the constitution gave virtually anyone the right to legislative initiative.[12] How a particular bill would arrive was thus not obvious, but how it would get on the agenda was. Drafts had to be submitted to the Presidium, and the committee chairs assigned one or more committees to be the "responsible committee" for each bill. On nonbudget legislation, though, no deadlines existed for committee action or the timing of floor action, nor were all committees expected to evaluate draft bills. The chair of the responsible committee decided these procedural matters. The first reading was on the overall conception of a draft law, and rejection was tantamount to killing it. On the second and final reading, the Regulations required votes only on changes made by the responsible committee after the first reading and on proposed amendments, not necessarily on every separate article.[13]

Aside from these differences, however, the budget followed the pattern for all Supreme Soviet legislation. Most important, the responsible committee always played the central role. At each stage, including floor debate, the responsible committee had the first and the last word. The rules made no mention of factions or parties, nor did they provide any role for the Supreme Soviet Chair. Both the Regulations and the Law on the Budget Process established a thoroughly committee-based and committee-dominated legislative process.

On the budget, the Committee was unable to adhere to the formal letter of the Law on the Budget Process, but it did try to follow the spirit of those rules as closely as possible. The greatest limitation was the fact that the government never met or even came close to meeting the deadlines for submitting the budget. Consequently, the entire process had to be substantially streamlined. This strengthened the Committee in some ways, as the contracted time line limited the ability of others to gain enough expertise to challenge its authority.

A second limitation, one that again increased the authority and the discretion of the Budget Committee Chair, was a lack of personnel. Of the forty-five-member Budget Committee, only a dozen or so were full-time members, and of these only the Chair and the Deputy Chair worked full-time on the budget.[14] This left the Committee Chair almost entirely free from constraints in organizing work on the draft. Aleksander Pochinok, a pro-government, reform-minded economist, used this freedom to create a collaborative environment for achieving budget consensus.

While Pochinok was undoubtedly inclined to consensus building, he was also constrained to pursue a collaborative process. Recognizing that two deputies and two staff members could never analyze and revise Russia's entire budget, especially given the tight time constraints, Pochinok convened a Budget Working Group.[15] It included any Budget Committee members who wished to attend, a representative from each sectoral committee, and representatives of the Finance Ministry.[16] In other words, the Budget Committee Chair gathered together as many additional experts as he could and charged them with thoroughly evaluating all budget provisions. Neither the Law on the Budget Process nor the Regulations envisioned such an extracommittee body, but the single-channel, committee-centered institutional design left the Committee Chair unconstrained to act. Former

Supreme Soviet and government participants alike view the close cooperation between various committees and the government as the Supreme Soviet's most notable achievement in the budget process.[17] This collaboration
was a model not only for consensus building on the budget but also for a
nonpartisan legislative process in general.

These structural features of the Supreme Soviet combined to compel an
intercommittee collaborative process. When the government's draft budget first went to the Presidium, it immediately became clear that all sectoral
committees had a strong interest in it. The Agriculture Committee was
concerned about spending on agriculture, the Defense Committee was
interested in provisions related to the military, and so on. The Committee
Chair recognized that the two active Budget Committee deputies focused
on the budget could never do their own work and the work of the others
and that he needed the support of the sectoral committees to win its ultimate passage; he therefore brought the interested sectoral committee
chairs into the process. He invited them to send representatives to a Budget
Working Group, to work together rather than at cross-purposes. The Presidium, then, provided a forum for committees to recognize where interests
overlapped, and a constraint on the committee chairs to respect those overlapping or conflicting interests and to work together to accommodate and
overcome them.

While the Working Group did the analysis, the Committee itself always
had the "final word" on proposals sent to the full Supreme Soviet for action.
As one participant explained, "When we had everything prepared we gathered the whole Committee." But "the informal Working Group did the real
analysis," with the full Committee "deferring to these experts."[18] What was
achieved in the Working Group was prior consensus on budget provisions,
with the sectoral committees and with the government. Representatives of
the sectoral committees came to the Working Group with their own proposals and demands, and they hammered out consensus in the informal
setting of the Working Group. Although they had further occasion to try to
push their separate positions later in the process, these expert leaders and
their colleagues invariably supported the outcomes achieved in this collaborative effort.

The norm of reciprocity in relations between Supreme Soviet committees is the subject of the next section. What is important to note here is the
authority of the Budget Committee Chair, the chair of the responsible
committee for budgetary issues, to organize the process as he saw fit. He
organized a Working Group that had no basis in the rules or in the law. His

authority to do so was a direct consequence of the nonpartisan, committee-centered design. It also confirms the expectations generated by students of Congress regarding the authority of House committees and their chairs when congressional parties were the weak institutional counterparts to the committees.[19] Whether the Supreme Soviet design emerged from or reinforced Russian traditions of deference to leaders and expertise, the effect was the same. It removed partisan politics from the legislative process, and extended wide latitude to the Committee Chair to exercise individual discretion in organizing the budget process.

RECIPROCITY BETWEEN COMMITTEES

In their Presidium meetings, the committee chairs quickly recognized a simple fact. The one thing they all had in common was that they all wanted to pass their legislation. Each wanted their legislative drafts enacted into law. Intercommittee reciprocity arose from their coordination in the Presidium. The goal of professional committees is to produce legislative output. With partisan organizations effectively excluded from the Supreme Soviet's design, organized partisan conflict was also minimized. The second fact that the committee chairs recognized was that they spanned the entire partisan map. So they focused on what they could agree on and all wanted to focus on — passing legislation. The relationship between the nonpartisan committees became a relationship of consensus building and cooperation as they pursued their one common interest.

The strongest manifestation of reciprocity between committees was mutual recognition of and respect for each other's autonomy over and expertise within their respective issue areas. This recognition and respect enabled the committees to manage conflict while drafting legislation and to produce extraordinary consensus on policy outcomes at the ultimate phase of decision making in the Supreme Soviet. By compelling coordination and joint work, for example on the budget, the chairs prevented competitive duplication on important legislation. The Presidium was the institutionalized forum sparking this coordination and consensus building, ensuring communication and cross-committee information on the progress and content of legislation. The Presidium thus became a committee of committees, binding the chairs together in a club of legislative leaders. The Budget Working Group was just one example of how this club implicitly constrained its members to work together, to see each other's legislation adopted. Exclusion and secrecy would breed competition and committees interfering in each other's work and blocking each other's legislation, which was against the interests of all members of the Presidium.

This is not to imply an absence of conflict. With an economy in shambles, rampant inflation, and budget deficits exceeding revenues, all sectoral committees were dissatisfied with their share of budget spending and with relative and absolute cuts in spending for their areas. They sounded their objections at every reading of the budget. During the 1992 Budget debate, the Transportation Committee complained that it had "given all the necessary materials and figures to the Budget Committee to make revisions. More is needed for railroads above all. We are sent this budget draft and have no idea where the figures come from."[20] A deputy from the Committee on Social Policy claimed his committee's proposals on the minimum wage for the 1993 Budget were "completely ignored without discussion."[21] Virtually every committee, on every budget document, submitted amendments for massive spending increases in their sectors over and above the government's draft. The total cost of amendments to increase spending at times exceeded the entire spending total in the baseline budget. The Budget Committee, however, as the experts responsible for analyzing the legislation and with a pro-government, reformist Chair directing those activities, saw its role as resisting sectoral committee demands.[22]

Objectively speaking, then, the budget was perhaps the most severe test of the Supreme Soviet's ability to reach internal consensus. The Supreme Soviet passed the test. It passed budgets with near unanimity each time it was called upon to do so. Some were dissatisfied with the budget's final provisions; one deputy was probably right when he said, "Nobody ever liked any of the budgets we adopted."[23] But rather than intercommittee rivalry and jealous competition grinding the budget process to deadlock and breakdown, the norm of mutual respect for responsible committee authority guided the deputies to pass budgets almost unanimously. The final vote on the 1992 Budget was 185–0, with three abstentions.[24] The Committee recommendation to return the first draft 1993 Budget to the government passed 138–4, with 14 abstentions.[25] The votes at the subsequent readings of the 1993 Budget were: first reading, 141–18; second reading, 153–0; and, on the revised budget, 176–0.[26]

The near unanimity reflects the norm of deference to the responsible committee on an issue, but the votes are less interesting than the process. Deference at the end was the result of cooperation and coordination throughout the process. On the budget, no sectoral committee had the knowledge and the information to challenge the Budget Committee on the budget as a whole, yet each possessed expertise on that part of the budget relevant to its particular area and could have challenged the Committee on that part of the budget. Struggles over sector budgets did characterize early stages of budget debate, and many sectoral committees saw their demands and proposals rejected by the Budget Committee. But those disputes never derailed final passage.

The Budget Committee secured final approval of its legislation because of the cooperation it was constrained to arrange with the sectoral committees. Each of those committees was made a part of the process, given a chance to argue its case. The Budget Committee Chair arranged several such opportunities during the budget process, above and beyond the Budget Working Group. For example, the Committee held extensive joint hearings on the budget, and it invited the sectoral committees to defend their demands before the Budget Committee itself. In the end, the sectoral committees felt that they had shaped the budget as much as had the Budget Committee; it was their budget too, for better or for worse.

The Committee held hearings on every sector of the budget. These hearings were important, although Russian legislative hearings hold little in common with those in the U.S. Congress. In fact, they are not committee hearings at all, but hearings on a topic sponsored by one or more committees. Rather than official, sworn testimony by government officials and outside experts before a committee in session, a Russian legislative hearing resembles a daylong, public conference at an academic institute or think tank. Russian budget hearings are held on days when there is no plenary session, and they are held in the legislative chamber. At the front, running the hearings, are the Committee Chair, any deputy chairs attending, and the chairs of any cosponsoring committees. The finance minister or one of his deputies and the relevant sectoral minister present also sit at the front. Everyone else, including any Budget Committee members and any other deputies attending, sits in the audience and listens to speeches from this list of officials, including speeches by the chairs of the Budget Committee and the cosponsoring sectoral committees. The Budget Committee Chair decides whether to allow questions to any or all of these speakers, and whether to allow shorter speeches by other deputies, Supreme Soviet staff members, or outside experts.

These hearings were extremely important to the sectoral committees. They gave everyone with an interest in some sector of the budget, whether social policy, education, industrial policy, or defense, an entire day to discuss that sector, to offer proposals, and to hear the government's response.

The Budget Committee held more than forty such hearings in each budget cycle, "to come to grips with each section of the budget." As one participant acknowledged, "On every serious question there was a special hearing."[27] Every issue for every committee was discussed in depth before the Budget Committee and any deputies wishing to attend, and with the attention of all relevant government officials.

The hearings preceded Budget Committee sessions to approve recommendations on the draft budget and proposed amendments to it, recommendations to be issued at the readings of the budget before Supreme Soviet plenary sessions. At some point between the hearings and these Budget Committee sessions, each sectoral committee had the additional opportunity to argue the case for its proposals directly before the Committee.[28] One deputy who made several such presentations described a highly collegial process.

> All committees came, one by one, and presented their proposals. We received as much time as we needed. We sat an entire Saturday once with representatives of the ministries, the Central Bank, and the Budget Committee. We considered the proposals in cooperation with the ministries and the Budget Committee and reached agreement. And that was all. Our disagreements were regulated. . . . All was discussed and decided in this conciliatory manner.[29]

This picture is perhaps too rosy. The sectoral committees were not always pleased with the Budget Committee. One committee chair complained on the floor: "The Budget Committee rejects everything. . . . I think this is absolutely inexcusable. You should call for and hold discussions, evaluations of the committee's proposals. These are not proposals of one lone deputy. . . . What right do you have to write 'reject' not having examined the proposals with them in your committee?" The Budget Committee Chair responded with characteristic sharpness: "To put it gently, I must say that A is lying. . . . We announced all hearings to all deputies. For one and a half months we have worked with all committees, and to say we did not hold hearings is absurd."[30] Three weeks later, the same sectoral committee chair complained that amendments his committee had submitted "were not discussed or examined in the presence of those who wrote them." The Budget Committee Chair again lashed out at his detractor's ignorance: "We spent a whole week discussing all amendments with all interested committees and the government and whoever wanted. . . . You were out of the country!"[31]

While such outbursts between committees on the floor were not un-
heard of, what is most remarkable from reading the Supreme Soviet stenographic record is how rare they were. Indeed, the instances above were the
harshest by far, the most direct exchanges that took place. On every occasion, the outbursts drew stiff reprimands from the Supreme Soviet Chair
for this "impermissible way to speak" about other committees in public.[32]
Such disputes were to be discussed quietly between their chairs in the
Presidium; unprovoked attacks on the floor were a clear violation of the
norm of reciprocity among committee leaders. When they did occur, they
were triggered by irresponsibility or ignorance, as when one deputy's pen-
chant for foreign travel caused him to miss a Budget Committee invitation
to participate in the process. Even on such a momentous issue as the annual
budget, when disputes that arose were not resolved in the joint committee
work described above, they were dealt with and resolved between the committee chairs in the Presidium.[33] The norm of giving all sectoral committees the chance to appear before the Budget Committee and to argue their
case was firmly established and followed. Tensions could arise when there
were deviations or suspected deviations by either party to those proceedings. The Budget Committee was expected to give the sectoral committees
time; in return the sectoral committees were expected to carry out a thorough analysis and to come before the Budget Committee prepared to competently discuss and negotiate their claims. Public criticism of each other by
committee chairs was exceedingly rare and elicited sharp and disapproving
reactions from the Supreme Soviet Chair, who reminded the deputies that
such conflict was expected to be worked out between the committee chairs
in the Presidium.[34]

Far more common, and evident throughout those same stenographic
records and in interviews with former deputies, was a feeling of satisfaction
with the process, if not with the outcomes. It confirms the importance of
institutional mechanisms for collaboration, such as the Presidium. Sectoral
committee members were satisfied that they had been respected as the experts within their given sectors, had been given ample opportunity to present and argue their proposals, had received a detailed response from the
government and the Budget Committee, and had the ultimate decision
explained to them in the context of the entire budget by those who they
accepted as the budget experts.[35] This reciprocal respect for committee
authority and expertise is what the deputies quoted earlier meant in praising
the Budget Committee for its "professional" approach to its work. The
consensus-building process ensured overwhelming approval of the budget
on the floor. This is why the Committee Chair organized that collaboration.

That he would behave in such a collaborative manner was the effect of the nonpartisan, committee-centered design, entrenched in the committee-dominated coordinating body, the Presidium.

COMMITTEE AUTHORITY ON THE FLOOR

When the Budget Committee Chair took the podium at a plenary session to lead debate on the budget, the outcome was rarely in doubt. He had every reason to be fully confident that the Supreme Soviet would approve the Budget Committee's recommendations on the budget as a whole and on proposed amendments. There were strong institutionally based constraints against blocking each other's efforts. These constraints had nothing to do with old Soviet-style decision making, as the entire legislative process bore no resemblance to Soviet-era legislating. Committees considered multiple drafts of legislation from myriad sources and every part of the political spectrum. Amendments came from any deputy, the executive branch, and the many other subjects of legislative initiative. Whether intended or not, the Gorbachev era entrenched principles of glasnost and plurality in the legislative process. Deference to the responsible committee did not result from fear or lack of access to the process, as was the case with the pre-Gorbachev Presidium and Communist Party Central Committee. Nor did it spring from omnipotent control by the Supreme Soviet Chair, Ruslan Khasbulatov.

On the contrary, it was the collaborative nature of the Supreme Soviet legislative process that guaranteed ultimate deference to the responsible committee. Collaboration prevailed because the measure of success in the nonpartisan, committee-centered Supreme Soviet was a committee's ability to get its legislation adopted into law. Supporting another committee today could reasonably ensure its support of your committee tomorrow. This is why the committee leading work on a bill was called the "responsible" committee. To be respected as responsible on their own issues, in addition to handling those issues competently committee members had to respect the responsible position of other committees on their respective issues. The implicit constraint flowed from the converse: blocking another committee's legislation today would virtually guarantee that it would turn around and block your committee's legislation in the future.

Although the Supreme Soviet Chair could, and often did, violate the rules by chiming in with support for or invective against individual speakers and specific provisions, such intrusions had little effect on outcomes. What

Table 2.1
Budget Committee Floor-Vote Success Rates on Budget Recommendations

Budget Law	Total Votes	Budget Committee Recommendations	Recommendations Followed	Budget Committee Success Rates (%)
1992 Budget	77	70	62	89
1993 Budget	180	164	156	95
1993 Revised Budget	222	215	196	91
Totals	479	449	414	92

mattered was the position of the responsible committee. When the Budget Committee recommended passage of a motion, it passed. When it recommended rejection, the motion was rejected. Supreme Soviet deference to Budget Committee recommendations was routine, as it was to all committees on their respective issues.

The most direct measure of Committee authority is the voting record of the full legislature on its proposals. Between late 1991 and late 1993 the Supreme Soviet cast 479 budget-related votes, on which the Committee made 449 recommendations (see table 2.1).[36] The vast majority of these votes were on amendments, for each sectoral committee had the last-ditch opportunity to try and persuade the entire Supreme Soviet to accept its amendments against the Budget Committee's recommendations. Such attempts rarely proved successful. These votes also included votes on entire articles and final votes on the budgets themselves. Of these 449 recommendations, 414 were carried, a Committee success rate of 92 percent.[37] By any standard imaginable, this was an impressive degree of authority. For a legislature with no organized partisan majority, without parties even, in only its second-through-fourth years of existence, and passing the country's first budgets, it is simply astounding. It matters little the time period, amendment author, or amendment type: when the Committee made a recommendation, the odds were overwhelming that the Supreme Soviet would follow that recommendation.

It is commonly thought that, over time, Khasbulatov seized decision-making power from the committees. The record defies this notion. Budget Committee authority was consistent and, if anything, increased over time. In July 1992, in voting on the 1992 Budget, sixty-two of seventy Committee recommendations, or 89 percent, were carried. In March 1993, at the second reading on the 1993 Budget, an incredible 156 out of 164 Committee

Table 2.2
Budget Committee Floor-Vote Success Rates on Amendments to Increase Budget Spending

Budget Law	Amendments to Increase Spending	Spending Increases Adopted	Budget Comm. Recs. to Adopt	Budget Comm. Recs. to Adopt Followed	Budget Comm. Recs. to Reject	Budget Comm. Recs. to Reject Followed
1992 Budget	37	26	24	20	10	6
1993 Budget	70	8	7	6	62	60
1993 Budget revisions	139	79	79	72	57	52
Totals	246	113	110	98 (89%)	129	118 (91%)

Total Budget Committee recommendations followed: 216 of 239 (90%)

recommendations, or 95 percent, were carried.[38] A few months later, of 215 proposed amendments to the revised 1993 Budget on which the Committee made recommendations, 196 of the recommendations, or 91 percent, were carried.

If the Committee remained dominant across time, it was equally dominant across amendment type. Whether for spending or revenue increases or decreases, regardless of whether the Committee recommended adoption or rejection, the Supreme Soviet supported over 90 percent of the Committee's positions. More than half of all amendments that were considered during this span were to increase spending (see table 2.2). Committee recommendations carried on 90 percent of these votes. Of its 110 recommendations to adopt the increases, the Supreme Soviet adopted 98, an 89 percent success rate for the Committee. The Supreme Soviet was even more supportive of Committee opposition to spending increases, following 91 percent of such recommendations. The Committee made recommendations on twenty-two of the twenty-four amendments to reduce spending during this period, and the Supreme Soviet followed 91 percent of these, including two of the three to adopt the cuts (see table 2.3). The Committee enjoyed a perfect record on all amendments affecting revenues, whether or not the Committee recommended adoption or rejection of an increase or decrease (see tables 2.4 and 2.5). Finally, on 139 amendments that did not affect spending or revenue figures and on which the Committee made recommendations, the Supreme Soviet followed 129 of those recommendations, a Committee success rate of 93 percent.

Regardless of the type of amendment in question, and regardless of whether the Committee's recommendation was to accept or reject, the Supreme Soviet deferred to the Committee's expert judgment. This deference was consistent across time and across different amendment types, and it was consistent at a rate of well over 90 percent.

Perhaps the greatest test of the norm of reciprocity was when the Budget Committee opposed the proposals of the sectoral committees (see table 2.6). The expectation generated by this analysis is that the Supreme Soviet would have deferred to the Budget Committee's expertise, as one would expect the members of the Budget Committee to defer to other committees on legislation pertaining to their expertise. Of the ninety-three Committee recommendations to reject proposals from sectoral committees, the Supreme Soviet rejected eighty-eight, an impressive 95 percent Committee success rate. On the surface, it seems significant that all five cases in which the Supreme Soviet overruled the Budget Committee were on amendments

Table 2.3

Budget Committee Floor-Vote Success Rates on Amendments to Decrease Budget Spending

Budget Law	Amendments to Decrease Spending	Spending Decreases Adopted	Committee Recs. to Adopt	Committee Recs. to Adopt Followed	Committee Recs. to Reject	Commmittee Recs. to Reject Followed
1992 Budget	2	2	0	0	1	1
1993 Budget	8	0	1	0	6	6
1993 Budget revisions	14	3	2	2	12	11
Totals	24	5	3	2 (67%)	19	18 (95%)

Total Budget Committee recommendations followed: 20 of 22 (91%)

Table 2.4
Budget Committee Floor-Vote Success Rates on Amendments to Increase Budget Revenues

Budget Law	Amendments to Increase Revenues	Revenue Increases Adopted	Budget Comm. Recs. to Adopt Increases	Budget Comm. Recs. Followed	Budget Comm. Recs. to Reject Increases	Budget Comm. Recs. Followed
1992 Budget	2	1	0	0	1	1
1993 Budget	3	0	0	0	3	3
1993 Budget revisions	10	2	2	2	8	8

Total Budget Committee recommendations followed: 14 of 14 (100%)

Table 2.5
Budget Committee Floor-Vote Success Rates on Amendments to Decrease Budget Revenues

Budget Law	Amendments to Decrease Revenues	Revenue Decreases Adopted	Budget Comm. Recs. to Adopt Decreases	Budget Comm. Recs. Followed	Budget Comm. Recs. to Reject Decreases	Budget Comm. Recs. Followed
1992 Budget	1	1	1	1	0	0
1993 Budget	40	0	0	0	33	33
1993 Budget revisions	1	0	0	0	1	1

Total Budget Committee recommendations followed: 35 of 35 (100%)

Table 2.6

Budget Committee Floor-Vote Success Rates on Amendments from Different Sources

Amendment Initiator	Total Amendments	Budget Committee Recommendations Adopted	Budget Committee Recommendations to Adopt[a]	Budget Committee Recommendations to Reject
Other committees	207	171 of 187 (91%)	43 of 47 (91%)	88 of 93 (95%)
Individual deputies	72	62 of 67 (93%)	5 of 6 (83%)	33 of 36 (92%)
Government	134	120 of 132 (91%)	48 of 53 (91%)	39 of 43 (91%)
President	10	6 of 8 (75%)	0 of 1	1 of 1
Budget Committee	33	31 of 33 (94%)	5 of 6 (83%)	
Regional Soviets	20	20 of 20	0 of 0	20 of 20
Khasbulatov	3	3 of 3	1 of 1	2 of 2

[a] For this and the column to the right, I have considered only amendments that affected overall spending and revenue figures, not the many miscellaneous amendments also voted on.

to increase spending in some area. However, such amendments were also the most numerous — eighty of the ninety-three. Thus, the Supreme Soviet supported seventy-five of the eighty Budget Committee recommendations to reject these spending increases, a rate of 94 percent. Even more impressive, this was *higher* than the overall 89 percent rate at which the Supreme Soviet approved spending increases that the Committee *supported*.

Even on other committees' amendments, the Supreme Soviet supported Budget Committee recommendations at rates of 90 percent or more. There can hardly be a better measure demonstrating the effectiveness of inter-committee collaboration in the nonpartisan Supreme Soviet. The norm of reciprocity and mutual respect for the authority of the responsible committees was a direct consequence of this institutional design and enabled impressive internal consensus, even on such objectively controversial legislative issues as the annual budget.

Similar rates of authority held on amendments from other sources. For example, the Committee made 132 recommendations on the 134 amendments submitted by the government. The Supreme Soviet followed 120 of these, a Committee success rate of 91 percent. The Committee position carried on sixty-two of its sixty-seven recommendations on amendments submitted by individual deputies, a success rate of 93 percent. On its own proposals, including final passage of the bills, the Committee enjoyed a 94 percent success rate. It made no difference within these categories what types of amendment were in question. Whether for spending or revenue increases or decreases, or on other amendments, and whether or not the Budget Committee recommended adoption or rejection, regardless of who submitted the proposal, over 90 percent of the Committee's recommendations were carried.

This evidence strongly belies the assumption of an all-powerful Supreme Soviet Chair. Khasbulatov did frequently trample on the rules by announcing his opinion immediately before a vote, more often than not with sharp invective against those holding differing views. On some occasions, he opposed the Committee's position, but more often than not, his words urged support for the Committee.[39] *In every instance* the Committee's position carried. This bears repeating. There was *not a single case* in which the Supreme Soviet supported Khasbulatov when he took a stand opposing the Budget Committee's position. The only possible conclusion is that the Chair's interjections could buttress the Committee's position but not significantly undermine it. Even without Khasbulatov's commentary, though, Committee positions carried.

The facts simply destroy any argument that Khasbulatov "wield[ed] substantial power over all aspects of the Supreme Soviet legislative process" or "coordinate[d] the entire legislative process."[40] He was far from omnipotent in the legislative process. Khasbulatov offered three amendments of his own to the revised 1993 Budget, near the apex of his political confrontation with the President in July 1993 and supposed power over the legislators. Only one passed; it was the one the Budget Committee supported. The Committee openly opposed the other two, and the Supreme Soviet supported the Committee, not Khasbulatov. Some might argue that Khasbulatov controlled the other committees and members and that their amendments were actually Khasbulatov's amendments in disguise. But the logic behind that view is shaky at best. If the Chair was so powerful, why would he have needed to disguise his proposals in the first place? In any event, the evidence presented here powerfully demonstrates that it was the Budget Committee's recommendations, not the position of the Supreme Soviet Chair, that determined the fate of budget-related votes.

The Supreme Soviet Norm

Committees supporting each other's legislation in the Supreme Soviet bore some resemblance to the logrolling familiar to students of the U.S. Congress. It was not logrolling in terms of the pork-barrel politics revealed by Fenno, Shick, Wildavsky, and others, in which members and subcommittees added each other's pet projects in amassing support for budget bills.[41] In the Russian Supreme Soviet, supporting another committee on its legislation today could reasonably ensure its deference to one's own committee's legislation tomorrow. Conversely, sabotaging another committee on its legislation could lead to the victimized committee's retaliating against your own committee in the future. The logrolling mechanism was on the order of, "You give my committee our bill today, and tomorrow we will support your bill." In this sense, it was similar to the sort of deals the various Appropriations Subcommittee chairs strike in Congress. In the Supreme Soviet, it confirmed the authority and the professional expertise that the committees enjoyed.

On other issues under its purview in the same time period, including taxation, banking, and currency issues, the Budget Committee enjoyed a success rate of 94 percent, and altogether 93 percent of the Budget Committee's proposals were carried (see table 2.7).[42]

The Budget Committee was far from atypical. Its success rate was nearly

Table 2.7
Budget Committee Floor-Vote Success Rates on Nonbudget Legislation

Issue	Budget Committee Recommendations	Budget Committee Recommendations Followed	Budget Committee Success Rate (%)
Taxation	135	127	94
Customs/tariffs	59	58	98
Currency	46	38	83
Banking	93	89	96
Total	333	312	94
Budget	449	414	92
Grand Total	782	726	93

identical to that enjoyed by the other committees. A sample of bills from nine other committees shows an average success rate of 94 percent (see table 2.8). At rates consistently well over 90 percent, the Supreme Soviet respected and deferred to the authority, autonomy, and expertise of the responsible committee.

If anything, this analysis *underestimates* committee strength in the Supreme Soviet. Most legislation was approved on just four votes. The first vote was adoption of the draft "in principle" to use as a basis for discussion. The second vote was to adopt at once the full block of amendments that the responsible committee recommended for adoption. Once passed, a similar vote was held to reject the full block of amendments that the committee opposed. The final vote adopted the law itself. Only if one of the package votes failed did voting proceed by individual amendments. Separate votes would also be held on any amendments on which the committee could not reach a consensus recommendation. On the vast majority of laws, the responsible committee received complete deference, and laws were passed on these four votes.

The bills used to compile table 2.8, therefore, were those on which the package votes failed and on which a number of outstanding, controversial points remained. They were, in other words, among the most contentious pieces of legislation the Supreme Soviet grappled with during the period. They were also, not surprisingly, among the most important bills the legislature faced, including a new Criminal Code, the Land Law, and the Law on Military Service. If any set of legislative issues would undermine the argument in this chapter that the Supreme Soviet's design produced an

Table 2.8
Floor-Vote Success Rates of Other Committees

Committee	Committee Recommendations	Recommendations Followed	Committee Success Rate (%)
Legislation, Legality, etc.[a]	237	216	91
Social Development of the Countryside[b]	112	106	95
Local Self-Government[c]	65	61	94
Veterans Affairs[d]	54	54	100
Culture[e]	15	15	100
Defense and Security[f]	22	21	95
Transportation[g]	18	17	94
Property[h]	27	26	96
Freedom of Consciousness[i]	17	17	100
Totals	567	533	94

[a] Votes on Criminal Code, Law on Illegal Trade, and Law on the Government.

[b] Land Law, Law on Selection Attainments, Law on Livestock and Animal Husbandry.

[c] Law on Capital, Law on Budget Rights.

[d] Law on Military Pensions.

[e] Copyright Law.

[f] Law on Military Reform.

[g] Law on the Road Fund.

[h] Law on Implementation of Privatization.

[i] Law on Freedom of Worship.

extraordinary ability to reach internal consensus on legislation, this is it. Yet even on these bills, the Supreme Soviet reached internal consensus and succeeded in adopting the legislation. The institutional mechanisms for internal conflict management proved effective, even on these most conflict-ridden laws. Precisely because these were such contentious bills, they demanded a great deal of effort by the responsible committees to arrive at final language. Any committee that interfered with passage of those bills after such a process had neared completion knew that it would severely compromise its hopes for passing its own legislation in the future. The mark of success in the Supreme Soviet was how one's committee fared in passing its legislative agenda. The way to secure this was to cooperate with one's fellow committees in passing their legislation.

Reciprocity in relations, centered on mutual respect for the autonomy and expertise of the responsible committees, was fostered in the close working relationship between the leaders of those committees in the Presidium. It was the basis for the Supreme Soviet's extraordinary success at conflict management and consensus building in its internal legislative process. Deputies deferred to the professionalism and the expertise of the full-time members of the responsible committees and to the authority of the committee chairs, the legislative leaders of the Supreme Soviet. As one committee chair summed it up, "We worked professionally in our committee. We had a professional attitude, and therefore had the complete understanding of the Supreme Soviet. Always, always the authority of the committee, the authority of the professionals, influenced the whole Supreme Soviet. We prepared the questions and the Supreme Soviet followed the committee. It never happened that we submitted an issue but the Supreme Soviet said, 'No, you are wrong.' Never."[43]

THE BENEFITS OF COORDINATION

That a nonpartisan, committee-centered institutional design resulted in a high capacity for managing legislative conflict, and that it produced inter-committee coordination and an efficient legislative process, confirms the expectations generated by various new institutionalist studies, including those focusing on legislatures. As students of organizational theory have argued, in situations of uncertainty and competition, organizations that develop internal forms of coordination improve their access to resources, their ability to stabilize outcomes, and their ability to remain autonomous from environmental elements seeking control.[44] The more coordination takes the form of a centralizing body, as was the case with the Supreme Soviet Presidium, the greater the internal efficiency in the workings of that organization.[45] In the Supreme Soviet, centralization and coordination were possible because of the single-channel design around committees; they were realized through the creation of the Presidium of committee chairs.

In many respects, the Supreme Soviet appears to mirror the traditional characterization of the U.S. Congress. Students of Congress praise the efficiency brought by its organization around a fragmented, decentralized collection of committees, whose independent decisions are ratified on the floor.[46] Without this design, there would be no cooperation and deference, no logrolling, and, as Wildavsky argues, the "members believe that the House would 'run wild.' "[47]

The Supreme Soviet's internal process also confirms expectations generated by more recent congressional scholars writing in the new institutionalism genre. With their control over the coordinating body and their command of the members' respect and deference, the Supreme Soviet committees can also be seen as "agenda setters in their respective jurisdictions," as wielding power by controlling what issues will be discussed, how they will be discussed, by whom, and when. The committees, by controlling these procedures, held the "building blocks" of legislative decision making much as House committees have traditionally been viewed.[48] By presenting themselves as the chamber's "representatives" on issues, they further constrain any attempts to interfere with their decisions.[49] Others see the source of committee power as the power of persuasion.[50] Committees persuade through their control over and use of information, again reflected in their control over rules, process, and expertise.[51] Again, using these measures developed for the U.S. Congress, the Supreme Soviet would have to be described as "a well-designed legislature."[52] At least internally, the constraints on behavior in the Supreme Soviet that guaranteed ratification of the work of the committees was a version of the "structurally-induced equilibria" that Krehbiel and Shepsle laud in the U.S. Congress.[53]

In the Supreme Soviet, it was the coordination among the committee chairs that ensured that their authority would hold on the floor. It established clear lines of responsibility between committees and prevented alternatives to draft legislation from interfering with the committee's version when a bill came to a plenary session for action. As one committee chair put it, "There were very clear lines of specialization on draft laws by committees. For example, a draft law on foreign policy was necessarily headed by the Committee on Foreign Affairs. The initiator may have participated in this work, but it was still led by the responsible committee." As in the committee-centered U.S. Congress, the barriers that a piece of legislation had to clear to reach the floor were high. It had to pass through the Presidium, the responsible committee, the Committee on Legislation, and expert legal analysis, and only then could the Presidium schedule it for floor action. Said one Presidium member, "Quite often at sessions of the Presidium someone from the Committee on Legislation or other committees express concerns that one or another act cannot be adopted. . . . It is not rare that such questions are then removed [from the agenda.]"[54]

If alternatives existed at an early stage, the Presidium organized joint work among the various interested committees. In so doing, it prevented surprises when legislation came to the floor: "When alternative drafts were presented directly as sessions, this was a negative moment and brought strong criticism. It was asked why a position was not agreed to in committees, and the issue was removed from the agenda and sent back to committee." If for whatever reasons the consensus-building mechanisms had failed or not been used, the Presidium removed the bill from the agenda until consensus was reached. Normally, the responsible committees had already considered and taken action on all alternatives, and before coming to the floor, draft laws had received the implicit, if not explicit, blessing of all committee chairs in the Presidium.[55]

Committee chairs discussed in the Presidium the progress their committees were making on important legislation. They kept each other informed and learned each other's opinions throughout the process. They could expect each other's support after such consultation, and they received it.[56] In turn, the chair's authority within his or her committee virtually guaranteed that the remaining members, particularly the part-timers, would defer to their expert advice. In the absence of gross errors of omission or commission, a committee could count on summary support of its proposals. Where such errors were found, action could be taken to correct them, either via amendment or by cutting off debate and returning the draft to committee for revision.

But the standard in the Supreme Soviet was that by the time a piece of legislation reached the plenary session agenda for final action, it had proceeded through and received detailed examination in committee. The responsible committee on an issue received respect for its authority over issues under its purview, authority carved out in the Presidium by the full-time, expert leaders of each committee. Their mutual acceptance of each other's leadership within their areas extended from the nonpartisan and committee-centered nature of the Supreme Soviet's design. That design removed partisan politics from the legislative process, enabling the committees to focus their efforts on producing legislative output on the basis of expert technical knowledge. It was reinforced by already inherent Russian traditions of respect for and deference toward leaders. Together, the design and traditions produced norms and behavior patterns that ensured that a committee's adoption and recommendations were the final critical barrier that draft legislation had to cross before adoption by the full Supreme Soviet. Once cleared, the full body would, with minor and rare exceptions, pass it in the form approved by the committee. In its internal legislative activities, the Supreme Soviet worked like a well-oiled machine, achieving extraordinary consensus even on the most objectively controversial pieces of legislation — a testament to its mechanisms for internal conflict management.

External Activities:
A Machine Out of Control

The Supreme Soviet was a legislative machine, but it was a machine out of control. There can be no dispute that Russia's first democratically elected legislature was a spectacular failure. It failed, in the words of one presidential adviser, because even though it "worked out a mechanism for preparing, discussing and adopting legislation," it remained "uncontrolled and unpredictable" in its political activities.[1]

Several accounts of the Supreme Soviet's demise exist. Some focus on the polarization of the political elite into pro-Yeltsin and pro-Khasbulatov camps as the cause of the conflict.[2] However, while these accounts accurately describe the polarization that occurred, they beg the question, why did the elites polarize? What factors enabled the gulf to become irreconcilable? Certainly, polarization was not unique to the Supreme Soviet. Why was it so much worse there than in other legislatures? Other accounts blame the conflict between the legislative and executive branches on the unwillingness of the major players to cooperate.[3] But these accounts are blind to the impressive cooperation on legislative issues such as the budget. Why was such cooperation insufficient to prevent the ultimate breakdown? These descriptive and noncomparative accounts are valuable as first cuts at history, but they are unable to answer questions such as these.

If we want to understand why that legislature failed where others, including its successor, have been more successful, we need to be more theoretical in our approach. If we want to learn about legislatures more generally, we must be more comparative.[4] The comparative institutional approach employed here enables explanation rather than mere description. A comparative institutional theory can explain why the branches were able to cooperate on legislative issues but were unable to manage conflict on extra-legislative issues. If the problem were merely "elite polarization," the impressive cooperation in the internal budget process could never have taken place. The inability to manage extra-legislative conflict was due to the nonpartisan design in a highly fragmented partisan environment. A comparative institutional theory can explain why the same institutional design that fostered internal conflict management and consensus building on legislation exacerbated conflict and produced deadlock in the Supreme Soviet's relations with the government and with the President. Because the framework is explicitly comparative, it can explain why similarly designed legislatures in Belarus and Ukraine faced similar difficulties.

Single-channel, committee-centered legislatures leave their members unconstrained in the exercise of individual discretion on political, as opposed to technical, legislative matters. In the Supreme Soviet, this design left the Supreme Soviet Chair, Ruslan Khasbulatov, virtually unconstrained in his competition for political power with the executive branch on extra-legislative issues. Similarly, it left committee chairs unconstrained in defining the political orientation of their committees. It was precisely the absence of partisan factions that robbed the institution of the capacity to control or check the political line of the chairs on their respective issues, or of Khasbulatov in relations with the executive branch more generally.

As such, a comparative institutional approach can also explain the significance of accounts describing the failure of political parties to coalesce in the Supreme Soviet or in Russian society.[5] For example, while the Budget Committee Chair pursued cooperation with the executive branch, it was the authority devolved to the committee chairs that enabled him to establish a collaborative relationship. Because of the peculiar institutional design, the individual occupying the committee chair position was unconstrained to determine what would be the nature of that committee's relations with the executive branch. While the Budget Committee Chair proved to be a consensus builder and a conflict manager, nothing prevented other committee chairs from steering their committees in the exact opposite direction by excluding executive branch input in their activities and by pursuing conflict and confrontation in their relations with the executive branch and in their legislative outputs.

In other words, while the lack of partisan entities enabled a nonpartisan approach and conflict management internally on legislative issues, that same design enabled confrontation in relations with the executive branch. In fact, it provoked such confrontation on extra-legislative, political issues. Because no partisan organization or party leaders existed to take an interest

in such issues and to manage conflict on them, and because no other legislative leaders were positioned to handle political relations with the executive
branch, a vacuum existed. The Supreme Soviet Chair stepped in and filled
the vacuum unchallenged. Just as the committee chairs were unrestrained
in setting the political orientation on legislative issues, the Supreme Soviet
Chair was virtually unchecked and single-handedly able to pursue a line
of confrontation with the government and with the President on extra-
legislative issues. The result was extended political deadlock between the
two branches, and the legislature's ultimate demise. Before discussing the
deadlock and breakdown on extra-legislative issues, it is worth taking a look
at the Budget Committee's own relations with the government, the content
of the budgets that the Supreme Soviet passed, and the nature of Supreme
Soviet–executive branch relations on legislative issues more generally.

External Conflict and Legislative Issues: Budget Content

President Yeltsin signed and sent tanks to enforce Decree No. 1400 abolishing the Supreme Soviet just weeks after the Supreme Soviet passed a
revised 1993 Budget. A conventional wisdom emerged that the Supreme
Soviet provoked its own destruction by saddling the government with uncontrolled spending and deficit increases against government objections
and resistance.[6] However, concrete manifestations of Supreme Soviet fiscal
irresponsibility are difficult to produce.

In fact, the Budget Committee together with the government worked to
keep budget deficits from rising in the Supreme Soviet. Even at the most
confrontational stage with the executive branch, 64 of the 139 amendments
to increase spending in the revised 1993 Budget were the government's own
proposals. On two-thirds of these government proposals, the Committee
supported the government's lower increase over a higher, alternate spending increase proposed by a Supreme Soviet sectoral committee. On the
other third, where the Committee supported the higher figure of another
committee or a deputy, the government agreed, giving its explicit consent
before a floor vote. Moreover, the single most inflationary amendment, not
only on this revised budget but also in the entire history of Supreme Soviet
budgets, was submitted by the First Deputy Prime Minister! It was no
trivial amount: the increase he proposed for "state investment in the economy" was nearly 10 percent of the total spending side of the budget. Can
the legislature be blamed for irresponsibility in supporting an amendment

authored by the Prime Minister's highest-ranking deputy?[7] As one official conceded, "The government itself was severely divided" on budget policy.[8]

At earlier stages, legislative-executive relations produced even more impressive levels of fiscal responsibility. Joint work between the Committee and the government on the 1992 Budget resulted in consensus on deficit figures, and the Supreme Soviet ultimately increased spending by only R3.3T, or just 2.3 percent.[9] The total number of amendments that the Supreme Soviet considered amounted to R850 billion, or more than 25 percent of total spending.[10] Committee-government consensus on the 1993 Budget was even more impressive. The Supreme Soviet increased spending from R17.1T to R18.75T, an increase of about 8 percent. Of the R1.6T increase, only R26 billion, just 1.5 percent of the increase and a mere 0.1 percent of total spending, was over and above the prior consensus reached by the Committee and the government.[11] Of 267 amendments, the Committee and the government agreed in full on adoption of 118 and rejection of 124. While all amendments taken together would have ballooned the deficit to levels exceeding total budget revenues, the Supreme Soviet adopted only three amendments over the government's objection, and these amounted to a mere 0.1 percent of total budget spending.[12] The Supreme Soviet was simply not a budget-buster.

It was Committee-government cooperation, initiated by the Committee Chair, that brought overwhelming consensus on budget content. As one deputy put it, "We worked together with the Ministry of Finance during discussion of the budget, and together tried to beat off the many spending amendments."[13] When the budget came to the floor, the Committee and the government had reached a united position. The Committee appears to have been quite responsible in trying to hold down the deficit, and in light of the evidence it was quite successful. While it is true that the legislature was less fiscally responsible near its end, in no case did it increase budget spending by as much as 10 percent over government proposals. The total for the entire period considered here was less than 3 percent of total budget spending, although the total cost of all amendments that the Supreme Soviet considered would have more than doubled total budget spending. And many of the provisions that the Supreme Soviet did pass over government objections had some powerful supporters within that government, as the example of the First Deputy Prime Minister's amendment demonstrates.

How was such consensus achieved? The answer rests in the distinction between legislative issues and extra-legislative, political issues, and in the authority of those bearing the title "Chair" in the Supreme Soviet. On legislative issues such as the budget, the committee-centered design gave committee chairs the autonomy and the authority to determine how to produce the bill that each committee deemed best, including how to organize the committee's relations with the government. In short, it gave the committee chairs unrestrained authority to set the Supreme Soviet's political line on those legislative issues. It did so because no party leaders existed to predefine that political line.

What a committee's relations with the government would be like, however, depended on the personality, predilections, and politics of the committee chair. The Budget Committee Chair, Aleksander Pochinok, chose to collaborate with the government because he was a reform-minded economist whose friends included high and midlevel government officials. Friends and foes of the Supreme Soviet alike attribute the close working relationship on the budget directly to the personality of the Budget Committee Chair.[14] Similarly, in other committees that worked closely with their sectoral ministries, it was the committee chair who enabled the collaboration.

Pochinok set up the Budget Working Group, and the results of the floor votes and the content of the budgets passed demonstrate the degree of consensus reached there. It took intense cooperation between deputies and government officials to reach that consensus; as one participant noted, "We sat from the beginning and did not leave anywhere. During the entire debate we sat and sat, and we reached agreement in spite of everything."[15] It was the "psychological pressure" of the Budget Committee deputies working closely with the government that resulted in compromise on increased spending. "Without this pressure, maybe the government would not have compromised to this degree," one participant suggested.[16] But it was not just that pressure existed, for other committees and the Supreme Soviet as a whole pressured the government on a whole range of issues.

Rather, the key to budget compromise was that pressure was exerted in a close, informal working environment, behind closed doors in the Budget Working Group. This environment existed because the Budget Committee Chair made it exist. Pochinok used his authority within the legislature's institutional design by acting to extend the internal norm of professionalism to encompass Committee relations with the government. Indeed, given the broader context of the constitutional struggle between the Supreme Soviet and the executive branch in 1993, the words of Supreme Soviet and government participants, respectively, are telling:

Relations between the Supreme Soviet and the government in preparing the budget are always very difficult. Some try at times to represent these relations as an irrec̶ ̶ncilable war, but it is not like that. We cooperate very closely.[17]

We carried out an enormous amount of work with ministers, their deputies, the heads of departments, etc. And in the discussion of issues we remained at a strictly professional level. We had no principle differences except on figures in the budget.[18]

We always reached a preliminary compromise with the Supreme Soviet. That is, the Ministry of Finance and the Committee agreed on a joint position, a joint compromise, and then defended this agreement in the [full] Committee. And these agreements ultimately passed almost automatically.[19]

Even as the legislature and the President spiraled toward a fiery confrontation over political power, the Budget Committee and the government "worked 24 hours and reached full agreement" on a revised budget for the third quarter of 1993.[20]

One final example demonstrates the distinction between the Supreme Soviet's greater ability to manage conflict on legislative, as opposed to extra-legislative, political issues. It would, of course, be as ludicrous as the conventional wisdom criticized here to argue that all was rosy in the Budget Committee's relationship with the government. Two areas of particularly intense disagreement existed. One centered on process, namely government delay in and routine ignoring of deadlines for submitting the budget and other documents. The other centered on budget content, namely the form in which the budget was submitted and the degree of detail that it contained. Although a budget must be submitted before it can be considered, I deal with these in reverse order, as the issue of detail relates to the content of legislation. The matter of submission of the budget to the legislature is a political issue, which I address in the following section on extra-legislative conflict.

The Budget Committee and the government gradually and consistently made great strides in resolving conflict over the form and level of detail in the draft budget and in accompanying documents. The best evidence of the success was the sheer length of the budgets. The first 1992 Draft Budget contained just ten spending lines, general lines for defense, culture, the economy, science, education, and so on. As the Budget Committee Chair wryly put it, "The quality and level of the presented documents does not allow them to be considered a budget."[21] The budget finally adopted in 1992, however, was eight pages long, consisting of eighteen articles and seventy-one spending lines, and the government agreed to and assisted in this expansion. Indeed, the Finance Ministry itself eventually presented the breakdowns.[22] Clearly, the level of detail increased, and it continued to increase the following year. The first draft of the 1993 Budget was nearly four times more detailed than the one adopted the previous year, and the final law adopted was twenty-five pages long, with twenty-two articles and a dramatically expanded level of detail within each provision.[23]

The Budget Committee regularly demanded that the government "give a complete account of state revenues and spending" and urged the sectoral committees to echo such demands.[24] Budget drafts lacked detail, and many required documents were lacking entirely, while those provided were "incomplete, contain many mistakes, typographical errors, and other errors." However, the Committee rarely resorted to public attacks in its efforts to improve the level of budget detail and supporting documentation from the government.[25] The issue of what should and should not be included in the budget was a technical matter over the provisions of the law and was a matter for negotiation between the Committee and the government. This negotiation took place in the Working Group, according to several active participants in the process. Together, the Committee and the government drafted a Law on Budget Classifications to specify the articles and provisions required in the budget. Even though only a first draft existed when the Supreme Soviet met its end — and by 1995 the State Duma had only passed the law on the first reading — the work brought such major changes to the way the Finance Ministry approached its work and, consequently, to the quality of the documents submitted that the Committee Chair could describe the draft 1993 Budget as being "on a higher plane compared to last year" and deserving of "very serious work."[26] "For the first time there is a section on budget-formation indices. This is the base. We now know what it is we are trying to deal with. This is very important for us. We now can follow the size of production, the proposed profits, and other budget parameters."[27]

The Finance Ministry began working according to new budget classifications, even though the law had yet to be passed, in preparing the 1994 budget. For example, agricultural spending in the past was spread out across four or five different sections in the budget, including Ministry of Agriculture spending, capital investments, and transportation. But the deputies insisted that to understand just what was being spent on agriculture, these had to be consolidated. This was changed in the draft Law on Budget Classifications, and the Ministry, having negotiated agreement with the Committee, did not wait for this law to be adopted to follow this principle.[28]

Increased budget detail may have been among the Supreme Soviet's greatest achievements, "but it was not easy," as one deputy said, and it was a continuing struggle.[29] The government initially saw many Committee demands as creating unnecessary friction. According to one official, "Some of these demands are irrational. Many of these demands are for details which are not envisioned in the law [on the Budget Process], and our principle is that it is not required to go beyond the requirements of the law. We are against widening this."[30]

Although the government did begin using the new classifications, much remained outside of the budget. For example, spending for ministries was ratified within the law. But spending within ministries was not; such breakdowns were presented merely in an appendix to the budget.[31] Similarly, spending articles were "opened up within the law," but the Russian budget was not a program budget. As one budget expert put it, "Many tens of programs' financing are determined by the executive branch, and the legislative branch turns out to be a myth."[32] Program financing was still determined by the executive branch, not by the budget, meaning that the legislature had no control over these extrabudget programs. But there can be no doubt that the Russian budget steadily became more detailed and more coherent in its form, and much of the credit must go to the Supreme Soviet Budget Committee and the close collaboration it carved out with government representatives in the Budget Working Group.

In short, the evidence strongly supports the view that the Supreme Soviet Budget Committee successfully negotiated a high degree of consensus with the government on budget content and that the Supreme Soviet overwhelmingly approved these agreements. The potential for conflict clearly existed, and conflict did exist. But negotiations in the Working Group environment created by the Committee Chair enabled Committee and Finance Ministry experts to reach consensus. As with the content of those provisions, the Supreme Soviet Budget Committee cooperated with the government to manage conflict and produce consensual outputs on budget-related legislation.

Any committee could cooperate with the government on legislation. For example, the committees on Defense and on Industry worked closely with officials in the Ministries of Defense, Security, Intelligence, Atomic

Energy, Economics, and Finance to reach agreement on defense spending, defense industries, and conversion policy.[33] Committees whose chairs were so inclined to collaborate with their respective government agencies on the technical work in writing legislation were free to do so. And such relations produced a much higher degree of agreement than is generally acknowledged.

However, had the Budget Committee Chair been a different person, with different political views, there could just as easily have been no collaboration and high confrontation over budget policy. Just as he was not constrained *to* pursue collaboration and conflict-management strategies, he was not constrained *against* pursuing confrontational strategies. Committee chairs opposed to the government and wanting to exclude the executive branch from the process were free to do so. Many committees did not cooperate with the executive branch. Unlike existing accounts of the Supreme Soviet's demise, which focus exclusively on confrontation, a comparative institutional theory can account both for the ways in which the branches were able to manage conflict and for the ways in which they were unable to do so. Indeed, if we want to understand how different features of a legislature's design affect cooperation and conflict, it is imperative to take such an approach.

In a single-channel, committee-centered legislature such as the Supreme Soviet, the committee chairs determine the nature of relations with the executive branch on their respective legislative issues. Supreme Soviet committee chairs were the full-time, expert legislators with the power to set the agenda and the procedures in their committees. An important part of the procedures is the nature of relations with the executive branch. This was a political decision, and because the legislature had a nonpartisan design, committee chairs were autonomous and unconstrained within their respective legislative areas. Each committee chair stayed out of the others' political affairs, by way of guaranteeing their own autonomy and authority in their own areas. And no party leaders controlled the positions of the committee chairs in the legislature or organized them along party platforms. With no parties or institutionalized partisan factions, the Supreme Soviet lacked mechanisms to check committee chairs in their political orientation toward and their political relations with the executive branch on their respective legislative issues, just as it lacked mechanisms to check the Supreme Soviet Chair on extra-legislative relations with the executive branch, as will be discussed in the final sections of this chapter.

A comparative institutional theory explains why some committees cooperated while others did not. It reveals the important cooperation that did take place and that existing accounts of the Supreme Soviet have generally ignored.[34] It also helps to explain the particular dangers posed by single-channel, nonpartisan legislatures. They yield maximum discretion to the committee chairs to follow whatever political orientation they prefer. In a design that gives maximum freedom to exercise individual discretion, everything boils down to individual personality and predilection. That is a dangerous formula. Committee chairs who opposed the government's positions or, for whatever personal or political reasons, sought a more confrontational approach could completely shun any cooperation with the government. As one deputy explained, such committee chairs "elevated themselves to the level of state policy" and tried to take the place of the executive branch rather than work with it.[35] The Committee on Social Policy and the Committee on Science and Education were two committees noted for a particularly confrontational stance.[36] The bills they produced provoked confrontation. The typical response of the executive branch, with the legislature lacking mechanisms to compel political negotiation, was to issue decrees on the same subject matter even after Supreme Soviet laws had been passed. While others have attempted to explain this deadlock, they have failed to offer a general, comparative theoretical explanation of the cause.[37] With no alternative to the responsible committee with whom to deal on legislation, and with no organized parties or factions with a clear institutional role, a government excluded from the process on that legislation could choose to ignore the decisions of that committee and of the Supreme Soviet; it could issue its own contradictory decrees and edits. In such instances, confrontation and deadlock resulted and propelled the two branches toward broader political conflict.

The following section explains the conflict and deadlock between the two branches on extra-legislative issues. It first explains the relative impotence of committees and their chairs to manage such conflict. It then turns to how the Supreme Soviet Chair came to dominate the Supreme Soviet in extra-legislative relations with the President and with the government. It is on these broader political issues that the lack of partisan organizations in the Supreme Soviet brought the most negative consequences and robbed that legislature of a capacity to manage, much less resolve, such conflict with the executive branch.

EXTERNAL CONFLICT AND EXTRA-LEGISLATIVE ISSUES

The Supreme Soviet had a low capacity for managing conflict with the government on extra-legislative issues, a complication that emerged directly from the legislature's nonpartisan design. Even the committees were impotent for handling such political issues. The Budget Committee, for example, had no means for resolving conflict with the government over repeated delays in submitting the budgets. Conflict over submission of the budget was not about technical content; it was about the legislature's role in broader government political priorities, the separation of powers and relations between the branches. The Supreme Soviet's inability to manage conflict on this matter stands in stark contrast to its success on the technical aspects of the budget and its content. It mirrors the Supreme Soviet's general inability to manage conflict on extra-legislative issues.

Government delay in submitting the budget was a matter of conflict from the get-go. Just weeks after the failed 1991 August Coup, as the USSR limped toward extinction and the Russian President and Supreme Soviet shared a joint euphoric high of triumph, the Budget Committee Chair warned the President about the budget: "According to the Constitution and our Regulations, the President must submit to the Supreme Soviet a draft [1992] budget and a conception of economic development by September. But this material, unfortunately, has yet to be submitted. . . . This work must be accelerated!" Another deputy put it more bluntly, charging, "The government is ignoring the law." Khasbulatov echoed these sentiments.[38]

Not only did the government continue to "ignore the law" until more then three months into the 1992 fiscal year, it then began submitting quarterly budgets rather than an annual budget.[39] These budgets were in fact simply requests for ratification of total spending and revenue ceilings rather than actual budgets. The Budget Committee was utterly helpless to affect the situation; as one member colorfully revealed, "Our Committee did not agree with [examination of quarterly budgets]. But, we were sent a quarterly budget. And what was left to be done? Even if you do not agree, even if the law demands an annual budget, if a quarterly budget is submitted instead of an annual budget, then, well, you have to examine a quarterly budget. You can demand an annual budget, but if the government submits a quarterly budget . . ."[40]

Without political links between the legislature and the executive branch, conflict of this sort was virtually unmanageable. No Working Group existed until a budget was submitted, so the Committee Chair could only resort to public attacks: "The government constantly violates the deadlines and orders for preparing the budget as ratified in our laws. . . . I will take the chance once again to simply remind our respected government that according to the law, the 1993 Budget should already be under examination. You need to act immediately and follow the procedure we ratified."[41] The Supreme Soviet had just received a 1992 Budget when by law the 1993 Budget was supposed to have been under consideration. The government was hardly cooperative, as the Finance Minister's matter-of-fact responses demonstrated: "If you want to know, we are only beginning work on the conception of the 1993 Budget, although we should have already submitted it long ago. There is simply no strength, simply no time in the organizational sense."[42] The Prime Minister quipped, "If we had the same economic conditions as Germany, we would have begun in September too."[43] The government and the President delayed submitting the budget and, in so doing, faced continued conflict, both public and private, with the Budget Committee.[44]

Given the Supreme Soviet's relatively smooth success in its internal work on the budget, particularly given the time constraints imposed by the delays and the massive economic crisis being faced, one deputy's feeling of helplessness in resolving this political conflict was particularly revealing: "Everything else was solved. The single unresolved problem [in the budget process] was the deadlines. The problem of the date of the submission of the budget. I do not have any idea how the legislature can solve this problem."[45]

The institutional design of the Supreme Soviet did not afford that legislature many options for handling such issues, except to complain publicly and loudly. Compared with its ability to resolve conflict on technical aspects of the form and content of the budget, and its ability to resolve internal conflict to produce consensus and pass those budgets in the form agreed on with the government, the Committee had no mechanisms for resolving conflict on these political matters regarding the government's political priorities and overall relations with the legislature. Committee chairs were not leaders of political parties or backed by political parties that coordinated or engaged in negotiations with the government. Such partisan organizations were absent, and this absence robbed even those chairs who may have been inclined to manage such conflict with the executive branch of any effective means of doing so. It is not merely, as Remington says, that "elites polarized."[46] They polarized because the design of the legislature compelled polarization on particular types of issues, even where the members of the legislature may have preferred negotiation and consensus building.

The Supreme Soviet's inability to manage political conflict with the executive branch becomes more dramatically evident when looking beyond budget issues. The Supreme Soviet Chair, Khasbulatov, dominated such matters as the constitutional balance of power between the different branches of government, the composition of the cabinet and other personnel matters, and the myriad crises that arose challenging economic and internal state security. On these issues, the nonpartisan committees and their chairs had no role.

The peculiar institutional design of the Supreme Soviet explains why Khasbulatov was able to pursue a line of confrontation with the executive branch. The absence of organized partisan factions meant also an absence of any political leaders in the legislature to check the powers of the Chair. The nonpartisan committee chairs were responsible for managing legislative issues; they had no interest in or means for dealing with conflict with the executive branch on political issues. The Supreme Soviet Chair had no committee responsibilities of his own and no formal role in the legislative process. High politics was the only game for the Chair to play. He thus became the single politicized deputy and as such was unconstrained in pursuing his individual political agenda. Moreover, the constitution encouraged the Chair to take that game seriously. It proclaimed the legislature the supreme political authority in the country, and it was as the Chair of that legislature that Khasbulatov staked his claim as head of state. Even after creation of the presidency, the locus of control over the government remained unresolved, and the constitutionally supreme Congress of People's Deputies provided the Chair with an independent power base under his sole control to wage a battle over control of the government. I will now deal with each of these factors in turn.

The institutional weakness and general disorganization of partisan factions in the Supreme Soviet provided the space within which the Chair could seize unchallenged control over the legislature's political agenda. The committees set the legislative agenda in the Presidium, but this planned agenda accounted only for legislative issues; it virtually ignored the ongoing political crises and issues that continually arose in the unstable postcommunist environment of the new Russian state. Such issues demand legislative debate and some sort of action, yet those interested in such extra-legislative political matters had only the last recourse of the floor to try to attach these issues on the plenary session agenda. The committees had their legislative items safely on the agenda, but those with more political interests had no institutional role in the Presidium where that agenda was drafted. With committee chairs uninterested and no partisan factions with an institutional role, there was no forum in the legislature for consensus building on these political issues; those taking an interest had no choice but to take their political battles to the floor. Floor debate of the agenda was unstructured and highly acrimonious, a free-for-all over these broader political issues that regularly exceeded an hour and often consumed entire mornings of Supreme Soviet plenary sessions.[47] Things indeed looked extremely polarized in the Supreme Soviet during these debates! But it was not universal polarization. Distinguishing between legislative and extra-legislative issues, and examining the roles of different institutional actors such as committees and partisan factions, enables us to explain the nature of that polarization, why it occurred and how, and its consequences.

Only one voice could restore order to the chaos on the floor, and that voice belonged to the Supreme Soviet Chair. Indeed, the Regulations made it his duty to maintain order on the floor. Just as committee chairs had wide authority on legislative issues within and pertaining to their committees, so too did the Supreme Soviet Chair have wide authority on extra-legislative issues within the full legislature. On this nonlegislative side of the agenda, Khasbulatov's positions, and his frequent comments before agenda-related votes, were normally decisive. Often, in blatant violation of the rules, he made agenda decisions spontaneously and unilaterally without even allowing a vote.[48]

Similarly, Khasbulatov controlled all perks and privileges of being a deputy in the legislature. As Remington details, Khasbulatov doled out office space, apartments, summer cottages, chauffeured cars, foreign travel, and other perquisites of power, and he did so as he pleased.[49] On such internal extra-legislative issues as the political agenda and control over personnel, Khasbulatov was absolutely unconstrained in his actions.

The committee chairs in the Presidium did not constitute a check on Khasbulatov's power over internal extra-legislative political and personnel matters. They did not challenge him on the agenda battles because they were happy to see such purely political debates cut short. Indeed, the Presidium actually encouraged Khasbulatov to summarily decide the political issues on the agenda, to prevent delay and expedite consideration of their own legislation.[50]

Had there been partisan organizations with leaders to organize the legislature, these would have provided a means for prior consideration of such issues and for reaching agreement on ordering their appearance on the agenda. They could have taken an interest in leading these issues and constraining the Chair's leeway for action. However, the legislature's design excluded precisely those institutional actors that "could play a conciliatory role in the political resolution of problems."[51] It left the Supreme Soviet with no leaders in a position to constrain the Chair in handling such political issues. Khasbulatov not only filled this vacuum to dominate the political agenda, but he also took full advantage of the lack of constraints in exercising individual political discretion. The lack of a "political filter" analogous to the legislative filter of the Presidium allowed Khasbulatov to pursue a confrontational policy with the executive branch, and he pursued it to its logical and disastrous end.[52]

This design did more, however, than simply leave Khasbulatov unconstrained to solve internal agenda and personnel matters in the Supreme Soviet. As presidential advisers and former deputies alike explain, it also left the legislature without political representatives with whom the executive branch could meet and attempt to find compromise.[53] Because the political decisions of the Supreme Soviet could be seen as Khasbulatov's rather than as a consensus reached among a wide range of political leaders representing all partisan political groups, the President and the government could feel justified in ignoring them. That is, the louder Khasbulatov yelled, the less relevant those outside the legislature took him to be. Rather than negotiation and consensus building, the results were breakdown and deadlock between the legislature and the executive branch.[54]

Deadlock came because the Supreme Soviet Chair saw himself as and acted as if he were the head of state. According to the constitution, the Congress of People's Deputies and its Supreme Soviet were, together, the "highest organ of state power."[55] Khasbulatov, as Chair of both, opened and closed the legislature's seasonal sessions with wide-ranging addresses on the domestic and international situation in the country, and in the scope, length, and tone of these addresses he took the air of a head of state addressing the country.[56] Khasbulatov was crystal clear on his conception of his constitutional authority: "I as Chair of the Supreme Soviet carry the same responsibility as the President for all that occurs in the country."[57] He rejected references to himself as "Speaker" and reminded anyone who dared to use that label that the title was Chair of the Supreme Soviet. "A Speaker is silent, the Supreme Soviet Chair is not."[58] Mimicking the President's broad powers of decree, Khasbulatov issued a steady stream of orders and resolutions on political issues outside of the legislative process, ranging from creating an armed "Parliamentary Guard," to waging battles with major newspapers and publishers, to matters relating to the ownership and control of property.[59] He had control over a special fund for "Social Relief of the Population," which he randomly distributed, like a political leader bringing perks to his charges, when he made personal visits to various regions.[60]

Without question, the most important extra-legislative battle that ensued was between the Supreme Soviet, embodied by Khasbulatov, and the President over control of the government. After creation of the presidency, the locus of control over the government was a bone of constant contention between the President and the legislature. Khasbulatov, again acting unilaterally and in the name of the Supreme Soviet, issued a steady stream of orders demanding government action, often directly contradicting decrees issued by the President. Most frequently, these took the form of direct contacts with ministers and deputy ministers and with lower-level officials who typically were uncertain about who had the legitimate claim on their loyalties and obligations.[61]

Former Presidium staffers and government officials tell unending stories of Khasbulatov's attempts to control the executive branch and thwart the policies of the President and the Prime Minister. Khasbulatov would call or personally appear at the offices of midlevel bureaucrats and, as the head of the Supreme Soviet, order them to not implement a presidential decree or to ignore an instruction from the Prime Minister, branding those decrees and instructions illegal or unconstitutional. Alternatively, he would order those same officials to carry out policies that the legislature had yet to adopt, had received a presidential veto, or had simply been rejected in the legislature but which he, Khasbulatov, favored. Whether on pension policy, industrial policy, agricultural policy, or the mass media, and whether at the federal, regional, or local level, no sector and no official was immune. Any could be visited by Khasbulatov's insistent and surprise interventions.

To whom did midlevel officials owe their loyalty? To whom were they responsible? To the President as head of state? To the Prime Minister as head of the government? Or to the Chairman of the supreme organ of state power? There was no obvious answer to this question. But there was an obvious answer to a different question for the vast majority of these officials who were put in such a predicament. The long and often brutal history of Russia and of the Soviet Union provided a crystal-clear lesson for how to act. The solution was to do nothing, because the consequences of making the wrong choice, of giving loyalty to the wrong side, had so often been life threatening.

By bringing executive action to a halt, not only in Moscow but in regional capitals as well, Khasbulatov brought with his actions increased levels of conflict and deadlock with enormous economic and political consequences. He remained unconstrained in these actions because no interested party organizations in the legislature existed to challenge and limit his range of action. The executive branch had no one to negotiate with in the legislature on relations between the branches except for Khasbulatov, and Khasbulatov was increasingly uninterested in negotiation and consensus building. The question of what the balance of power between the branches would be, therefore, was unresolved.

Whether by oversight or intent the legislature left this major constitutional question utterly unresolved, even when it created the presidency. The Chair of the Committee on Legislation argued, "Neither the parliament nor the President has the right to give direct orders to the government, or to separate ministers."[62] By this interpretation, *nobody* controlled the government! Clearly, this was not a viable formula for resolving a conflict over power between the President and the legislature. Another committee chair, while less categorical, saw the main political crisis in the country as stemming from the lack of clarity regarding what aspects of the government were the control of the President and what aspects were the responsibility of the legislature.[63] The President, as chief executive, claimed responsibility for the entire executive branch, meaning the entire government and the ministries. The Supreme Soviet, led by Khasbulatov, maintained that as the constitutionally mandated supreme authority, it should have such control.

Not only were formal lines of responsibility unclear, but the Supreme Soviet Chair also saw it as his duty to continually provoke the legislature into conflict with the government, and no political leaders were around to either step in or compel Khasbulatov to engage in conflict management rather than in unconstrained conflict. Khasbulatov saw obstructionism as his duty: "We came to parliament to take upon ourselves the role of critics. And the rationale for a parliament is to be the natural opponent of the government."[64] Many committee chairs rejected such a conception of their work and did not proceed in this confrontational manner.[65] But their work was limited to the technical work of writing legislation. On matters of political power and control, the Supreme Soviet's positions were those of its Chair, not of the committees. What the Supreme Soviet lacked was a cadre of partisan political leaders interested in cooperating with the executive branch in the name of the legislature. But Khasbulatov dominated those relations, taking pride that his oppositional stand was not that of "some specific groups or factions," but of "the very Supreme Soviet."[66]

With such unchecked authority, Khasbulatov's politics quickly became the politics of conflict and confrontation, waged with invective and scheming, rather than a search for compromise. He branded members of the government "little kids in diapers," saying, "I have open contempt for these people, they are like worms." He addressed one as a "D-student," branded the Finance Minister "a worthless professor, he must be recalled," and another minister "a little boy." He then literally screamed at deputies accusing him of violations of ethics and the Supreme Soviet Regulations.[67]

Khasbulatov started out a political unknown loyal to Yeltsin. But "power has its own laws," as one Presidium staff member reflected, and Khasbulatov was "the wrong personality in the wrong institution at the wrong time."[68] In the political vacuum created by the absence of partisan factions, he seized the political initiative in the Supreme Soviet. He cemented his position by using the larger and constitutionally supreme Congress of People's Deputies as an independent power base. In the "political show" of the CPD, the Supreme Soviet Chair was not even checked by committee chairs in the Presidium. The Congress Presidium was made up of the Supreme Soviet Chair and his deputy chairs, who firmly controlled the organization of the congresses and their agendas. With over a thousand deputies, the congresses were not about legislating. That was the realm of the smaller Supreme Soviet. But "when they get together for only a few days, something happens to them," one commentator observed.[69] The CPD was an unruly and reactionary body, the place for discussing political and constitutional "turning points," for sounding off about political crises, and for waging a battle over power against the President and the government.[70] Khasbulatov convened congresses at every political or economic crisis, to hold highly raucous debate; he called government members to speak, to publicly chastise them.[71] Khasbulatov had virtually unchallenged authority at the congresses "to reject, destroy and silence those who disagree," and he "relished his dominance" over the deputies.[72]

A conflict over power was built into the constitution's ambiguous triangular design. Institutional mechanisms for managing such complex political relations were excluded from the Supreme Soviet's institutional design. On these extra-legislative issues, the political balance of power, control over the government, and other political crises that emerged, the legislature lacked organized partisan entities and recognized partisan leaders with whom the executive branch could have negotiated. The Supreme Soviet Chair's steady stream of public challenges to executive branch authority and direct interventions aimed at seizing control over government action raised questions of legality and responsibility in the minds of government officials at all levels. With no means to manage or control Khasbulatov's handling of such extra-legislative, political conflict, the battle between the

Supreme Soviet and the executive branch disintegrated into extended deadlock and the final bloody confrontation that was the legislature's demise.

SUMMARY

The single-channel, nonpartisan Supreme Soviet was able to get things done. The Budget Committee reached an extraordinary degree of consensus with the government and enjoyed nearly automatic Supreme Soviet approval of that consensus in passing annual budgets. That the former happened depended on the Committee Chair; the latter was a norm of committee authority throughout the Supreme Soviet. Both were the result of a nonpartisan institutional design centered on the committees and their chairs. With partisan political conflict minimized in its internal political activities, consensus was achieved and legislation was adopted to an impressive degree. In its last session alone, the Supreme Soviet passed 114 laws and 149 resolutions, and it passed 30 additional laws on the first reading.[73]

In this sense, the Supreme Soviet did indeed work like a "well-oiled machine" in its legislative activities, even on such objectively controversial legislation as the budget and even with the massive economic and political instability. Government officials continue to remember the Supreme Soviet as a "professional" legislature.[74] Those who have described the Supreme Soviet's demise have routinely failed to account for these legislative achievements.[75] They have done so because they have lacked a general theoretical framework for comparing legislatures.

The exclusion of partisan organizations in the Supreme Soviet's design, combined with the centralization of the legislature around the committees and the concentration of the committee chairs in the leadership, made the committee chairs virtual dictators on their issues. They determined the technical process of legislation writing in their issue areas. Intercommittee coordination and the lack of partisan organization kept political conflict in the Supreme Soviet's internal legislative activities to a minimum. On the budget, conflict was effectively managed through intensive and varied communications channels among the committee leaders, coordination organized by the Committee Chair.

But there was a flip side to this dependence on the committee chairs. The political line of a committee, in particular its orientation toward either cooperation or confrontation with the executive branch, was also in the committee chair's hands. Had the Budget Committee Chair been different or of different mind, he could have taken the approach of some other committee chairs, who isolated themselves from and took a confrontational orientation toward the government. The Supreme Soviet, in other words, had a clear and functioning process that ensured consensual legislative outcomes, but the direction of the content of those outcomes was heavily dependent on the predilections of the committee chairs. In many instances, the line taken provoked confrontation with the executive branch, confrontation that the Supreme Soviet lacked political mechanisms to manage.

Deputies could and did oppose legislation they disapproved of. But it was rare that they could garner enough rebels to stop a piece of legislation from passing, again, largely owing to the dominance of the committee chairs. The budget is a perfect example. The Committee on Social Policy, for example, could rebel en masse against a Budget Committee recommendation to oppose one of its amendments. But those votes would hardly be enough to defeat the Budget Committee, and other committees had no interest in similarly bucking the head committee on an issue. In other words, the only hope to "roll" the responsible committee was for enough committee chairs to band together in opposition. But if this were possible, then the issue would never come to the floor, for with a majority in the Presidium the issue would simply be taken off the agenda and sent back to committee.

Just as the committee chairs determined the political profile of their committees on legislative issues vis-à-vis the executive branch, so the Supreme Soviet Chair did so on extra-legislative issues. With partisan factions excluded from the legislature's institutional design, the Chair was left virtually unchecked in pursuing political confrontation with the executive branch. The result was a legislature unable to manage conflict with the executive branch, culminating in irreconcilable conflict, deadlock, and the ultimate demise of the Supreme Soviet.

These are the consequences of the single-channel, nonpartisan legislative design, and the consequences are general to that design. Stanley Bach describes a similar pattern of high capacity for lawmaking but a low capacity for managing relations with the executive in Ukraine's Supreme Rada. The Rada, from 1990 to 1994, was designed around a complex committee structure, with party organizations excluded from that design.[76] Similarly, in Belarus the President abolished the legislature, again a single-channel, nonpartisan body, when deadlock between the branches stymied policy making in spite of a legislature actively passing legislation.[77]

This design pattern, in an environment of weak or nonexistent political parties, seemed a logical choice to leaders in many of the newly independent states of the former Soviet Union. Committees are professional and issue-oriented, and the postcommunist states were in desperate need of legal reform across the entire range of legal issue areas. Minimizing the institutional role for partisan organizations that were themselves unstable seemed desirable in this environment because what was needed was action in legal reform, not necessarily a legislature debilitated by partisan squabbling and instability. But this choice caused unexpected consequences. The Supreme Soviet, like the Supreme Rada in Ukraine and the Supreme Soviet in Belarus, lacked any internal political checks and balances to compel compromise internally and externally across the range of legislative and political issues that came before it.

Those who designed the new Russian State Duma took as an important lesson from the experience of the Supreme Soviet that legislatures, if they are to function successfully, must incorporate partisan organizations into their institutional design. They may be incorporated in different ways, however, with dramatically different effects. The following chapters show that the Duma's design seems to have resolved the problem of conflict on extra-legislative issues, particularly in its external activities, by constraining legislative leaders across the board to pursue consensus-building and conflict-management strategies. However, the way the partisan factions have been included has exacerbated the problem of internal, legislative conflict by turning individual deputies into split personalities free to switch allegiances between their committee and faction identities. But the Duma's founding fathers seem correct in their perception that the Supreme Soviet's virtual exclusion of legislative parties and factions did hold consequences for its internal and external activities that were worth trying to avoid. By incorporating factions into the Duma's design they hoped to force political and technical consensus on legislative issues while preventing any one individual from dominating extra-legislative issues. In other words, the factions would serve as a check against the domination of the committees and their chairs, and against the domination of the Speaker over the political line of the new legislature.

PART 2

The Russian State Duma: Complete Chaos, Under Control

Only three months after the Russian Army bombed the Supreme Soviet into the past tense, the Russian electorate approved a new constitution and elected a new legislature.[1] But in spite of all the change, it appeared at first that little had changed. The new State Duma shares many of its unfortunate predecessor's characteristics: it has a large membership dispersed among roughly two dozen committees; its leadership body is called a "Soviet" and controls the work of the legislature; and ambiguity persists in the legislature's triangular relations with the government and the presidency — the government neither springs from nor is responsible to the legislature, while the President retains extensive decree powers that encroach on governmental and legislative prerogative.[2]

A fourth continuity also exists, one highly fortunate for the purposes of testing a comparative institutional theory: the socioeconomic environment in which the new legislature appeared was virtually identical to that of its predecessor. This fact is relevant because there is one significant and evident difference in the Duma's institutional design. Whereas the Supreme Soviet excluded partisan factions, the Duma has a dual-channel design with both committees and partisan factions. In spite of the weakness, instability, and lack of societal roots of Russia's postcommunist partisan organizations, the Duma's creators essentially grafted a faction-based structure onto the Supreme Soviet's design. With other environmental and institutional variables remaining constant, this affords an unusual opportunity to test the effects of institutional design on legislative behavior. What are the implications of increasing the strength of partisan organizations in legislatures in states with high levels of political fragmentation? If ever a political scientist could test the consequences of institutional design and attribute variation in performance to institutional design features, this would seem to be it.

A comparative institutional approach enables explanation of the differences in behavior between the Supreme Soviet and the Duma. The Duma's two organizational channels are unlinked, a condition that undermines that legislature's capacity to manage internal conflict on legislative issues. The lack of links removes constraints against the exercise of individual discretion. Such a design provokes conflict among the members while minimizing opportunities for and incentives to manage that conflict. On precisely those issues on which the Supreme Soviet was most adept at managing and resolving conflict, the Duma proves most inept.

The Duma's experience vividly demonstrates that simply including partisan organizations does not solve a legislature's problem of managing conflict. How they are integrated relative to legislative committees determines whether the combination of incentives and constraints compels legislators to pursue conflict management strategies or leaves them unconstrained in the exercise of individual discretion, even if this means breakdown and deadlock. The Supreme Soviet's nonpartisan, committee-centered design constrained deputies to pursue collaborative, conflict management strategies on legislative issues while leaving them unconstrained to pursue confrontational political strategies in the legislature's political, extra-legislative activities, particularly in relations with the executive branch.

The Duma's unlinked, dual-channel design, in which partisan factions and legislative committees exist as parallel, autonomous channels of organization, provides exactly the opposite incentives to members. The lack of links does not merely allow competition and conflict in the legislative process; it downright encourages it at every stage. In the Supreme Soviet, legislating was about writing and adopting laws. In the Duma, legislating is about political sabotage, procedural breakdown, and decision-making deadlock. Committee work is uncoordinated, leaving committees free to compete and fight each other, effectively blocking each other's initiatives. The factions control the Duma's leadership body and have little or no respect for committee authority on either legislative or procedural matters. Indeed, the notion of issues "belonging to" committees, such a central feature in the Supreme Soviet, is increasingly foreign in the Duma. Factions compete not only with each other in their partisan battles but also with the committees, provoking confrontation that stifles legislative action.

In other words, the Duma's unlinked, dual-channel design leaves individual deputies unconstrained in their actions, free to play the two channels of organization off each other, shifting back and forth in their allegiance to either their committee or their faction to suit their personal political ends. This situation leaves the Duma plagued by procedural breakdown and deadlock in its internal legislative processes. The institutional constraints to pursue consensus on legislative issues that characterized the Supreme Soviet are conspicuously absent in the Duma, where the stronger incentives are to pursue conflict and confrontation.

However, legislative-executive relations in Russia have improved with the advent of the new legislature. The organization around faction leaders provides the Duma with conflict management mechanisms the Supreme Soviet lacked for resolving conflict on extra-legislative, political issues, both internally and in relations with the executive branch. On issues ranging from forming governments, to filling internal leadership posts, to declarations of political amnesty, to the balance of power between the legislature and the executive branch, the Duma's design constrains deputies to pursue political consensus and to manage conflict with the executive branch.

The State Duma:
An Unlinked, Dual-Channel Design

The State Duma is a far cry from the well-oiled machine of the Supreme Soviet. Deputies describe the Duma's internal legislative process as *bardak* — complete chaos.[1] The root cause of the "chaos" is the Duma's unlinked, dual-channel institutional design. The Duma's committees and partisan factions are autonomous internal structures vying for deputy loyalties. The lack of links between them leaves deputies unconstrained in exercising individual discretion and renders the Duma convulsed by chronic deadlock in its internal legislative activities.

Duma committees, like their Supreme Soviet counterparts, exist to produce technically competent legislation. But unlike their predecessors, Duma committees are excluded from the legislature's leadership. One committee chair explained, "We have a matrix structure in this parliament. On the one hand are the factions, on the other are the committees. The Duma needs to improve the balance between the factions and the committees."[2] The partisan factions control the Duma's leadership and constitute a distorting filter through which all legislation must pass before final action. The notion of a "responsible committee" for a piece of legislation is significantly diluted by partisan competition between the factions. It is further diluted by intense competition between the committees themselves, for their exclusion from the leadership denies them any mechanisms to coordinate their activities. This chapter describes this peculiar design of Russia's new legislature.

ONE CHANNEL: PARTISAN FACTIONS

A party system did not emerge during the Supreme Soviet's life span, nor did one appear during the three months before the opening of the Fifth

State Duma.[3] However, fostering the development of political parties has been accepted by analysts and politicians in the West and in the former Soviet states as a necessary component of democratization. The electoral system employed to elect the Duma deputies, and the design that those deputies instituted in the new legislature, reflect this concern for creating Russian political parties. But the effort "to make the parliament a party parliament" brought instead a "highly fragmented parliament."[4] Half of the Duma is elected by a proportional representation (PR) vote from "party" lists in a single national district. Of the thirteen electoral blocs that contested the PR race in 1993, eight passed the 5 percent barrier to gain representation and automatically became factions in the new Duma.[5] The other half of the Duma's members are elected from 225 single-member, territorial districts.[6] As Robert G. Moser has found, most of these ran as independents and expressed a desire to remain so.[7] Indeed, a recent study found that 78 percent of Russian voters shun any party identification, making independence the politically astute choice for Russian political candidates.[8]

The electoral design in Russia may itself be described as an unlinked, dual-channel design. The PR and plurality elections are "two separate electoral arrangements operating side by side" with little "cross-contamination" between the two ballots.[9] They are largely independent of each other: party labels on the one do not appear on the other; nomination procedures and campaign processes are separate from one another.[10] This lack of coordination proliferates the number of partisan organizations competing in and produced by both sides of the election. The Duma created is intensely fragmented, sporting roughly ten registered factions and a number of other smaller groups.[11]

In spite of the literature's expectations on party behavior in legislatures, these myriad factions fail to produce a partisan majority. The literature assumes that the factions have an incentive to do so, but this is in fact an empirical question. Duma factions lack any institutional incentive to form a majority. As is the case during elections, the premium is on going it alone.[12] As Remington and Smith correctly describe, the factions work to protect their collective "procedural rights."[13] The necessity of belonging to a faction became clear to all members from the outset, when the leaders of the original eight factions began meeting before the opening of the Fifth Duma to determine the internal organization and the rules of the new legislature.[14] Predictably, the faction leaders decided it would be they, not the Speaker[15] or the committee chairs, who would control the Duma's leadership body, the Duma Soviet. These partisan leaders in the Duma Soviet created the committees, divvied up leadership posts from the Speaker on down to committee chairs, and distributed deputies among the committees.

Even the independent deputies quickly recognize that the only advantage of maintaining "independence" is that it enables one to proudly proclaim no partisan affiliation to an electorate highly suspicious of anything called "party" or anyone associated with an organization using that label.[16] Virtually all consequences within the Duma are not merely negative, however; they are downright painful! In the end, almost all deputies elected as independents join an existing faction or form one of their own. One late joiner explains why: "I was not going to join a faction, until I realized that I had become 'Mr. Nobody.' I had no rights. I was a second-class Deputy."[17]

The disadvantages of independence were made clear in the Fifth Duma by the experience of the December 12 Union, formed from among independents elected from single-member districts. The rules required a faction to have thirty-five members to be registered.[18] The "Decembrists" initially had twenty-three and waged an unsuccessful battle to reduce the number required for registration. The Decembrists complained of being "treated as inferior deputies," for without status as an official faction they were excluded from the Duma Soviet. They were unable to influence the agenda, unable to command time on the floor on legislation, and lacked usable office space. In short, they were virtually excluded from the legislative process from beginning to end.[19] They eventually accumulated the requisite thirty-five deputies to gain official registration and the status that went with it.[20] But within months a handful of members bolted, and they again lost their status. One of its leaders complained, "The threat to our faction's registration is very serious, because it would mean our deputies would lose their offices, that we would lose the possibility to openly present our opinions in the parliament. . . . We would be unable to participate in the work on the agenda."[21] Such was the fate of the December 12 Union, which disappeared in January 1995. Its members scattered to other factions, or joined with defectors from other factions to form new ones in the fluid environment leading to the 1995 elections.

Particularly in its first months, when the Duma led a nomadic existence, most deputies lacked offices. But those who were members of factions could retreat to the faction office or meeting room. Independent deputies had nowhere to hide and were left to congregate in the leather lounge chairs in the corridors of the parliament building, unable to escape the whirring Dictaphones of the Moscow press corps — and one American political scientist!

So not only are there a multitude of factions in the Duma, but they also have a special place in the Duma's institutional design and clearly "are more powerful than they were in the Supreme Soviet."[22] A deputy who is not a member of a registered faction can hardly be considered a full-fledged deputy.

Factions may be institutionally stronger, but as one deputy put it, they are "still very weak. They are weak in managing their members, the leaders are weak within them."[23] Such has been the trend across postcommunist Europe. Partisan factions are highly unstable. As David M. Olson describes, from Albania to Russia, "Once in parliament the parties combine and recombine in new formations. . . . Neither the number nor the size of party groups remains constant."[24] In Russia, most factions have radically diverse memberships. Deputies join electoral blocs in the PR campaign as a matter of convenience, to increase their chances of election rather than to support a shared political platform.[25] Expediency certainly drove those independent deputies, such as the Decembrists, to join factions. Not surprisingly, fluidity in membership is the norm for all factions, small and large.

The low internal cohesion became evident as the 1995 elections approached. Factions like the Decembrists collapsed, and new ones formed almost on a weekly basis. Of the thirteen original factions that competed in 1993, only five ran in 1995, and even their memberships and candidates had changed dramatically. In the meantime, thirty-eight new electoral blocs sprung up to compete.[26] As of this writing, 28 electoral blocs are on the ballot for the 1999 Duma elections. Again, the vast majority are new organizations formed for electoral convenience, rather than true political parties. The unlinked, dual-channel designs of both the legislature and the electoral system gives Russian politicians far greater incentives to go it alone than to cooperate. Such partisan fragmentation is common across postcommunist Europe, but Russia's peculiar institutions exacerbate the problem.[27] As authors such as Hough and Moser have argued, party development in Russia since 1993 is most notable for its failure, and the Duma's design has only impeded party consolidation.[28]

At the same time, parties are extremely hostile to and suspicious of each other. Russia's many small partisan factions are each led by politicians seeking to build and lead a new political empire after the demise of the Communist Party dynasty. The leaders all view themselves as the future president and have created personalized cliques promoting their candidacies.[29] Not surprisingly, they are hostile to and suspicious of each other.

Still, being a faction member actually means something in the Duma, and it certainly means more than it did in the Supreme Soviet, where factions resembled dining clubs more than legislative parties. As a reflection of this enhanced institutional role, deputies perceive greater partisanship in the legislature's operations. One Duma leader complained, "There is still a widespread tendency to approach sessions as political demonstrations, and that destroys legislative work."[30] The Speaker echoed these words at the end of the legislature's first seasonal session: "Many deputies still have not come to terms with the nature of deputy work. Several representatives of certain factions approach their work as a political demonstration [and] rush to the microphones and shout, demonstrating their obvious lack of professionalism and lack of the qualities required for high state office."[31]

The increased role of factions is the most startling institutional change from the Supreme Soviet to the Duma. In such a splintered partisan environment, this change has meant increased partisanship throughout the Russian legislature. The consequences flow from the way those factions interact with the other organizational channel, the committees.

A Second Channel: Legislative Committees

The inclusion of factions has blurred the distinction of committees as being "professional" as opposed to "political." One Duma deputy presented a new view: "Committee activities should reflect not only professional legislative work, but also factions and the political spectrum of society."[32] The rules of committee work changed very little in the Duma compared with those of the Supreme Soviet, but the circumstances of that work changed a great deal. For one, all Duma deputies are full-time legislators. The standard comparative legislative studies literature, which suggests that the presence of committees makes legislative work full-time, appears in need of some adjustment because in the Duma this change coincided with the introduction of partisan organizations.[33]

A second difference flows from the way committees are formed. Committee assignments are the result of a bargain struck by the faction leaders in the Duma Soviet.[34] Leadership posts in the Duma — the Speaker, deputy speakers, committee chairs, and deputy committee chairs — are each assigned a number of points. The points are then totaled, and each faction is allocated a portion corresponding to its percentage representation in the Duma. A faction with forty-five members receives one-tenth of the points. The leaders then bid in a sort of auction for leadership posts, with each faction "spending" its points for desired positions. For example, in December 1993 the Agrarians got the speakership "and immediately ran out of points."[35] Meanwhile, deputies submit their desired assignments to their faction leaders, who distribute them accordingly. The Duma Soviet approves the final package, which the full Duma ratifies.

Tidy though this appears on paper, it created quite a mess in practice. The first consequence of involving every faction leader in allocating leadership posts was to thoroughly undermine the vision of a Duma of few committees. The designers of the constitution hoped to create "mini-Dumas" of a dozen or so committees whose political profiles would mirror the political makeup of the Duma as a whole. Said one participant, "Our conception was to have few committees with large numbers of deputies from all factions. They would function as mini-parliaments. They would carry out all serious discussion and debate, and then at plenary sessions we would not have such long, routine work on amendments and conception of laws. If there were six or eight committees, then there would have been more deputies working in them, more would have participated."[36] The combination of faction affiliation and committee membership would, they thought, bring a balance the Supreme Soviet lacked. Not only would committee members become "experts" in their designated areas, the committees thereby producing "professional" legislation, but that legislation would also reflect a multipartisan consensus acceptable to all.

Things have not worked out that way, to say the least. Rather than compromising with partisan enemies, the competing faction leaders ballooned the number of committees to an eventual twenty-three.[37] The existing literature on legislatures has long suggested that the greater the number of committees that a legislature has and the more "complex" the committee structure, the more "institutionalized" and stable is the legislature.[38] David E. Price even suggests that it is precisely in states with weak legislative parties that a complex committee system will contribute to internal stability.[39]

The Russian case thoroughly undermines these expectations and demonstrates the utility of a comparative institutional framework for explaining the conditions that produce stability and those that produce instability. The proliferation of Duma committees has not produced institutional stability, because that proliferation had nothing to do with legislative necessity and everything to do with partisan politics. At the first meeting of the faction leaders in the Fifth Duma, leaders from diametrically opposed factions demanded the chairmanship of the Budget Committee. So the Duma Soviet created a Committee on the Budget, Taxation, Banking, and Finance, giving the chair to the pro-reform faction, and a Committee on Economic Policy, giving the chair to an anti-reform faction. When Yabloko and the

Liberal-Democratic Party of Russia (LDPR) both demanded control over the Committee on Foreign Affairs, under threat of preventing any conclusion to the committee-formation process, the faction leaders simply added a Committee on Geopolitics and gave the chair to LDPR. This dynamic repeated itself to such an extent that for any committee in the Duma another may be identified that claims responsibility for the same issue area. What are the boundaries between the Committee on Foreign Affairs and the Committee on Geopolitics; between the Committee on Ecology and the Committee on Natural Resources and the Environment; or between the Committee on the Budget, Taxation, Banking and Finance and the Committee on Economic Policy?

No doubt the Duma has many committees, but despite the expectations in the literature this is not an obvious good. With no coordinating mechanism between them, and with chairs who are sharply hostile partisan opponents, committees with muddled boundaries provoke rather than ameliorate legislative conflict.

A second consequence of this method of committee formation is a thin stretching of deputies across committees. None of the numerous factions have enough numbers to place members on all two dozen committees. Some simply have fewer members than there are committees — in the Fifth Duma, the Democratic Party of Russia had only fifteen members — and no deputy may serve on more than one committee. Other factions have a disproportionate preference for one or two committees, which drains their membership and precludes representation on other committees. For example, twenty-one of the Committee on Agriculture's twenty-six members came from the Agrarian faction, meaning six factions gained no representation on that committee and leaving the Agrarian faction, the Fifth Duma's fourth largest, with no representation of its own on three other committees. In all, seventeen of the twenty-three committees in the Fifth Duma lacked representation from at least one faction, while the average for the factions was five committees without representation (see table 4.1). Moreover, three committees had fewer than the minimum of twelve members required by the Regulations, while one had more than the maximum of thirty-five.[40]

Duma committees thus have nothing resembling proportional faction representation. One committee chair explained this result according to the old distinction between "professional" and "political" committees: "I think it is very difficult in our conditions to hold strictly to this principle [of representation of all factions on committees] because deputies still try to hold to their specialty. A professional wants to make use of his professional

Table 4.1

Number of Committees on Which Factions of the Fifth
State Duma Lacked Representation

Women of Russia	10
Democratic Party of Russia	9
Yabloko	7
Party of Russian Unity and Accord	7
Agrarian Party of Russia	3
Liberal-Democratic Party of Russia	3
Russia's Choice	1
Communist Party of the Russian Federation	1
New Regional Policy	1
Liberal-Democratic Union of December 12[a]	14

[a]The Decembrists formed after distribution of committee posts.
When they are excluded, the average number of committees on
which a faction lacked representation was 4.7.

knowledge, and as a result the make-up of committees does not reflect the
opinions of the whole Duma."[41] Most deputies, however, argue that the
primary reasons for the large number of committees and for the discrepan-
cies in faction representation across them are the large number of small
factions and the unbounded partisan political aspirations of their leaders.[42]

A third destabilizing consequence of the committee formation process
in the Duma is a lack of partisan consistency within and across committees. The committee formation process suggests that the faction leaders
sought to prevent, rather than to foster, creation of a consistent partisan majority. Said one committee chair, "Our committee is dominated by
Russia's Choice, Yabloko, and PRES, that is parties of a certain wing, although its chair (myself) is from the other side."[43] The faction leaders
span the entire partisan map, and each sits on the Duma Soviet with one
vote. Every faction receives at least one committee chair post and, as is
the case with the Speaker and the deputy speakers, a committee's chairs
and deputy chairs must be from different factions.[44] Moreover, the chair
of a committee may often be alone, with no faction colleagues on the
committee and sometimes with no deputies from factions of the same part
of the partisan spectrum. One committee may be entirely dominated by
a single faction, such as the Agrarian-dominated Committee on Agriculture, while another committee may be dominated by more liberal factions. The chairs and the various committee majorities range across the

political spectrum from far left to far right, while within committees the chair and the majority are often from opposite ends.

The increased institutional strength of factions came at the expense of committees. Veterans of both legislatures cite this as the greatest difference between the Supreme Soviet and the Duma.

> There has been a very serious reduction in the status of committees in the Duma. In the Supreme Soviet factions were anemic. Leaders of factions were not members of the Presidium, and this was a problem. But today the picture is stood on its head. Now committees have been made weak and this is bad.

> Not only are committees here weaker, but so are the chairs of the com-mittees. The chairs lack many levers they had before. They do not vote in the Duma Soviet.

> The strength of the committees was far greater [in the Supreme Soviet]. There, people were not in parties, this did not exist.[45]

The stunning weakness of Duma committees would seem to demand in particular a reconsideration of the expectation of strong legislative commit-tees in presidential systems. The constitutional system appears less impor-tant than the design of the legislative body itself. Others have found that introducing committees to a single-channel, partisan legislature weakens the parties.[46] In Russia, adding partisan organizations to a single-channel, nonpartisan design has weakened the committees. As discussed in the intro-duction, most of the literature expecting strong committees in presidential systems is in fact based on studies of the U.S. Congress. However, a com-parative institutional approach enables explanation of the weak status of Duma committees and can encompass explanations of changes seen in the Congress itself in recent years. It is not only the inclusion of the parties but also the weak links between the channels that have most undermined the status of Duma committees. Wildavsky and Schick in particular have re-cently noted a similar erosion of the power of congressional committees and have tied that to the increased institutional autonomy that congressio-nal parties have asserted in recent years.[47]

Two Unlinked Channels

In the Supreme Soviet, committee chairs also spanned the partisan map, and this did not prevent internal conflict management. In the Duma, however, the dual-channel design means committee chairs have dual organizational identities. The competing channels spell trouble for the Duma, as no link exists between one's partisan orientation and one's committee affiliation. One frustrated committee chair bemoaned the chasm between factions and committees: "In the [Duma Soviet] the heads of the factions meet. They do not sit on any committees at all, yet they nevertheless decide the fate of legislation. The leaders of factions do not work in committees, and the committees are not part of the Duma Soviet. The biggest problem with the Duma, the most obvious problem, is that there is no working coordinating body."[48] In a dual-channel design, if the channels are linked through either a leadership or a coordinating mechanism, the point at which they are linked may gain the authority and the means to manage conflict between and across disputing actors within the institution. The benefits of linkage are elaborated by Philip Selznick, who speaks of "dual power"; Peter Evans, who speaks of "dual hierarchies"; and Simmel, who speaks of "dyads."[49] Linkage imposes constraints on the exercise of individual discretion, constraints that compel the pursuit of conflict management rather than confrontational strategies. Linkage facilitates information exchange, communication, and negotiation; in short, it is essential for consensus building.[50] Linkage promotes negotiation and agreements, which reduces uncertainty and increases predictability and stability of outcomes. Without them, members of the different channels are free to shift between their dual allegiances. This shifting denies an organization all the advantages just noted; it results in a high degree of institutional instability and conflict rather than consensus building and conflict management.[51]

There are several ways to link the channels in a dual-channel legislative design. Each method promotes coordination and conflict management. A strong Speaker, a coordinating body incorporating both channels, and effective "enmeshing" of one channel by the other (for a legislature, this would mean consistent faction or coalition control of all committee chairs and committee majorities) are the three most common options.[52] The Duma lacks all of these.

The framers of the constitution and the rule makers for the new legislature sharply constrained the powers of the Duma Chair in the wake of the experience with the Russian Supreme Soviet Chair and the USSR Supreme Soviet Chair before him.[53] That the Chair of a legislature can serve as a unifying political force is testified to even by Khasbulatov's most stringent political opponents: "The Supreme Soviet was more authoritative, with the strong influence of Khasbulatov on all political questions. This is on the one hand bad, but on the other hand it allowed the Supreme Soviet to reach a united position."[54] The weakening of the Duma Chair stems less from the defined powers of the office than from institutionally entrenched constraints on his freedom to act. The constraints come from the factions. The Speaker is beholden for his position to the faction heads and to their political agreement in the bargain over leadership posts. Were he able to appoint his own deputies and committee chairs, were the Duma Soviet to consist only of the Speaker and his deputies, the office could serve as a unifying force between factions and committees. The Speaker would become what Selznick terms the "central focus," with the authority to compel cooperation, induce coalition formation, and resolve crosscutting conflict over priorities and strategies.[55] As a source of authority the Speaker would become Simmel's "third who benefits" and who benefits the organization as a whole.[56] Most significant, with such powers the election of the individual would be of greater moment, compelling the factions to reach a working coalition agreement that would preserve for that coalition all leadership posts.

But the Duma Speaker lacks all such powers. The faction leaders jealously guard them, and unlike the apolitical Supreme Soviet committee chairs who formed the Presidium, the faction leaders in the Duma Soviet are highly partisan. Their interests are not in the technical aspects of legislation, but in partisan politics and the battle for political dominance. Their shared interest is in ensuring that together they maintain political control over the institution and in constraining each other from usurping control. No faction leader has an interest in ceding authority to anyone else, and all have an interest in politically constraining the Speaker.[57]

The Speaker is confined to running the daily session, overseeing order in the hall, and serving as a mediator between feuding faction leaders in the Duma Soviet. While it is no trifling point that the Speaker of the Fifth Duma, Ivan Rybkin, was obviously quite a different personality from Supreme Soviet Chair Khasbulatov, the institutional design is most directly responsible for constraining the powers of the Chair of the new Russian legislature. This is vividly evident in the behavior of Rybkin's successor, Communist Party member Gennadiy Seleznev. Seleznev was a vociferous and "irreconcilable" opponent of the President and of the government, but after becoming Speaker his behavior was virtually indistinguishable from Rybkin's. Unlike Khasbulatov, Duma Speakers face imposing constraints limiting their ability to act. Any independence meets swift counterattack by the faction leaders in the Duma Soviet. A Duma Speaker, therefore, is unable to compel coordination and is unable to use his position to subordinate or unify the group, to use Simmel's terms, because he is not recognized as a true leader of the institution.[58] He must work through and with the factions, unlike Khasbulatov, who was free to act for or as the Supreme Soviet.

A second means of linkage is through a "central coordinating organization," which Jeffrey Pfeffer and Gerald R. Salancik argue is the most effective option "when there are many small competitors."[59] The Duma's multiple factions and two dozen committees clearly fit that description. The Duma Soviet could be an effective linking mechanism, but because it excludes an important class of "competitors," it is not. Faction leaders do not sit on committees, and committee chairs do not sit on the Duma Soviet, leaving committees unrepresented in the Duma Soviet. The Duma Soviet is a place for political coordination and for negotiation and cooperation between "political interests," but it is not a "central coordinating body" of the sort Evans speaks of, which can unify all suborganizational interests.[60] The "professional interests" of the committees are excluded. Were the committee chairs also to sit on the Duma Soviet, it could perhaps serve such a linking function. But they do not, and it does not. This should not be taken to mean that the Duma Soviet is a weak body. It is so only in the "professional" legislative sense. Its duty is to resolve conflict on extra-legislative political issues, and as chapter 6 shows, it is often effective at doing so. But whereas the Supreme Soviet Presidium served as a committee on committees, the Duma lacks any analogous body.

A third means of linking factions and committees would be to compel consistent faction or coalition majorities across committees. Organizational theorists have found that where dual channels exist, enmeshing each in the other's networks makes relationships more binding and more stable.[61] The multiple factions of the Duma have not recognized any interest in coalescing into majorities, nor have the rules compelled such coalition building.[62] Were the 450 members of the Duma divided among two or three parties or coalitions with the majority controlling the leadership, the committee leaderships, and the majorities on committees, the benefits of linkage could be realized. The factions would become more party-like in their platforms, membership, and internal cohesion than are the small leader-based cliques that currently populate the Duma. It is highly likely that there would be far fewer committees, perhaps twelve or fifteen, and none of the existing duplication. Consistent partisan control would ensure coordination of strategies and priorities across committees and the faction or coalition of factions that controls those committees. It would induce consensus building throughout the process.

Duma faction leaders have failed to create any of these forms of linkage, with lasting consequences for that legislature. The myriad small factions stretch across nearly two dozen committees, and a single faction member on a committee often finds it difficult to speak for the entire faction or to return to the faction and expect adherence to agreements reached in committee. The links are extremely tenuous. Some deputies publicly stated that the lack of a majority would be a good thing for the Duma. Said one prominent member, "In the Duma not a single political structure has an absolute majority, and this, to be honest, is good for Russia."[63] In just six months the frustration of persistent internal deadlock on legislation led this same deputy to propose virtually any means conceivable to force creation of a majority in the Duma.[64]

That the Duma factions failed to create consistent majority control throughout the legislature suggests a weakness in the literature on the role of legislative parties. That literature tends to assert in universal terms that "parties control party and staff ratios on committees, appointments and scheduling."[65] It assumes that party leaders share legislative priorities and commitments with the committee chairs, that "the majority influences the committee chairs," in short, that a partisan majority will "stack the deck" to ensure favorable outcomes in a legislature.[66] But legislative parties do not always form majorities. Sometimes, they may face stronger incentives to remain fragmented. The mere existence of parties does not magically mean that committees are no longer autonomous, as some recent literature suggests.[67] A comparative framework can explain this concept by examining the consequences of alternative institutional designs. Parties may indeed play a role in structuring a legislature, but they have many ways of going about that structuring. For understanding legislatures in general, rather than understanding simply the U.S. Congress or the British Parliament, we must look at the institutional incentives and rules determining how that structuring takes place, for the consequences for legislative behavior are substantial.

With a weak Chair, with committees excluded from any leadership or coordinating role in the legislature, and with no consistent partisan majority controlling leadership or committee posts, the two channels in the Russian State Duma — factions and committees — are about as unlinked as they can be. Such a design in a highly fragmented partisan political environment creates strong incentives for members to pursue strategies of sabotage and

confrontation rather than those of consensus building and conflict management in the internal legislative process, as chapter 5 demonstrates.

The Constitutional Triangle: Persistent Ambiguities

Were the Duma required to form the government, the factions would have
to reach some sort of coalition agreement of cooperation, which could
provide an external inducement to conflict management and linkage.[68] But
the triangular relations between President, government, and legislature are
nearly as ambiguous under the new constitution as under the old. The
President names the head of the government. Constitutionally, the Duma
gives its approval to this appointment, under threat of dissolution if it
refuses. The Duma may also vote no confidence or, when the government
so requests, confidence in the government, again under threat of dissolution.[69] The Duma is thus relegated to an essentially silent role in naming
the government, removing the potential incentive for coalition building
and the creation of a partisan majority in the legislature.

Relations between the President and the legislature are clearer under the
new constitution in that the days of the legislature being the "highest organ
of state power" are gone. The Duma's powers are notably circumscribed
compared with those of the President and its predecessor.[70] Yet important
ambiguities remain. The Duma is the legislative organ of government, yet
the President retains and regularly uses broad decree powers. So when the
Duma rejects or decides not to act on a given law, "the mandarin," as one
faction leader branded the President, can simply legislate by decree. The
Duma has authority over budget and revenue legislation, but the President
continues to issue a stream of economic and tax decrees that either contradict or render irrelevant Duma legislation. Indeed, the Russian Constitution says that presidential decrees "*should not* contradict the Russian Constitution or federal laws," not that they may not.[71] Such loopholes for
presidential transgression into the legislative arena are evident throughout
the constitution, leaving open the question of authority for legislation in
Russia.[72]

It is also no trifling matter that the President controls the Duma's property and budget. The first battles between the President and the new legislature were over the residence of the latter. The Duma was something of a
traveling circus during its first years. It first met in the old Comecon building, a building one-third the size of the bombed-out White House for a
legislature twice the size of the Supreme Soviet. Adding insult to the injury

of not being given the White House, the Duma shared its first residence with banks, television studios, and International Monetary Fund (IMF) offices that refused to vacate. Most deputies and committees lacked offices. Indeed, one of the most pressing issues was how to stay warm in a drafty building, in which temperatures dipped into the 50s, in a country where it is a cultural taboo to wear jackets and other outer clothing indoors. The Duma then moved to the old Gosplan building just off Red Square, but the building was in such disrepair that the Duma soon abandoned it while it underwent renovations and moved to the Hotel Moscow across the street.[73] Some committees moved as many as seven times during the Duma's first year. This nomadic existence created novel problems. For example, the Moscow Professional Union refused to vacate the Duma's final residence and continued to occupy the wing of offices that was targeted for the Budget Committee. After issuing several letters and demands, the Budget Committee threatened to go on strike and to picket the corridors of the Duma, and it very nearly voted to instruct the Committee Chair to burn the budget in effigy on Red Square![74] Security forces ultimately had to deny entry to the Union members and break down a door to enable the Budget Committee to move in and work on the already late budget.[75] In the end, the Duma has roughly a third less space than the smaller Supreme Soviet enjoyed.

But the most pressing and persistent constitutional ambiguity lies in questions of relations with and control over the government. With no partisan majority linking the government to the legislature, some feel that the government is free to ignore the Duma.[76] The legislature can approve the President's nomination to head the government and may express confidence or lack thereof in the government, but it exercises these powers under the threat of dissolution.[77] The President can choose to ignore the resolution and to dissolve the legislature if it repeats its no-confidence vote. The government therefore has little to worry about. As one minister said on one such occasion, "Even if no confidence is expressed in the government—and I personally doubt this will happen—all the same there will not be any practical or political consequences whatsoever."[78]

If the President is more likely to dissolve the Duma than to remove the government, and if Duma members are aware of this, the government has little reason to worry. Still, it is clear that at least to some degree the government must work with the legislature, particularly on legislation crucial to its functioning such as the budget and other economic issues. The government initiates and implements such legislation, and the Duma is responsible for adopting it; so, by definition, these branches must work together to some extent. As chapter 6 demonstrates, the Duma's dual-channel design constrains deputies of all stripes to engage in conflict management and consensus building with the executive branch and to avoid pursuing strategies of confrontation.

A final constitutional issue that must be noted is the massive duplication in the executive branch, indeed the very difficulty in defining the executive branch in Russia. It is itself an unlinked, dual-channel design in which departments in the Presidential Administration parallel those in the government ministries. Relations between the two are unclear at best.[79] Even a member of the government called on the President to "take organizational and other measures to remove the duplication between the functions between the Presidential Administration and the government."[80] The duplication and the lack of coordination between the presidential and the government structures look much like that between the Duma committees and between the factions and committees. Although beyond the scope of this study, the nature and consequences of the dual-channel design of the Russian executive branch are worth serious examination and comparison with the findings of this study of legislatures.[81]

Before turning to an examination of how this peculiar institutional design affects the Duma's ability to manage internal and external conflict, we turn to an examination of the Budget Committee itself for a microlevel picture of the Duma's design.

THE BUDGET COMMITTEE: A PARTISAN COMMITTEE

Duma Budget Committee deputies, and above all the Committee Chair, suffer from split personalities. On the one hand, they orient their positions toward their faction because, as one deputy said, "On key questions the faction is decisive." The Budget Committee, like all Duma committees, is a partisan committee. On the other hand, deputies work in the committees and become "experts" in preparing legislation. Committees are still supposed to be "professional." So while "the position of factions is of course more important" to how a deputy will act, it is also true that "the personal views of a deputy will depend on how the Committee works."[82] Sometimes deputies wear their faction "hats," and other times they wear their committee "hats." They are unconstrained, free to choose which hat to wear and to switch hats as they please.

The Budget Committee was the most popular committee among the

Table 4.2
Faction Representation on the Duma Budget Committee

Faction	Total Members in Budget Committee	Budget Committee Leadership Positions
NRP	9	1
RC	8	3
C12D	6	2
APR	4	1
LDPR	4	1
PRES	4	1
Yabloko	3	2
CPRF	2	1
WR	2	0
DPR	1	0

deputies. More requested membership on it than on any other committee, and each faction demanded and received seats on the Committee.[83] As a result, it was the largest in the Fifth Duma with forty-three members. As with all Duma committees, there was no majority or minority. The most any one faction had on the Committee was nine members, not close to a majority (see table 4.2).[84] The Committee Chair was a Yabloko faction member, while the four deputy chairs and the subcommittee chairs spanned the entire political map.

One Committee member called the partisan nature of the Committee "the most surprising aspect" of being a Duma deputy:

> I never even imagined I would think about how many we have from Russia's Choice, how many from the Agrarian Party, etc. The idea at the first meeting of the Committee, you remember it, was that the Committee should not take up any political debates, that it should take only a professional approach. But political battles exist in the Committee. Everyone believed the Duma was divided purely politically and the Committee was professional. But it turns out you need to account for the political divisions in the Committee too. Therefore when the Duma makes a decision you must know the Committee is not only a professional Committee. Maybe 70%, but the rest is political.[85]

With forty-three members from ten factions, partisan debate often takes over Committee sessions.

Partisan interests are constantly higher here [than in the Supreme So-
viet]. Perhaps this is more democratic, but it is less productive. The problem is the quantity of factions. And also, in the West if a party leader says
something, this is something the party will do. This strict discipline holds
them together. Here things are simply very clear. When we have two or
three clear tendencies and follow discipline, then all will be normal.[86]

Instead, the norm is partisan squabbling, right down to such matters as
the composition of the Committee staff. At one closed session of the Committee, a Yabloko deputy branded the staff as "unqualified" and called for
firing the staff, as they did not come from Yabloko. Since Yabloko chaired
the Committee, it should appoint the staff, this deputy reasoned. A second
Committee member disagreed. "You should note that those you speak of
worked many years in the Supreme Soviet staff, these people did not have a
single complaint against them, these people sat and worked evenings and
nights. And aren't you embarrassed to say these words about those people
who here, too, sit and work evenings and nights? You can verify that they do
in the records of orders for cars for transport home. If you think this is not
work, then I do not know what work is! Moreover, they voluntarily stayed
here. I think after what you have said I would simply spit in your face and
leave!"[87] The following exchange ensued:

> Second Deputy: To work on such insults against your own staff, destroy-
>   ing work from the very outset, I simply cannot understand why you
>   have done this.
> Yabloko Deputy: It is your staff!
> Second Deputy: It is the Committee staff.
> Yabloko Deputy [shouting, inaudible]: We did not ratify it!

The first deputy was more interested in whether the staff was "ours" or
"theirs" than in how the staff worked. She was more interested in a partisan
staff membership than she was in having technical budget experts. While
this deputy lost this fight, such partisan tensions continued and intensified
throughout the entire term of the Fifth Duma.[88]

Further enhancing the split personality syndrome is the fact that while
more partisan, the Duma Committee is simultaneously more professional
than was its Supreme Soviet predecessor. First, all deputies now are full-
time legislators and are expected to work full-time on legislative work.
While absenteeism is rampant even in Committee work, the expectation of
deputies as a result is higher.[89] Second, more Committee members have

budget, finance, and economic expertise than was the case in the Supreme Soviet. The Fifth Duma's Budget Committee had as members a former Supreme Soviet Budget Committee Chair, a Russian Finance Minister, a first deputy Finance Minister, a deputy Finance Minister, a head of the Finance Ministry currency department, a deputy chair of the USSR Council of Ministers, several regional government officials, and also businessmen, bankers, and accountants. One Committee member observed, "To be modest, well, we could in our membership make up a small Finance Ministry of a small country."[90] By comparison, as one high government official who called the Duma Committee "not bad" pointed out, only one or two Supreme Soviet Budget Committee deputies had any budget expertise.[91] Of the forty-three Duma Committee members, only seventeen lacked either an educational or a professional background in economics, finance, or banking. Of these, half were "entrepreneurs" — heads of small or medium-size businesses or trade associations.

In a sense, then, the "professional" identity of Committee membership has eroded with the increased partisanship. Yet Duma members still try to maintain a "professional" and a "partisan" identity, as Remington and Smith correctly note.[92] Committee members have their partisan identities, rooted in their faction affiliation, and their professional identities, rooted in their prior experience and in the professionalism that remains the ideal of Committee work. Committee chairs in particular "try to distinguish their committee work from their duty to the faction."[93] The chronic breakdown and deadlock in the Duma, however, are testimony to their inability to do so. The distinction is simply not as clear in the Duma. The way in which Russia's legislature is designed maximizes partisan conflict among its many factions. This unlinked, dual-channel institutional design leaves Duma deputies unconstrained and able to shift between these very different orientations toward legislative work. The consequence is chronic breakdown and deadlock.

Procedural Breakdown and Deadlock in the Duma

When the Duma passed the 1994 Budget halfway into the year, it did so in one fell swoop. It approved the Budget Committee's recommendations on a single vote, rather than casting votes on each of the nearly 400 separate amendments as required by the Law on the Budget Process and by the special Regulations passed by the Duma for the 1994 Budget Process. It is tempting to interpret this blanket adoption of Committee recommendations as reflecting even greater Committee authority and smoother decision making in the Duma than in the Supreme Soviet. However, this would be a complete misinterpretation of what transpired and of the Duma as an institution. In fact, this blanket adoption was a dramatic manifestation of procedural breakdown and deadlock, the product of constant conflict between the committees, the factions, and across these two channels of the Duma's design. The Committee Chair opposed the swift adoption of the budget, and the Committee was never afforded the opportunity to consider the proposal. The instance highlighted the weakness of Duma committees, and the unpredictability and instability in the Duma's process that extends across all legislative issues in the new Russian legislature.

The Duma's unlinked, dual-channel design is the culprit. The lack of linkage between the two channels leaves deputies unconstrained to pursue strategies of competition, conflict, and sabotage rather than compelling or providing incentives for conflict management and consensus building. This chapter explains the collapse of the budget process in the Committee, in relations between Duma committees, and on the floor. It then demonstrates the chronic condition of breakdown and deadlock on legislative issues beyond the budget.

The Process on Paper: The Committee's Procedures

The strength of a legislative committee in large part depends on its control over the process of consideration of its legislation. The Duma Budget Committee defines the formal rules of the budget process. The Committee's formal authority derives from the same Law on the Budget Process passed by the Supreme Soviet and from temporary procedural rules and laws the Committee writes and the Duma adopts each year.[1] The temporary provisions were needed because the government continued to be either unable or unwilling to submit draft budgets in time to allow for eight months of examination as the law required.[2] These resolutions compressed the time line for budget examination and introduced at least two major innovations to Russia's legislative budget process: a distinction between the nature of the different readings of the budget and restrictions on the content of valid amendments. Establishing a clear distinction between each reading was, at least on paper, a major advancement. In the Supreme Soviet, the entire budget was discussed at every reading, but the new rules set up a "top-down" budget sequence. The first reading would ratify the "conception" of the budget and the government's economic prognosis, including predictions on inflation rates, gross domestic product (GDP), the ruble-to-dollar exchange rate, and other indices upon which Russian budget figures are based.[3] The second reading would ratify the "basic characteristics," which include overall revenue, spending, and deficit ceilings, and subceilings for each "sector" of the budget.[4] The third reading would approve specific spending articles, or "line items."

This multitiered approach sought to prevent continuous inflation of the three macrolevel parameters at each successive reading. Once the basic characteristics were approved, figures within sections could change, but the spending, revenue, and deficit ceilings could not.[5] The Committee would evaluate amendments based on these guidelines, and amendments violating these ceilings would be invalid, and thus not be considered. This, then, marked a second procedural innovation. All amendments had to be balanced. As one Committee member explained, "Amendments that do not have sources of funding for spending increases are simply dismissed. In a nutshell, stupid amendments are not examined. This is extremely good."[6] To increase spending in one area, one had to propose equal cuts from another or demonstrate how additional revenue could be raised. Amendments without such "sources" would not even be considered.

In addition to these innovations, the Duma's new rules also required ratification of quarterly spending targets within each budget spending provision and ratification of each spending item as a percentage of total budget spending. With these measures, the Committee sought to strengthen oversight by preventing the government from arbitrarily spending resources if the prognosis proved faulty and rendered specific budget figures meaningless. If exchange rates, inflation, or revenues diverged from the prognosis, the government would have to follow strict guidelines of equal sequestration across the budget the Duma had approved, rather than independently deciding how much to spend and on what.[7] Such provisions seemed to recognize the specific difficulties of "budgeting in poor countries" elaborated by Naomi Caiden and Aaron Wildavsky. The danger was that the legislature would appropriate more than the government could raise, producing an "illusory budget." Rather than "abdicating control to the executive," the Duma adopted this innovation to prevent such executive independence.[8] The rules also defined what action the Duma could take on each reading. For example, on the first reading the Duma had a choice of either adopting the budget, rejecting it and returning it to the government for revision, or rejecting it and forming a "conciliation commission" with the government to revise the basic characteristics.[9] On the third reading, the Duma was required to vote separately on each amendment submitted and approve each independent article of the budget law.[10] For each vote, the Committee was to present its recommendation for Duma action.

On paper, then, the rules seemed to entrench Committee control over the budget process. In reality, however, the Committee is virtually powerless to enforce these rules. It faces and is unable to manage conflict within its sessions and on the floor from other committees and from the factions. The actual process followed bears little resemblance to these formal rules.

PROCEDURAL BREAKDOWN IN COMMITTEE

When asked what worked well in the Duma's budget process, one Committee member was stumped: "Let me think. [Pause]. No, I don't think I can name anything positive. We set a goal for ourselves, in terms of the budget process, and the main thing was for the deputies to follow that process and understand [it]. We failed."[11] Government officials also lament the failure: "Of course for us it would be advantageous to rush through discussion of the budget, but it is more important not to break the law on examination of the budget because if deputies break the law once they may do so again."[12]

This is the crux of the problem in the Duma. There are no constraints to follow the rules, which leads to conflict and confrontation.

The budget process broke down at virtually every stage in the Fifth Duma and continues to do so. When others, notably Remington and Smith, have examined the Duma's legislative process, they have failed to delve beyond the formal rules.[13] However, in Russia formal rules rarely seem to matter. The Budget Committee failed to abide by its own rules. Without a single exception, every sectoral committee that came before the Budget Committee with amendments to the 1994 Budget either neglected or consciously refused to show sources for their proposed spending increases, and faced no sanctions for doing so. The rules declared such amendments invalid and not to be considered. But the Committee, instead of refusing to consider these "invalid" amendments, examined them all.[14] The Budget Committee received no answer when it asked the Committee on Federation Policy, "Where are the sources of financing?" for the R7.3T increase it requested in 1994. Nor did it get answers from any other committee. It told the Committee on Industry, "You need to give concrete proposals for this spending increase! You must show it, the procedure is clear." It told the Committee on Education, "According to the regulations, when submitting amendments you must show sources for your proposals to increase spending. Your proposed amendments that you are speaking about today simply lack these sources of funding." The Budget Committee sang the same song to every committee that came before it. None followed the rules![15]

It demanded sources and threatened not to consider amendments lacking them, but the sectoral committees responded with silence, feigned ignorance, or openly scorned the rules. The Committee on Science and Technology representative was indignant: "What? You want specific sources? I will not take this on myself! I can speak as much as you like about the need, but I think sources should be specified by professionals." By this, he meant the Budget Committee, the Finance Ministry, anyone but himself. A member of the Defense Committee, which in 1994 sought a massive spending increase, said, "We did not even embark on submitting an amendment to find resources for the increased spending, because this should not be the Defense Committee's problem. It should be the problem of the Budget Committee. Our concern is defense spending. We told this to the Budget Committee."[16]

The Budget Committee was hardly amused when other committees dodged responsibility for their proposals. Committee members fired back:

No, it must be YOUR committee that says where the cuts should come from!

No, YOUR proposal! According to the regulations amendments must be paired — you must show increases in spending and from where the money will come.

The Agriculture Committee fell back on the old Soviet-era argument that "the agriculture sector has never clashed with other economic sectors." The Budget Committee attacked this view.

I beg your pardon! There are rules for submission of amendments, rules adopted by the Duma, according to which you must simultaneously show spending increases at the expense of what, or where additional revenues will come from, or redistribution. At the cost of what?!

Otherwise we simply will not be able to examine your amendments. We will not even be able to include them in the table of amendments to be voted on by the Duma.

We will not have the right to adopt them — look for yourself![17]

These proved to be idle threats. These sectoral committees gambled on the weakness of "responsible committees" in the Duma, and it was a successful gamble. The Budget Committee in the end considered every amendment rather than rejecting them all as invalid. It feebly justified abandonment of the rule as a necessary evil in order to move the process along. But the sectoral committees forced the move with conflict and threats of deadlock, and they were able to do so precisely because no institutional constraints or structures exist in the Duma to compel intercommittee collaboration and consensus building. The responsible committees, in this case, the Budget Committee, lack the authority over the legislative process enjoyed by their predecessors.

These experiences triggered a domino effect and nearly complete procedural breakdown. When the Committee later tried to defend the rules, it did not have a leg to stand on. Allowing consideration of these unbalanced amendments undermined the basic characteristics. The rules stated that, once ratified, the overall spending ceilings and the subceilings for each major section of the budget, in other words, the structure of budget spending, could not be changed. But as one Committee member said, "It did not work. It was in the rules, but there was no way to enforce it because everyone ignored it during discussion of amendments to spending articles."[18] The expert budgeteers could not constrain the other committees or deputies driven by squabbling factions. The Committee never even bothered trying to set individual spending articles as percentages of total budget spending, approving instead only the raw sums for each item. "We just ignored the rule," one deputy said.[19]

The important point is not that the Duma deviates from the rules. The Supreme Soviet Budget Committee did so as well. What is important is the context of and motivation behind the deviations. Every organization at times bends or forsakes rules in the name of building consensus, reaching decisions, and acting. In the Duma, however, rule breaking is about preventing action, not reaching consensus, and is a symptom of intercommittee and partisan confrontation. This is a vastly different environment from the ad hoc Working Group's consensus-building environment in the Supreme Soviet.

As the Duma's budget procedures crumbled, the Committee ceased to follow even the most basic elements of its rules. For example, after repeated failure to gather enough members for a quorum to discuss the budget, the Committee started calling closed sessions.[20] The Duma's Regulations forbid closed meetings, except for situations concerning state secrets. The Budget Committee ostensibly closed its sessions to discuss the military budget, but they in fact closed them to break the rules and pass decisions on the entire budget without a quorum. Members who regularly attended simply decided to emulate the sordid example of other committees that had been ignoring the quorum rule.[21] Subsequently, even when there was a quorum to vote on budget proposals, the Committee closed its session in blatant violation of the Duma Regulations; it evicted all deputies from other committees who came to observe the debate and decisions on their proposals. "Voting by kicking them out," as one deputy put it, was a "violation of the rights of deputies of other committees."[22] It was a reaction to the inherent intercommittee suspicion built into the unlinked design and did nothing to ease that mutual suspicion.

Other violations had a more direct bearing on the substance of the budget. The Committee had three options for its recommendation to the Duma for the first reading of the 1995 Budget: adopt the budget on the first reading, reject it and return it to the government for revision and resubmission, or reject it and form a conciliation commission with the government to make the revisions. The Committee Chair told the Committee, "These are the choices before us according to the regulations, and in connection with this we should recommend to the Duma one of these variants."[23] But again the deputies found the rules inconvenient and ignored them. One member proposed a novel variant, one that he had previously proposed on the floor during plenary session debate on tax reform legislation and that had carried even though it had received no prior discussion in Committee. The proposal was to accept the draft as "information" and to immediately form a "conciliation commission" between the Budget Committee, the factions, other committees, and the government. Opponents called this "a sad precedent of neither war nor peace."[24]

The telling point was that both supporters and opponents of this idea used the weakness of the Committee in resolving conflict and in carrying its decisions in the Duma to make their case. One deputy argued that the Duma "works through factions," not committees, and therefore a conciliation commission "is the single means we can use on controversial matters to find some kind of joint decision." Such a body, he said, "allows us to quietly consider all arguments" rather than "take a fighting position toward these issues." When asked why the committees, with factions represented on them, do not provide this role, this deputy offered a response that beautifully captured the confusion deputies have regarding their dual affiliations and the weakness of committees in this design: "Between factions and committees, because factions are also represented in committees, every committee is also multi-factional. So we also need a conciliation commission between committees, and between factions, and with the government."[25] In this fumbling way, one deputy captured the fact that the Duma is organized around factions and committees, that factions are loosely distributed across committees, and that there is no coordinating mechanism whatsoever between committees. He argued for a conciliation commission to unite the two channels as a way to overcome the deadlock that was sure to emerge between the two. The proposal to effectively by-pass the Committee reflects a sense that Duma committees lack the authority and the power to make decisions that would carry any weight in the full Duma. The factions and, not surprisingly, other committees expressed their "readiness to actively and constructively participate in the work of the conciliation commission."[26]

Opponents pointed to Committee weakness as a powerful argument against forming a conciliation commission: "I am against this procedure. I do not support it because it is unregulated, and because in this procedure the Committee and the Duma lose their voice. This is the whole problem. In this procedure, when the Duma starts to work, it is already tied to some agreement with the government."[27] Another deputy issued this stern warning to the Committee: "If we again ignore our own rules, which we specially adopted ahead of time, we will have an endless string of conciliation commissions and will rob the Duma and the Committee of its authority. I do not see the logic behind your proposal. This is a bad precedent to set."[28]

But the Committee set that precedent, and lost to the government, to other committees and factions, and to the whole Duma the last vestige of authority it had over the legislative budget process — the authority to carry out the main analytical work on the budget. This work would now be done in the conciliation commission. Committee weakness precipitated the decision to bypass the Committee procedure on the 1995 Budget, and this decision entrenched that weakness for each year to this writing.

LACK OF COORDINATION BETWEEN COMMITTEES

The lack of links between the two channels has undermined in the Duma the type of close, intercommittee coordination that characterized the budget process in the single-channel, nonpartisan Supreme Soviet. Consensus building and conflict management have given way to confrontation and jealous competition. From the Defense Committee on the defense budget to the Agriculture Committee on the agriculture budget, all sectoral committees compete with the Duma Budget Committee on budgetary issues. The Committee also faces persistent competition from the Committee on Economic Policy, for the simple reason that neither logic nor the Duma's Regulations provide a clear distinction between the responsibilities of a Committee on Budget, Taxation, Banking, and Finance and a Committee on Economic Policy. In the Supreme Soviet, committees worked together in a working group. The dominant strategy of Duma committees, however, is to fight to block each other's proposals from being adopted.

Intercommittee relations in the Duma are relations of confrontation more than of consensus building. The Budget Committee, for example, structures consideration of the budget around budget topic rather than inviting each committee to present its proposals. Instead of having a time for the Defense Committee, for the Agriculture Committee, for the Education Committee, and so forth, there is a time for defense and security issues, for social-cultural issues, and so forth. One sectoral committee may have its proposals broken across several of these sessions while, on any given topic, two or three committees may be scheduled to speak. As a result, each committee has far less time before the Budget Committee than was the case

Table 5.1
Schedule for Sectoral Committee Appearances before the Duma Budget
Committee, 1994 Budget

Budget Issue	Committees Invited	Total Time Allotted (hours)
Federal territorial budgets	on Local Self-Govt. on Federation Policy	2
Northern territories	on Federation Policy on Industry	2
Sectors of the economy	on Industry on Economic Policy	1.5
National defense	on Defense	1
Law enforcement	on Security	1
Social-cultural affairs	on Education and Science on Health Policy	1.5
Science and technology	on Education and Science	1
Agriculture	on Agriculture	2
Debt service	Budget Committee	1
State administration	Budget Committee	1
Foreign economic activities	on Economic Policy	1

in the more collegial Supreme Soviet. As one veteran of both budget committees observed, "In the Supreme Soviet there were more joint meetings with committees and they were deeper. Before, we had entire working days with committees."[29] In the unlinked, dual-channel Duma, committees averaged roughly one hour before the Budget Committee; several committees, including Foreign Affairs and Environment and Natural Resources, received no time at all (see table 5.1).

The closed hearings are a dramatic manifestation of intercommittee hostility. Wearing his committee hat, the Committee Chair viewed the sectoral committees with suspicion and, in the competitive intercommittee environment, saw no reason to allow members of other, potentially hostile committees into his sessions. Wearing his faction hat, he did not want committee chairs from other factions exacerbating partisan battles in his

Committee's sessions. The Duma's fragmented design provides powerful incentives to go it alone and presents no constraints against doing so. Such retrenchment serves to reduce understanding between committees and to exacerbate conflict at all stages of the process.

The reduced coordination is also abundantly evident in intercommittee communications. One Defense Committee deputy sought to change the budget process to enable closer participation by sectoral committees such as his. When asked if he had submitted amendments to the Law on the 1995 Budget Process that the Duma had recently passed, he responded, "It was just adopted on the first reading. I plan to talk to the Budget Committee about making changes to it." When informed that the vote had in fact been to adopt the law immediately in full and not merely on the first reading, he almost exploded with anger. "It was adopted in full? They promised time for amendments! Again the Budget Committee has deceived us!"[30]

Similar illustrations abound. During the 1995 Budget process, the Committee on Federation Policy held hearings on the relationship between the federal and the local budgets. These hearings concerned such issues as the size of subsidies to the regions from the center and the tax obligations of the regions to the federal budget. Budget Committee staff were never notified or consulted, had never met or even spoken to the other committee's staff member, and, as a final insult, were left off the list of those allowed into the meeting hall.[31] The Duma staff member bearing primary responsibility for technical work on the budget was barred from participating in or even attending a major hearing on the budget because a competing committee organized that hearing. The two committees were, at best, strangers to each other almost a year into the legislature's work and after an entire budget cycle in the legislature had already been completed.[32]

The Committee evaluation of the government's draft budget provides a physical illustration of the chasm. Rather than crafting a single consensual evaluation of all committees, the Budget Committee simply collects the independent evaluations of each sectoral committee, writes its own evaluation, and staples them all together. It calls this a "joint evaluation."[33] But in fact it is nothing of the kind. The evaluations are fraught with internal contradictions, leaving the government with no idea what to make of them. Said one Finance Minister on the Duma floor,

> I have no idea what the Committee opinion is. The joint evaluation is a collection of those evaluations submitted by the Duma committees. And you see that there are many internal contradictions, very many. For

example, some committees feel that revenues are exaggerated in the budget, many feel that way, while other committees, including the Committee on Economic Policy, believe they are sharply underestimated. . . . Many committees, especially sectoral committees, demand increased spending, while the majority of committees feel that the budget deficit must not be increased. Therefore it is hard for me to say what I think of these evaluations.[34]

While the Supreme Soviet's joint evaluation was an intercommittee consensus hammered out between the Budget Committee and the sectoral committees, in the Duma the committees fight against each other in their evaluations. There is no such coordination.

The fiercest intercommittee conflict swirls around relations between the Committee on Economic Policy and the Budget Committee. The Committee on Economic Policy distributes its own evaluations of budget documents, including long, detailed analyses of the government's draft budget and proposals for how to respond to it. It holds its own press conferences and hearings, publicly criticizing the government for its budget policies and the Budget Committee for its actions.[35] In return, whether intentionally or not, the Budget Committee did not notify the Chair of the Committee on Economic Policy of at least one crucial meeting on the 1995 Budget, causing a public scandal between the two committees.[36] In short, what was unthinkable in the Supreme Soviet has become routine in the Duma.

Conflict between these two committees is therefore not only real but public, ongoing, and occasionally hostile. Public and sustained intercommittee confrontation was inconceivable in the Supreme Soviet. In the Duma, it stems from lack of definition of spheres of responsibility. What are the boundaries between the Committee on Economic Policy and the Committee on the Budget, Taxation, Banking, and Finance? With overlapping profiles, chairs from diametrically opposed partisan factions, and no coordinating body between them, Duma committees are free to compete with each other for responsibility over legislative issues, and compete they do. The Committee on Economic Policy, for example, sees no reason why it should not control the budget process:

Two committees should carry out the evaluation of the budget, ours and the Budget Committee. As it stands it is very difficult to influence the budget. It is difficult just to make contact with the Budget Committee.

In all civilized parliaments, the Budget Committee is responsible only for the revenue side of the budget and macroeconomic spending and deficit figures. The **Committee on Economic** Policy answers for the structure of the budget among **spending articles**. This is what we want. When one committee does it all, **you get a monopoly.** In fact it becomes a Ministry of Finance representative **in parliament.** This is absurd.[37]

With no constraints against doing so, the Committee on Economic Policy simply acts as if it had equal responsibility for the budget, publicly and combatively competing with the Budget Committee. It knows that other committees will fight to block its initiatives, and that the measure of its strength is its ability to do the same in return. The Budget Committee calls the pretensions of the Committee on Economic Policy "ridiculous."[38] It refuses to acknowledge for any other committee any role beyond the submission of evaluations and amendments to the Budget Committee for consideration.

The Duma's institutional design, rather than alleviating conflict between committees, provokes and exacerbates that conflict. Rather than "inducing equilibria" and stable outcomes, the committees perpetuate instability.[39] Krehbiel's argument, developed in reference to Congress and which seemed to apply to the Supreme Soviet, clearly is not universal to all legislatures or even to all legislatures in presidential systems. A comparative institutional theory can explain the conditions under which legislatures induce equilibria, as in the Supreme Soviet, as opposed to those in which they provoke conflict, as in the unlinked, dual-channel Duma.

The large number of committees with overlapping responsibilities, combined with the absence of established forums for intercommittee coordination, leaves committees and their members in competition and in conflict with each other over the budget process and budget content. This predominance of confrontation and competition, instead of consensus building and conflict management, extends to and increases on the floor with the intrusion into the process of a second autonomous channel of organization for the deputies — the partisan factions.

PROCEDURAL BREAKDOWN ON THE FLOOR

Confrontation remains the dominant strategy on the floor, where the factions enter the fray. Procedural breakdown, internal conflict, and often-crippling deadlock plague the Duma. The contrast with the Supreme Soviet could hardly be more dramatic. If the committee-centered Supreme Soviet was a "well-oiled machine," the unlinked dual-channel Duma is truly "complete chaos." Shepsle and Weingast's assertions that legislative committees have the power to enforce rules and control agendas clearly do not apply to a legislature designed like the Duma.[40]

On the floor, the budget falls prey to the internecine battles between the factions, the committees, and the deputies playing these two channels off each other. Neither the Committee Chair nor anyone else has the slightest idea what its fate will be. All players are free to pursue conflict virtually without constraints. Intercommittee competition continues on the floor, but when the budget leaves the Committee, the numerous partisan factions immediately begin to fight for control over the process. Following the work of legislative scholars like Cox and Krehbiel, who praise the stabilizing effects of parties, Remington suggests that including party leaders in the Supreme Soviet's organizational structures would "stabilize political conflict within the legislature."[41] But it is how partisan entities are included that is important, not merely their inclusion, as a comparative institutional approach demonstrates. In an unlinked dual-channel design, conflict erupts.

For example, when the Committee was unable to complete its work before the first reading of the 1994 Budget, the Chair left for the Duma Soviet meeting assuring the Committee that he would tell the faction leaders of the need to delay debate on the budget until the Committee could complete its work.[42] Imagine the surprise of the press and observers, not to mention the Committee members, when the next morning they found the budget on the agenda! The faction heads did not care whether the Budget Committee was ready for debate. They were ready, and debate and votes there would be. Six of ten faction leaders opposed the Committee "because they had an agreement with the government for quick adoption of the budget."[43] A similar negotiation between the Duma Soviet and the Prime Minister had been reported nearly a month earlier.[44] The Committee unanimously voted for a delay, but the vote was irrelevant to the agenda decision.[45]

Two weeks later, it was déjà vu. The Duma Speaker announced, "The Budget Committee submitted to the Duma Soviet yesterday a final draft budget for examination on the second reading [in two days]."[46] But the Committee had not even finished printing all of the amendments and still had more than 100 to consider. It had no "final draft" to submit! "We heard only this morning that he said, 'we're ready,'" one stunned Committee member said, referring to the Committee Chair. "It was a surprise to everyone."[47] He assumed that Mikhail Zadornov had unilaterally told the Duma Soviet that the budget was ready. In fact, the faction leaders had ignored Zadornov's protest that the Committee should be allowed to complete its work, and did so because they had a deal with the Prime Minister to have a budget by the end of that week, even though the Committee was not ready.[48]

In the Duma, it is not important whether the Committee or a piece of legislation, even the budget, is ready for debate. What is important is the political mood of the partisan faction leaders. The Committee's lack of control over the fate of its legislation is astounding. Indeed, it is dubious even to refer to "a committee's legislation" in the Duma.

With committees and factions engaged in crosscutting partisan and highly personal battles, in a legislature like the Duma individual deputies fill the void as just that — individual deputies. Both process and outcomes become highly unstable. At the crucial second reading of the 1994 Budget, a single deputy, out of the blue, proposed adopting the budget in one fell swoop.[49] He suggested a single vote, rather than hundreds of separate votes on each item and on each amendment as the law required. This proposal was an explicit rejection of the Committee and of its Chair, who only moments before had spelled out the rules to the deputies for voting on the nearly 400 amendments. First, they had to vote on each article of the budget. When they reached the articles on spending, first votes would be held on all amendments to reduce spending. Then they would turn to amendments to increase spending. Such a process would enable them to stick to the rules against altering the basic characteristics of overall revenue and spending figures.[50] He might as well have been speaking to a pile of stones. The Committee again proved irrelevant. First, the Defense Committee had for weeks been demanding an increase of R18T, while the Budget Committee granted only R4T plus an empty provision to target for defense extra revenues collected from privatization. Second, there was no agreement on what could reasonably be expected from privatization revenues in the first place. The Committee on Economic Policy believed that the budget underestimated these revenues by a factor of twenty, and dozens of other estimates swirled around the corridors of the legislature. These arguments promised to derail final action on scores of amendments and on the budget itself. With literally dozens of alternatives on each issue, and with deep, public, even hostile divisions between the committees and partisan competition between the faction leaders, the prospects of the Duma's reaching a majority position on the amendments or, in the end, on the budget were minuscule.[51]

Moreover, the official rules were already a joke. One deputy who proposed an invalid amendment on the floor made this clear: "Of course, this is a violation of the regulations. But I think you will agree that the regulations were already abandoned long ago."[52] When in response to an exasperated deputy's question the government representative said that "defense increases are impossible" and called increased revenue proposals "unrealistic," that deputy proposed adopting the entire budget on a single vote. As a member of the Agrarian faction, supporting a budget that had secured R16T in agriculture spending increases, nearly 10 percent of total spending, was understandable. Any increase elsewhere would have threatened to cut into the agrarian gains. But this was the proposal of a single deputy who had not consulted with and did not speak for his faction, and who had not sent the proposal through the Committee for evaluation of its effect on the technical merits of the overall budget.[53]

The proposal failed by more than eighty votes, but the Speaker called a meeting of the Duma Soviet, where the faction leaders met for forty minutes to discuss how to overcome the deadlock. The Committee was excluded, and its members paced the halls impatiently, wondering what the fate of the budget would be and on what basis it would be decided. In that meeting, the Communist leader announced that he would support fast adoption of the budget, provided that separate votes were held on amendments to increase privatization revenues and defense spending. Every other faction leader immediately demanded votes on their own preferred amendments. Again, deadlock loomed. If any amendments were to be voted on, all 400 would have to be voted on, and everyone knew that even after the several hundred votes, the budget would never pass. No amendments would pass because each issue had several alternative proposals, ensuring that none would garner the required majority for adoption. Committees and factions raise alternatives to block passage of opponents' proposals, knowing that they cannot amass the votes to pass their own. The strategy of each faction and committee is to sabotage the proposals of the others by springing competing alternatives. At the final vote, everyone is dissatisfied, and the bill goes down in flames. This scenario repeats itself on countless pieces of legislation at every session.

But the budget is not just any legislation. As one leader at the Duma Soviet meeting observed, the faction leaders "were scared off by the sheer number of amendments" and the time that it would take to hold all of these pointless votes. To put it bluntly, the faction leaders do not like to work nights. Who can blame them? When everyone knows the final result will be deadlock and failure, why expend all the time and effort? So the leaders "decided to just adopt the [1994] budget" on a single vote.[54]

The Speaker returned to the hall and announced that the proposal to hold a single vote was a procedural matter and thus had passed, since more voted in favor than against. Virtually everyone, even the deputy who had made the proposal, agreed that it was anything but a procedural matter and that calling it such was itself a massive violation of the rules.[55] The Duma's Resolution on the Examination and Ratification of the 1994 Budget established a budget process. Amending that resolution required passage of a new resolution, and that required a majority of all deputies. It was therefore not a procedural matter, as was quite clear even to those unschooled in the rules of parliamentary procedure.

But in the Duma, rules and procedures are less important than interpersonal and partisan battles between the heads of the rival factions. One Duma leader emerged laughing from the hall after the vote, exclaiming, "We adopted the budget on the second reading!" When asked how this happened, he replied, "Uhhhh. By two votes!"[56] It is not that he did not understand the deeper significance of the question. Events had moved so fast with so little consideration of the practical and policy consequences of this "blind adoption" of the country's budget that he could not immediately comprehend what had transpired. What was clear was that the Committee had little to do with its passage. It was not consulted either on the floor or by the faction leaders about this proposal. The Committee in fact opposed blind adoption of the budget because it meant that the merits of the budget's provisions would not even be considered. But in the Duma, the Committee controls only the formal rules; the faction leaders decide the process that the Duma actually follows, and they do so based on partisan interest (the Agrarians stood to gain the most) and expediency (400 votes would take too much time), not on the technical merits of the budget.

For the 1995 Budget, the Committee did not even make a pretense of trying to stick to the rules. The Committee Chair revealed to the deputies that they would not have to vote on the more than 600 amendments or even on every article at the third reading of the 1995 Budget. This was not his or even his Committee's idea, however. The faction leaders again devised ad hoc voting rules. The Chair explained these to the Duma:

> The Duma Soviet yesterday discussed the rules for today's work. It arrived at the following scheme. The majority of factions agreed to this. . . . We can put to a vote the amendments the Committee supported. I think there should not be any fundamental disagreement. We agreed we would then hold a recess of approximately one hour to allow the factions to

consult and select from among the amendments the Committee rejected two or three (maybe, one or two) which each faction considers necessary to still discuss additionally before a vote on rejecting all of the opposed amendments is held. . . . Then after this recess we can hold a discussion and we can vote on the opposed amendments, having selected the most important ones from among them.[57]

In other words, there would be a single vote on the "package" of amendments that the Committee supported and then a vote on the "package" of amendments it opposed, with the exception of an amendment that each faction could single out. After the package votes, separate votes would be held on these specified amendments.

This process had no basis in the Regulations that the Duma had only recently adopted and was based purely on political agreement among the partisan leaders rather than on technical budget considerations. The amendments singled out were neither the most contentious nor those on which the Committee was most divided. They were thus not necessarily the most important from a technical budget standpoint. They were merely those amendments most politically important to the factions and, in particular, to the leaders of those factions. All faction leaders had pet proposals for specific programs or to damage their opponents which they wanted debated and voted on, and the faction leaders devised a procedure that would give them an abundance of floor time to wage these personal and partisan political battles. The "real" budget could be adopted with summary votes, as the real budget was not the real issue to these faction heads.

On the surface, this situation appears to confirm the arguments of Cox and McCubbins that parties structure legislatures and control outcomes, that they control logrolls and deal making to make legislatures "efficient."[58] But the similarity is superficial; the Duma betrays the fallacy of such generalization about the role of partisan organizations in legislatures. In the Duma, the factions demonstrate no regular or predictable patterns of behavior, except that they are unpredictable! Their actions are spontaneous, ad hoc behavior. Were these ad hoc procedures in the name of consensus building and overcoming conflict to produce policy, it could increase legislative efficiency. It is not deviation from the rules per se that is indicative of inability to manage conflict. But ad hoc procedures in the fragmented Duma mean instability and unpredictability and, therefore, greater rather than managed conflict.

This was evident to observers, who howled with laughter as the Duma passed the Committee-supported amendments but failed to reject the package of amendments the Committee opposed. Individual deputies and sectoral committees, it turned out, had their own pet interests beyond those of the faction leaders, and they could cite the Committee-supported formal rules to demand their consideration. Duma deputies have two channels that they can play upon. Nothing in the rules compels linkage between the channels. The existing literature assumes such linkage. Legislative scholars such as Cox, Kiewiet, McCubbins, and Olson all assume that parties control majorities or produce them through coalitions and maintain them throughout the legislature.[59] Such linkage, however, is not automatic, as a comparative institutional approach demonstrates. The rules must compel such linkage, and in the Duma, they do not.

Deputies are like free agents, and in this instance many bucked their faction leaders and the agreement they had reached in the Duma Soviet; they pointed instead to the Committee in defending what was in fact highly individualist action. These were often the very same individual deputies who had undermined the Committee procedures at earlier stages, being guided by their factions. Agreement of the faction leaders alone is not enough in the Duma. While the leaders could agree to single out a few amendments each, the rank and file had either amendments from their own committees or their own pet favorites, and they used the space provided by the Duma's design to act on these. A free-for-all nearly broke out when one faction demanded a vote on not just a few but all of its several dozen amendments. Since the Duma Soviet agreement had collapsed, it argued that the original rules applied.[60]

The Duma's design leaves deputies virtually unconstrained in pursuing individual action, even if such action undermines the legislature's ability to manage and overcome conflict, that is, to act. Individual deputies, representing at times other committees, at times their factions, at times simply themselves, frequently rise to propose alternative amendments from the floor, which, although explicitly banned by the rules, are nonetheless often considered and voted on. This occurred in 1994 on the aforementioned amendments to increase defense spending and privatization revenues; these amendments were not only considered but also repeatedly voted on even after they had failed.[61] And it occurred the next year, with the Speaker at one point begging the deputies for "mercy" against "a flood of requests to return to amendments which have already been voted down."[62] Said one Committee member, "Individual deputies could not move from political motives to economic motives in their amendments. Once we had already discussed and voted on a question, someone raises the very same question again. This has nothing to do with economic interests or budget characteristics, it is political games."[63] The political games are aimed at preventing final action on the bill. They are games that even Committee members are not immune from playing. At the third reading of the 1995 Budget, one Committee member raised on the floor an amendment to redistribute funds within the defense budget, an amendment the Committee had previously rejected.

During debate on the second reading of the 1995 Budget, a Committee member from the Agrarian faction played a political game of his own on the floor. He falsely argued that agricultural spending had been cut from R12.5T in 1994 to R7.5T in the draft 1995 Budget, or only 2.3 percent of total spending. In fact, he knew this was false. Agriculture spending was distributed throughout many budget articles in direct and indirect spending, and agriculture spending in the draft budget amounted to almost 8 percent of total spending. Even when the Committee Chair reminded him before the entire Duma that based on his participation in Committee discussions, "you understand this perfectly well," this Agrarian deputy did not veer from his political advantage. He knew that the majority of deputies would see simply the line in the draft showing R7.5T for the agriculture sector. He therefore knew that he could score trillions more for the agrarian sector. He demanded a special tax to raise an additional R5.7T for agriculture, a proposal that had never been submitted in written form and that had never been submitted to the government or to the Committee for "expert analysis." The Duma voted "spontaneously" and passed the provision.[64]

The instigator of this incident was a Committee member. But once the budget went to the floor he had a separate channel that he could play for his personal and partisan interests, and he abandoned his responsibilities to the Committee, to its decisions, and to its rules. Earlier, when a different Committee member threatened a similar maneuver, this same deputy had argued, "Excuse me, but I simply do not understand what this Committee is for. We came here to work in this Committee, are paid by the taxpayers to do this. We made a decision. It is one thing to disagree, but another to undermine the committee in which you work. This is also a matter of ethics and etiquette."[65] This deputy danced with the greatest of ease between his Committee and faction affiliations, a dance familiar to all Duma deputies. Ethics, etiquette, procedure, previous "decisions," and the technical merits of the content of legislation be damned, the Duma's design highlights partisan politics, individual power, and prestige.

Similarly, the Communist Party proposed on the floor to increase spending on scientific research. An enfeebled Committee Chair spoke against the proposal: "An amendment can be voted on only after concrete financing sources are specified. What has been stated here gives no clear understanding of what the sources for financing this amendment are, although we agree it is very important to fund science."[66] A source was proposed from the floor — the ever popular cuts in spending on "state administration." The problem was that that section could never cover a R1.7T increase in the first place. The Committee Chair was not even given a chance to speak. When he tried to intervene to explain that there was no money from this source and that massive cuts in state administration would entail huge cuts even on the Duma's own meager budget, the Speaker cut him off, telling him to "sit down and settle down."[67] The proposal carried. In the Supreme Soviet, the Committee Chair dictated the process and the outcomes on the floor. In the Duma, when the Committee Chair tries to explain the consequences even of objectively absurd proposals, he is told to "sit down."

Procedural breakdown means more than that procedures come to a halt. It means that the procedures that form the expectations for roles and actions of legislative and nonlegislative players alike, procedures that by definition are meant to lend predictability and stability to legislative activity, are cast aside by legislators embroiled in conflict over partisan politics or intercommittee rivalry. The "guide" for members on how to act disappears.[68] Where no institutional mechanisms exist to manage such conflict, procedures designed for predictability and stability become inconvenient. They are replaced with ad hoc, extralegal rules of convenience that undermine predictability and stability of expectations, roles, and outcomes.

The framework used here to explain deadlock in the Duma may also explain increased breakdown in the U.S. Congress. Schick and others describe how increased partisanship and increased autonomy for the parties in Congress have undermined consensus building and conflict management in the congressional budget process.[69] They have transformed what was high collegiality into "breakdown," "improvisation," and an "inherently unstable process."[70] The comparative framework used here puts this into perspective and explains it according to a shift in the institutional design, a shift providing greater autonomy for, and fewer and weaker links between, parties and committees. Congressional parties have increasingly asserted autonomous decision-making and procedural powers. The costs are "fractious and volatile" with outcomes uncertain and unpredictable; big problems are "left to fester."[71] This framework can explain the proliferation of "gimmicks" that perturb Wildavsky.[72]

The "unintended consequences [of] structural and procedural norms" are predicted by a comparative framework sensitive to variation in organizational design.[73] When a dual-channel institution lacks links between the channels, anything can happen. Gimmicks and ad hoc procedures are a recipe for deadlock. We turn now to the issue of legislative budget outcomes, first in terms of voting on the floor.

FLOOR VOTES ON THE BUDGET:
UNPREDICTABILITY AND DEADLOCK

When budget votes are held in the Duma, no one has any idea what the outcome will be. As one deputy put it, "It is always difficult to predict what the multi-fractured Duma will do."[74] In the committee-centered Supreme Soviet, it was important for the Budget Committee Chair to remind the deputies that all committees had participated at its sessions, that all had been given the opportunity to appear before the Committee on several occasions, and that the Committee had taken their proposals into consideration. In the Supreme Soviet, consulting and respecting the sectoral committees ensured that they would in turn defer to Budget Committee recommendations.

The Budget Committee Chair in the Duma must appeal to the factions, reminding the deputies that the Committee is a partisan committee: "In the Committee sessions we, representatives of every faction in parliament, were able to reach consensus and introduce for your examination a complex of proposals."[75] In the Duma, it is the factions, not the sectoral committee representatives, who make the co-speeches after the Budget Committee Chair has presented the budget. It is thus a partisan political discussion, not a discussion of technical issues of budget content. The Budget Committee must try to appease the numerous factions.

One need look no further than the Duma's first Budget Committee Chair to see the conflict between committees and factions. Mikhail Zadornov was widely described as suffering from a "split personality."[76] As Committee Chair, he promoted the Committee's recommendations and warned of the negative consequences that failure to adopt the budget would hold for the sputtering Russian economy, for the legislators' popularity, and for the legislators' work schedule should budget work drag on.[77] He was a relentless lobbyist for the budget, warning deputies against returning home with no money for agriculture and industry in their regions.[78] But not once did Zadornov himself actually cast a vote for the budget in 1994 or in 1995. His faction opposed the budget outright, and since only faction affiliation could explain his ascent to his lofty position in the Duma, he defected from his own Committee and from his own budget.

When a Duma deputy finds it convenient to vote with the faction, a deputy votes with the faction. When it is convenient to vote with the committee, a deputy votes with the committee. There are no significant sanctions limiting this freedom of movement between the two channels. As one of the Duma's leaders put it, "The Duma's biggest problem is that the representatives of parties and factions poorly translate the conciliation and their line in the Duma. And the same low level of influence goes for the corresponding committees. The thing is that in factions the deputies are somehow united, but when they arrive in committee and at sessions, then their views somehow turn out not to be so."[79] Committee chairs have a reverse image; they feel there is often unanimity on votes in committee, but when deputies go to their factions or are on the floor, their positions change.[80]

One moment a deputy is Sybil, the next she is Martha. In a Duma of 450 split personalities, outcomes are highly unpredictable. Like the Budget Committee Chair, all deputies dance between their committee and professional identities and their partisan identities. One observer explained Zadornov's predicament: "On the one hand, he should follow the decision of the faction, on the other he should facilitate the fastest possible passage of the budget through the Duma."[81] When a deputy confronted the Committee Chair with this dilemma, the Speaker could only murmur, "It is very complicated, of course."[82] With a design promoting competition between these dual affiliations, deputy decisions are often made willy-nilly at the last second on the floor. Outcomes are unpredictable at best.

One consequence of the Duma's emphasis on political agreement rather than on budget content is that the Duma casts far fewer budget votes than did the Supreme Soviet. The Duma's predecessor, like a machine, cast hundreds of votes each year on budget sections, articles, and amendments. The Duma has shunned such detailed examination of the budget, casting a combined total of ninety-one budget votes in 1994 and 1995. Committee recommendations were carried on seventy-three of these, a success rate of about 80 percent, some 10 percent lower than its Supreme Soviet counterpart (see table 5.2).

Yet even this picture vastly exaggerates the Committee's strength and vividly demonstrates how numbers can distort when context is ignored. In the Supreme Soviet, votes on budget amendments had everything to do with the position and the strength of the Budget Committee. A vote cast against a Committee recommendation was in essence a vote against the Committee in much the same way that observers like Fenno and Wildavsky interpreted floor votes on amendments to appropriations bills as tests of the strength of the U.S. House Appropriations Committee. Budget votes in the

Table 5.2
Budget Committee Floor-Vote Success Rates on Budget Recommendations

Budget Law	Total Votes	Budget Committee Recommendations	Recommendations Followed	Budget Committee Success Rates (%)
1994 Budget	12	12	6	50
1995 Budget	79	79	67	84.8
Totals	91	91	73	80.2

Duma, though, rarely have anything to do with the position or strength of the Budget Committee. Most are amendments from factions and are a test of their relative strength in the Duma. Such votes are about partisan jockeying, not about the technical aspects of the budget or disputes with the Budget Committee. Typically, the Budget Committee has neither seen nor deliberated on these amendments, nor has it had the opportunity to voice its opinion on them on the floor. The Budget Committee is simply a second-class actor during floor debate on the budget.

Only a few votes, then, truly test the Committee's strength. Most important are the package votes and the final votes on the budget at each reading. Unlike the unanimous, automatic final passage in the Supreme Soviet, achieved because compromise had been achieved in the legislature's inter-committee process, in the Duma the Committee has less than a 50 percent success rate on final votes, three or four of which are often necessary at each reading. In 1994 and 1995, the Duma held nineteen final votes at seven separate budget readings, or nearly three votes per reading. Outcomes were so uncertain that bets were taken, and deputies, journalists, and observers fell silent, excitedly watching the monitors for the results. So did the Committee, which was only eight for nineteen, a success rate of just 42 percent[83] (see table 5.3). On each reading of the 1994 Budget, the Duma failed on several attempts to pass the Committee's recommendations on these final votes. It took three attempts to adopt the budget on the first reading, and the budget passed by only eight votes. The third reading spanned two sessions and three failed votes and provoked an uncharacteristic outburst by the Speaker, who demanded that all travel by deputies be canceled and that those away from Moscow be recalled for the next day's session and vote.[84] The next year the story was much the same. For example, it took four attempts to adopt the 1995 Budget on the second reading alone.

Table 5.3

Budget Committee Floor-Vote Success Rates on Final Votes on the Budget

Budget Law	Proposals to Reject the Budget[a]	Budget Comm. Recs. Followed	Proposals to Adopt the Budget	Budget Comm. Recs. Followed
1994 Budget	3	1	6	2
1995 Budget	2	1	8	4
Totals	5	2(40%)	14	6(43%)

Total Budget Committee recommendations followed: 8 of 19 (42%)

[a]Includes proposals to return budget to government or conciliation commission.

It did not matter whether the Committee recommended passage or rejection of the budget. On proposals to reject, the Committee was two for five; on proposals to adopt, it was six for fourteen — both around 40 percent. The same unpredictability held for the "package" votes on blocks of approved and opposed amendments discussed above. On twenty-nine votes the Committee's position carried only twelve times, an almost identical success rate of only 41 percent. On significant votes, then, the Budget Committee had a success rate of well below 50 percent.

The failure of the Duma Budget Committee relative to the Supreme Soviet Committee clearly confirms Hall's prediction that making committees more partisan results in greater conflict and weakened committees on the floor.[85] The presentation here not only confirms that expectation but also explains it in a comparative perspective with the power to extend it to legislatures more generally. The weaker the linkage between the channels, the greater the conflict will be and the less able committees will be to carry positions on the floor.

Such spectacular and repeated Committee failure was unthinkable in the Supreme Soviet. Deference to committee expertise clearly does not drive floor voting in the Duma. As on all legislation, after the budget comes out of Committee, the Committee's recommendations face discussion within the factions. The decisions of the faction are unpredictable, as are deputy actions after those decisions. One deputy, when asked what happens when forced to choose between differing faction and Committee positions, said, "More important to me is my own personal opinion. If the Committee's decision conforms to my personal view, if I myself voted for the position [in the Committee], then I will vote my own personal convictions. If I and my faction were convinced [against the Committee], then of course I would vote not the way the Committee recommended. My own view may conform to one or the other." When asked how other deputies act, however, this same deputy said, "The majority are guided by their faction, not the Committee. Especially those who were elected by electoral blocs. I was elected by my electorate [from a single-mandate district]. They answer to their factions."[86]

But many committed faction members still express their individualism in their voting behavior. When one faction decided to vote against the budget in June 1994, one of its most prominent members exclaimed to a throng of journalists that his faction "has lost its mind! Even if they will vote against the budget, I will vote for it in any event. Even if they make a decision to hold a 'solidarity' vote."[87]

In fact, recent survey research demonstrates that more than one-third of the deputies rate their faction as more fragmented than united. More impressive, more than three-fourths of the deputies say their factions have been on the wrong side of at least one vote, and most felt this on more than three occasions. When asked what they do when they disagree with their faction, fewer than one in four say they usually vote with their faction. More than 40 percent vote against the faction, and an additional 27 percent abstain. Since the Duma rules require a majority of all deputies to pass legislation, rather than a simple majority of those voting, those abstentions are tantamount to nay votes. These responses mean that nearly 70 percent of the deputies would oppose their own faction if they disagreed with its affirmative position on a piece of legislation[88] (see table 5.4). These findings confirm those of others, who report that members see themselves as independent and that factions do not dictate the behavior of their members.[89] This study goes further, however, by explaining why this individualism is able to persist and the consequences that result.

Factions make two types of decisions regarding floor votes. They can vote to express a position on the floor but leave individual deputies to vote as they see appropriate, or they can decide to hold a "solidarity vote" on which all are supposed to toe the faction line. But in practice there is little difference, as there are no effective sanctions against those who stray. There is no "imperative mandate." Deputies cannot be kicked out of the Duma for abandoning their faction; leadership posts cannot be taken away.[90] More important, these are not parties. Only six of the ten factions that existed in late 1994 competed in the Duma elections in December 1995, and two of those had radically different memberships. There is no effective shadow of the future to hold deputies in line, nor any guarantee that loyalty will bring

Table 5.4
Actions of Deputies Who Oppose Their
Faction's Position on an Issue (%)

Side with the faction anyway	23
Vote against the faction	41
Abstain or don't vote	27

advancement or even preservation of one's position. Indeed, Zadornov himself was dropped from Yabloko's list in the 1995 elections. He was compelled to battle for a single-member district seat, in spite of the fact that he had always remained loyal on budget votes even when under the greatest of pressure to support his Committee.[91] He did so because he owed his position as Budget Committee Chair to that faction and its leader, and he believed that such loyalty would enhance his status in the faction. In terms of the expectation, this was clearly a political misjudgment. For deputies more astute to the unstable nature of these organizations, this uncertainty regarding the future, regardless of how they voted, severely weakened their links to their factions when it came time to vote.

So counting votes on the basis of faction decisions is a shaky proposition at best. This layer of the decision-making process was entirely absent in the Supreme Soviet. The Duma's unlinked, dual-channel design provides the deputies with two separate identities. How they behave is only partly and often not mostly a factor of their committee commitments. Most Duma votes are based "less on the priorities of ideas as on political posturing."[92] The vote on the 1994 Budget is a perfect example. One faction leader whose position had flip-flopped several times at successive readings explained his faction's final position to adopt the budget: "We did not support the budget, we do not like it. But our position extends from a consideration of action. Anyone can see that today you cannot do anything better here. It was either accept this one or make further concessions to the LDPR. That is all. We based our decision on the LDPR . . . from the conviction of the necessity of preventing political games around support of the budget by the LDPR."[93] The ranting of LDPR members demonstrates that they followed the same strategy of voting to block one's enemies rather than voting based on the technical merits of legislation. "I remove my vote for, since Gaidar voted for the budget. That is all," said one LDPR member after the vote on the 1994 Budget. This hardly reflects a rational-technical approach to legislative decision making.[94]

That the Committee Chair's faction opposed the budgets also demonstrates that technical merit does not guide a faction's position. Yabloko voted against the budget, even though over 70 percent of its amendments, including the most significant in terms of spending and revenue amounts, were adopted.[95] Their vote cannot be explained by the technical merits of the legislation. It can only be explained by a political decision of the faction leader to oppose the government and the President on every vote possible, in the hope of enhancing his own prospects in the next presidential campaign.

THE INABILITY TO MAKE POLICY CHANGE: DEFENSE VERSUS AGRICULTURE

The chronic deadlock in the Duma is best characterized by votes on amendments. None of the more than 600 amendments to the 1995 Budget passed. The reason is simple. Three or more alternatives existed on each issue: the version in the government's draft, the amendment under consideration, and one or more additional alternatives from sectoral committees, factions, or independent deputies. If Russia's Choice had its own amendment on spending on basic research, Yabloko was sure to have its own. Yegor Gaidar was hardly going to vote in favor of Grigoriy Yavlinskiy's amendment, and vice versa. Moreover, on the few amendment votes that were held, the Budget Committee was not afforded the chance to voice its position on the alternatives. Not that this would have mattered much. The Duma's design renders it too splintered between committees, between factions, and across these two channels to be able to overcome the deadlock that ensues when alternatives appear.

The struggle between defense and agriculture offers a nice illustration of this phenomenon. The contrasting strategies of and the corresponding outcomes for these sectors perhaps indicate something about the relative strength and weakness of the defense and agriculture lobbies. But they also demonstrate the weakness of the State Duma as a forum for seeking major policy change. The Duma is in fact a lousy place to try to make policy, as the defense sector learned. The Defense Ministry and defense industries primarily sought policy action for their cause in the Duma. They consistently lost. The agriculture sector relied on the government for major changes in its budget. It consistently won, using the Duma only to preserve and consolidate those gains.

The 1994 Budget was "the battle over 18 trillion rubles."[96] The Defense

Ministry initially requested R87T from the Finance Ministry. An early, internal government draft of the budget gave the defense sector R55T, but when the Defense Ministry complained at a meeting of the full government and demanded all R87T, the Finance Ministry did just the opposite and cut the defense budget to R37.1T![97] The draft budget the government submitted to the Duma contained this lower figure. The next year the Defense Ministry requested R111T, an absurd 77 percent of all budget revenues. The Finance Ministry set defense spending in the draft budget at R45.3T, and the Defense Committee, supported by the Defense Ministry, lobbied for R56.1T.[98]

These actions cause more than a little confusion for deputies. The government claims that it submits the draft budget with unanimous support. The Speaker, too, on at least one occasion sought to defuse rumors that the government was severely divided: "The government voted on this matter, on the budget, unanimously, with all ministers voting."[99] But with the Defense Ministry openly lobbying against the government's budget in the corridors of the Duma even while the budget was being debated on the floor, the Budget Committee Chair mused, "This is a very strange situation. . . . We received a budget from the government, which it agreed to. And again a number of ministries and above all again the Ministry of Defense speak here at the session about its reservations on spending, which makes up a fifth or more of all spending!"[100] One deputy active on defense budget issues explained, "Since the Ministry of Defense, the government, the Ministry of Finance, and the Ministry of Economics work in isolation from each other, they did not reach agreement."[101]

Contrary to popular Western perceptions, the Russian military, like its Soviet predecessor, has traditionally been a weak political actor, and its influence has if anything steadily declined since the beginning of Soviet reforms in the late 1980s. The size of the army has been cut, arms procurement has dropped, missions have been scaled back, and spending has been slashed.[102] The Defense Ministry warns of threats to "defense preparedness" and the "preservation of defense industries" and warns that the budget does not support the "bare minimum" required for upkeep of the services.[103] But somehow it fails to persuade the government. The Defense Minister reportedly does not actively participate in the budget process while that process is still within the government, and one deputy claims that the Defense Minister "does not even see the draft budget before it leaves the Finance Ministry."[104]

The defense sector is virtually excluded from the budget game in the government, and by the time the draft goes to the full government for approval it is too late in the game for the Defense Ministry to win significant changes. The Prime Minister, when asked about the army's demands for an R18T increase, told the deputies, "I do not know who, from whom, or where this matter was discussed."[105] At the first reading of the 1995 Budget, the Finance Minister informed the deputies that nobody from the Defense Ministry had approached the Finance Ministry about defense spending. On both occasions, government officials urged the deputies to adopt the draft and discuss amendments at later stages. But as of the final government meeting that formally approved these budgets for submission to the legislature, the defense sector demands appeared not even to have been heard.

So the Defense Ministry has either chosen to rest its hope for spending increases on the Duma or has been left to do so. But given the massive changes that the proposed increases would demand of the entire budget structure, by the time the budget gets to the Duma, it is far too late in the game. The Finance Minister tells the deputies, "This draft budget is the opinion of the entire government. . . . I can say that neither the Minister of Defense, nor his deputies, nor the head of the Main Finance Administration [of the Ministry] has approached me personally."[106] If the Defense Ministry hadn't even bothered to approach the Finance Ministry about the increase, why should the Duma listen?

In fact, even the defense sector's supporters in the Duma could not get very far in pushing such a major change of R18T in a draft budget with total spending of R183T. Some sources argued that the Defense Minister had made a "strategic error" by failing to court deputies in his lobbying effort, but the strategic error was his relying on the Duma in the first place. First, when the budget hits the Russian legislature, almost every sector seeks either an increase or a reversal of cuts made in its own budget. With the Russian economy in a shambles, every sectoral committee and every ministry, from education, to culture, to science, to health care, seeks to recoup losses in the current draft budget and from budget debts owed in the previous year. The few sectors that gained increases fight to either increase or consolidate their gains.[107] Under the budget rules, any increase in one sector must come from corresponding decreases elsewhere. Which sectors could be so dramatically cut to allow an R18T increase in defense spending? No deputy was willing to take responsibility for slashing any area except the budget for the "state administration." In 1994, the draft budget set this line item at R3.8T, and every other sector, not just defense, sought to claim money from there. Major cuts in spending on industry, health care, education, culture, or any other area to pay for a 33 percent defense increase would be a major policy decision, given that these other sectors had already undergone massive cuts.

The Duma is simply too politically fragmented and too partisan in its decision making to produce such major policy change. Whenever there is an attempt to do so, individual deputies, factions, and committees send a flurry of alternative proposals to the floor to ensure that no such change takes place. Simply suggesting the existence of alternative proposals just before the vote blocks action on the floor. Dozens of alternatives to an R18T increase were put up by those defending the spending levels of their own pet areas. "Cut somewhere else!" was the battle cry. Presenting alternatives guaranteed deadlock, and that one's own favored area would be safe from cuts to pay for increases in defense.[108]

The agriculture sector, by contrast, sought major increases in spending but did not use the Duma as the vehicle for pursuing these increases. The original draft 1994 Budget set spending for agriculture and foodstuffs at R5.3T, but the one that made it to the Duma more than doubled this amount, to just over R12T. Agriculture supporters in the Duma fought mainly to preserve this gain, and won. That the agriculture battle was waged and won within the government is evident from the Defense Minister's words long before the Duma even saw the 1994 Budget: "The obstacle for me is Deputy Prime Minister Zaveryukha, whose rank is higher and who is by character more pushy. You cannot pull the blanket entirely onto your side. You have to allow a bit for everyone."[109] Aleksander Kh. Zaveryukha was the top government official responsible for agriculture, and he secured that sector's budget gains in the government long before the Duma entered the picture. While he did not pull the entire "blanket" onto his side, he pulled enough to prevent the defense sector from increasing its share. Clearly, the Defense Minister was not "pushy." He and his associates apparently did not even play the government game, and proved inept at the Duma game.

At first many from the conservative Agrarian Party of Russia (APR) faction supported the large increase for the defense and other sectors. But when they realized that the enormous increase would necessitate cuts in their R7T gains, they balked. One APR deputy came up with an ingenious plan, which he sprang unexpectedly during floor debate: take any extra and unexpected revenue from privatization that exceeded the planned amount and use it to create a special fund for the defense sector. In one stroke he robbed the antiprivatization crowd of their bluster and gave the supporters of the defense lobby the ability to say they voted for potentially unlimited defense increases.

The Agrarians understood that the government was the place to fight for policy and content. The Duma was the place to play politics. This decision to create the special fund was not about substance — almost everyone understood that there would be no unanticipated revenues from privatization. Indeed, the government knew it would be hard pressed to collect the amount already written into the budget! But everyone could appear to be critical of the wildly unpopular privatization *and* cast a vote supporting the financially decimated defense sector.[110]

Spending trillions more rubles for decrepit defense industries would have been a bad decision, and this certainly is one reason why the huge increase did not pass. But the Duma is too fragmented and too partisan to be able to make such major policy decisions. Hostility and jealousy between committees and factions alike render the Duma incapable of effecting major policy change. That is why the deputies turn to ad hoc procedures to reach political agreements that ultimately do not entail solutions to the most pressing problems, be they the privatization program or defense spending. This situation is in sharp contrast to that of the Supreme Soviet, which was highly capable of acting, although the decisions it made on many issues may not have been the most desirable, at least not to the executive branch. The two legislatures prove to be diametrically opposite in their capacities to manage internal conflict over legislative content on the one hand and internal political conflict on the other.

LEGISLATIVE DEADLOCK: THE DUMA NORM

The Duma has passed budgets each year despite the "complete chaos," but chronic procedural breakdown and deadlock are far from ideal conditions for legislating. The difficulties on the budget reflect general conditions of poor coordination across committees, inconsistent political coordination across factions, and a lack of constraints on individual action that causes debilitating breakdown and deadlock in the legislative process. With a confusing lattice of committees with crosscutting profiles and no institutional mechanism to coordinate committee work, jealous competition and wasteful redundancy stifle the legislative process. In the Duma, as one member nicely put it, "Everyone works for himself and nobody watches over the work of the whole system."

In the Supreme Soviet, there was a very clear specialization of draft laws by committees. For example, a draft law on foreign policy was necessarily headed by the Committee on Foreign Affairs. This work was led by the profile committee.

In the Duma, this is not preserved. Here draft laws may be distributed to several committees, and how the initiator works may be peripheral. That is, there is no observance of any clear profile role for committees, and therefore there is no responsibility of committees for legislative drafts.

The lack of a coordinating mechanism exacerbates conflict: "The leaders of factions do not work in committees, and the committees are not part of the Duma Soviet. Therefore there is no filter to control against weak laws and duplication, and legislative work is uncontrolled and spontaneous."[111] The lack of coordination exacerbates conflict between committees and, in the fragmented partisan environment, renders consensus extremely elusive.

A repeated cry of committee chairs is, "Other committees are interfering in our sphere of competence!"[112] For example, there was nothing to prevent and many incentives to encourage the Committee on Legislation and Judicial Reform to write and introduce a Law on Indexation of Pensions, even though the Committee on Social Policy, which logic would suggest should have responsibility for such a law, was also working on a draft. Both committees brought drafts to the floor, no coordination was attempted, and the existence of competing alternatives produced deadlock. This deadlock was precisely the goal of the Committee on Legislation's Chair, who harbored great personal dislike for the Social Policy Committee Chair and wanted to prevent his bill from being adopted.[113] The deputies either divided their support between the alternatives or, more commonly, had no idea which to support, so they simply abstained, leaving neither version to pass.

The existence of alternatives virtually guarantees deadlock on the Duma floor. Their existence alone is concrete evidence of the lack of coordination among legislative actors. As the Speaker said, "We dream about alternatives. Alternatives earlier were an 'enemy.' " But in the Duma alternatives are the result of a "failure of coordination" and "far from embody opposite points of view."[114] The reflect partisan political bickering, not a search for optimal policy solutions. Consultation and unofficial cooperation are virtually absent from the Duma's legislative process. At the end of 1994, at least seventy-seven items on the legislative calendar, more than one-third of the laws before the Duma, were plagued by competition among three or more drafts.[115]

One committee may have primary responsibility for a given piece of legislation, but there are likely to be one or more other committees that feel that they should have the responsibility for the same legislation. As one experienced Russian legislator observed, "They begin to compete with each other and duplicate each other's work on drafts. And experience shows that when there are alternative drafts, not one of them will pass. They will not gather the necessary number of votes, and then we have a problem of trying to avoid duplication of work."[116] The committee chairs do not meet together in any intercommittee body; they are each from different factions spanning the entirety of the partisan map. In short, because the Duma's two organizational channels are unlinked and autonomous, the first place that these committee chairs meet is on the Duma floor. Conflict erupts at such a late stage. By voicing objections and suggesting alternatives, a committee can torpedo decision making on the floor, as in the example above. Floor activity becomes a game of blocking the proposals of others rather than of ratifying compromise and consensus and adopting laws. There is no consensus to ratify.

The factions follow the same strategy, based on the same logic. Procedural breakdown and decision-making deadlock go hand in hand. The crosscutting conflict between committees and factions and the freedom of individual deputies to roam between these two channels renders decision making on the floor highly conflictual, unstable, and unpredictable. The factions screen documents a day or two at most, and normally only hours before plenary session debate. In other words, factions take up draft legislation only after a committee has completed its work. While they may also examine drafts and submit amendments at earlier stages, they tend to discuss items on the plenary session agenda at meetings just before sessions, during recesses of sessions, and during the sessions themselves. Their conclusions and behavior are impossible to predict.

The typical reaction of factions is to "block anything that emerges from political opponents," rather than to base decisions on the content of the legislation in question.[117] The lack of a legislative majority and the incessant competition between numerous small partisan factions, each of whose leader sees himself as a presidential candidate, makes reaching decisions on the floor extremely difficult. The manifestation of this is the proliferation on the floor of alternatives to legislation under debate. Merely suggesting the presence of an alternative draft is normally enough for a faction or a deputy to torpedo passage of any item in the Duma. For one faction seeking to block the advancement of another's bills for partisan, political reasons, introducing an alternative is a sure way to bring deadlock and grind the legislative process to a halt. An actual alternative draft need not in fact exist; all one has to do is to suggest that one does.[118]

Of those seventy-seven bills that faced alternatives in 1994, the Duma was able to overcome the conflict to adopt legislation only twice. As one deputy observed, "We have only two, only two laws that passed in the face of alternative drafts. But we have not a single other instance, and there have been dozens of cases. We had several Water Codes — none passed. We had several draft Land Laws — none passed. And on the state symbol and hymn, too. Not one was adopted. We could talk about such examples without end."[119]

Indeed one could. The sharpest example of decision-making deadlock in the Duma, came in June 1994, as the Duma debated the government's program for the second stage of privatization. Multiple votes failed to pass any of at least eight alternatives. Several sessions of debate and long nights of intense "conciliatory" negotiations produced agreement between government officials and the most disparate partisan leaders and experts in the Duma. One deputy mused that if the government official in charge of privatization, a radical reformer, could reach agreement with the Chairs of the Duma Committees on Property and on Economic Policy, both sharp antigovernment, antireform deputies, there was "nothing for the Duma to do but approve the agreement."[120] This agreement entailed nearly forty changes to the program inspired by all Duma factions and committees. But after more than half a dozen failed votes the Duma had to give up. The continued existence of alternatives from two different factions and three independent deputies ensured that no plan at all would pass.[121]

Some deputies simply refused to vote for any document associated with the name of the controversial Chair of the State Property Committee, Anatoliy Chubais. Some refused to vote for any document associated with the names of the two antireform deputies. Still others refused to sign any document lacking the approval of one or another of these participants. The deadlock was less about the program's content than about partisan battles and poor internal Duma coordination. The Duma closed for its summer recess with no program, the legislative deadlock opening the way for the President to enact the program by decree.[122]

Other less dramatic examples abound and make the Duma podium an uncertain and unpleasant place to be for a committee chair or for a leader on a given piece of legislation. The draft Law on Voting Rights had the support of the Central Election Commission and two Duma committees.

But Yabloko had its own version tied to a draft electoral code, and as a result nothing passed.[123] The debate on the Water Code provided a humorous example of how alternatives can torpedo progress on the adoption of legislation in the Duma. The Committee on Natural Resources submitted its draft which it reported was agreed to by the government and by the regions. The committee chair said that three committees had worked on the draft "and that no alternative exists or can exist." Minutes later, though, LDPR presented an alternative. It had not been submitted to the Duma Soviet as the Regulations required. It had not been sent to the territories as the Regulations required. But LDPR submitted it on the floor and complained that its ideas had not been heard, and movement on the Water Code screeched to a halt.[124] The Duma could not even ratify the state trappings. The Communists proposed reinstituting the old Soviet flag and anthem, nationalists proposed Tsarist symbols, while the President's draft, of course, would have established those in de facto existence since 1991. By raising the alternatives they knew would never pass, the Communists and others could guarantee deadlock and prevent any law from passing.[125]

A more hostile debate broke out over the Law on Fighting Organized Crime. The Committee on Security submitted a draft initially authored by the Ministry of Internal Affairs, the Foreign Counter-Intelligence Service, and other security organs. It contained a number of radical, anticonstitutional provisions that directly violated virtually every international human rights convention and that sparked a raucous debate more reminiscent of a political demonstration than of a professional legislature. The Committee on Legislation submitted a hasty alternative to prevent its adoption. Its Chair explained, "The situation of examining two draft laws was raised in the Duma Soviet. I said to the respected Duma Soviet that, in my opinion, the matter is not ready to be examined in plenary session."[126] Again, deadlock was the result. These are only a few examples from among many, just in the Duma's first year of existence.

Committee recommendations are routinely subject to criticism and questioning on ground already tread and negotiated by its members. The Speaker blamed the faction leaders, who are "consumed by pure politics" and engage in "political machinations" instead of focusing on the technical merits of legislative solutions to the problems in society.[127] A faction leader may take the floor at any time to speak on legislation under debate and may grind the process to a halt by announcing the existence of an alternative draft. But as seen, they do not bear sole blame. Other committees may present unexpected criticism, opposition, or alternatives. As a result, decisions of the responsible committee on legislation are subject to uncertain alteration or rejection by unpredictable and undisciplined factions and by other committees. Compared with the Supreme Soviet, floor activity in the Duma is not merely more conflictual, it is an unmitigated mess.

Extra-legislative Conflict Management in the Duma

The Duma has better mechanisms for and somewhat better success in managing internal conflict on extra-legislative, political issues. On the budget process this was evident in the political agreement regularly achieved in the Duma Soviet for bringing the budget to the agenda. It was also evident in the hurried, last-minute meetings among faction leaders during breaks in the plenary session, when they agreed to ad hoc procedures for debate and votes. While these were decisions based on political expediency rather than on the technical merits of the law, the instances do demonstrate the Duma's ability to reach such internal political compromise. Again, the budget serves as an example of the broader trend in the Duma.

The clearest and perhaps most significant example of the Duma's ability to manage internal conflict on extra-legislative issues came on the first major conflict it faced in the first week of its existence. The Fifth Duma opened on January 12, 1994. By January 17 it had elected its entire leadership — Speaker, deputy speakers, and committee chairs. Within weeks it had passed its Regulations. The Supreme Soviet took over six months and multiple votes to elect its leaders and complete work on its rules.[128] The Duma's mechanism for political conciliation among faction leaders is indeed "a work mechanism until now never seen before in Russia."[129] That the faction leaders were able to agree so quickly on the distribution of posts, and that the package they presented was immediately and overwhelmingly approved by the deputies, was immediate evidence of the fallacy of predictions that the fragmented partisan nature of the Duma would prevent it from resolving internal political disputes.[130] The inclusion of the factions in the design is precisely what enables the Duma to resolve such disputes better than its predecessor did. The Duma Soviet, an institutional forum for the leaders of the partisan factions to coordinate, negotiate, and resolve political disputes, enables such agreements in the new Russian legislature. This first instance set an important precedent for interfaction coordination, repeated regularly in the leadership's coordination on the budget, in

the consensual resolution of "housekeeping" functions, and in the formation of "inter-faction conciliation commissions" for drafting resolutions
such as those on amnesty and internal security.[131]

The faction leaders repeat this conflict resolution weekly in the Duma
Soviet, where they draft and agree upon the plenary session agendas.[132]
Agenda formation perhaps most clearly demonstrates simultaneously the
successes and the failures of extra-legislative conflict management in the
Duma. The Duma approves a long-term legislative plan covering all bills
that the Duma seeks to consider during the course of a given seasonal
session. From this plan, two calendars are formed, one for the month and
one for the coming two weeks.[133] The Duma Soviet in turn forms the daily
agendas from these two-week calendars. Nominally, it does this on the basis
of what legislation is ready to come out of the committees. In fact, the
agenda is based on those issues that the faction leaders happen to feel like
discussing.[134] Nevertheless, they do reach political agreement on the longer
legislative plan and on the calendars, as well as on what issues will be
included and what excluded from each plenary session agenda. The agreement may not conform to the activities of the committees, because they are
not represented in these Duma Soviet meetings. But it does reflect political
conflict management between the leaders of the Duma's partisan factions.

Still, this agreement between the partisan leaders has little noticeable
effect in easing conflict in agenda setting on the Duma floor. Even though
"it is extremely difficult to change the agenda from the floor," proposals
from individual deputies are allowed and empty agenda debate regularly
takes up an hour or more of the Duma's morning.[135] Duma agenda debates
are as long and even more contentious than were the Supreme Soviet's.
Debates are frequently so loud and so partisan, even to the point of physical
conflict, that they leave the deputies in a "non-working mood" when they
finally do get around to considering legislation.[136]

Neither the original Duma Regulations nor revisions to them envision a
time limit on agenda debate. As a result, the Fifth Duma wound up "every
day discussing the agenda practically from scratch."[137] A verbal agreement
set a standard for agenda debate of twenty minutes: ten minutes for proposals to be made, ten for brief explanation and votes. However, during a
span of fifty-one sessions between March and December 1994, the average
time spent on the agenda was just short of one hour — fifty-five minutes.
Only seven times during this period did the Duma succeed in limiting
agenda debate to twenty minutes or less. Forty-one times agenda debate
exceeded this amount, and twenty-three times it consumed over an hour of

the Duma's time.[138] The longest agenda debate during this span lasted a whopping two hours and thirty-three minutes — the entire morning![139] The twenty-three agenda debates lasting over an hour produced *a combined* ten changes to the agenda. On fourteen of these occasions, not a single change was made, and only once was more than one change made.[140] As seen above on budget votes and on alternative bills, with the agenda as well, one or two factions can be enough to block passage but not enough to carry a proposal on the floor.

So on July 21, 1994, the agenda debate lasted over an hour and a half when the agenda itself already included twenty-one items, one of which was the program for the second stage of privatization. This issue had already consumed a full day and a half of plenary session time, and nothing approaching a solution had been reached. On October 21, 1994, when the only item on the agenda was a speech by the Prime Minister and debate on no-confidence in the government, the agenda again took up nearly ninety minutes of the morning. One deputy notorious for raising what can only be called idiotic proposals once consumed the agenda debate with a complaint about being able to purchase a "pornographic journal" in the Duma corridor for R10,000. The Speaker, along with everyone else, laughed and chimed in, "What are you throwing your money away on!"[141] Over time, though, the deputies became accustomed to such antics. When this same deputy accused another of murder, the accused responded, "Virtually every day in this hall, Mr. Marychev insults someone for laziness or whatever, including myself, and today even raised serious criminal accusations. The Speaker, ignoring his responsibilities, does nothing to silence the slander and insult. We have frequent boorishness and lack of culture on the floor. *But the most dangerous thing is that we are becoming used to this.* "[142] One Duma leader charitably blamed this on the "political energy of the deputies."

A more precise explanation for the agenda breakdown stems from the internal weakness of the factions combined with the high partisan fragmentation in the Duma. Agreement in the Duma Soviet does not translate to formal approval of the agenda on the floor, just as Duma Soviet agreement to approve the budget on package votes did not bring approval of those packages. First, the agreement between the faction leaders is virtually never consensual. Since faction organization does not end with the Duma Soviet, a faction whose position in the Duma Soviet is a minority due to the one-faction, one-vote principle may feel that it has a majority on the floor. More often, a faction or deputy can use multiple agenda proposals as a form of protest against the decision of the Duma leadership. Or, they may realize that even short of a majority to pass an initiative, they may have a large enough minority to prevent a majority of 225 deputies to gain passage of the agenda to enable the Duma to move on to its legislative work.

This partisanship affects far more than just passage of the agenda. Many items never get acted upon because of poor time management. One Duma leader complained, "The main function of the Duma is legislating. And what do we see? Sessions are twice a week, five and a half hours a day. Of these we waste about an hour on the morning's agenda, and the last 30 minutes on Friday for political announcements, 40 if not 50% of our working time is relegated to political discussion."[143] They also fail because partisan leaders lack legislative expertise in setting the agenda. As one faction leader unwittingly pointed out, "I go to the Duma Soviet and see nine laws on the agenda for one day and say, 'What is this?!' Each one is given twenty minutes for debate, when we can't even adopt the day's agenda in one hour."[144] At one session the day's agenda had twenty-one items, including the privatization program that had undergone nearly two full sessions of debate with no action close to being taken. At another session, the Civil Code was given twenty minutes for debate when it required three hours, and still it was not passed. Agreement in the Duma Soviet may resolve or manage political conflict, but it can bring unrealistic decisions that are impossible to implement, resulting in procedural breakdown and deadlock in the legislative activities of the Duma.[145]

Evaluating the Unlinked, Dual-Channel Design

The Speaker graded the Duma a "B-" after its first six months, saying, "Our engine is the multiplicity of political divisions. . . . Too much time is wasted on this division and electors must know how their representatives act. It is time to end this situation of party interests being higher than everything and turn to normal legislative work."[146] He attacked "certain factions" whose members behave as if at a "political demonstration" rather than in a legislature.[147] The Duma Speaker was referring to the Liberal-Democratic Party of Vladimir Zhirinovskiy, whose members dominated the raucous agenda debates, issued the vast majority of ludicrous proposals, and were responsible for at least four fistfights and shoving matches on the floor with members of other factions.[148] But partisanship runs through all corners of the Duma, and partisan conflict is so sharp that observers can say that the deputies "display no respect for each other, for other opinions, or for the very organ to which they have been elected."[149] One faction attacks another as being everything from "criminal" to "traitors," and the other responds that the first is "hooliganist," "raising hysteria," and "destroying the Duma sessions" with "incompetent behavior" of the type described above.[150]

The point is not that there is partisanship in the Duma. There is partisanship in any legislature in which party or partisan faction organizations are represented. The point is that the Duma's design creates incentives for deputies to pursue strategies of competition and confrontation rather than constraining them to pursue consensus building and conflict management. Sharp partisan conflict between the factions, competition between the committees for control over legislative issues, and competition between committees and factions for control over the process and for the loyalties of the members prevails because of the lack of links between the two channels. The Duma lacks all of the advantages linkage could provide; to use Pfeffer and Salancik's terms, there is poor information flow, disjointed communications, and no reliable means of negotiation and networking.[151]

These findings are hardly confined to Russia. The advantage of a comparative institutional approach is that explanations are generalizable. Applicability to changes in the U.S. Congress has already been discussed. However, in other dual-channel legislatures where links are weak or absent, the consequence is similar internal breakdown and deadlock on legislative issues. Hungary's legislature is a particularly instructive case, for Hungary has a parliamentary system, yet its legislature has extremely weak links between its factions and its committees. Attila Ágh and Istvan Soltesz each describe a highly fragmented partisan body in which all factions are represented in the leadership and all have committee chair posts. The legislature therefore shares with the Duma some important organizational features. Ágh finds that legislature internally ineffectual in all major tasks.[152] Clearly, the findings here do not apply only to presidential systems. Legislatures can have unlinked designs in parliamentary systems as well and suffer similar consequences.

Ukraine also offers a nice comparative confirmation of the findings here. Before 1994 its legislature looked very much like Russia's Supreme Soviet, but in 1994 it changed its legislature's design to mirror that of the Duma's. As Bach describes, its factions were even more fragmented and weaker before there was a PR election to that legislature.[153] A similar unlinked chasm between factions and committees in the Rada brought chronic, persistent deadlock to that legislature.[154] The Rada has a "limited policy-making capacity" due to intense "ideologization of the legislative process."[155] It is plagued by multiple alternatives and repeat consideration of the same issues while being unable to arrive at solutions to those issues. A reform to elect half the Rada by PR lists as in Russia did not help. Nine factions organized the first Rada so elected, exactly as the Duma is organized. Twenty-four overlapping committees with chairs span the entire ideological spectrum, all faction heads sit in the leadership, and no majority or coalition exists across legislative posts. One difference in the Rada that confirms the relevance of the linkage concept here is that it has included the committee chairs in that leadership council. The consequence is that those chairs work together more closely than do their counterparts in the Duma to produce and evaluate drafts. Joint responsibility rather than competing alternatives is more the norm in the Rada. This result lends support to the expectation that such linkage improves intercommittee coordination.

However, this linkage is the only one in Ukraine's Rada, and the factions still submit their own alternatives to block each other's legislation on the floor. Rada deputies report a "complete inability to agree," and "factions are unable to reach consensus" to overcome deadlock on legislative content. They describe the legislative process as "chaos" and "breakdown"; as one Rada member put it, "agreements all go straight into the garbage" when legislation hits the floor.[156] They may not use the word *bardak*, but they do describe internal chaos and breakdown that leaves the members highly frustrated. Even Ukraine's President recently bemoaned the lack of "mechanisms that could induce the parliament to form a majority and operate as a responsible, efficient legislature."[157] He was calling for the factions and the committees to be more thoroughly linked throughout the legislature's design.

Unlinked, dual-channel designs, therefore, provide constraints on deputy action that are only partially effective. Conflict management takes place in the Duma Soviet between the faction leaders only in setting the agenda and in resolving procedural and leadership issues. These are important achievements in and of themselves and represent in each case advances in internal, extra-legislative conflict management compared with the Supreme Soviet. But when the agreements among the faction leaders concern legislative issues, the lack of links leaves deputies free to act as individualists who sometimes vote with their faction, sometimes vote with their committee, and sometimes go it alone. The result is not only procedural breakdown but also decision-making deadlock in the Duma's internal legislative activities.

External Activities:
Negotiation and Cooperation

While the Duma's two channels are unlinked, its design does entrench the partisan factions in the leadership. Chapter 3 demonstrated the dangers of a legislature lacking a political body able to negotiate with the executive branch on extra-legislative issues. The Supreme Soviet's political orientation at all levels was dependent on and determined by the personality of an individual — by Khasbulatov on extra-legislative issues and by individual committee chairs on their respective legislative issues. At no level of the Duma is this true. Russian legislators are now constrained in their ability to single-handedly influence the Duma's political orientation.

The expectations of theory are clearly borne out in the Duma: increasing the partisan nature of a legislature makes internal decisions more difficult to reach.[1] The Duma's internal legislative process routinely breaks down in deadlock under the weight of debilitating conflict. However, as Remington suggests, including partisan leaders in the legislature's leadership does constrain those legislators to cooperate with the executive branch.[2] Decisions the Duma does reach reflect a consensus struck by a broad range of partisan views, and such multipartisan consensus is more likely to be acceptable to the executive branch. Additionally, all factions share an interest in buttressing the strength and prerogatives of the Duma in their relations with the executive branch. They simultaneously act together and constrain each other to pursue conflict management in the Duma's external activities.

Some peculiar aspects of recent Russian history have also helped to ease conflict in the Duma's external relations. First, the new constitution dramatically reduces the authority of the Duma compared with that of the Supreme Soviet. Eugene Huskey's recent work describes the "presidential leviathan" and the enormous advantages that the executive branch in Russia enjoys over the legislature.[3] Nevertheless, that executive branch does not ignore the legislature outright. All officials seek to avoid a repeat of the sort of confrontation that produced the violence of October 1993. This violence was a traumatic experience for the political elite and for society alike. Also, the Duma's membership reflects and the institution is built around all major political orientations in society, lending it a political authority that its predecessor lacked. This partisan composition robs the executive branch of the argument that the legislature does not reflect the political landscape of Russian society. Such a claim regarding the Duma would be difficult to sustain.[4]

A comparative institutional approach explains why Russian legislators are now constrained to cooperate with the executive branch when so recently they were free to pursue strategies of confrontation and conflict. While the lack of links between the two channels leaves the Duma riddled by internal procedural breakdown and decision-making deadlock, the inclusion of the factions has transformed relations with the executive branch. These relations are marked by conflict management and consensus building. This chapter first explores legislative-executive conflict management on technical, legislative issues, budgetary and nonbudgetary, and then turns to extra-legislative, political issues. On legislative and extra-legislative issues, the Duma's design constrains deputies to pursue collaborative and conflict-management strategies, constraints that were absent in the single-channel, nonpartisan Supreme Soviet.

CONFLICT MANAGEMENT ON BUDGET CONTENT

Like its predecessor, the Duma Budget Committee cooperates with the government. But the Duma's design roots this cooperation in more than the personal predilections of a committee chair. All committees now cooperate with the President and the government. The increased institutional role of the factions ensures broader and deeper cooperation with the executive branch across all committees and on all issues.

The Duma and the government continued and even expanded on the cooperation on the budget begun with the Supreme Soviet. Finance Ministry officials say of the budgets:

> We reached agreement on these parameters jointly with the deputies, and in the government's opinion this demonstrated the potential of such an approach, in which a whole range of matters are worked out in coopera-

tion between government specialists and departments, and deputies and Duma experts.

This is an acceptable compromise, reached in close cooperation between the government and the Duma. Don't destroy the cooperation which we feel has become so productive and which we are prepared to continue in the future. We are prepared to resolve the remaining questions in a businesslike manner, as they say.[5]

The literature on budgeting in poor countries notes that government officials often see legislators as "stupid" or "irresponsible" for adopting unrealistic provisions.[6] There are indeed Russian officials who in private refer to Committee members as "idiots." But even these embrace the closer cooperation and urge still more: "We in the Finance Ministry probably need to learn to work with the Duma, and the deputies need to learn to work with the Ministry. This is called experience. We need to meet more often, to discuss problems, swear at each other, maybe. Drink vodka together."[7]

In the Duma, the partisan factions control relations with the executive branch, and together they ensure that these will be collaborative. Legislative-executive conflict management on budget content is manifest in every aspect, in the form of the budget itself, the macroeconomic characteristics at the heart of the budget, and in specific revenue and spending provisions. I will address each of these in turn.

Although each year the Budget Committee acknowledged that the draft budget was "advanced in comparison with that presented in previous years," a number of serious disputes regarding its form remained.[8] Among the most important were that the budgets excluded figures on federal programs and that the level of detail generally needed to be radically increased. In spite of initial government resistance, the Duma has made great progress in collaborating to resolve conflict over the form of the budget.

The demand that the budget show federal programs was hardly new. One deputy reminded the Finance Ministry that the Supreme Soviet had demanded this since 1991: "For the third year already we are asking for something that is not at all dangerous. We are asking only . . . how much each program costs, what is the breakdown of the spending, and where in the budget the federal programs are. We understand they are in many sections. But how much concretely is being spent on which federal programs? It would be interesting to simply look at how much our programs cost and how much we are spending this year. This is very important to show!" The Finance Ministry tried to deflect responsibility to the Ministry of Economics, but deputies continued to press; they knew that the Finance Ministry had the information: "We have already ordered, requested, there was a Duma vote, the Committee has expressed its opinion, to ask you to present these figures. We need these figures. They should be here."[9]

The Ministry never provided the information in 1994, but the next year the Budget Committee was pleased to see it included with the draft from the beginning. The Ministry and the Committee reached a tacit agreement that if the Committee dropped the issue for 1994, the Ministry would submit the figures for 1995.[10] With the 1995 Draft Budget, the government submitted a List of Federal Programs, a twenty-page document outlining spending on forty-eight federal programs, and included article 15, which ratified these program spending provisions.[11]

Another aspect of the budget's form concerned the level of detail in revenue and spending provisions. Cooperation between the Committee and the government yielded impressive results in resolving conflict over the issue of budget detail. One of the most contentious Committee demands was for quarterly breakdowns of revenues and spending to allow the Duma to monitor budget implementation during the course of the fiscal year. The Finance Ministry initially said that such breakdowns did not exist. As Caiden and Wildavsky note, governments in economically troubled countries see it "as their job to say 'no.'"[12] The Committee knew better, however, as several of its members were former Finance Ministry officials. One of these shot back, "It exists, and you also have monthly breakdowns which we can demand if we want!"[13]

Some Ministry officials said that the demand reflected a lack of professionalism: "What do they need this for? If the Duma decides this should all be ratified in the law, then any change required during the year would have to be adopted as an amendment to the law. This is a function of the government. The Duma's function is merely to examine in what way different priorities will be financed and at what level."[14] But the two sides met halfway on the 1994 Budget. The Ministry admitted that it had the information and agreed to provide it "in working form," that is, unofficially for purposes of background information only. But the Ministry begged not to be required to submit it officially or as part of the law.[15]

The Committee positively noted this informal presentation in its review of government action on its demands.[16] The next year, however, its Law on the 1995 Budget Process required that the breakdowns be included in the budget itself. Finance Ministry officials were furious:

Well, fine. Fine! If we need to transfer spending from the first quarter to the second quarter and vice versa, does this mean we need to adopt a change to the law? We have thousands of such changes during the year. Does this mean we have to debate thousands of amendments to the law? In the Committee, in the Duma, two readings, the Federation Council, and a presidential signature just like any law? The Duma won't be able to work on anything else!

Also, the Duma wants these quarterly breakdowns right away. We have never done this before! It will take at least two months for purely technical reasons. They want these in two days. This is unrealistic. How can you explain to them that this is impossible? But fine, we'll try.[17]

But the Ministry had submitted a document providing these quarterly breakdowns, again not in the law itself, almost two weeks before this official made these comments.[18] This must have satisfied the deputies, because the issue never arose publicly again in 1995 and quarterly breakdowns did not appear in the law.

The Duma even made progress on that issue that all legislatures press — the level of detail in budget items, particularly spending items. Each year, government officials and deputies alike hailed the expansion of budget detail. Said one Finance Ministry official,

On expanded figures on the majority of spending articles in the 1994 Budget, I have to say that, and I think Aleksandr Petrovich [Pochinok] will confirm that in this instance the draft budget as submitted, I can't even say, in comparison with the 1993 Budget it is probably three times more detailed. And the main thing is that it is submitted with every ministry visible. If some other expanded statistics are needed, concrete ones, then let us look at this and we will give what we have in the Finance Ministry. I think this can take place in the context of the Committee's work, and the sectoral committees' work, as needed.[19]

There could be no argument here, and the Duma succeeded in consistently increasing the level of budget detail. The 1994 Draft Budget was twenty-six pages long and consisted of twenty-nine articles. The budget adopted was forty pages long and consisted of thirty-nine articles. Even more significant is what happened within article 16.[20] The draft had less than nine pages for spending items. The final budget had over twelve pages, so the Duma increased the breakdown of spending detail by more than

30 percent. The next year, the draft budget was only marginally more detailed, with forty-three pages, forty-six articles, and again, only nine pages of spending detail. The 1995 Budget adopted, however, had fifty-three pages and sixty-three articles. Spending detail was more spread out throughout the document and the nearly sixty pages of appendices ratified by the law. Moreover, each year the Committee received several tomes of appendices showing revenue and spending breakdowns. This was provided as information only and was not part of the law but nevertheless provided the legislature with a level of budget detail previously unknown in Russia, and the deputies used these appendices to push for expansion of the law itself.

Perhaps the most dramatic area demonstrating the Duma's success in expanding the level of detail in the annual budget is the most controversial area — national defense. While most sections of the 1994 Draft Budget reflected an increase in detail over previous budgets, on defense no detail was provided whatsoever, signaling a regression in government openness. The 1993 Budget contained ten items within the defense section, but the 1994 Draft Budget had just one line: national defense. At R37.1T, it was the biggest item in the budget by far. One report lamented, "One can only guess how many and what kind of soldiers, officers and generals, planes, tanks, etc. are needed. Why are they not in the budget[?] Yes, there are military secrets, but in the US these make up only 10–12% of the general defense budget. It should at least show those things which fall under other ministries, such as spending for housing for demobilized soldiers."[21] The Duma Defense Committee was appalled and sought to open up the budget and to give the Duma control over a large amount of detail along the lines of the U.S. defense budget. The only increase in detail they achieved initially was in closed committee sessions, and programs were not revealed at all by the end of 1994.[22]

Still, they did manage to open up the defense budget in 1994. The final budget contained six subpoints. Compared with the previous year, lines for the following were lacking: mobile forces, spending for the Commonwealth of Independent States (CIS) united forces, spending for families and children of servicemen, spending on realization of arms control treaties, and spending on military law enforcement organs. The 1995 Draft Budget for defense looked much the same in structural terms as that adopted in 1994, but the final 1995 Budget contained twenty-one items under defense and a separate article on the size of cuts and the cuts required for each service. The new detail included spending amounts for salaries, food, hous-

Table 6.1
1993 Russian Defense Budget

Law on 1993 Republican Budget of the RF	
Spending on Defense	R3.15B
Including:	
Upkeep of the Army and Navy	1.56
Arms and Military Technology purchases	.57
in first half of 1993	.41
Scientific-Research and Testing	.22
Capital construction	.51
for construction of housing for servicemen in conjunction with the	
resolution of the 8th Congress of People's Deputies of 3/13/93	
on the Russian Referendum	.01
Pensions and welfare for servicemen	.12
Ministry of Atomic Energy spending on Ministry of Defense orders	.05
Upkeep of mobile forces	.03
Russian share of forces of the CIS	.00

ing, energy, transportation, communications, arms purchases, and research and development. Under several points, debts owed to the Defense Ministry from the previous year were written into the law. This new detail represented roughly a fourfold increase (see tables 6.1, 6.2, and 6.3).

What explains the increased detail in the Russian defense budgets? Above all, it is the result of close cooperation between the Defense Committee, the Defense Ministry, and the defense industrial sector in a Defense Budget Working Group formed during debate on the 1994 Budget.[23] In this multipartisan environment, deputies and government officials organize and resolve their differences by finding middle ground on current legislation and agreements regarding future provision of information. Most important, the deputies receive additional, if secret, materials on an "eyes only," background basis. One deputy noted at the plenary session discussing the 1995 Budget on the first reading that a separate hearing was held, and it was decided that separate lines were needed for the navy budget. Because he did not see it in the draft being considered on the floor, he asked the Budget Committee Chair where the line was: "I would like to say that in general we need more detail — not five or six but perhaps twenty or thirty positions — with strict control over its implementation, precisely on those articles to remove the disagreements which arise among us." The first deputy said that there should be 700 lines in the defense budget or even more, like in the

Table 6.2
1994 Russian Defense Budget

Draft Law on the 1994 Federal Budget	
National Defense	R37.1T
Law RF on the 1994 Federal Budget	
National defense — total	R40.6T
Including:	
Upkeep of the Armed Forces	22.1
Arms and equipment purchases	8.4
Research, development and testing	2.4
Capital construction	4.8
Pensions	2.0
Ministry of Atomic Energy	.9

United States. The Budget Committee Chair offered a more moderate response: "I am not a supporter of such a radical step. We will make a significant step this year if we have not five but twenty to thirty positions; this would be a big step forward."[24] While most deputies do support such radical steps for the defense budget, they do not take the highly confrontational approach of pushing for such radical steps immediately. Rather, they take what they can get in informal or secret "eyes only" releases from the government to be used for their background information only. In the meantime, they continue to press for modest expansion of the budget law itself to include more and more of this detail given initially on this informal basis.[25]

Defense was only one of many advances in budget detail. The 1994 Budget was the first to fully display foreign economic activities and credit operations. It was thus the first to provide the "hard currency budget" that the Supreme Soviet long demanded and never received. Moreover, the entire revenue side of the budget was expanded in detail. The Duma Speaker listed these as the Duma's major successes in its first session: "We demanded of the government, and the government and President eventually agreed, that all sources of revenues without exception be shown in detail — from foreign economic activities, all hard currency receipts — all that was concealed from the eyes of the citizens and lawmakers in recent years."[26] As one Committee member said, "It goes without saying that the 1994 Budget was prepared better than its predecessors. The methodology of its development improved, there is a virtual lack of secret and closed articles, the section on foreign economic activities fundamentally changed, [and] for the

Table 6.3
1995 Draft Federal Budget

Draft Law on the 1995 Federal Budget	
National defense — total	R45.3T
Including:	
Construction and upkeep of the Armed Forces	41.3
Current upkeep of all systems for defense of the state	23.0
Arms and equipment purchases, special equipment and communications for military formations	8.4
Research, development, and testing for national defense, law enforcement activities, and state security	3.8
Capital construction and purchase of equipment and systems for the Ministry of Defense	6.1
Pensions	2.7
Ministry of Atomic Energy military programs	1.0
Mobile forces	.2
Law on the 1995 Federal Budget	
National defense — total	R48.6T
Including:	
Construction and upkeep of the Armed Forces	43.3
Upkeep of the Armed Forces	21.2
Including:	
Servicemen salaries	7.5
Salaries for civilian personnel	1.3
Food	1.7
Clothing	1.6
Energy (purchase and storage)	2.4
Repair and building of arms, equipment, and other items in defense industries	1.1
Salaries for servicemen and civilians	1.1
Transport	1.4
Communications	1.0
Other spending for securing activities	
of troops	4.8
civilian salaries	3.1
Arms purchases	10.3
Debt from 1994 budget	1.3
Research, development, and testing	4.9
Debt from 1994	.7
Pensions	4.0
Ministry of Atomic Energy spending	1.0
Support for mobile forces	.2

first time it is proposed to introduce a system of transfers for support of underdeveloped Federation subjects."[27] Clearly, the Duma and the executive branch made impressive strides toward managing conflict over the form of the budget.

A second major issue of conflict over budget content concerned the macroeconomic prognoses on which the budgets are based. In 1994, the government submitted the draft budget with no prognosis whatsoever, in direct violation of the Law on the Budget Process. The government argued that the constitution required submission of a budget only, not a prognosis. This brought shouts from the deputies and a devastating response from two in particular.

> First, if you read the Constitution carefully, you find a funny phrase there. It says that the government submits not a draft federal budget, but simply the federal budget. Not a draft law, but the budget! So again, to follow the spirit and letter of the Constitution at times is not very correct. On the other hand, the Law on the Budget Process has not been repealed or changed.
>
> The government resolution of March 9, 1994, concretely orders the Ministry of Finance and Ministry of Economics to prepare a draft economic prognosis for economic development for 1994 and to submit it together with the budget to the Duma. How can you speak of it not being permitted to submit the prognosis?! How are we supposed to evaluate the budget?[28]

In 1995, the government did submit a prognosis with the budget, but by the time it did so, the prognosis was so unrealistic on so many parameters as to be obsolete. First, it envisioned an average exchange rate for the ruble of R3200 to $1. But the day the budget was submitted the exchange rate was already R3187 and falling by 5–10 percent daily. The idea that the exchange rate would not change at all in 1995 was laughable, and it was obvious that the entire budget for foreign economic activities required recalculation. Second, the draft envisioned no change in the minimum wage, when the Duma had already voted an increase. Budget spending is based on the minimum wage, and changes in this parameter required changes in virtually all social spending, from budget salaries to student stipends to pensions.[29] These two basic indices were, then, entirely unrealistic and required "a recalculation of the basic characteristics in the budget."[30]

In the face of such fundamental disputes over macrolevel budget characteristics, the rules offered the Duma two choices: to reject the budget outright and return it to the government, or to accept the faulty figures. However, the faction leaders did away with formal procedures and formed a conciliation commission between the deputies and the government. The commission was made up of five Budget Committee members, one representative from each sectoral committee, and one representative from each Duma faction, in addition to government representatives.[31] The commission was given ten days to rewrite the prognosis and to recalculate the budget based on the new parameters. The Duma therefore neither adopted nor rejected the budget but called for its revision and resubmission and mandated that the Duma would have a hand in the revising.[32]

Again, some government officials took initial exception. After the Duma made the decision to form the conciliation commission, several government officials surrounded the Committee leaders, some literally yelling at the deputies, "What is it you want to do? Write an entire prognosis and budget in two weeks?"[33] Others argued that the changes the deputies demanded were not of a "principle nature" and could be dealt with through amendments. The Committee was correct, however, that the amendments would have changed the "basic characteristics." They were thus principle changes. The government held to its strong stand at the first meeting of the conciliation commission, where Finance Ministry and Economics Ministry officials presented an inflexible face. One minister even proposed that the Duma not adopt the budget at all but rather allow the government to operate without Duma control. The deputies exploded at this arrogance, and the meeting ended in discord.[34]

But discord yielded to political agreement. Both sides recognized the need to reach agreement, and that all political forces were represented in the room. Faced with a united front of factions spanning the entire political spectrum, the government at first yielded on the issue of the exchange rate, suggesting R4000 to the dollar as an average rate for the year. Then it negotiated upward to R4400. It agreed to increase the prognoses for inflation and for the drop in industrial production and included the minimum-wage indexation.[35] One deputy who opposed the ad hoc procedure of an early conciliation commission nevertheless acknowledged the benefits of the cooperation:

There is a more clear government position on various questions, and more clear positions of deputies. There is a certain agreement of positions and arguments. Deputies better understand the government, they better understand and examine concrete matters and problems, and then deputies bring this to the attention of the whole Duma. That is, there is a clearer understanding of positions. And second, the government has begun to move on a whole range of questions.[36]

So while the government was at first belligerent, the multipartisan and multicommittee conciliation commission eventually agreed on the budget. Such commissions have become commonplace at early stages of the legislative process and are a hallmark of legislative–executive branch conflict management.

Duma-government conflict also concerned actual figures. Unlike the Supreme Soviet, which voted on and adopted hundreds of amendments with the Committee's and the government's positions known before each vote, the Duma rarely makes substantial changes to the budget on the floor. It is therefore less obvious how the Duma changes the budget from the government's wishes, and to what degree and on which provisions the government disagrees with the budgets that the Duma adopts.

In 1994, the Duma raised revenues from R120.7T in the draft budget to R124.5T in the final version, an increase of 3 percent. However, it increased spending by 6 percent, from R183.1T to R194.5T, and thus increased the deficit from 34 percent of total spending to 36 percent of total spending. In 1995, the Duma raised revenues from R144.2T to R175.2T, an increase of nearly 18 percent, but increased spending by just 13 percent, from R216.3T to R248.3T. So in 1995 the Duma actually reduced the deficit from 33 percent of total spending to 29.5 percent.[37]

Such figures, however, exaggerate the changes the Duma makes. The Duma returned the initial 1994 Draft Budget to the government for revision. It made the changes, mostly based on Duma demands, but it was the government that made the revisions to increase revenues to R124.5T and spending to R193.3T. So the Duma in the end increased 1994 spending only by R1.2T, or just over 0.5 percent.[38] In 1995, the government again changed its own initial budget figures, this time the result of agreement in the conciliation commission set up to revise the draft for the first reading. Although the Duma mandated that revisions be made, the government participated in the conciliation commission and reached agreement there. The draft the government came back with had revenues at R160.3T and spending at R232.0T. So the Duma actually increased revenues R14.9T, or 8.5 percent, and spending R16.3T, or 6.6 percent, and thus reduced the deficit in relation to total spending by less than 1 percent.[39]

The government was in no way obligated to change its initial draft budget. Particularly given the ad hoc, extralegal nature of the procedures followed, it had reason to refuse to make the changes. It could have resisted and forced the legislature to take responsibility for the changes. But this would have been a highly confrontational approach, and was unnecessary. It was unnecessary precisely because the multipartisan Duma had ready institutional mechanisms for political negotiation to overcome such conflict and to reach consensus.

Above all, the government and the Committee agreed on the need to hold to the basic characteristics once they were approved on the first reading. One Finance Ministry official, commenting on the Duma's failure to abide by this during adoption of the 1994 Budget, praised the Committee's cooperation against the partisan activity on the floor:

> We need to do what the Supreme Soviet never succeeded in doing. First adopting general parameters of the budget — general ceilings for spending, revenues and the deficit. And then within this examine specific articles. Because all say, "I don't want my area cut, cut someone else's." Last year during discussion they [the Duma] did not hold to these ceilings. The factions' initiatives torpedoed this agreement; they said, "Let's change these." *I and Zadornov [Budget Committee Chair] labored extremely hard to prevent their reexamination.* This is the main thing. We need to establish this norm.[40]

This approach runs counter to the expectations of legislative behavior in poor countries elaborated by Caiden and Wildavsky.[41] The institutionalized role of the factions has made the legislature more cooperative with the executive branch, not less.

These "basic characteristics" do yield ambiguous evidence regarding the Duma's effects on the content of the budget. But these effects were not the central issues of conflict between the Duma and the government during this period. The main issues of legislative-executive dispute concerned the government's figures for revenues, particularly privatization revenues. Virtually everyone in the Duma argued that the revenue figures in the government's budget were grossly unrealistic, most arguing that they were wildly inflated. But several deputies felt they were underestimated by more than 10 percent.

Indeed, many government officials privately admitted that the government's budget figures, particularly on revenues, were often highly unreliable. They pointed to the Soviet system's traditions of falsification of data as a legacy that the current Finance Ministry and government were struggling to overcome.[42] Deputies who believed the government's figures were exaggerated had a lot of concrete evidence to back up their claims. One Committee member asked a Finance Ministry representative, "By my calculations, the tax side will be collected at R53–54T. The [1994] budget sets taxes at R93T. Do I understand correctly? If you have some other variant, then explain it to us. I keep asking and never get an answer." He never got one that day either, although during a break at the first reading two weeks earlier, the Finance Minister nodded his head in response to the same question.[43]

He didn't need an answer, though, because one consequence of the government's submitting the budget well into the fiscal year is that the early results of its implementation are already known. The Duma adopted the 1994 Budget in June, when it knew the results for the first third of the year. They were not good. Revenues stood at only 8 percent of GDP, half the planned level. The Committee Chair argued that this confirmed "the non-reality of the revenue sums" in the draft.[44] The following year, the Committee complained about massive increases in expected privatization revenues in the draft 1995 Budget. In 1994 these revenues were collected at only 10 percent of planned levels.[45] The government had added by a factor of eighty-five to what the deputies perceived as an "artificial base" from 1994.[46] Like the Supreme Soviet Committee before it, the Duma Budget Committee continually blasted the Finance Ministry's bogus revenue figures.

As if to highlight the partisan basis of Duma action, this action did not stop the Committee from introducing still further revenue increases. In 1995, for example, the Committee increased the value-added tax (VAT) on imports, oil excise fees, and export tariffs on gas and eliminated a number of exemptions on export and import tariffs.[47] Just why the Committee and the Duma would criticize the government for exaggerating revenues on the one hand while increasing them on the other demands some explanation. The best explanation lies in partisan politics, not in the technicalities of budget content. Since the deputies did not expect revenues to be fulfilled anyway, raising them further made no difference. In exchange, they could then increase various popular spending provisions, phantom increases that would never be fulfilled due to revenue shortfalls. This would let the faction leaders later blast the government for not meeting budget spending for pensions, education, and other social areas, using this political capital in future political campaigns. The factions had nothing to lose. If the amendment game required revenue increases to offset demands for spending increases, so be it. It was all just on paper anyway, and the budget itself was not the real issue. These actions seem to confirm the expectations generated by Caiden and Wildavsky regarding unrealistic budgets adopted in poor countries. However, in the Duma the environment is one of partisan cooperation, including cooperation with the government, to pass the budget that the government wants.

This analysis explains the actions of the Agrarians, who proposed from the floor a special tax to be targeted for agriculture spending in the 1995 Budget. As will be recalled, agriculture spending had been broken up into several sections of the budget, making it appear to a casual observer that agriculture spending had been cut. In fact it had not, and the Agrarians on the Committee knew this well. But the argument was complex, and they knew they could score points by demanding preservation of the special tax and thereby increase the agriculture section of the budget by more than R5T.

This increase had nothing to do with real agriculture needs. Those needs were met in the original budget provisions, and it was clear to all key players that neither the revenue nor the spending side of the amendment could be implemented.[48] It was simply a partisan political victory aimed at scoring uncertain future political points for the faction.

The same explanation applies to the debate that raged over privatization revenues in the Fifth Duma. The Committee on Economic Policy led by its Chair, Sergey Glazyev, argued from the start of the 1994 Budget debate that privatization revenues could be collected in the tens of trillions of rubles, instead of the hundred billion in the initial draft. Even when the government increased the figure to R1T, many deputies continued to side with Glazyev. In fact, the debate was less about actual revenues than it was a campaign against privatization itself.[49] So while the Duma on the one hand lambasted the government for submitting exaggerated and unrealistic revenue figures, it demanded astronomical revenue increases that left the government baffled.[50]

Still, the macrolevel characteristics ultimately adopted differed little from the government's own provisions. On the 1995 Budget, the Duma actually approved a lower deficit figure than the government had proposed. The government urged adoption of the budget at each reading, explicitly endorsing the amendments made. The Duma and the government cooperated and reached agreement on the technical form and on the detailed content of the budget, and the cooperation depended on the partisan nature of the Committee and on the entrenchment of the many partisan factions in the Duma's design and leadership. That the factions, not the

Committee Chair, control the relations with the government means such collaboration extends to all committees and legislative issues, as the following section demonstrates.

LEGISLATIVE-EXECUTIVE CONFLICT MANAGEMENT AND NONBUDGET, LEGISLATIVE ISSUES

The Supreme Soviet also cooperated with the government on the budget, but in the Supreme Soviet this cooperation depended on the predilections of the Committee Chair. Many other committee chairs pursued confrontation. In the Duma, cooperation with the executive branch is more broadly based. Committee chairs still span the entire political spectrum, but the partisan nature of those committees, the prominent institutional role of the partisan factions in the Duma's design, and the partisan-dominated leadership ensure cooperation on all legislative issues. If a committee chair tries to exclude government participation or cooperation, a deputy chair from a different faction and his colleagues ensure that he fails. When any faction initiates meetings with the government, no faction has an interest in excluding itself, and all send representatives. Unlike committees in the Supreme Soviet, no Duma committee can systematically exclude presidential, government, or ministry officials from participating in the legislative process. All notify and invite relevant officials to their sessions and work with those officials.

The formation of a conciliation commission early in the legislative budget process in 1995 was controversial with deputies. However, legislative-executive conciliation commissions have become commonplace as a way for the two branches to forge compromise on legislative issues. These commissions include representatives of both channels of Russia's "dual executive" — the President and the government — and representatives of the relevant ministries. From the Duma, they include members of all of the factions and all interested committees. As Huskey describes the frequent convening of these commissions, they compel a diverse group to "work intensively in closed sessions to find language that will accommodate the interests of all sides." Huskey recognizes that even such agreements as these fail to be adopted by the full Duma, but these multibranch commissions "in the institutional interstices between executive and legislative power" do give the legislature influence on the content of policy. For if the Duma fails to adopt the measure, the President has the option of decreeing the measure into force. Using Huskey's terminology, the commissions are a way for the executive branch to "rule with" the legislature before using the decree route to "rule around" it.[51] Other manifestations of this multibranch standing cooperation are the Consultative Council, which discusses general trends in Russia's political and economic development, and regular meetings between the President, the Prime Minister, and legislative leaders.

As a result, cooperation on legislative issues is more broadly based and consistent across committees in the Duma and, in the end, far more influential with the government. The story of privatization is perhaps the best example of the Duma's increased ability to manage conflict with the executive branch on even the most controversial legislative issues — even though the agreements reached ultimately failed to break the deadlock on the floor. Privatization was certainly a controversial issue in the Fifth Duma. Virtually every morning, one or more deputies took the floor to blast the entire process. Some threatened to put the Chair of the State Property Commission (GKI) in jail if they came to power, alleging all sorts of criminal activities on his part.[52] For most of these deputies, it was privatization itself that was criminal. The Duma rarely got through an entire plenary session without someone taking the floor to denounce the "deceit of the people" and the "stealing" of people's money and demanding that the government "make an account of the results of voucher privatization" and be "made responsible" for the "tears and suffering" it caused.[53]

The GKI Chair, Anatoly Chubais, having been accused of "thievery," "deception," and worse, responded "in kind," as he put it, to his attackers.[54] Confrontation was sharp and it was two-way. He warned the deputies,

We will be watching how the deputies behave. Today, irrespective of the details, facts remain facts. The privatization program was not adopted. This means that the Duma deputies lack the minimum level of wisdom of statesmen, and even an elementary conscious understanding of their role in the machine of state authority. But since they did not adopt a program, I think the events may develop in a variety of ways. The President now has no obligations before the Duma, and the deputies may discuss it for a month, a year, twenty years, this is their problem. In my opinion, the response of the President is clear. He will enact the program by decree....

My God, what is unexpected in this?! Do you really expect anything different with the likes of [these deputies]? What do they have new to say? Of course, I never consult with any of them. Look at the insulting venom they display toward me! My response will be exactly the same as the tone of their questions. And their reaction shows they do not like it when they receive an equal response.[55]

This same Chubais, however, immediately turned around and cooperated with the Duma's leadership, and the deputies cooperated with him. For fourteen days in 1994, July 7–21, representatives of the GKI, the President's administration, the Duma committees on property and on economic policy, and every Duma faction worked together to amend the privatization program. The two committee chairs were among the severest critics of Chubais personally, and of privatization generally. Not only did they meet, they reached consensus on dozens of major changes to the program. As one report put it, "Chubais thinks that he deceived them, and they think that they ran him over. This is a compromise."[56]

The partisan factions make such cooperation possible. They delegate representatives to a conciliation commission, and the relevant committees include their own representatives. Such a linking mechanism exists only in cooperation with the executive branch. Russian legislative committees no longer have exclusive control over legislation. The partisan factions, the other channel of the Duma's design, are at least equal players, and they demand that their own representatives take the lead in discussions with the government. In so doing, they guarantee that multipartisan cooperation with the executive branch takes place on all issues. If Yabloko and Russia's Choice deputies are going to meet with the government to negotiate on privatization legislation, it is certain that representatives of the Communists, the LDPR, and the Democratic Party of Russia (DPR) will demand equal representation in those negotiations. The same holds for the relevant committees, who distrust the faction leaders. No one individual can dominate the political tone or direction of Duma policy on any issue, regardless of the policy or committee in question. Since on any issue at least one faction will seek cooperation with the government, all participate in that cooperation, and all committees cooperate with the executive branch across legislative issue areas.

The Duma failed to pass the program despite the support of all of the committees working on it and the most politically diverse faction representatives. But the Duma's mechanisms for managing its external conflict with the executive branch are significant. While the internal breakdown and deadlock prevented it from adopting the law, the cooperation with the executive branch did pay dividends. The President enacted the program by decree the day after the Duma broke for summer recess, but the program he signed into action was the one with the dozens of amendments agreed to by the disparate groups. Instead of decreeing the original program into force, the President retained the consensus reached in the conciliation commission with the Duma factions and committees. Some government representatives admitted that the changes made resulted in a stronger program, one that fixed problems discovered in the original draft. The Duma rejected it for purely partisan political reasons, but the President and the government were satisfied enough to honor the results of the cooperative effort. Some have expressed outrage at the frequency of presidential decrees, saying that they violate the important principle of separation of legislative and executive powers that is so crucial to a liberal democracy. However, there have been many other instances like the privatization program involving issues just as demanding of policy action. While enacted by decree, this example is unfairly categorized as an instance of "ruling around the parliament."[57] The content of the decreed program was very much influenced by Duma players of all stripes but would not have been so without the interbranch commission and compromise.

Cooperation between Duma and government representatives did produce concrete results, and the President honored the results of this multipartisan collaboration even after the Duma proved unable to act. When the Supreme Soviet pursued its line of political conflict, the President issued decrees that sharply contradicted the line pursued by individual committees or by the Supreme Soviet Chair. With the Duma, cooperation with representatives of all of the partisan factions brought a consensus on legislative content that the President could enact by decree even after the Duma proved incapable of taking action. While passage may not have been the sense of the majority of the Duma, there can be no doubt that the legislature had strong influence on the final content of the program, and that all partisan groups in the Duma played a role in reaching that consensus.

CONSENSUS BUILDING ON EXTRA-LEGISLATIVE, BUDGET-RELATED ISSUES

Consensus building between the two branches on extra-legislative, political issues is still more impressive and is the direct result of the institutional role of partisan factions. Two political issues in particular related to the budget highlight this increased conflict-management capacity: the deadlines for submission of the draft budget and the supporting materials accompanying it.

Since Russia had no legislature in the last quarter of 1993, it was clear that the 1994 Budget would not be submitted and could not be deliberated until after the beginning of the fiscal year. But there was no objective reason why the government could not submit the budget at the opening of the Fifth Duma after the New Year. It delayed for months, though, with one deputy complaining in mid-March, "The Duma still has not received a draft budget. This is in spite of our frequent, official appeals to the government. Virtually immediately after the beginning of the work of the Duma, this question was directed to the government, and ten days ago we formulated an official inquiry to the government, showing that financing for the second quarter of this year will be impossible without a necessary draft law. But I repeat, as of today we have not received a draft budget."[58] The Duma issued numerous "official inquiries." With the Duma only two weeks old, the Duma Soviet instructed the Speaker to remind the Prime Minister of the laws on and deadlines for budget submission and to demand that he "instruct the ministries and departments" to submit the budget together with a list of nine other documents.[59] Two months later, with the Duma still lacking a budget, the Duma Soviet had the Speaker scold the Prime Minister in another sharp letter.[60] The Committee issued a similar statement blasting the government for avoiding control and oversight over budget spending.[61]

As with demands on budget content, the government at first ignored the Duma. Some Committee members threatened to pass a new law containing "sanctions for violating deadlines for submitting the budget," that is, monetary and criminal penalties for violating the law.[62] The existing law contains deadlines but no such sanctions.

The Duma, however, found cooperative rather than confrontational methods for improving government compliance. The first resolution on the 1994 Budget, it will be recalled, was a political compromise neither to adopt nor to reject the budget but to consider it "submitted" and to return it to the government for revision. The Duma added a demand that the government "present along with the Draft Federal Budget a budget for the third and fourth quarters of 1994, and to submit in September 1994 a draft 1995 Budget, so that we can move toward normal procedures for examining the federal budget."[63] The Duma's faction leaders folded a request into their decision not to reject the government's draft 1994 Budget, a request for reciprocal good intentions from the government, to be expressed in timely submission of the next year's budget. The linkage contained a thinly veiled warning of potential consequences if the government did not reciprocate the goodwill. The pro-government factions in the Duma Soviet and those critical of the government forged this compromise. The Committee pressed the point about budget submission in future meetings with the Finance Ministry, and the Minister himself accepted this requirement for submission of the 1995 Budget. With this agreement, later resolutions accordingly dropped the somewhat accusatory provision.[64]

The requirements reappeared, however, when the Committee wrote a Law on the 1995 Budget Process. It included a provision requiring that the budget and all accompanying documents be submitted by October 1.[65] When Committee members asked if even the prognosis could be submitted on time, the authors of the law reported, "Neither the Ministry of Finance nor the Ministry of Economics has raised any problems with these deadlines."[66] And again, on the floor before final adoption, one deputy asked, "Is there any guarantee that the government can in principle come to grips with this demand placed upon them, that is, will the 1995 Draft Budget be prepared for submission by October 1 given the pitiful practice which we have seen in recent years?" The Budget Committee representative replied, "As for the deadlines for submission, the government believes it can meet the October 1 deadline. . . . I think there is reason to believe it can meet it. As for the materials required, here there are doubts."[67] The President vetoed the procedural law, delaying the entire budget process by several weeks. When the Duma overrode the veto, its first veto override, the Finance Ministry completed its final work on the budget and submitted it two weeks later.[68] Had there been no veto, the documents would have been submitted on time. There is no basis for Russian press accounts that the Finance Ministry urged a veto to buy time to finish work on the budget or to constrict the amount of time the legislature had to work on it.[69]

No partisan group in the Fifth Duma supported government delays. Every faction and every leader, including those closest to the government, demanded that the budget be submitted on time, as did every member of the Committee. In the conciliation commission formed to revise the 1995 Draft Budget, government representatives again heard from all factions on the delays, and all factions demanded that the 1996 Budget be submitted early. Similar demands came in the Duma Soviet's meetings with representatives of the President and the government. By mid-1995, the government was striving to submit the 1996 Budget to the Duma as early as possible because, in the face of unanimous partisan demands in the Duma, it had no political interest whatsoever in delaying. It submitted the 1996 draft only three weeks past the deadline set in the Law on the 1996 Budget Process, and was clearly cooperating by consistently submitting the draft budget to the Duma at an earlier date than it had in the previous year. On the 1996 Budget it agreed on the immediate formation of a "working group" similar to the conciliation commission of the year before, again including all partisan groups, in an effort to pass the budget for the first time before the end of the fiscal year.[70] The effort proved successful, so the draft was submitted in time to meet this goal.

In some ways reciprocal to its pressure on the government not to delay submitting the budget, the Duma Soviet repeatedly reached agreement with the government not to itself delay considering the budget. As seen in chapter 5, even when the Committee was not prepared, the faction leaders held to their bargains with the President and the Prime Minister on the schedule for debate and votes on the budgets. The Duma Soviet serves as a link between the legislature and the executive branch. While not as strong a linkage as in a parliamentary system, where a partisan majority controls the government, it is active in reaching agreement and following through on those agreements. In this sense, then, the Duma Soviet provides a powerful demonstration of the benefits of linkage.

Similar success is evident in resolution of conflict over budget-related documents. The government argued that it either did not have or did not have to provide the additional materials that the Committee and the factions wanted. Similar negotiation mechanisms served to successfully overcome this conflict. The same official inquiries by the Speaker and the Budget Committee on budget deadlines included demands of the government to submit a package of additional materials, including accounts of implementation of previous years' budgets, and a draft consolidated budget for regional and federal budgets.[71]

Following its traditional pattern, the Finance Ministry at first argued that it had provided everything it could or should.[72] The most heated argument swirled around the Duma's demand for a consolidated budget. The Finance Ministry argued, "We are not presenting this for constitutional reasons. None of the federations in the world demand a consolidated budget."[73] Another government official explained, "The Duma asks for such materials that require changes be made to the Constitution, materials that cannot be presented on the federal level. A consolidated budget, for example. They want a consolidated budget with the same details as the federal budget. We are a federation. The regions have autonomy, the right to self-government. They pass their own budgets. How are we supposed to know what these are ahead of time? We cannot do this, simply from the principles of our Constitution."[74] The Committee, however, maintained that the Duma would not examine a budget without the consolidated budget and all other supporting materials: "Formal issues are not formal for us.

This is not something we can ignore or look at separately. In fact this means that we do not have a draft budget in the full sense. The Committee and the Duma do not have the documents which will allow us to examine the budget with open eyes and take a responsible decision before ourselves and the voters."[75]

Even after the government did comply with most of the demands by providing most of the documents, this issue remained one of conflict, even within the Committee. At one point the following exchange between two Committee members took place:

> Deputy A: I simply don't understand. Why when the government in reality ignored these demands we made, why should we now support their figures?
> Deputy B: I would not say it ignored us because they responded with 44 pages — it is difficult to say this is ignoring!
> Deputy A: It is not the 44 pages we asked for!

The government had provided forty-four pages of tables and explanations of 1994 Budget spending and revenue figures. The Committee's own review noted that the government had provided the following: quarterly breakdowns for the initial budget figures, preliminary results of implementation of the 1993 Budget, and even a draft consolidated budget![76]

The Committee demand for a consolidated budget in the Law on the 1995 Budget Process was the main reason the Finance Ministry recommended that the President veto that law. To break the impasse, the Committee softened its demand. Instead of calling for ratification of the consolidated budget, it instead asked only that it be submitted "for analytical purposes."[77] The Finance Ministry suggested a different approach: "We can possibly present this after the fact for examination. But we cannot present it until the subjects adopt their budgets. And they cannot pass their budgets until they know what they will be getting from the federal budget. This poses a vicious circle for the Finance Ministry."[78] The Committee seemed to accept this offer as the issue did not arise publicly again.[79]

Cooperation between the government, the Committee, and the factions resulted in the government's eventually providing all available data for information and analysis of the budget. That some of this was less than initial Duma demands is evidence of the negotiation and compromise on these politically charged budget issues. The Prime Minister was most emphatic regarding the government's conciliatory approach at the first reading of the

1994 Budget: "We openly showed what we have, what our resources are now and what we will have until the end of the year. I can tell [Budget Committee Chair] Mr. Zadornov this too. I can say only one thing. We presented everything we have today to go with the budget. We have held nothing back."[80] After the budget failed to pass on the floor, the Prime Minister stood cheek to cheek with Zadornov and, with uncharacteristic animation, berated him while several of the Prime Minister's security guards surrounded them both. When Zadornov opened his mouth to speak, the Prime Minister jabbed his finger in Zadornov's face and continued his onslaught as he backed the besieged Committee Chair into the elevator with him.[81] The Prime Minister's anger was over being publicly accused by the Committee Chair, on the Duma floor, of refusing to supply budget-related information to the deputies.

Ultimately, even the Committee agreed that the material went beyond anything the Supreme Soviet was ever able to pry out of the government. Said one Committee member, "Like never before we have received additional information and accounting material. That is, on all budget articles we requested much additional material that was eventually submitted. The level of examination as a result was much deeper than before."[82] The government certainly agreed with this assessment: "They want to see still more, and the demands for material are understandable. We as a rule send the materials, because what is the sense of hiding anything? We present all materials, all details."[83]

When the government submitted its draft 1995 Budget, its representative told the Committee that the Finance Ministry had presented all materials that it had. As if to underscore the government's cooperative posture, he further promised the deputies that if they required still more information, it would be provided upon request.[84] None in the Committee challenged this statement, as the draft budget was accompanied by more than 300 pages in dozens of documents. When the Committee wanted additional analyses of figures it believed to be controversial, such as revenues from privatization and securities issues or spending on the war in Chechnya, once it specified these requests to the government, the latter complied within days. For example, the Committee issued a demand on January 16, 1995, for detailed information on spending required for military and other operations related to the Chechnya conflict, and the government provided the documentation on January 18.[85]

The fruits of the earlier collaboration brought progressively less confrontation over Duma demands for information. The government recognizes that the Duma Budget Committee has among its membership "all political groups" in the country. As a result, it feels that "closer relations are needed" than was even the case with the Supreme Soviet Committee. And these "closer relations," particularly with representatives of the Duma's factions, result in more understanding regarding the importance of meeting the deadlines and the need to open up budget detail and analytical materials.[86] Committee members also cite among their greatest achievements in the Fifth Duma that they achieved "positive normal cooperation with the government and certain ministries. It was cooperative work, and not confrontation."[87] The conciliation commission in particular brought "agreement of positions" between the two branches. It served as a multipartisan mechanism for mediating political conflict between the two branches in the budget process.[88]

CONSENSUS BUILDING ON NONBUDGET, EXTRA-LEGISLATIVE ISSUES

Duma relations with the executive branch depend on the multiplicity of partisan factions and on their several and collective relations; they do not depend on, nor are they controlled by, the Duma Speaker. This is particularly evident on extra-legislative, political issues. The multifaction Duma Soviet constitutes a standing multipartisan body for managing conflict with the executive branch. The factions ensure that no single individual or orientation dominates. Instead, they constitute a group of partisan leaders with whom the President and the government can negotiate to manage, channel, and overcome political conflict between the branches. The Duma Soviet links the legislature to the executive branch and thereby serves as an effective consensus-building structure.

The most visible and perhaps the most important cooperation between the branches has been in the area of personnel policy. From Huskey's perspective, the President has been instrumental in "defusing rising hostility" by making concessions on government personnel.[89] It could be argued equally as strongly that the concessions were the legislature's. In fact, both sides cooperated. They have been able to cooperate thanks in large part to the existence of the Duma Soviet as a political coordinating body or to the legislature. Several significant government reshuffles and two prime minister replacements all occurred in consultation with the Duma's faction leaders. One of the first ministerial changes that occurred after the Duma's creation was the replacement of the Finance Minister in 1994. The President and the Prime Minister worked with the Duma Soviet, and with the Budget Committee, to appoint the head of the Budget Committee staff as the new minister.[90] One of the charges of the new minister was to carry out an order given to all ministers, in the wake of the Agreement on Social Accord (discussed below), to cooperate with the legislature. Midlevel officials keenly felt the pressure: "The Minister of Finance demanded a Deputy Minister be present at the Duma at all sessions of the Committee, the [Budget] Subcommittee, etc. Earlier we sent a head of a department, that is, from the lower ranks. Now I have been here four times already just this week. How am I supposed to do *my* work?!"[91] While this official bemoaned the "waste of time," it clearly reflects a collaborative atmosphere.

Such cooperation became the norm. In 1995, Yeltsin appointed a member of the Agrarian faction as Minister of Agriculture, in part in exchange for that faction's votes on the 1995 Budget. In 1996, in another government reshuffle, the former Budget Committee Chair, Mikhail Zadornov, became Finance Minister. Aleksander Pochinok, the deputy Budget Committee Chair, became head of the Tax Service. Negotiations with the Duma Soviet were instrumental in these appointments, as they were in 1996 and in 1997 in the replacement of the General Prosecutor, the Interior Minister, the head of the State Property Committee, and the Foreign Minister.

Several of these changes took place in the wake of a successful no-confidence vote in mid-1995. Changes also have come after unsuccessful confidence motions or to ward off such motions. Similarly, in February and August 1998, the President replaced his Prime Minister. New heads of government were named and new governments formed, on both occasions in close cooperation with the faction leaders in the Duma Soviet.[92] In each instance, the cooperation between the Duma and the executive branch on personnel policy helped to avoid deadlock, to improve relations between the branches, and to move specific policies, particularly economic policies, forward. Where the Supreme Soviet plunged the country into deadlock over such personnel matters, the Duma Soviet enables the branches to negotiate and to reach consensus. Sometimes the Duma makes concessions to approve the President's nominee, as was the case with the approval of Sergei Kiriyenko in early 1998; other times the President makes concessions to the Duma, as he did in August 1998, when he substituted the doomed candidate Viktor Chernomyrdin for a second stint as Prime Minister with a candidate more amenable to the Duma. Yeltsin could have stuck to his guns, nominated Chernomyrdin to a third unsuccessful vote, and dissolved the Duma, provoking a massive political and constitutional crisis.

Instead, he made use of a means to negotiate a mutually acceptable way out of the crisis, a means that was possible because of the existence in the Duma of a multipartisan forum for negotiation and conflict management, the Duma Soviet.

This is not to say that things got off to a smooth start, however. The Duma's first major decision, a month into its existence, was to grant amnesty to President Yeltsin's fiercest political enemies, the respective leaders of the 1991 Coup and the October 1993 Uprising. As a result, the likes of former Supreme Soviet Chair Ruslan Khasbulatov and former Vice President Aleksandr Rutskoi were freed from prison without ever having gone to trial. The initial amnesty idea was the President's, to amnesty those imprisoned under old Soviet laws for economic crimes that reform had made not merely obsolete but entirely legal and even desirable behavior. The Duma took this proposal and added to it a direct political challenge to the President.[93] The Duma's partisan leaders claimed that the decision meant "reconciliation" and the "prevention of sharp confrontation," while the President saw it as a provocation and sought to block its implementation.[94]

The most important consequence of the experience was to spark a massive expansion of direct contacts between the political leaders of the Duma on the one hand and representatives of the President and the government on the other. All major actors realized that unlike the Supreme Soviet, which lacked a body to lead or even to engage in such political discussions, the Duma has clear partisan leaders who meet regularly. Each at least in theory represents a significant number of deputies and a segment of society. These political contacts immediately began to improve political cooperation between the legislature and the executive branch.

First, the President initiated regular meetings with each of the Duma's partisan leaders, on a rotating basis, to discuss broad political concerns and goals face to face.[95] Faction leaders all attend because they do not want their political opponents to be seen meeting with the President and looking presidential while they are left out. Each faction leader wants to appear presidential, with views on the major political issues, and wants to be seen in the Kremlin and interviewed in the media on those issues. Moreover, none of the faction leaders want the others to cut deals with the executive branch that would undercut their positions.

Second, he added the Duma Speaker to the membership of his Security Council.[96] There the legislative leaders sit with the President's security team to discuss and negotiate policy on political and security matters facing the country. Third, and perhaps most significant, the President and the

Prime Minister each hired representatives for the presidential administration and the government, respectively, to the Duma to serve as liaisons between their offices and the deputy corpus.[97] The President not only has a representative to the Federal Assembly, he also created the post of Adviser for Cooperation with the Federal Assembly, Other Branches of Power, and Political Parties. This Adviser serves as a sort of mediator, "not for the purpose of pushing through legislative initiatives of the President, but with the goal of creating favorable conditions for cooperation among the branches."[98] Later, the Prime Minister ordered every ministry to designate its own representative to the Duma. The Prime Minister sought better information flow between the branches: "Each ministry should know what is happening, just as the deputies should know, at the least should closely work with, those who today work on the problems in the economy in their sectors."[99]

These executive branch representatives to the legislature serve as go-betweens for their respective bosses and the Duma leadership. They meet primarily with the faction leaders and attend as observers their meetings in the Duma Soviet. At these meetings they present the legislators with the views and the positions of the executive branch. Similarly, they forward to the Prime Minister and to the President the plans and positions of the Duma's partisan leaders, as well as their own analyses of political trends and the political atmosphere in the legislature.[100]

Perhaps the most significant role of these liaisons is to serve as a political buffer. This was most evident when the President signed the Law on the Status of Deputies on May 8, 1994, but at the same time sent a letter to the Duma complaining of "clear contradictions with the Constitution."[101] The letter served simultaneously as a critique of the quality of the legislation and as a demand for numerous amendments he wanted made to avoid an appeal to the Constitutional Court. This approach of signing the bill into law with requests for subsequent amendment, rather than of issuing an outright veto, indicates the depth of the desire for cooperation. The decision to take this approach was the brainchild of the presidential Adviser, who used his knowledge of the Duma's faction leaders to urge the combination of signature and appeal for amendment. The conciliatory approach proved successful, as the deputies approved most of the desired changes.[102] The approach and its success were possible because of the close and continuous contacts between the Duma's political leadership and the executive branch representatives. The contacts themselves were made possible by the existence and the institutional importance of the partisan wing of the Duma's dual-channel design.

The existence of the Duma Soviet has caused the greatest contrast between the old legislature and the new in managing conflict on extra-legislative issues with the executive branch. In the Supreme Soviet, when a committee with a confrontational chair produced legislation unacceptable to the executive branch, the latter had virtually nowhere to turn. Obviously, that committee chair was unsympathetic and frequently had excluded government participation from the committee's process. The Supreme Soviet Chair dominated the legislature's political relations in its external relations, and he pursued a confrontational line as well. The executive branch's option was to simply ignore the law and issue contradictory, competing decrees, leaving government departments in the middle to figure out where their responsibilities lay and which policy to implement.

The Duma Soviet, however, is an institutional forum of political leaders continuously available for political collaboration and negotiation, the type of forum the nonpartisan Supreme Soviet lacked. The Duma Soviet may either accept the executive branch's arguments and bring them to the full Duma, refer the matter back to the appropriate committee, or organize a conciliation commission including representatives from the factions, the committees, and the government. Whether before the Duma Soviet, the committees, or the full Duma, executive branch representatives may appear to lobby for the executive branch's positions and to seek agreement. But it is the existence of the Duma Soviet, made up of the partisan leaders, that has provided a mechanism to manage political conflict and avoid confrontation.

One of the more tangible manifestations of the increased political collaboration between the Duma and the executive branch was the Agreement on Social Accord.[103] The document was something between a peace treaty and an alliance between the executive branch, the legislature, and other political organizations. The agreement was written jointly by officials in the President's office and representatives of all Duma factions.[104] The factions negotiated to ease the responsibilities borne by signatories to the agreement, to make the agreement itself more mild in tone, and to add pet demands such as the Agrarian demand to include a government commitment to support the agricultural complex. In the end, the signatories included the President, the chairs of both houses of the Federal Assembly, the Prime Minister, and all but three of the Duma's factions.[105] In the agreement, the President dedicated himself "to regularly meet with representatives of all organizations signing the Agreement" and formed a consultative commission of representatives of the President, government, federation subjects, Federal Assembly, and political organizations to "coordinate their work." In return, the participants to the agreement recognized in writing "their great responsibility before society to fulfill the obligations they have taken upon themselves" to cooperate.[106]

For their part, the Duma's leaders created a precedent of forming conciliation commissions of their own to revise, rather than reject outright, legislation submitted by the government or the President. Two such instances have already been discussed, regarding tax legislation and the 1995 Draft Budget. The first instance was on changes to tax legislation; the government representative agreed that this was "a good compromise variant" that would break political deadlock on the floor regarding the various proposals for massive changes to the tax system.[107] Deputies directly refer to the Agreement on Social Accord as compelling, if not requiring, cooperation and consensus building.[108]

The findings here, coupled with those Huskey describes, suggest a need to reexamine some assumptions about legislative-executive relations in presidential systems. Arend Lijphart, for example, asserts that a strong president sees no need to collaborate with deputies or to negotiate with a legislature.[109] Lijphart cannot explain the close cooperation that emerged between the Russian executive and the Duma. Similarly, Scott Mainwaring sees a necessary deterioration in relations between the branches when the legislature is highly fragmented and unable to pass legislation.[110] However, it was the legislative machine of the Supreme Soviet that ran afoul of the executive branch, while inclusion of the partisan channel, fragmented though it is, has enabled the Duma to negotiate and to reach consensus. It is not that legislatures are or are not able to cooperate with the executive branch in presidential systems. What is important is to understand the circumstances that either promote or impede conflict management and consensus building. A comparative institutional approach to studying legislatures helps us to reveal those conditions.

One may question this analysis of cooperation between the Duma and the executive branch, citing highly visible and contentious conflict over the makeup of the government itself. In its two-year existence, the Fifth Duma twice held votes of no confidence in the government, and the second one carried.[111] Expressions of no confidence are a strong manifestation of conflict between a legislature and a government. The Sixth Duma continued this tendency to periodically raise questions of confidence in the government, and even of impeachment of the President.

But context is essential for understanding. In parliamentary systems, expressions of no confidence topple governments and bring early elections. They are thus dramatic, momentous, and therefore rare occurrences. In the

Duma, however, no-confidence motions are toothless in the ambiguous triangular relations between the Russian President, the government, and the legislature. The government need not change in the aftermath of a successful no-confidence vote, as it does not spring from the Duma. The President names the Prime Minister, and the constitution gives the President the right to ignore a Duma vote against the government. He need take no action against the government; and if the legislature dares to repeat a no-confidence motion, the President can take action against the legislature itself rather than act against the government.

Faced with the threat of dissolution, the deputies predictably remained silent when the President ignored their expression of no confidence on July 21, 1995, rather than repeating the move and potentially losing their positions. Similar provisions virtually prevent the Duma from rejecting a President's appointment for Prime Minister. Therefore, because they carry little consequence, one or more factions can raise no-confidence votes in an effort to gain public visibility in expressing its dissatisfaction with the government and its policies. But that is where it ends. The constitutional provisions concerning votes of no confidence mandate that the Duma cooperate with the government, and vice versa.[112]

And cooperate they do. Debates and votes on confidence are events that seem to culminate in heightened collaboration, not confrontation, between the legislature and the executive branch. The threat of a no-confidence motion combined with the pressures outlined in the previous sections to compel the government to submit the 1995 Draft Budget on October 27, 1994. The no-confidence motion ultimately failed, but only barely. Even though it had failed, within days of the vote the President, to try to allay some of the factions' clear dissatisfaction with the government, replaced the Finance Minister with the former head of the Duma Budget Committee staff. He did so after consulting with the Committee and with the faction leaders in the Duma Soviet.[113] Several other personnel compromises between the Duma and the executive branch are the result of these no-confidence debates.

SUMMARY

Mainwaring, Lijphart, and others expect "prolonged impass" and high "polarization" in legislative-executive relations when a presidential system is combined with a highly fragmented partisan environment in a legislature.[114] However, the Russian State Duma, when compared with the nonpartisan, committee-centered Supreme Soviet, has a far greater capacity to manage conflict with the executive branch. The comparative institutional framework applied here powerfully demonstrates the effects that an unlinked, dual-channel institutional design has on a legislature's ability to manage internal and external conflict. Internal legislative processes, smooth as clockwork in the Supreme Soviet, routinely grind to a halt under debilitating procedural breakdown and deadlock in the Duma. The lack of institutional links between the partisan factions and the legislative committees leaves individual deputies free of constraints in their actions on legislative issues. Their incentive structures compel them in a multitude of ways to pursue strategies that confound consensus building and exacerbate conflict, rather than to channel and manage conflict to produce consensual outcomes.

The Budget Committee writes the rules for the budget process in the Duma, and the Duma adopts those rules with virtual unanimity. But the Committee is unable to hold to its own rules, much less compel anyone else in the Duma to hold to them. The Budget Committee, like all Duma committees, does not control legislative procedures. The Committee does do the bulk of the detailed work on the budget, but its recommendations to the Duma are regularly rejected.

Committees and factions are two parallel, unlinked channels of organization in the Duma. Committees lack any coordinating mechanism between them, and they engage in wasteful duplication and debilitating competition on legislative issues. The partisan factions are in political competition with each other and thus also compete for internal dominance and, ultimately, for political popularity. Most significant, in the absence of coherent linkages between these two channels, factions and committees find themselves in competition over legislative procedure; the final passage of bills depends on who wrote a draft and who else supports it rather than on the content of the law itself. Partisan competition between factions, and jealous power struggles between factions and committees, result in the appearance of "alternative" drafts at the final stages of the legislative process, which more often than not bring deadlock rather than legislative outcomes. Individual deputies are free to side with one or the other channel as they see fit; they regularly shift their allegiances in unexpected and, from the perspective of legislative efficiency, destabilizing ways.

When internal conflict in the Duma is resolved, when deadlock is overcome, it is the result of partisan political compromise in the Duma Soviet. Rather than detailed debate on legislative content, political agreement and bargains struck among the leaders of the partisan factions, who have no committee affiliations or legislative expertise of their own, are the only mechanisms available to break through the deadlock.

The Duma Soviet is a forum for political negotiation. Its existence enables the Duma to manage political conflict with the executive branch through negotiations and regular contacts between executive branch officials and the partisan leaders of the legislature. The Supreme Soviet lacked such a multipartisan organizational entity. But the Duma's political leaders span the partisan spectrum, are all gathered in the legislature's leadership body and meet regularly, and can each claim a degree of popular support for their own partisan orientation. Their entrenchment in the Duma's leadership body brings closer political relations with the executive branch, thereby preventing the Duma's external relations from descending into the sort of uncontrollable political conflict that was the bane of the Supreme Soviet.

The case of the Duma thus demonstrates the potentially perverse effects of including partisan organizations like parties and factions in a legislature, particularly in new states where partisan lines are highly fragmented and parties are weak and unstable. The Duma's design has essentially grafted a partisan layer onto the nonpartisan, committee design of the Supreme Soviet. While parties are normally considered essential for effective legislative procedures, the way they have been included in the Duma has brought breakdown and deadlock where legislative processes previously worked quite smoothly.

It is also somewhat surprising in light of the existing literature that making a legislature more partisan would lead to smoother relations with the executive branch. But again, this is the case. The evidence here suggests that such a design is far more able to manage conflict than is one that excludes partisan entities, even where the partisan environment is highly fragmented. Institutional design defines the space within which individuals may exercise political discretion. In the Duma, the members are constrained to cooperate. The inclusion of factions and their institutionalization in the leadership guarantees that no individual may dominate the way individual committee chairs dominated the political orientation on legislative issues and the way the Supreme Soviet Chair dominated extra-legislative issues in the Supreme Soviet. In the Duma, no individual deputy can single-handedly take over the legislature's political orientation either in the Duma's internal affairs or in its relations with the executive branch. Political conflict, both internally and with the executive branch, is managed through multipartisan negotiation.

PART 3

The Estonian Riigikogu: The Benefits of a Linked, Dual-Channel Design

How Linkage Promotes
Conflict Management

One 1993 report hailed Estonia for having "assumed the pioneer position among the post-Soviet republics in implementing political and economic reforms," and in its progress toward democracy and a market economy.[1] In 1998 Estonia led most East European states and all former Soviet states in moving toward membership in such international organizations as the European Union, World Trade Organization, and other leading economic and political institutions. Estonia's success is also visible in the stability of its political institutions, success attributable to the choices that its independence leaders made for the design of those institutions, including the legislature. The success of the institutions is at least partly if not largely responsible for the success of the reforms. Those independence leaders looked West, to make a clean break with the Soviet-era institutions and a clear break with the path chosen by Russia. They chose a parliamentary system, picking and choosing elements from a number of West European and Scandinavian states, including Germany and Finland.

In Estonia's parliamentary system the legislature's two channels, parties and committees, are linked throughout, and consensus building and conflict management are the norm internally and in relations with the executive branch, on legislative and extra-legislative activities alike. The broad consensus that emerges as a result of this design and the processes it fosters help explain Estonia's impressive economic and political success since gaining its independence.

Estonia's success, far from rendering it illegitimate for comparison to other postcommunist states, makes such comparison all the more important. Estonia belongs squarely in the same category of states as Russia and the other former Soviet and East Bloc states. For forty-five years, it was straitjacketed into the Soviet political and economic system. The Soviet army, the State Security Committee (KGB), and the Communist Party crushed most Estonian political and economic institutions after occupying the country in 1944.[2] But while communism was introduced by Russia, it was, as one analysis put it, "embraced by tens of thousands of locals who then became the grist for its oppressive, monopolistic system."[3]

Moreover, when Estonia gained independence it faced the same set of difficulties as did the other former Soviet states. It sought to shake off Soviet political institutions and to replace them with new, Estonian institutions. It proclaimed democracy as its goal, even though it lacked democratic traditions.[4] It had to create political parties and other elements of civil society out of a virtual void. As in the other states, Estonia's leaders sought to transform a centrally planned economy into a market economy, meaning that Estonia had to create market institutions such as private property out of an economic apparatus in utter ruins. As in most other former Soviet states, Estonia has ethnic divisions that are territorially based with which it has to struggle. In Estonia's case, most of its large Russian population populates the northeast region of the country. Finally, the collapse of communism ruptured trade ties across the former Soviet Union and Eastern Europe, and Estonia sought to reorient its links toward the West.

Estonia began the same tasks at the same time and with roughly the same starting characteristics as did the other states in the region. It is thus in the same class of states as the others, and we should resist the temptation to consider it unique simply because just a few years later it looks so different, most glaringly from Russia, in its impressive economic and political development. Comparison is essential if we want to understand what contributes to success on the one hand and difficulties on the other.

Some may argue that its small size compared to Russia explains Estonia's more successful transition. However, other small states have fared less well after the fall of communism. Bulgaria and Belarus are also small compared with Russia, for example, and are suffering a much more difficult postcommunist existence, while Hungary is much larger than Estonia yet it has also enjoyed successful economic and political transformation. Size is clearly not a determining factor. Others may point to Estonia's choice for a parliamentary system of government as negating any fruitful comparison with Russia. Linz and Lijphart in particular have extolled the virtues of parliamentary government.[5] However, while parliamentary government brings important links to the executive branch, the design of the legislature itself remains important. For example, in Estonia as in any parliamentary regime the prime minister and the cabinet emerge directly from the majority party or coalition in the Riigikogu, the legislative body. The government's survival depends on maintaining this majority, as do the ministerial jobs of the leaders of that majority. In Estonia, the linkage extends to the legislature. The majority controls all leadership posts, including all committee chairs, and maintaining control depends on maintaining the majority. The two channels are tightly linked, and this linkage in politically fragmented legislatures like those in postcommunist states provides a powerful incentive for small, weak partisan organizations to preserve internal coherence and cooperate with each other. This is far from true for all legislatures, even in parliamentary systems. They may be designed with tight links between the channels, as in Estonia, or with weak links, as is the case in Hungary, for example. While the legislative body in a parliamentary system may be the weaker partner relative to the government, it still must perform legislative and political functions, internally and in relating to the executive branch. The linkage between the parties and the committees in the Estonian legislature's design enhances consensus building and conflict management in both internal and external activities, on legislative and extra-legislative issues alike.

What is important for the legislature is the degree of linkage between the two channels. In either presidential or parliamentary systems linkage may be strong or weak. This examination of the Estonian legislature's design and behavior demonstrates the utility of comparative institutionalism as applied to legislatures, for this approach explains Estonia's greater conflict-management capacity according to the linkage in its dual-channel legislature and yields insights applicable to other legislatures, including Russia's. The analysis of Estonia's legislature can ultimately suggest ways that legislatures such as the Russian State Duma may be designed to enhance legislative and political consensus building and conflict management.

The Riigikogu: A Linked, Dual-Channel Design

Unlike in Russia, there is no ambiguity in the triangular relations between President, government, and legislature in Estonia. Indeed, a triangle is the wrong image. Estonia has a figurehead presidency, a symbolic head of state who is not directly elected and does not control the executive branch.[6] Executive power rests with the government, headed by the Prime Minister, who springs from the legislative majority. Legislative elections determine which party or coalition of parties will gain a majority and therefore control the government.[7] The strongest incentive to create and maintain party discipline is the fact that the leader of the largest legislative faction is first in line for the post of Prime Minister, the most important position in Estonian politics.

As in all postcommunist states throughout the region, Estonian parties at the time of independence were weak and fragmented, and they remain so.[8] The 1993 elections yielded representation for nine legislative factions in a legislature with only 101 members. The largest faction, Isamaa, garnered twenty-nine seats, well short of a majority. But as the largest faction in the legislature, it took the lead in putting together a majority to form a government. The coalition it forged with two other factions numbered a mere fifty-one members, a majority of just one.[9] With such a slim majority, it is difficult to imagine a more stringent test of the virtues of linkage than Estonia's first postcommunist legislature. The government had five ministers plus Prime Minister Mart Laar from Isamaa, three from the Estonian National Independence Party (ENIP), four from the Moderate faction, and one independent.[10] The 1995 elections yielded somewhat more coherent results. Seven factions gained representation in the legislature, but this time two were able to form a governing coalition numbering fifty-seven members. The Coalition Party led by Prime Minister Tiit Vahi, with forty-one legislative seats, took ten ministerial posts; the Centre Party, with sixteen members, took five.[11]

Even with so many factions in such a small legislative body, the imperative of discipline has turned the fractured, multipartisan Estonian legislature into something resembling a bipolar system. The need to form and preserve governing coalitions provides powerful incentives to the small, fledgling parties and factions to maintain their internal integrity. The incentives of parliamentary systems for interparty collaboration that operate in the West, as persuasively argued by such proponents as Lijphart and Linz, operate similarly in Estonia.[12] Estonian legislators have less room to act as individualists than their Russian counterparts—they must always have an eye to their own faction and their partners, for if too many stray the government might fall.

The Russian Duma demonstrates the absurdity of the assumption that parties produce majorities which then control committees and agendas.[13] A comparative institutional approach demonstrates those institutional design features that can bring about such a circumstance. A comparative institutional theory of legislatures explains the incentives for party cohesion and cooperation within the Estonian legislative body. When such incentives prevail, leaders do "internalize their party's collective interests" and "stack the deck" in the legislature to favor themselves, or their coalition.[14] The incentives to coalesce extend from a design that links the two channels throughout the legislature's organization.

This coalescence occurs in spite of the fact that Estonia lacks a stable party system. In 1998, Estonia had thirty-three parties poised to contest the next elections, with increasing fragmentation rather than coalescence. "Personality differences" have been cited as the primary barrier to such coalescence, even where platforms of the tiny organizations are indistinguishable.[15] Peet Kask finds that most Estonian legislators refuse to even recognize themselves as "members" of their respective parties.[16] The parties are new and unstable, and consistent with the findings of Olson and Norton across east-central Europe, legislative factions can be amorphous in the Estonian legislature.[17] Coalitions are not immortal, parties are tenuous entities, and legislative factions appear and disappear. As seen in Russia, as elections approach, coalitions become weaker and shift.[18]

In the last several months of the first Riigikogu leading up to the 1995 elections, there was no governing majority. The government relied on a minority of as few as nineteen members after two coalition partners bolted, and the number of factions increased as the parties themselves split apart.[19] As one report put it, "The Estonian Parliament shattered into a lot of small competing groups. . . . Even ideologically close parties cannot establish contacts due to mutual personal hostility."[20] Various ministers have been forced or have opted to resign, and governments have fallen under the weight of corruption and scandal. Nevertheless, such events pass with barely a shudder in Estonia's legislature. Consensus building on legislative and political matters proceeds without a glitch.

If the comparison is to established Western democracies, Estonian parties and legislative coalitions appear unstable and even incoherent, and the conclusions here could be challenged by such comparison. But evaluating a new postcommunist legislature according to the standards of more institutionalized Western counterparts is hardly fair. When making a fair comparison, such as to Russia's postcommunist legislatures, one finds Estonian partisan organizations impressive for their stability and coherence. In this respect, Estonia more resembles Ágh's portrayal of parties in Hungary. As in Hungary, Estonian parties seem to play "an exaggerated role" given their societal weakness, but one sees greater stability in their political profiles and in their organizational integrity than is the case in Russia.[21]

However, Ágh also describes a Hungarian parliament in which the links between parties and committees are weaker than they are in Estonia. Despite the parliamentary system in Hungary, all factions have equal representation in the legislature's leadership and committee chairs are divided proportionally among all factions.[22] Parliamentary systems do not guarantee linked legislative designs, any more so than presidential systems guarantee unlinked designs. A linked design constrains individual members to pursue consensus building and conflict management on legislative and extra-legislative issues both in internal activities and in relations with the executive branch. In Estonia it affords greater coherence in the development of political parties and greater effectiveness in its legislature.

Unlike Hungary, Estonia's legislative parties extended coalition control to compel linkage between the two channels throughout the legislature. The benefits of linkage follow. In the Russian Duma and in Hungary's parliament, leadership posts and committee chairs are distributed among all factions with no consistency in political orientation across committee chairs, memberships, or on the floor. None of this is possible in Estonia, where the majority that forms the government is a majority throughout the legislature's design, from leadership posts to committee chairs to committee membership. The Speaker comes from the same faction as the Prime Minister, the leading faction in the coalition. The deputy speakers come from either the same faction or from the smaller coalition partners. One's position at any level of the Estonian legislature is tightly linked to one's partisan affiliation. Either one is a member of a majority faction with access to leadership positions, the floor, and the government, or one is part of the opposition and largely excluded from these benefits of the majority.

The formal legislative leadership is sharply constrained. The constraints extend from the greater linkages in the design, just as the greater constraints in the Duma compared with the Supreme Soviet extended from the inclusion of partisan factions in the design. The Speaker of Estonia's legislature has an almost purely formal role. He introduces speakers, names bills being put to a vote, and announces the results. The leadership approves the agenda prepared by the coalition leaders in their own meetings.[23] The leadership formally distributes the members across committees, ensuring coalition majorities on every committee. The committees then elect the chair, ensuring that all committee chairs are controlled by the coalition.[24] In fact, the faction leaders present their requests, which the leadership "confirms," and the coalition majorities confirm the coalition leaders' agreement on the committee chairs.[25] With a consistent majority and minority across all leadership posts and committee memberships, the effect is to thoroughly link the factions and the committees throughout the legislature's design. As a result the Estonian legislature has fewer committees and is free of the duplication and incoherence that plagues committees in its Russian counterpart.[26]

Estonian deputies generally speak of committees as the place for "specialized" and "intense" work on legislative issues.[27] They see them as a route to expertise and information. Perhaps this is their ideal, but the reality is far removed. Estonia's legislative committees suffer the same limitations found by scholars of committees in other parliamentary systems.[28] Committees face severe shortages of space, resources, and personnel. In fact, they take proposals from factions "and decide what to do with them."[29] A nearly complete lack of resources renders committees the subordinate channel to partisan factions in the Estonian legislature. Compared with the Riigikogu, even the Duma's quarters are luxurious. The Estonian legislature shares with the government an old palace perched atop the old city. The legislature has access to roughly half of this building, with a mere fifty to seventy-five small rooms housing 101 legislators, ten or so factions, ten committees, and the entire technical and support staff, including library and archives.[30]

Most legislators do not even have their own desks, to say nothing of offices, phones, or staff. Factions do have offices — one or two rooms to carve up as they see fit. Typically, only the faction leader and one or two secretarial staff have desks. And this is spacious compared with what is left for the committees! Most committees have a single room for the chair that doubles as a meeting room for the committee. The single expert staff member and the secretary share a small adjoining room. Only one or two committees, one being the Budget Committee, have two rooms. The chair uses one, while the other doubles as a committee meeting room and an office for the deputy chair when the committee is out of session. The staff and secretary share the entryway connecting the two rooms. Except for the offices of the Speaker and the Deputy Speaker, this is the entirety of office space for the Estonian legislature. Technical support such as computers, fax machines, and copy machines are even scarcer than desk space.

Walking around the Estonian legislature, one gets a sense of a collegial atmosphere for talk but a nightmare for serious work. The complaints of Estonian legislators recall Polsby's description of arena legislatures, and the many descriptions in the early comparative legislative studies literature that expressed shock over the relative lack of resources that other legislatures have compared with those of the U.S. Congress.[31]

> We lack offices for individual members. Committees have their rooms and factions have their rooms . . . but if a faction includes a dozen or so members, then members have no work space.
>
> We have no staff members, especially qualified staff. There is no authority in this work, no glamor. Younger people seek better salaries and glamor in business and the private sector than we can offer.[32]

Indeed, the cabinet's meeting hall occupies the main connector hallway between the two wings of the building, meaning that when the cabinet is in session the path is closed and one must go up, over, and down again to reach destinations on the other side. What better example could there be of the blurring of boundaries and the legislature's lack of resources?

As if to compound the problem, the membership itself is shifting. Those appointed to the government only suspend their status as legislators. Their places are taken by "substitute" or "reserve" members who are next on the respective party list. When original members leave the government, they return to the legislature and the replacement steps aside. In the first Riigikogu, as many as a dozen replacements served at some stage in the legislature, a hefty number considering an overall membership of only 101. Such a shifting membership severely hampers the ability of the committees and of the legislature as a whole to establish an intensive work rhythm.

The remaining sections of this chapter demonstrate how this linked, dual-channel design promotes consensus building in all of the legislature's activities. The consensus building flows from the majority-versus-minority cleavage, and from the consistency of the linkages between factions and committees across the legislature. The discussion will first examine the relations between the legislature and the government and then turn to the internal workings of the legislature.

RELATIONS WITH THE GOVERNMENT:
EXTRA-LEGISLATIVE, POLITICAL CONSENSUS

The linked, dual-channel design maximizes the imperative to pursue consensus building and conflict management, even in a highly fragmented partisan environment. The partisan factions must closely collaborate to maintain their coalition, and thus control of the government and their own predominance within the legislature. Those excluded from the majority band together as an opposition poised to take over the reigns should the coalition dissolve.

The consensus building that counts occurs among the coalition factions. Consensus building with the government is natural. Government ministers come from the leadership of the parties that make up the coalition. Estonia's system thus duplicates "the efficient secret" of cabinet government lauded by Cox and others as the advantage of parliamentary government, advantages that derive from links between the government and the legislature's parties.[33]

As one report puts it, "The selection of the Prime Minister, the formation of a working government, and the success of a legislative program depend on the cooperation with parliament."[34] Actually, the cooperation is among the partisan factions. A candidate for Prime Minister must satisfy enough of those factions to gain at least the fifty-one legislators necessary for confirmation. That support is garnered by offering representatives of those factions government portfolios. One nominee, Siim Kallas, failed to offer any portfolios to one faction on whose support he counted. That faction went with the opposition, and Kallas lost the confirmation vote. "If we are not wanted in the government, we can't back Kallas," said one of that faction's leaders.[35]

Kallas revealed his lack of understanding of Estonia's political system in his retort, "I would have become Prime Minister if I had promised 50 seats in the government," or one for every confirmation vote in the legislature.[36] This may be the case in an unlinked, dual-channel design like Russia's State Duma, where every deputy is an individualist and each particular member must be satisfied in order to gain his or her vote. But it is not true in a linked design such as Estonia's. Garnering the support of the faction leaders in the legislature is enough to ensure the votes of all faction members, as it is fealty to the faction that can lead to advancement and future government posts for the average member. That support can be won with a judicious distribution of the basic perks of such a system — government portfolios. Without the perks and the positions of responsibility, there is no incentive for any faction to join a coalition.

With those perks, however, there is little incentive to leave the coalition. As part of the government, a coalition faction's role in the legislature is to work with its partners to ensure approval of its government's legislative and political policies. Issues of political strategy and resolution of political disputes are handled in both separate and joint meetings of the coalition factions in the legislature. Each faction's government representatives attend these meetings, where political concerns are discussed behind these closed doors.[37] Under normal circumstances, after these discussions the government, not the legislative factions, handles public management of these extra-legislative issues. The legislature's input comes in the meetings of the coalition factions, attended by the members of the government.

Of course, coalitions once formed can fall apart, and the Estonian legislature, having formed a government, can also bring it down. Estonian governments and their coalitions have met such a fate, at times the result of policy disagreements, at others the product of corruption and scandal. Estonia's first government, headed by Prime Minister Mart Laar, experienced both, first fragmenting due to internal policy disputes and then collapsing in scandal. Policy differences can cause a faction's government representatives to resign and the faction itself to withdraw from the coalition. This happened in mid-1994, when one faction failed in its effort to replace Laar over a disagreement on the government's financial policy. Having lost its bid, it withdrew from the coalition, its two ministers resigned from the government, and the faction went into opposition. From that point the coalition was actually a minority within the legislature.[38] The government soon fell completely under the weight of a financial scandal involving the Prime Minister. Prime Minister Laar had carried out a financial deal involving old Russian rubles in Estonia without consulting his coalition partners, and then compounded the scandal by trying to cover up the deal.[39]

The coalition that formed after the spring 1995 elections had its own internal problems. Prime Minister Tiit Vahi fired his Interior Minister, who happened to be the leader of Vahi's main coalition partner, over allegations that he had ordered secret and illegal wiretapping of senior politicians. Vahi then disbanded the coalition and offered the government's resignation, preempting a no-confidence motion. He then forged a new coalition with the next largest faction in the legislature and regained his post as Prime Minister.[40] The former Interior Minister's faction went into opposition.

Each time that a coalition partner has withdrawn or a government has fallen in Estonia, the factions quickly reconstituted new coalitions and formed new governments. Close cooperation between the two branches continued virtually uninterrupted. Policy differences or scandal may force government ministers, coalitions, and governments to fall in Estonia. But the need to form a government places the strongest imperatives on legislative factions to form governing coalitions, and on members of the government and leaders of the coalition factions to collaborate. It is this cooperation and political consensus that are the norm.

The linkage in the dual-channel design, then, in addition to fostering consensus building and conflict management between the two branches on political issues, also serves to clearly distinguish the roles between governing and opposition factions within the legislature. The opposition is excluded from this legislative-executive collaboration. The opposition in a parliamentary system exists to engage in partisan competition, and the Estonian legislature's opposition plays this role well. However, the opposition factions do attempt to provide a united front against the coalition. So the same design that encourages consensus building among the coalition factions also encourages cooperation among the opposition factions, creating something resembling a bipolar partisan alignment, even in a highly fragmented partisan environment. The primary activity used by the opposition in the legislature is to ask questions and to make critical speeches during the thirty-minute "Information Hour" at the first and third Monday sessions of each three-week legislative cycle.[41] The Prime Minister and other ministers may be called on to deliver speeches or to answer the written and oral questions of legislators, normally from members of the opposition.[42] Opposition factions may also call for no-confidence votes to be held, and often do so to test their strength.[43] The speeches they make in both instances give members of the opposition the ability to make public their disagreements with the government and its policies. Beyond such public speeches, though, the opposition factions have little political role in relations with the government. This situation is in stark contrast to the regular meetings held in Russia between the government and all faction leaders, from all points on the political spectrum.

This linked design promoting clear majority and opposition has served Estonia well, better than the unlinked designs where they have been applied. In Hungary, Ágh describes the "failure to produce a policy agenda" and the continual legislative-executive battles,[44] the products of the unlinked legislative design that even a parliamentary system cannot completely overcome. While Estonia may seem to support the arguments of the advantages of parliamentary government, legislative design determines how the legislative body will behave.

RELATIONS WITH THE GOVERNMENT: CONSENSUS ON THE BUDGET

Relations on legislative issues such as the budget are just as marked by consensus building. This should hardly be surprising, given the symbiotic relationship between the branches. From submission to the level of budget detail to the legislative budget process, strong collaboration and consensus building mark relations between Estonia's legislature and its executive branch.

Submission of the Budget

The first noticeable difference between Estonia and Russia is that in Estonia budget deadlines are not an issue. They are written in law and the government follows the law. The 1992 budget cycle was the last one prior to the adoption of the Law on the Estonian Budget, and the 1992 Budget was the last one submitted after the onset of the fiscal year. Every year, without exception, the government has submitted the budget on time, a full three months ahead of January 1, as required by the Law on the Estonian Budget.[45] The Finance Ministry was three days early with the 1995 Budget, and one Budget Committee member acknowledged, "We can't have any complaints about this!"[46]

The government has no reason to delay. The legislative majority is its majority; its budget is the coalition's budget. To guarantee that this is so in fact and not just in theory, the government drafts the budget in consultation with the coalition leaders in the legislature. The consultations are informal and at the highest levels. In fact, they are so high-level that most legislators and government officials are unaware that they take place. Ordinary coalition members, the entire opposition, and midlevel government officials all seem to be in the dark. The conviction is widespread among coalition and opposition legislators that the government writes the draft budget in isolation. Even Budget Committee members are surprised to learn of consultations between coalition faction leaders and the government. Estonian deputies state confidently that before the legislature sees the budget "only the government" works on it.[47] Even government officials in the Finance and Economics Ministries maintain that legislators are not consulted, that they have no role in drafting the budget. Indeed, Finance Ministry officials look with abhorrence on the mere suggestion of advance consultations with legislators.[48]

However, the leaders of the coalition factions do consult with the government on the budget, even before it is finalized for submission to the legislature.[49] They hold formal and informal discussions in regular meetings of the separate parties and factions, and in joint meetings of the coalition partners. The formal collaboration occurs after the Finance Ministry has sent its draft budget to the cabinet for initial approval. The Ministry, having gathered the proposals of the sectoral ministries and compiled a draft based at least in part on these requests, sends the draft budget to the government in August, one month before submission to the legislature.[50] The leaders of the coalition factions are invited to attend this government meeting and to take the opportunity to express their views.

Although they attend and speak, one government official said that these faction leaders do not make demands for specific changes to budget provisions at this meeting: "No! No! In general they do not. Of course, they could, but they do not do so. They already know what proposals will come from the government, because it wants the legislature's support."[51] This, of course, begs the question, how do they know?

They know because they have already held discussions at earlier stages of the process. Coalition factions hold several types of meetings. Most common are meetings of coalition leaders in the legislature. Less frequent meetings are held for the broader membership in the legislature and in the government. Once or twice a year the entire membership meets, including those in society at large. These meetings are normally to discuss the party's general political strategy; however leaders of the party's legislative faction may meet privately with their representatives in government to discuss important issues such as the budget. Coalition meetings are normally attended only by the leaders of its legislative factions, the Prime Minister, and selected other government ministers. They are precisely for discussion of policy issues such as the budget, and it is at these meetings that coalition leaders in the legislature and their counterparts in the cabinet discuss budget strategy and ensure that goals remain united across the coalition. They also discuss specific budget priorities and demands.[52] Government civil servants do not attend such political meetings, which explains the ignorance of Finance and Economics Ministry officials.

It is these joint meetings of the coalition leadership, and the separate meetings held by the leaders of each coalition faction with its representatives in the cabinet, that are most influential on the budget. A leader of one coalition faction said:

Our party is better positioned than others, because our representatives are in high government offices, and the Prime Minister, too, is from our party. So we can discuss the draft budget before the government gives it to parliament. And we can discuss problems in the budget before this, too, and we do so. Our contacts with the government mean that our position and the government's position must be the same. It is different from other factions and particularly from opposition factions. Our contacts with the government are quite good as a result, and this gives us influence on draft laws like the budget.[53]

No faction leader in the Russian Duma would even think of uttering such words! The Finance Ministry gets its priorities in drafting the budget from the cabinet, led by the Prime Minister. Those priorities are sounded out with the leaders of the coalition factions, as the government must maintain the integrity of the coalition. This is Cox's "efficient secret" in action, and Linz's basis for promoting the advantages of parliamentary systems.[54]

Unlike in Russia, in Estonia there is a very clear distinction between who does and who does not take part in these informal consultations. First, and most glaring in comparison to Russia, the Budget Committee is virtually a nonplayer. As one government official said, "The Committee did not play any role at all in the preliminary process. None at all, because, well, maybe this is not right but this is simply how it is in Estonia."[55] Most Committee members are surprisingly content with the situation: "This is not for us. . . . We have two branches of power, legislative and executive, and they should work separately, so that we don't mix up everything and then nobody answers for anything. A lack of responsibility is the biggest problem of all, when everyone works on all questions and nobody answers for anything."[56] Even Committee leaders were unaware that these discussions take place, and expressed extreme surprise to learn they were misinformed in the conviction that "there were absolutely no consultations of any kind prior to the budget's submission, none at all." One claimed to have been invited to attend one government meeting, and went "because I am a very curious person." This member was never invited again, "nor did they inform me at all."[57]

Second, the Speaker and deputy speakers also play no role in these budget consultations between legislature and government. In Russia, the Presidium and the Duma Soviet after it were and remain engaged in the process. But the leadership of the Estonian legislature is strictly a formal leadership. As one member of the Riigikogu Board revealed, "We will not enter into the subject of government drafts. It is not our responsibility . . . but of course coalition members do."[58] The first Speaker of the Riigikogu saw his main role "as mediator" between the coalition and the opposition during sessions of the legislature. "I don't interfere with day-to-day politics or make controversial statements," he said, and he remains disengaged from "state matters."[59] The Board does not engage in discussion of specific legislation, particularly with the government. The true leadership of the Estonian legislature is not its formal leadership, but the leaders of the coalition factions. The formal leaders exist as mediators between the factions, particularly on the floor.

Nor do rank-and-file members have such access to the government. Even members of the coalition factions betray utter ignorance of prior consultations on the draft budget between their leaders and the government.

As for the opposition, whether faction leader or rank-and-file member, opposition legislators profess to being shut out at virtually every stage of the process. They simply scoff at the notion that they would be included in any consultations with the government, whether before or after submission of the budget.[60] They don't expect such consultation, don't get it, and are not upset by it. The opposition in a parliamentary system exists, as Wildavsky puts it, to issue "a string of criticism" of a general political nature.[61] Estonia's opposition appears to fit this description perfectly and to be content with this system.

The only legislators who meet with the Prime Minister, the Finance Minister, and the Economics Minister in preliminary discussion of the budget are the leaders of the coalition factions. The discussions most commonly concern general budget priorities rather than specific provisions. The legislative leaders may, for example, express a desire that one sector or another receive more money and state, if necessary, at the expense of which other sectors. These discussions may take place at meetings of the cabinet where the draft budget is being discussed and finalized before being submitted to the legislature or, more significantly, at earlier stages, during regular meetings and informal discussions between the coalition leaders in government and coalition leaders in the legislature.

In this way, both sides ensure that their positions "must be the same" by the time the budget reaches the legislative arena.[62] This prior consensus obviates any reason for the government to delay submitting the budget to the legislature. That only a handful of legislators are engaged at early stages of the budget process should not leave the impression that such input is unimportant. Preliminary consent of the coalition leaders assures the government that its proposals will safely pass once the budget is submitted.[63]

Supporting Information and Budget Detail

After the government submits the budget, cooperation between the two branches expands. The Budget Committee, which is also responsible for banking, finance, and tax issues, has only a dozen or so members and one professional staff member. As a result, only a handful of people in the Estonian legislature actively works on the budget. The Committee is not able to carry out independent expert analysis because it lacks the expertise, resources, and staff necessary to do so. The same applies to other committees on nonbudget issues.[64] The members are highly dependent on cooperative relations with the government on legislative issues.

What is interesting and even surprising is that few Estonian legislators complain, even when pressed on the subject. While one Budget Committee member bemoaned the "little information" available, in particular the lack of detail regarding specific items being funded within each ministry's budget, that same member also said, "If we need such information we turn directly to that ministry [and] they respond very well."[65] The government provides enough information to satisfy the legislators, and neither legislators nor government officials report any complaints from the Riigikogu regarding the quality or objectivity of the information provided.

The Estonian Budget Committee is limited in its ability to perform an independent legislative function, largely because it lacks sufficient expert staff to independently gather and analyze budget information. It is thus dependent on the government for both information and analysis. Coalition members express few reservations about such reliance on the government. What is surprising is that leading opposition deputies betray no qualms about turning to "contacts with officials" in the Finance and Economic Ministries as a primary source of information. Rather than complaining about the lack of an independent analytic capability, one opposition deputy said, "I don't know . . . the Finance Ministry is responsible to answer honestly. These are civil servants."[66]

Most legislators actively working on the budget agree with the Finance Ministry's assessments:

> You can get all the information about the content of all spending and revenue provisions from that yellow book that is called "explanatory notes on the draft budget." It explains all spending and revenues.[67]

> If they say there is no detail in the budget it means they simply do not want to read the budget. It is easier to criticize than anything else. When they ask their questions at the first and second readings, virtually every answer is here in this book [the appendix to the budget].[68]

These explanatory notes grow each year, meaning that the government provides more information every year. The 1993 Budget was accompanied by fewer than 150 pages of explanation, while the 1994 Budget came with more than 180 pages and the 1995 Budget with nearly 250 pages.[69] One Budget Committee leader even called the 1995 Budget a "program budget," even though the information was not part of law itself.[70] It was enough that the information was provided, even in an appendix.

Estonian legislators have been content and do not feel a need to pressure the government for greater detail in and information on the budget. Indeed, the government makes many of the changes on its own. Driven by a desire for integration into European economic and trade institutions, the Estonian government is most interested in transforming its economy to "correspond to international demands," as one official put it.[71] On the advice of experts primarily from Finland and Sweden, the government has voluntarily made changes to the structure and the level of information provided in the budget.[72]

The Finance Ministry has gradually been transforming the structure of the budget to mirror Finland's, first, by including the appendix as explanatory information on spending by ministry, then, by including part of that appendix in the law itself. Advice for what to include and where to include it has come directly from representatives of the Finnish Ministry of Finance.[73] The 1993 Budget contained only a few revenue lines, and spending fit on about seventy lines on four pages.[74] The 1994 Budget had some thirty revenue lines and twenty-one pages of spending provisions.[75] The 1995 Budget was nearly two times longer than that.[76] These government actions may have the tangential effect of providing legislators with more budget information and greater detail in the law to oversee government action, but even Budget Committee members acknowledge that this result is not a consequence of legislative demands or pressure on the government.[77]

Some legislators even feel that they already have enough detail. There is only so much that the small Committee can process.

> We should ratify spending on overall directions of spending, such as education. I agree we may ratify how much for higher education, for general education, and it seems to me this is sufficient. This is politics. The legislature should ratify the politics of the economy. But how much to every little thing? Please God this is for the government to decide! It is explained in the explanatory notes. . . . It is not the legislature's affair to say how much to spend on one school and not on another. This is not a political question but one for the executive branch to decide. The legislature is not competent to decide this, this is not its function. Please God let them [the government] take responsibility for this![78]

Increased detail under education, including breakdowns for higher and general education, did arise from negotiations between the coalition leaders in the legislature and in the government. Within most ministerial budgets, the only breakdowns given before the 1994 Budget were for salaries, capital construction, and "other" spending. The increase in detail was a coalition priority. Coalition members on the Budget Committee reached agreement with Finance Ministry officials on which objects should be detailed in the budget, but their role was in seeing through a political decision already made by the coalition faction leaders and government ministers. The technical details of the breakdown and the amounts to spend, issues on which the Duma Committee is intimately involved, are beyond the scope of the Riigikogu Budget Committee.[79]

Budget Provisions, Amendments, and Adoption

The close cooperation extends to deliberations and consideration of amendments in the Committee. A Finance Ministry official attends every budget-related Committee session. "It is excluded that we could meet without a Ministry representative present," said one legislator, who added, " We have very close and good contacts. We understand each other well. . . . We have absolutely no complaints at all."[80]

Representatives of other ministries may also appear before the Budget Committee, but unlike in Russia, "in no case do we invite all ministries," one Committee member revealed. "Some we invite, others we do not."[81] The Committee invites a sectoral ministry only when specific questions arise. For example, when an opposition-sponsored amendment to cut defense spending and transfer the money to the Ministry of Culture was being discussed, "We did not understand the amendment, or the explanation in the appendix, really. So we asked the Defense Ministry. We were divided and we did not understand and so we invited a representative of the Ministry. We argued about an hour and a half and the Budget Committee Chair also could not understand, so we again invited a representative of the Defense Ministry. And we also called a representative of the Ministry of Culture."[82] In the end, the government prevailed on the coalition to reject the amendment, and the Budget Committee recommendation reflected this position.[83]

The main government participant is the Finance Ministry representative, and he appears before a mostly friendly crowd in the Committee — the majority of Committee members are from the governing coalition. As one official described it, over the course of four hours he speaks and answers questions, after which "the Committee decides to adopt [the budget] on the first reading."[84] These words are shocking compared with the tumult in the Duma. In Estonia, Finance Ministry officials know even before entering the room that the Committee will approve the budget. Moreover, this happens "at the first session" during which the Committee discusses the budget. "They say yes, adopt it, and they set the date of the first reading on the floor."[85]

The discussions take the form of coalition members and Ministry representatives fighting against opposition amendments. The character of these amendments is discussed in the next section. What is important here is that an amendment will be adopted only if it has the agreement of the coalition, headed in the Committee by the Committee Chair, and the Ministry. These two conditions are virtually reflexive — one exists when the other does. Committee and Ministry positions are almost always identical. At every reading, the Finance Ministry representative can tell the full legislature, "We do not have any disagreements about amendments with the Committee in our Ministry and therefore the government will not make any counter-proposals." The Committee Chair says virtually the same regarding agreement with the Ministry.[86]

From the government's perspective, the most important result of meetings with the Committee are not the substantive give and take. Finance Ministry officials literally scoff at the notion that technical budget discussions with the Committee are important or even take place. What is important is the political tone of the meetings: "It prepares us for the tone on the floor. The legislature can use the budget to bring down the government if it wants. The budget can be good but they can say, 'We don't like it.' This is theoretically possible. So we use Committee meetings to figure out how to speak in the hall. Will it be a light or sharp debate? This should be clear."[87] In other words, Committee sessions prepare the Finance Minister and the Prime Minister for the reception from the full legislature, for the nature and tone of questions they will face. The important aspects of Committee-government cooperation are political rather than technical.

Implementation and Legislative Control

One final area of cooperation between Estonia's legislature and its government on legislative issues is control over implementation. This area crosses the boundary into extra-legislative, political issues, because the main mechanism of legislative control over the budget is to bring down the government with a vote of no confidence if it discovers improprieties. The government provides quarterly material on budget implementation to the Committee and every year presents accounts of the previous year's implementation on the floor.[88] Each year, the Committee learns of violations. In 1994, the President spent nearly $1 million on reconstruction of the President's residence, an expense that the legislature had rejected during consideration of the budget. The President spent the money anyway, but "there was nothing we could do. We can only discuss," one Committee member said.[89] In another instance, the Committee learned that one ministerial department had illegally used budget funds for commercial activities to form an internal enterprise. "This happens and the legislature cannot do anything," this same member said.

This is not entirely true. The legislature could, of course, cut or eliminate funding for the department in question. But as one deputy said, "Nobody wants to punish. It is possible, but nobody wants to."[90] At least, nobody in the coalition wants to, as admission of guilt would discredit the government and could propel disintegration of the coalition, loss of government positions, and loss of leadership in the legislature. The shadow of the future is a compelling constraint in the linked, dual-channel Estonian legislature, where it was almost absent as a constraint in the unlinked design of the Duma. Oversight thus comes down to the legislature's listening to long accounts from ministers and asking questions. Finance Ministry officials see their accounts as "only for information, that is all. We do not feel any control from the legislature at all," although they admit that when the legislature asks for information, "we cannot say no."[91] The ministry officials give the accounts, and members of the coalition and opposition alike are allowed to make speeches and ask questions. Opposition speeches may be highly critical, but that is normally the limit of any such criticism of the government in the Estonian legislature. The Riigikogu does reserve the option of disbanding the coalition and bringing down the government in a no-confidence vote. The violations would have to be severe indeed for any of the partners to see any self-interest in taking such a step.

In all of the respects discussed to this point, Estonia's Riigikogu follows the pattern of Polsby's "arena" description of legislative bodies in parliamentary systems.[92] As Walter Bagehot describes the British Parliament, the cabinet is itself the legislature in a sense and gains legislative approval of all of its acts.[93] The opposition exists to publicly state its position with an eye to the next election. It can ask questions and make critical speeches against the government but not affect policy. Much as Cox and Jogerst describe the British experience, the ability of an individual legislator to effect policy change is severely constrained, while the role of the majority party or coalition and, in particular, the leaders of the party or coalition are dominant on legislative and political issues.[94]

A Frustrated Opposition

As one might expect given this picture of government-legislature relations on the budget, opposition deputies feel largely shut out of the process, and for good reason. A familiar lament from opposition deputies is, "I cannot receive such information," "I cannot meet with government representatives," and so on.[95] In terms of preliminary consultation with the opposition, the simple fact is there is none. The opposition's work on the budget, as on other legislation, begins with the government's submission of a draft to the relevant committee.[96]

Once the budget has been submitted, opposition factions may invite a Finance Ministry or sectoral ministry official to attend faction meetings at which they prepare their amendments. But one government official said, "This is rare. Normally they invite opposition legislators from sectoral committees, not us." The reason is simple: "We are fighting to prevent any of these amendments from passing!"[97] Still, when invited these officials do attend.

A leading opposition member of the Budget Committee summed up the situation quite succinctly: "In general the ability of the opposition to influence the budget is practically zero, because if the coalition has the support of the legislature, then they can just talk amongst themselves."[98] Other opposition leaders agree: "I have very little influence on the budget and all questions surrounding how to make the budget. I can influence as a member of the opposition only by asking questions. And in this way I can send a message that I believe our budget is incorrect in various aspects."[99] On legislative and extra-legislative issues the role of the opposition is primarily limited to making speeches on the floor and asking questions of the government. As will be seen in the following sections, opposition amendments to the budget, as for all legislation, do not pass. The few victories it may score on the budget are fleeting — they are quickly and easily overturned. In Estonia, relations between the legislature and the government are controlled by the coalition, whether on extra-legislative, political issues or on legislative issues such as the budget. Again, in this respect the Estonian experience follows the expectation of legislatures in parliamentary systems. As will now be seen, the legislature's internal activities are similarly marked by a high degree of consensus, a consensus again forged and dominated by the majority coalition.

INTERNAL CONSENSUS: THE LEGISLATIVE BUDGET PROCESS

When the government sends the budget to the legislature, the game may shift to the Budget Committee, but the reins of power remain in the hands of the coalition, which maintains a controlling majority on that as on all committees. Formally, the Committee has responsibility for the law, but in fact, committees are a junior partner in Estonia's legislative process.

The Formal Budget Process

Unlike in Russia, Estonia's formal rules for the legislative budget process are extremely brief. Only four short articles in the procedural Law on the Estonian Budget pertain to the legislature; the remaining forty detail the process that the government and particularly the Finance Ministry are to follow. This reflects the Finance Ministry's dominance over the budget. The constitution states only that the budget must be passed by a majority of the legislature's membership, not by a simple majority of those voting.[100] All that the budget process law adds is that the budget must be balanced and that all amendments introduced in the legislature that affect spending and revenues must be balanced.[101] The brevity of specific rules for the budget process means that in the Estonian legislature the process of consideration and adoption of the budget is virtually identical to that for all other legislation. This is in fact the case, and comments in the following sections thus apply to all legislative issues in the Riigikogu.

Committee Weakness

If anything, the brevity of specific rules for the legislature's budget activity reflects the legislature's and the Committee's limited prerogative. Committees are the weak channel in the Estonian legislature. Said one committee chair, "My lesson from the last two years [of work in the legislature] is that if there is a political line, then this is more important than specialists."[102] In other words, the Budget Committee may work as "specialists," but if "politicians" from the factions set a political line on an issue, the Committee opinion becomes irrelevant. Committees are the anemic channel in Estonia's legislature, as in most parliamentary systems. They are not, to use Jogerst's terms, "legislative-drafting and information-taking committees." They lack the resources, as do legislative committees in parliamentary systems more generally, for an independent legislating capacity.[103]

One factor inhibiting committee strength in the Riigikogu is the terrific lack of qualified staff and resources. That the Budget Committee has only one staff member for all of the issues it handles, including taxation, monetary policy, and banking, translates to a severely limited Committee capacity to seriously analyze the budget. Budget Committee members repeatedly complain that they "are not competent" to decide specific issues of budget policy. At the second reading of the 1995 Budget, for example, the Committee Chair, on at least half a dozen occasions, announced to the legislature that she and the Committee opposed an amendment because they were "not competent to decide" how much money should be spent on the President's staff, how to distribute funds within the defense industry, how to decide matters of investment in military construction programs, and so on.[104] They lacked competence because they lacked the resources to critically analyze the enormous span of budget issues.

Government officials seem to view the entire Committee process as superfluous: "It is not a professional discussion in the Committee, because it is too much material. They only see there is so much for this and for that and they ask questions. The analysis as a whole only scratches the surface."[105] Most Estonian legislators, including Committee members, believe that neither the Committee nor the legislature should even try to become involved in budget details. The Estonian legislature "should ratify the politics of the budget," but not the microlevel program details, says one. Another says, "Strategy is more important than specific amendments or details. We should decide principle questions." And recall the "Please God, no!" exclamation of the member quoted above, in reaction to suggestions that the legislature should ratify a detailed program budget.[106]

The situation is no different in the sectoral committees. Few Estonian legislators outside the Budget Committee are seriously engaged in budget issues. One Budget Committee member expressed a typically skeptical view of non-Committee colleagues: "Several [deputies] work actively on the budget, but not one does so wisely. . . . We do not see anyone in other committees capable of working seriously on the budget. We haven't seen this. Many haven't even read a budget."[107]

The coalition's dominance means that Estonia's legislature resembles a system of "party government."[108] Even though many fragmented factions must cooperate in the coalition, they still control the direction and the priorities of policy through their leaders in the government. As Jogerst's analysis of the British experience demonstrates, introducing committees into even a Westminster-style parliament does not undermine the partisan political nature of legislative activity so long as the channels remain firmly linked through majority control. Such is certainly the case in Estonia.

In stark contrast to those in Russia, Estonia's committees submit far fewer amendments on the budget than do the factions. Moreover, the Budget Committee "rarely" invites representatives of other committees to appear before it when discussing the budget. There is no scheduled time for Defense Committee or Agriculture Committee representatives to appear and present their arguments. One member of the Economics Committee said, "We do not work on the level of the budget. . . . Our committee can do nothing."[109] Compare this with the combativeness of intercommittee rivalry in the Russian State Duma!

Such committee weakness was not always the case in Estonia. In the Estonian Supreme Soviet of the late 1980s through 1991, as in the old Russian Supreme Soviet, all sectoral committees examined the budget and presented evaluations and proposals to the Budget Committee. The latter compiled these and presented its own detailed analyses. But independence brought a sharp break with all things Soviet, and a new institutional design in which the partisan factions have displaced the committees. As one with experience in the old and the new Estonian legislature observed, "Now there is no formal procedure written in black and white. Committees may examine and present their proposals and evaluations . . . but far from all of them do and if they are given any time at all it is very little."[110] The Budget Committee Chair initially lobbied to set up legislative hearings on the budget. At one session she said, "We believe there must be debates about the budget outside the official debates in the Riigikogu, as is normal in other European countries. This means there must be discussions between deputies and representatives of the government to clarify issues both on the budget and the overall economic situation. . . . We cannot discuss all questions at the plenary sessions. Therefore our Committee hopes the members will be interested in holding hearings outside of the official sessions."[111] Not one member responded to her call! She tried again at a later session: "I want to hear in your speeches your opinion about holding hearings on the budget with the government outside of our official sessions of the Riigikogu. There you could ask any questions of the members of the government about specific budget provisions."[112] The legislators again ignored her attempts to organize hearings, and none were held that year or the following year.[113] Estonian legislators are not interested in detailed discussion of the budget, but rather in partisan political discussion.

Faction Dominance: A Politicized Budget Process

The lack of interest is due to the dominance of the factions over the legislative process. Budget Committee decisions are decisions of the coalition, and they pass. There is nothing other committees or the opposition can do if they disagree. Said one frustrated opposition deputy, "Over 90 percent of the time we will lose."[114] But this result extends from the institutional strength of the factions, not from the Committee. The Committee may need to be satisfied for a budget to pass in the Estonian legislature, but the means to this end is through the factions. As one Committee member observed, "Committee decisions are the decisions of the factions, because the Committees have proportional representation of the factions. . . . And some Committee decisions may be changed because information from the Committee to the factions takes too much time, so the coalition meets and decides what to do."[115] Most Estonian deputies echo this perception that the factions do the most relevant work on legislative issues. Committee members find budget amendments from the factions technically superior to those from sectoral committees. As one Committee member put it, "The most principled and defended [proposals] come from factions, not from committees. This is how it seems to me."[116] This Budget Committee member presents the dominant view among Estonian legislators, that not only are factions more political in their orientation, but that this is the most relevant orientation in the Estonian legislature.

This is exactly the opposite situation from that of the Russian legislature, where the Budget Committee sees amendments from the factions as either superfluous, unprincipled, or even destructive. It confirms, however, expectations from Lijphart and others regarding the role of parties in parliamentary systems.[117] It also confirms the expectations of the role that parties play in legislatures when they do control majorities. Estonian parties do influence committee chairs and committee positions on issues, and they do indeed "stack the deck in their own favor" to dominate not only the legislative agenda but legislative content as well.[118]

The "global" rather than the technical economic nature of budget activity in the Estonian legislature is evident in the amendment activity, floor activity, and general perceptions and goals of the leaders of the legislature's budget process. The vast majority of amendments come from the factions. On the 1994 Budget, for example, of 247 amendments offered, only 46 came from committees, and the vast majority of these were from the Budget Committee itself in collaboration with the Finance Ministry. The remaining 201 were offered by factions or individual legislators representing their factions, almost all of them from the opposition.[119] The next year, of 194 amendments, 126 were offered by the factions, while 45 were from other committees. The Budget Committee submitted the remaining twenty-three.[120]

A quick glance at the amendments from the factions demonstrates that they are purely redistributive; they are not technical economic proposals focused on budget details. As one government official put it, the factions say, "take from here and give it there."[121] Such amendments are seen as being "political" rather than "economic" because they lack foundation or explanation accompanying them. They are not merely redistributive; they are demands for redistribution lacking detailed justification. On the second 1994 Supplementary Budget, for example, the main debate swirled around a number of amendments offered by opposition factions to take EEK 2 million from the Defense Ministry and give it to the Ministry of Culture. One Budget Committee member, exhausted from examining "stupid" amendments of this nature, complained that virtually all of the hundreds of amendments offered by the factions to the budgets during in 1994 and 1995 were of this type.[122]

The rule requiring that all amendments be balanced necessitates in part that amendments be of the form, take from A and give to B. But the rule does not require that this be done blindly! Factions offer amendments "with no idea what hinges on this, or what basis the switch in funds has."[123] The figures in such amendments are "random," as legislators have no independent source of information on which to argue "why change this much, or why not leave that much" in one or another area.[124] Neither in Committee nor on the floor is there concrete discussion of which programs are ripe for cutting in one area, or of what needs to be added to the other to warrant the spending increase. Similarly, there is no substantiation of the figures suggested for rescission and addition.

Rather than being based on a technical analysis of different economic sectors, these amendments reflect a political desire of the factions and their leaders and, in particular, of opposition factions and their leaders to be seen and heard. The amendments have no chance of adoption as evidenced by the fact that the Budget Committee rarely invites the authors to, and the latter rarely attend, Committee sessions at which decisions on recommendations on amendments are made.[125] The decisions are foregone conclusions.

The game is not about getting these amendments adopted, and the important moment in the game for amendment authors is therefore not the Committee's decision-making process. The important moment is the opportunity for the amendment author to rise on the floor and make a speech in defense of the particular sector for which he or she is proclaiming support. A coalition deputy explained, "Now we have politicians who can appear on TV and say they demanded two million more for culture and two million less for defense. They are content to give the government the power and the responsibility, while they speak loudly, with no analysis."[126] Government officials agree: "This political battle for power doesn't enable them to work very professionally or objectively. It prevents them from serious work. They simply want to make a political statement, the main thing is to speak . . . and show that they support everyone. All of this puts pressure on the government, because the government is guilty of everything!"[127] After asking their questions of the government representative and of the Committee Chair, opposition deputies make their speeches, defend their factions' amendments, and then withdraw them without even demanding a vote. They withdraw them because the result is not in question, and the exercise is not about changing the budget. Having made their speeches on the floor and criticized the government and its policies, the opposition members have achieved their goal.

The most political aspect of the legislative budget process in Estonia is the surprisingly universal view that rejection of the budget would mean the fall of the government.[128] Neither the Law on the Estonian Budget nor the constitution states that budget votes are votes of confidence. Article 98 of the constitution states that the government may tie a vote on any legislation to a vote on confidence, but no budget has been so tied.[129] Nevertheless, almost all legislators and government officials believe that this is automatically the case with the budget, and they behave accordingly.[130] The conviction that a negative vote on the budget will bring down the government is a powerful incentive for members of coalition factions to toe the party line, further cementing coalition dominance over the legislative budget process.

Coalition Dominance on the Floor

Jogerst, when pondering the significance of including committees in the single-channel, partisan British Parliament, worries that adding this second channel will enable the members to defect from their parties more frequently. If they can point to their committee identities and loyalties, this would provide them with a foundation for greater independence in exercising their individual judgements.[131] However, a comparative institutional approach demonstrates that the real question is how the channels are combined, not whether both are present. In Russia, for example, including parties was what caused the effect that Jogerst describes, but the effect occurred by the undermining of committee dominance. The question is one of linkage. The tight links between the two channels in Estonia demonstrates how to avoid such internal chaos. As long as the channels are linked in Britain's legislative body, Jogerst's worries will not be realized.

The coalition's dominance predetermines the fate of the vast majority of amendments and the outcome of the vast majority of votes in the Estonian legislature. It is not the vote that is important; the game is not about getting amendments passed. If the initiator for whatever reason seeks to press the political point to the extreme, the initiator may demand a vote. But the amendment will fail. Only amendments with the blessing of the government and of the coalition pass, and these easily pass. Such amendments may correct a mistake that the Finance Ministry made when drafting the budget. These may be caught by the Budget Committee, by one of the coalition factions, or by the Ministry itself. In such instances, the government and the Committee agree from the outset to make the change. For example, an amendment to reduce by nearly EEK 9 million social security funds for unemployment in the 1995 Budget corrected for an error in predictions for unemployment figures for 1995. Predicted unemployment when the budget was being drafted in the spring of 1994 exceeded actual unemployment when the budget was being considered in the legislature in November.[132] The amendment was made by the Budget Committee in close consultation with the government. When an error is caught by a coalition faction, that faction will submit the amendment, again in close cooperation with the government in drafting the correction.

The other type of amendment likely to gain government support is one that corrects changes made at earlier readings of the budget. On occasion, "unintended" or "strange" amendments have been adopted either in the Committee or on the floor due to the absence of one or more coalition members at a session.[133] The opposition may use its temporary majority in Committee to adopt an amendment. The confusion extends to the floor if members miss the Committee Chair's argument warning members to overturn that opposition victory. Those members hear the signal for a vote and vote according to Committee recommendation on the papers distributed.

Coalition members may thus "inadvertently" vote for the "strange" opposition amendment. At the next reading the government will, through the coalition factions, introduce amendments reversing these fleeting opposition victories. As one Finance Ministry official noted, "These are in fact the government's amendments, but formally they come from the factions."[134]

During discussion of the 1994 Budget, for example, an opposition amendment sought to include in the state budget all profits of the Bank of Estonia. The debate took place during the day, but the proposal did not come to a vote until late at night, when many coalition members were absent. The amendment passed in spite of its direct violation of the Law on the Bank of Estonia and the constitution, the negative recommendation of the Budget Committee, and the opposition of the government and of the coalition. The chair of the Bank, who was also a member of the legislature, then began to lobby with all factions and particularly with coalition members to repeal the amendment at the next reading. The counterproposal was formally submitted by a coalition faction but in fact came from the government and the Bank.[135] It passed easily, reversing the apparent opposition victory. The coalition's domination of the process thus gives the government the opportunity to correct mistakes made either in its own drafting of the budget or in the legislature.

Amendments may also pass under more normal circumstances, only to be severely challenged by the government after the fact. One amendment in 1994 eliminated funding for the Board of Tourism. This amendment passed during the second reading, but the government argued afterward that the move would eliminate an important revenue source. The Committee, at the next reading on the demand of the government, restored the funds.[136]

The most common amendments to pass, however, reflect the political priorities of the coalition above and beyond the economic priorities of the Finance Ministry. The best example is the increase in spending that the legislature approved for education and culture in the 1995 Budget. The coalition majority, led by the Budget Committee Chair, consistently sought to increase spending for culture and education.[137] The spending increases granted during the 1995 Budget debate totaled nearly EEK 70 million. Nearly half of this increase was for the general category of "investments." As the Budget Committee Chair pointed out on the floor, this and other increases in that year's budget were made possible by a recalculation of VAT revenues by the Ministry of Finance itself, after the budget had been submitted to the legislature.[138] The remaining increase resulted from coalition-led reform of the pension administration.[139] That the money went to such a general category reflects the political rather than the technical nature of even these amendments.

No other sector received anything approaching this level of increase in the 1995 Budget. Indeed, the final adopted budget was balanced at EEK 8.8 billion, an increase of only EEK 100 million over the draft submitted. So the budget expanded by a mere 1 percent after submission to the legislature. The government's budget is the coalition's budget, and the coalition controls legislative outcomes. In most sectors where there were spending increases, these were offset by decreases within the same sector. One powerful example of this was the appropriation for the Ministry of Internal Affairs, where EEK 27 million was added for municipal rescue agencies (paramedics and fire), while EEK 23 million was cut for the nebulous expenditure "regional support."[140] Similarly, increased support for new farms was largely offset by cuts in loan subsidies and "development" expenses within the Agriculture Ministry. The areas that sustained cuts were the legislature's own administrative costs (EEK 13 million) and defense (EEK 14 million). Such amendments reflect the political priorities of the coalition factions and of the government itself. The government continuously adjusts the Finance Ministry's figures to meet these priorities while the budget is being drafted, and the actions of the Budget Committee and of the coalition are fully consistent with and reflective of these priorities, and fully supported by the government.[141]

The coalition factions, not merely the factions, dominate Estonia's budget process. The opposition can speak, but that is normally the extent of its role. The first government enjoyed a majority of only three in the legislature, and two of its supporters were independents not affiliated with any party or legislative faction. Nevertheless, coalition leaders in the legislature had swaggering confidence that, "if the coalition decides one way, it cannot be another way."[142] Even when the opposition scores a victory, it is fleeting and due to attendance abnormalities or uninformed voting. The coalition overturns these victories by simply presenting counteramendments to repeal them. As Wildavsky describes budgeting in parliamentary systems, the opposition can criticize government and coalition policy, but it lacks the information that the government controls to have much effect on that policy.[143]

The most startling confirmation of coalition dominance came in late 1994, during and after the crisis that brought the collapse of the Laar government. While the coalition was beginning to splinter, the government was down to a minority government, and the Prime Minister was nearing a no-confidence vote that he would lose, the legislature debated that government's supplementary 1994 Budget and draft 1995 Budget. The first passed with virtually no amendments to the draft. The only abnormality was the virtually universal sentiment among all legislators, coalition and opposition alike, that the government should have more accurately predicted revenue receipts so that such large supplementary budgets would not be needed.[144] Similarly, after the Laar government fell, its 1995 Budget continued to sail through the legislature and was passed in mid-December. The difficulty in agreeing on a new Prime Minister, discussed above, and the change in several cabinet ministers, including the Finance Minister, hardly disrupted the process of adoption of the budget.

In the coalition-dominated Estonian legislature, internal consensus on legislation is thus largely predetermined, even on the annual budget. Only in its first year of existence did the legislature fail to adopt a budget before the beginning of the fiscal year. It adopted the 1993 Budget on February 9, 1993, with a vote of 65–17, meaning that eleven opposition deputies joined the coalition in approving the budget. All of Estonia's budgets since that date have been adopted before January 1 of the new fiscal year. The 1994 Budget passed on December 15, 1993, with a vote of 56–12; the 1995 Budget was adopted December 14, 1994, on a vote of 67–4; and the 1996 Budget passed on December 29, 1995.[145]

Similarly, action on amendments is highly consensual. Most notable is the fact, discussed above, that after speaking on the floor in defense of their proposals, opposition legislators normally withdraw their amendments without even demanding that a vote be held. For example, of 122 amendments to the second 1994 Supplementary Budget, only 52 were put to a vote by their authors, and nearly one-third of these were supported by the Committee and by the government and adopted on their recommendations. So of 105 amendments that the Committee and the coalition opposed, only 35 went to a vote. Only one of these was adopted. Similar patterns hold for votes on the base budgets.[146]

CONCLUSIONS: THE ROLE OF THE ESTONIAN LEGISLATURE

That so much of the Estonian legislative budget debate focuses on politics and strategic priorities rather than on the technical, economic details reflects the general nature of legislative debate in the Riigikogu. A common sentiment has emerged among legislators and government officials alike on how to improve the quality of the discussion and the overall legislative process. Government officials call for still earlier consultations with the legislature, or for the legislature to begin its consideration of budget priorities at an earlier stage in Estonia's budget process. Said one official, "The parliament's priorities should be specified earlier, because now when all the work has already been done and we begin to argue about priorities it is a waste of time, work and of money. Why not have these statements of priorities earlier? Then we can try to do things differently if we must. . . . It seems to me parliament could have a discussion in the spring about its budget priorities, not have this after the draft budget is already submitted."[147] In other words, let the legislature have its say on broad priorities at the early phase, and then let the government decide the details.

Many legislators agree that they should have their most important say on these political issues. The Budget Committee Chair, during floor debate on the 1995 Budget, expressed her belief that the legislature should determine relative proportions for budget spending across sectors; in other words, it should discuss and ratify the government's strategic budget priorities. She even suggested changing the procedural Law on the Estonian Budget to require the Finance Ministry to submit its strategic priorities in May.[148] Presumably, the autumn discussion would ratify these percentages once again, but as specific spending and revenue figures. The important point, however, is that wide agreement exists among government officials and legislators alike on the political and macro nature of budget debate in the Estonian legislature. The argument, and the suggestion, could easily be extended to encompass the legislature more generally.

On the surface, the findings here could be said merely to confirm the observations made by other scholars that parliamentary systems lead to more stable government and favor democratic consolidation, particularly in a highly fragmented partisan environment. Scholars such as Lijphart, Linz, Shugart, and Fred W. Riggs have all trumpeted those virtues.[149] Parliamentary systems such as Estonia's do have institutionalized means for resolving conflict, as Mainwaring suggests.[150] The danger of impasse in legislative-executive relations is normally eased in a parliamentary system.

However, this comparative institutional study as applied here focuses on the particular effects of legislative design. The advantages of Estonia's design lie in the links created by the demand on the small, partisan factions to cooperate within the legislature. As Donald L. Horowitz argues and as this discussion demonstrates, the presidential-parliamentary debate is not the relevant issue for legislative performance. What is important in either constitutional system for democracy to stabilize and to succeed is to get dis-parate and mutually suspicious elites to engage in consensus building and conflict management.[151] The Estonian case is instructive to students of legislatures precisely because of the comparative distinction with respect to the Russian cases.

The thorough linkage between factions and committees in the Estonian legislature helps ensure consensus building internally and in relations with the executive branch, on legislative and extra-legislative activities. The combination of the linkage between these two channels and the constitu-tional linkage between the partisan factions severely constrains the political space in which legislators may act, particularly compared with the current Russian legislature. The legislators are far less free to maneuver than are their counterparts in the Duma. As the Estonian Speaker put it, "Party discipline and inter-party arrangements inevitably set limits on the mem-bers' activities."[152] Positions are determined in meetings of the factions and of the majority and opposition coalitions, and the imperative of party disci-pline necessary to maintain the majority leaves individual legislators with little room to stray. Consensus thus reached among the leaders translates to support among the broader membership and action on the floor of the legislature. In these respects, the Riigikogu resembles more institutional-ized European parliaments.

As a result of the linkage, the Estonian legislature gets things done. Jogerst describes the inclusion of committees in the British Parliament as an expression of the desire of MPs "to get things done."[153] But clearly it is not just the existence of committees that has this effect, in spite of the protestations of such legislative scholars as Krehbiel, Shepsle, and Wein-gast. The Estonian legislature gets things done largely in spite of its com-mittees, defying the expectation that committees necessarily control agen-das or induce equilibria.[154] Rather, it is the degree of institutional linkage between the two channels that induces equilibria and enables legislative effectiveness in managing conflict. The parties-committees debate appears inappropriately cast as an either-or proposition. The works on postcom-munist legislatures that repeat this dichotomy continue to prevent compar-ative legislative theory from making much progress in explaining variation in legislative behavior and performance.[155] What is important is whether the two channels are combined to induce conflict management, or are unlinked to provoke conflict and deadlock.

Estonia's legislative design features close institutional links between the factions and the government and internally between the factions and the committees. In addition, and in part extending from this situation, the committees are clearly the weaker partner in the Estonian legislature. The ties between parties and government largely determine the close cooperation between the legislature and the executive branch. However, were the coalition not so thoroughly to control the legislative levers, the government's programs would meet with far greater difficulty in the legislature, and the links would likely eventually break down.

It is possible to link the partisan and the committee channels in a legislature without resorting to a parliamentary system, however. The Estonian case reveals the advantages, particularly in a multipartisan legislature with weak and underdeveloped parties, of having a consistent legislative majority coalesce from among the partisan factions. It reveals the advantages of having a consistent majority across leadership and committee posts and committee majorities. It reveals the advantages of having fewer committees and, as a result, less duplication and competition between them. The concluding chapter discusses these and other possible changes, some derived from this comparison to the Estonian legislature, others derived from the Supreme Soviet-State Duma comparison. These changes could be adopted to create a linked, dual-channel legislature in a presidential system such as Russia's to enable internal and external consensus building and conflict management on legislative and extra-legislative issues.

CONCLUSION

Designing Legislatures: Prescriptive Lessons, for Russia and Beyond

Upon hearing a description of this project at a recent conference, a fellow "new institutionalist," invoking the title of a recent book, asked, "So, do institutions matter?"[1] Happily, this book does more than say that institutions matter. By developing and applying a comparative institutional theory of legislatures, this study demonstrates how they matter. They matter because institutional design defines the space within which individuals may exercise political discretion. Institutional design determines a legislature's ability to manage, channel, and overcome conflict of various types by determining whether the combination of incentives and constraints compels members to pursue strategies of consensus building and conflict management, or if it leaves them unconstrained to pursue noncooperative, confrontational strategies. By demonstrating how institutional design affects the conflict-management capacity of legislatures, this study takes a much-needed step toward developing a theoretical framework for comparative legislative studies. While a first step toward theory building in this burgeoning field, this study is clearly a fruitful merger of institutional theory, comparative methodology, and legislative studies, one that hopefully will attract efforts at refinement and expansion.

This concluding chapter demonstrates the value of a comparative institutional approach by suggesting its practical implications for those designing legislatures, whether in postcommunist states or elsewhere. As the references throughout the preceding chapters make clear, several valuable and highly informative studies have been recently published on postcommunist legislatures, including Russia's and Estonia's.[2] Guided by earlier works in comparative legislative studies, they identify relative strength and weakness of various legislatures and provide useful descriptive interpretations of these new legislatures. However, as with earlier efforts in comparative legislative studies, no general theoretical approach has emerged. Nearly all of these works are collections of single-case studies, and when volume editors attempt to make broader, more general statements beyond these single cases, they flounder. The lack of a general theoretical approach has denied students of legislatures any broad explanatory power or the ability to generalize their findings. The best these studies can provide are fairly empty statements that "postcommunist parliaments do indeed evolve and develop."[3]

My comparative institutional framework enables us to explain why these new legislatures differ from each other, to explain why some have succeeded where others have failed. It is a general theoretical approach that explains variations in legislative performance according to differences in institutional design. It also affords the opportunity to suggest to legislative designers the advantages and the disadvantages of various design choices. As Hahn notes, whether stable democratic institutions arise depends on the design of and the rules in those institutions.[4] Earlier works have failed to systematize the comparative examination of legislatures and to develop a systematic comparative framework to enable explanation and true comparison. The promise of comparative institutionalism is that it will take us beyond the desire "to say something comparative" to an ability to engage in systematic comparative analysis and explanation across a variety of legislatures.[5] This is the ambition of this project.

Mezey makes a timely and important appeal to students of postcommunist legislatures to adopt "a larger comparative context" when examining those legislatures. The call is equally relevant to students of any legislatures. The comparative institutional approach developed here is an important step toward developing "theory and explanations that help us to understand legislatures in general."[6] To understand what contributes to the emergence of stable democratic legislatures we need to be able to understand what works and what doesn't work, and why. Indeed, we need to know what we mean by "works." My comparative institutional framework seeks to develop and apply a truly general theory of legislative organization and performance.

"Politics is premised on inconsistencies and conflicts," as March and Olson put it, and it is "critical" for democracy that "the use of 'other means'" resolve those conflicts.[7] As such, new legislatures and their designs should be evaluated according to their capacity for managing political conflict. Institutions may create the conditions that enable the peaceful resolution of conflict. They may also impede conflict resolution. Whether they do one or the other in large part depends on how they are designed. Nowhere is this more evident than in the comparison of Russia's two post-communist legislatures. However, because of the paltry state of theory in comparative legislative studies, those designing legislatures to this point have been left without any prescriptive suggestions to guide them in designing legislatures that will be able to manage conflict of various types. The framework developed in this book and in this concluding chapter seeks to provide such practical guidelines for future legislative designers.

A word is perhaps in order about embarking on a prescriptive conclusion in a study such as this. It seems safe to say that there will never be another wave of postcommunist transformation, at least not on the scale of 1989–91. However, state formation and regime change to and from democracy continue around the world, and new states and regimes must confront the question of how to design their legislatures. Given the high stakes involved, those who design legislatures would benefit enormously by having a blueprint of the different types of legislatures and the various consequences that pertain to choosing one design over another. With such a blueprint, one would know when designing an unlinked, dual-channel legislature like the Duma what sort of institution would result. With such a blueprint, those who redesigned Ukraine's Supreme Rada to mirror the Duma's unlinked design would have had no reason to be surprised when internal processes in that legislature degenerated into chaos. A useful blueprint could have suggested to the designers of those institutions the trade-offs of those design choices and suggested alternatives that may have served those legislatures better.

Just as this book is a first step in theory building, this conclusion is a first step in developing such a blueprint. The comparative institutional theory developed here isolates as a variable how partisan entities — parties and factions — are incorporated into the design of legislatures. In postcommunist states, the partisan map is highly fragmented. What passes for parties are small, unstable personality cliques, rather than societal organizations with consistent platforms and deep roots based on well-established social cleavage structures. These characteristics may be fairly identified as general characteristics of the partisan environment in any new state that has arisen under conditions of dramatic socioeconomic-political upheaval. Therefore, findings regarding the effects of different ways of incorporating such partisan entities into the new legislatures in postcommunist states are by no means limited to those states but rather suggest generally applicable lessons for new legislatures in new states.

As an opening statement of a comparative institutional theory of legislatures, the lessons drawn must be tentative until further elaboration of the concepts and corroboration of the findings can take place. Prescriptive judgments offered to those designing new legislatures must be even more cautious. However, even cautious prescriptive statements within a theoretical framework represent a vast advantage over the void that currently exists. Legislative designers currently have only descriptive single-case studies but nothing in the way of comparatively derived prescriptive frameworks to guide them. A comparative institutional approach enables us to begin to draw lessons that are theoretically grounded and backed by multiple-case evidence. While only the most solid of such conclusions can be advanced here, this study should already be of enormous value to future legislative designers.

The central lesson of this study is one argued by students of institutions in other contexts, dating at least to the writings of Georg Simmel on dyadic organizations, or what I have termed "dual channels." The lesson is, that for effective conflict management in such institutions, the dyads, or channels, must be linked. The less they are linked, the less effective conflict management will be. As Simmel and others have argued, the most effective linkage is one that creates a third element that draws from the channels or otherwise enmeshes them.[8] Other lessons emerge that relate to the various ways of including or not including partisan entities in a legislature. These lessons speak directly to the dilemma that new states and new regimes normally face where political parties are either nonexistent or extremely fragile and unstable. There are costs and benefits to consider in choosing whether or not to include political parties, and if so, how. The comparative institutional approach provides us with the explanatory power to present these costs and benefits.

The Benefits of Including Parties

Any suggestion for how to link parties and committees in a legislature presupposes the inclusion of both. The assumption that legislatures include parties is universal in the legislative studies literature, including the recent literature on postcommunist legislatures cited in the opening of this chapter. As this study makes clear, though, this should not be assumed. New regimes face a dizzying array of tasks: political, economic, and social. It is easy to understand the temptation to exclude the tiny, new, unstable, and raucous personality cliques that pose as parties, whether the weakness of political parties and the party system was due to years of suppression by dictatorial or authoritarian regimes or to other causes.

Russia is just one state that has followed this path of excluding partisan organizations from its legislature. The experience of its Supreme Soviet strongly warns against a nonpartisan legislative design. Its spectacular failure, and similar difficulties experienced by other legislatures so designed, suggest that despite the weakness of parties and the party system, new states are ill-advised to exclude those partisan organizations from the legislature's design. This is in spite of the demonstrated internal efficiency that that design brings to the legislative process. The nonpartisan, single-channel Supreme Soviet was impressive in its capacity to manage internal legislative conflict. In fact, it was too effective in this regard. As chapter 2 demonstrates, the Supreme Soviet was a legislative machine. Its committees dominated the legislative process much like House committees in Congress have been described as dominating the legislative process. It was not a dictatorship of the Supreme Soviet Chair. Rather, committee chairs coordinated their activities in the Presidium to ensure that differences between committees were worked out in the early stages of drafting and revision, before final action. Committees shared the common interest of wanting their legislation passed, and they recognized and deferred to each other's authority and expertise. The reciprocal relations brought mutually beneficial results. Supporting another committee today ensured its support of yours tomorrow. Legislation was adopted without partisan bickering and maneuvering, as these were designed out of the legislative process. This single-channel, nonpartisan design was an attractive option beyond Russia and brought efficient conflict management in the internal legislative process to other legislatures so designed, including those in Ukraine and Belarus during their first few years of post-Soviet independence.

These findings resonate with the long tradition of scholars of the U.S. Congress who highlight the stabilizing role of congressional committees and committee strength, some even to the point of ignoring the parties altogether. In spite of this seeming internal efficiency, however, the lesson of the Supreme Soviet is a powerful lesson to legislative designers in new states everywhere and to theorists of legislatures. Committees may matter, but so do parties. This is not an either-or proposition for a legislature, at least not without dire consequences. Legislative studies, including studies of Congress, that ignore the role of parties are incomplete and of limited theoretical value for the study of legislatures generally.

The comparison between the Supreme Soviet's and the Duma's relations with the executive branch dramatically demonstrates the benefits of including partisan entities in a legislature. Take, for example, interbranch relations on legislative issues. In the State Duma today as in the Supreme Soviet previously, committee chairs span the entire partisan map. Some are devout Communists, some ultraright or nationalist, some social democrats, while still others are neoliberal or libertarians. In the Supreme Soviet, where partisan factions were excluded, those committee chairs enjoyed enormous freedom in exercising individual discretion. They single-handedly determined the political direction of their committees and what relations with the executive branch would be like on issues under their purview. Some supported the government and, like the Budget Committee Chair, structured relations to enable their committees to work with government officials to produce legislation agreeable to both. Others, however, were vehemently antigovernment and excluded the executive branch from their proceedings, producing legislation that the executive branch could not accept and would not implement.

If one could imagine "looking down" on the Supreme Soviet, its posture toward the executive branch on legislative issues was highly unpredictable and unstable. It was dependent on the personal predilections of the committee chair responsible for the issue in question. The Supreme Soviet lacked institutional constraints on the political actions of those committee chairs, resulting in repeated and intense confrontation and deadlock between the two branches.

However, the Duma contains such institutional constraints on the exercise of individual discretion, constraints that derive from the inclusion of the partisan factions in its design. Even though Duma committee chairs are scattered across all factions, the inclusion of those factions constrains those chairs to pursue collaboration and conflict management with the executive branch. Because duplication and overlap between committee profiles was the result of interfaction jealousies, overlapping committees are chaired by members of factions on diametrically opposite ends of the political spectrum. One might wish to shun collaboration and pursue confrontation with the executive branch. But if the other seeks cooperation and negotiation, the first, out of suspicion and hostility if nothing else, will want to be privy to those meetings with government officials. This very dynamic operates across all legislative issues, and therefore, all committee chairs participate in negotiations and consensus building with the executive branch. There will always be some factions that cooperate with the executive branch, organizing their own meetings or attending those organized by others to inform relevant government officials of progress on legislation in their committees. Once this process starts, no faction stands for being excluded. The end result is that every committee in the Duma engages and negotiates with government representatives, and conflict management with the executive branch across legislative issues is far more consistent than it was with the Supreme Soviet.

This evidence alone confirms the powerful benefits of including parties in legislatures, for regardless of their societal weakness they seem to promote consistent interbranch cooperation on legislative issues. The evidence on extra-legislative issues provides still more powerful evidence. Inclusion of the partisan organizational channel in the Duma imposes institutional constraints on the Duma Speaker that the Supreme Soviet Chair did not face. For example, all Duma faction heads collectively decide questions of internal leadership positions. The presence of these partisan leaders means that the Duma is able not only to resolve these leadership questions but also to do so quickly, whereas the Supreme Soviet took months to finally elect its Chair. Once elected, though, the Supreme Soviet Chair faced no partisan organizations or leaders to challenge his authority on extra-legislative issues. Khasbulatov could decide housekeeping issues and dominate the nonlegislative agenda in the Supreme Soviet. Partisan politics were essentially ceded to the only politicized actor in the Supreme Soviet, the Chair. In the Duma, however, the factions and in particular their leaders impose severe constraints on the political space within which the Duma Speaker may act. The faction leaders in the Duma Soviet make such decisions, not the Speaker. The faction leaders set the daily agenda and collectively decide what extra-legislative issues come to that agenda. Again, it is not a single individual who controls such decisions as was the case in the Supreme Soviet. The inclusion of the partisan channel and the constraints on the individual whims of the Speaker that it entails must be considered an advancement in the Duma over the arbitrariness of the Supreme Soviet when it comes to internal conflict management on extra-legislative issues.

While Supreme Soviet relations with the executive branch on legislative issues were unpredictable and frequently conflict-riven, it was relations between the two branches on extra-legislative issues that ultimately doomed the Supreme Soviet. A legislature that excludes partisan entities altogether will find it extremely difficult to manage extra-legislative conflict with the executive branch. Like committee chairs on legislation, the Supreme Soviet Chair determined the legislature's orientation toward the executive branch on these broader political issues and was virtually unconstrained by any entity within the legislature. Perhaps a different personality would have steered those relations in a different direction, but it must be remembered that Khasbulatov started out as a political unknown who was beholden to and a loyal ally of President Yeltsin. The institutional incentives and environmental stimuli drove him in a different direction. Even had Khasbulatov remained a loyal consensus builder with the executive branch or had a different personality occupied the position, the fact that the fate of such a crucial relationship between the two branches was so dependent on the personality and the predilections of that single individual indicates a highly unstable institutional arrangement. For while a different individual may have pursued conflict management and consensus building, the institutional design afforded virtually unhindered space for such exercise of individual political discretion. Lacking institutional constraints that would compel managing and defusing political conflict, the design was not merely open to catastrophic breakdown but prone to it.

Including the partisan factions in the legislative design brings those constraints. The improved interbranch relations enjoyed by the Duma are powerful confirmation of the benefits of including partisan organizations in a legislature, regardless of the weakness of parties or the absence of a party system. The Duma's dual-channel design removes that ability of a single individual to determine the nature of the legislature's extra-legislative relations with the executive branch. Just as it constrains committee chairs in their relations with the executive branch, it constrains the Speaker and all faction leaders in the Duma Soviet. They together, not the Speaker or any other single leader, are the principle players in the relationship. As a standing body of the partisan leaders, the Duma Soviet constitutes an institutional forum to which the President and the government can and do send liaisons to hear the positions of the factions, to explain their own positions, and to negotiate to resolve political crises and defuse potential conflict between the two branches. In addition to these collective meetings, executive branch leaders and representatives also regularly meet individually with the leaders of each faction to exchange in a political give-and-take. It is not that the Speaker is now excluded from meeting with the President and the Prime Minister. He meets with them, and even sits on the President's Security Council. The point is that he is not the only or even the most influential deputy, and as such he is unable to act individually. To the extent that he does act, he acts at the pleasure of the Duma's faction leaders. He must consult with and be guided by those leaders, to whom he is beholden for his position in the first place. Those faction leaders are engaged in their own regular consultations and political negotiations with the President and the government, for if one has such access, all demand equal access for reasons of personal ambition, public prestige, and political influence. The result is that the executive branch and the legislature now consult and negotiate to manage political crises over personnel, economic, security, and other political matters.

This is perhaps a surprising finding. The nonpartisan Supreme Soviet, which excluded tiny, bickering, partisan factions, was the legislature least able to manage political conflict with the executive branch. The Duma, which includes myriad competing, mutually hostile partisan factions, is better able to manage political conflict and negotiate political agreements with the executive branch to avoid the deadlock of its predecessor. Entrenching partisan organizations in a legislature has a constraining effect on the ability of any individual legislator to dominate the legislature in pursuit of an independent and confrontational political line.

THE BENEFITS OF LINKAGE

Simply including parties does not, however, solve all problems of conflict management. How they are included, and in particular the extent to which they are linked with committees, is what matters. Again the legislative studies literature assumes such linkage. Those authors writing about the U.S. Congress or British Parliament may perhaps be excused for this assumption; however, for understanding legislative performance generally this is a deeply flawed assumption. The degree of linkage varies enormously and determines the depth and breadth of conflict management in any particular legislature. The benefits of linkage are dramatically apparent when considering its absence. Internal conflict management on legislative issues is most compromised by an unlinked, dual-channel design such as that in the Russian State Duma. The design denies the legislature of institutionally based means for coordination between its suborganizations. The resultant incentives compel committees to compete with each other rather than to cooperate, and they compel factions and committees to struggle against each other for control over procedures and outcomes. Most significant, the lack of links denies all incentives for coalition building and cooperation between the partisan factions, thus exacerbating the natural tendency of such organizations toward sharp and pervasive competition and conflict.

The legislative game in such a legislature is about blocking opponents' initiatives rather than collaborating to reach consensus. Individual deputies, committees, and factions all work to torpedo the proposals of their rivals. The incentives for legislators in an unlinked, dual-channel legislative design all point to confrontational rather than collaborative strategies, while constraints on their ability to pursue such confrontation are virtually absent. In the Duma, this was abundantly evident on the budget as on other issues. Duma deputies become split personalities; their actions are highly unpredictable, as they may switch allegiances unexpectedly, frequently, and without sanction. The mark of one's stature and strength in the Duma is measured by one's ability to prevent actions by opponents, rather than to generate outputs through consensus building. The intrinsic weakness of the factions combined with and exacerbated by the weak linkages between the factions and the committees mean that the faction leaders often prove unable to enforce on the floor the political consensus they reach in their meetings. Individual deputies may defect, either because of the lack of sanctions or because of the lack of conviction that loyalty will mean future advancement, or indeed for both of these reasons. Duma deputies are unfettered in their exercise of individual discretion, and political agreement reached among the faction leaders frequently evaporates on the floor.

When comparing the Duma with the Supreme Soviet, this finding becomes somewhat surprising. It appears that the inclusion of partisan factions in the Duma has stymied internal consensus building. This is surprising because we normally think of parties as essential for effective legislating, as they organize partisan interests and provide organizational coherence to the myriad partisan and policy preferences of individual politicians. But the nonpartisan, single-channel Supreme Soviet was more effective in internal legislative conflict management than is the Duma, which includes partisan organizations.

The problems of unlinked dual channels are not unique to Russia. It is a general condition confirmed by similar findings in other legislatures so designed. In 1997, Ukraine redesigned its Supreme Rada to mirror that of the Russian Duma, and the effects of the unlinked design on the internal legislative process have been just as astounding as they have been in Russia. Similarly, in Hungary, where links are absent or weak, analogous tendencies toward chronic breakdown and deadlock demonstrate the institutional disadvantages of unlinked dual-channel designs. The Hungarian case dispels the inclination to attribute the problems of weak links to strong presidentialism. Hungary has a parliamentary system, yet its legislature suffers the internal disadvantages of weak internal linkage. It is the institutional design of the legislative body itself that is important. Including the factions as a parallel, autonomous organizational layer erodes a legislature's capacity to manage conflict in its internal legislative activities.

As this comparative institutional framework demonstrates, it is not the inclusion of factions, but the way they are included that is the source of the Duma's internal difficulties. A linked, dual-channel design is far more effective at managing internal conflict, particularly on legislative issues. Estonia also went from having a nonpartisan design to a dual-channel design including an array of small partisan factions. But the Riigikogu has a linked, dual-channel design in which the factions face powerful and immediate incentives to coalesce into majority and minority coalitions, and in which those coalitions penetrate all levels and structures of the legislature. As a result, the majority and the opposition compete, but the majority coalition controls all leadership posts and committee majorities. The committee chairs are all from the same coalition of partisan factions, and they work together in coalition meetings; committee work is thus coordinated in these sessions. The factions also internally coordinate their efforts within the majority and opposition coalitions. Coordination, conflict management, and consensus building are thus the hallmarks of legislative work in the Riigikogu. The Riigikogu-Duma comparison demonstrates that for internal conflict management to become the norm in a dual-channel legislature, the two channels must be linked in a coherent way throughout the legislature.

Such linkage provides the most effective capacity for internal, extra-legislative consensus building. In Estonia, party leaders actually lead something. The leaders of the majority coalition run the government, all coalition partners have government positions, and the coalition controls the leadership posts in the Riigikogu and all committee chairs. They also control all committee majorities. The imperative of forming a government compels the factions to collaborate and coalesce, meaning they are constantly working to manage and resolve interfaction political differences to maintain the coalition. The imperative of holding this majority together raises the imperative of maintaining faction discipline, as the potential future rewards of loyalty are compelling. What this means in terms of extra-legislative issues in the legislature is that the Riigikogu leadership is the legislative coalition leadership. It does not span the entire political map as it does in the Duma. The coalition resolves internal political disputes and sets its political agenda at internal meetings of the coalition factions, and these decisions sail through the legislative body because those factions comprise a majority. The conclusion is almost intuitive: questions of internal organizational politics are much more easily resolved by a leadership of like-minded factions than they are by a leadership that spans the entire partisan map.

Similarly, a linked design provides the most comprehensive capacity for conflict management with the executive branch. Chapter 7 elaborates the close links between the legislative majority and the government in Estonia's parliamentary system. The government consults the leaders of the coalition factions on its legislative proposals, including the draft budget, before submitting that legislation for legislative approval. It does so in part to ensure that the strategies and the priorities of the coalition leaders remain consistent and coordinated. On the flip side, it does so to avoid any unpleasant surprises on the floor. Those surprises could potentially arise if government initiatives stray to far from the desires of one or more of its constituent factions. If this were to occur, the coalition could begin to crumble. To keep the coalition stable and viable, its leaders in the government and in the Riigikogu meet regularly to keep legislative priorities, policies, and strategies in tune. Once legislation is submitted to the legislature, the close coordination continues across all Riigikogu committees, each of which is chaired by and has a majority controlled by the same coalition. With the broad sweep of legislative content already agreed to by the coalition leaders, the committees fill in the details in a collegial relationship with government officials on their respective issues.

On extra-legislative issues, the coalition's political leaders dominate. The coalition sets and coordinates its political strategy and goals in its internal meetings, and the leaders in government run that strategy. The legislature plays a purely rhetorical role, with the opposition making speeches denouncing the government and the coalition defending its government and its leaders. Legislative-executive relations on extra-legislative issues are those of coalition negotiation and government implementation. When crisis or scandal causes one or more factions to leave the coalition and to bring down the government, the legislative factions engage in the process of forming a new coalition to form a new legislative majority. The new coalition then takes control of the government, with corresponding changes in personnel, political strategy, and goals.

Of all types of legislative design, a linked, dual-channel design appears to produce the most effective, most comprehensive, and most stable means for managing political conflict. Across all types of conflict in all settings, a linked, dual-channel design has the highest capacity for managing conflict. It imposes the severest constraints and the strongest incentives for individual members to pursue consensus-building and conflict-management strategies.

HOW TO EFFECT LINKAGE

Having established the institutional benefits of including parties and having demonstrated the benefits of linking them to the committees, the obvious questions are how can linkage be created and how can links be improved where they are weak, as in the Duma? It is important to recognize an assumption being made in this exercise, namely, that linkage is beneficial. From the perspective of the institution itself, linkage is beneficial for the greater conflict-management capacity it brings. It is reasonable to question this assumption from a different level of analysis. Is it always desirable to have an internally efficient legislature, or might there may be situations in which legislative designers might deem it desirable to create an unlinked legislature that is unable to legislate efficiently and effectively? I will address this in the final section. From the perspective of the legislature itself, however, linkage is clearly beneficial. So accepting for the moment an objective of improving internal conflict management in the Duma, how can the links between the factions and the committees be strengthened? What general lessons does this study provide for those legislative designers wishing to effect links in new legislatures?

There are several ways to link the partisan and the committee channels of a legislature. These may fairly be grouped into two categories of solutions. The first approaches the matter from the direction of the parties, aiming at creating consistent partisan control of committee formation and personnel and creating a majority within the legislature. In effect, such methods seek to weave the partisan identity through the professional identity of legislators. Options that may be considered include constitutional mechanisms, giving several powers to the Speaker, or limiting access to the leadership of the legislature. The second approaches linkage from the direction of the committees, seeking to better integrate committees both with the partisan organizations and with each other. Options to consider here include allowing committee chairs access to the leadership, giving them a forum of their own, and limiting the number of committees. While these categories and their specific design features are elaborated separately, they are far from being mutually exclusive or incompatible. Indeed, the more that are adopted the stronger and more comprehensive the links, and therefore conflict management, are likely to be.

The most obvious way to create consistent faction majority control over the legislature is indicated by the Estonia case study, which suggests linking the legislative factions to the government as the most effective approach. A parliamentary system requires the factions to cooperate in organizing the legislature. They would have to coalesce into majority and opposition coalitions and to coordinate their legislative and political programs and strategies. As seen in the Estonian case, the imperative of intrafactional discipline would rise dramatically, and there would be fewer instances of agreement among the faction leaders disintegrating on the floor. In the Duma, individual deputies would be more constrained in their internal activities to actually be led by their faction leaders.

The lesson of the comparative institutional theory developed in this book, however, is not that parliamentarism is the solution. First, as the case of Hungary alluded to in earlier chapters suggests, weak linkage may arise even in legislatures in parliamentary systems. Second, and more to the point, parliamentarism would require fundamental constitutional changes, and such changes are not necessary to create an effective legislature. Effective legislatures may be designed within the same type of presidential system that currently exists in Russia. Parliamentary systems are not necessarily better than presidential systems, and their legislatures are not necessarily superior at managing legislative and political conflict. Rather, legislatures in presidential and parliamentary systems may be designed to maximize their capacity to manage conflict, and this can be effected in Russia short of redesigning the constitution. It is true that the Russian Constitution retains a confusing triangular relationship with unclear lines of responsibility between President, government, and legislature. However, evaluation of the desirability of changing that constitution is best left to studies of the executive branch and constitutional design.

In any case, the Duma's difficulties managing conflict in its internal legislative process can only be solved through design changes internal to the legislature. Changes that create links between the factions, between factions and committees, and between the committees would be required to improve the Duma's internal legislative processes. And in this context the more specific lessons of the Estonian case are extremely relevant. Strong linkage brought by a consistent legislative majority throughout the institution has enormous benefits for internal conflict management. The goal of legislative designers, then, and for those who may seek one day to reform the Duma should be to induce the formation of such a majority. In the Duma, having the leadership span all factions, from the Speaker and his deputies to the Duma Soviet to all committee chairs and deputy chairs, with no such thing as a "majority" in the committees or in the legislature generally, is the design feature that pries the channels apart. The culprit preventing formation of a majority is that all faction leaders participate in an auction system for delegating leadership and committee assignments. The general prescriptive lesson lies in a variety of alternatives to this means of forming and appointing members to committees.

The question to answer is, how can a majority be created in a legislature so splintered by tiny partisan factions? There is ample room for creativity in answering this question. What one state chooses might be different from what another chooses, as local conditions are likely to affect the solution preferred. What is important for the legislature is linkage and that a viable answer to that question be found and implemented.

In the Duma, for example, an obvious solution with substantial domestic historical precedent would be to empower the Speaker to appoint committee chairs. A Speaker would presumably select chairs from his or her own and from like-minded factions, producing greater partisan consistency across committee leadership posts. Similarly, the Speaker could be empowered to appoint the deputy speakers to make for a truly consistent partisan leadership. Under such a system, whether one was or was not eligible for a leadership post would depend on one's faction affiliation. Committee and faction identities of the members would be linked throughout the legislature. Such increase in authority would make the election of the Speaker a momentous event. It would require collaboration among like-minded factions to agree on candidates for committee chairs whom the Speaker they support would be committed to appoint. Bargaining among the factions, including negotiations over committee chair posts, would mirror the bargaining among Estonian legislative factions when forming coalitions to produce a government. Just as they negotiate over the allocation of cabinet posts in their proposed coalitions, the factions electing such an empowered Speaker would negotiate over allocation of committee leadership posts. But the change would come as a result of an internal design and rule change, not as a result of a constitutional redesign.

To demonstrate the importance of local conditions and that no particular linkage mechanism may be advanced as universally applicable, one need look no further than Russia itself. Such a scheme was simply unacceptable to virtually the entire Russian political elite in the wake of the experience with Khasbulatov and a long line of criminal legislative chairs before him dating at least to Stalin. But while not viable for Russia, it is important to note that such a system need not produce an all-powerful Speaker. The Speaker in the U.S. House of Representatives enjoys such formal powers; however, the virtual revolving door for occupants of that office over the last decade or so demonstrates that checks on individual Speakers can be substantial. As a general prescriptive option for inducing linkage, it should be comfort to legislative designers wary of investing too much power in the Speaker that the holder of that post faces various constraints in his actions. The various factions pose a constraint, for should the Speaker stray too far for their comfort they could remove that Speaker. Such a mechanism could be explicitly included in the rules. If the coalition of factions that elected the Speaker falls apart, for example, a new coalition could elect a new Speaker, who would reward that coalition by appointing a new set of committee chairs. That is, the legislature could be designed so as to link the Speaker to the committee chairs as a cabinet is linked to a Prime Minister in a parliamentary system. Such a no-confidence option would bring the added benefit of compelling continued cooperation and conflict management among the coalition factions, and the benefits of this linkage could be enjoyed while retaining constraints against the rise of a tyrant. Other creative solutions are possible, but the important point is that endowing the Speaker with such powers would link the partisan and committee channels without necessarily bringing tyranny.

Other design features are available for inducing partisan consistency across leadership posts in a legislature and thereby linking the two channels. For example, it would be possible simply to require that all leadership and committee chair posts be filled by a single faction. The faction leaders would then be forced to work to form a majority coalition and to make the appointments from within that majority coalition. The effect on forcing coalition forming among the factions would be the same and perhaps even more compelling over the long run than the first option described above — more compelling because it would compel the coalescence of factions into larger organizations that could perhaps foster the development of more stable political parties. With the opposition excluded from the leadership, the consequences of belonging to one or another faction would be real. One's position and role would be linked at all levels to one's partisan affiliation.

A third and related linking mechanism focuses on membership in the top legislative leadership. The Duma Soviet includes all faction leaders, as do the legislative leadership bodies in Ukraine and Hungary, as described in chapter 5. This was a strong temptation in the "hyperdemocracy," to invoke M. Steven Fish's terminology, of early postcommunism.[9] With all factions having access to the leadership, the institutional significance of belonging to one faction or another disappears. However, instead of each faction having one vote in the leadership, that leadership could be limited to the majority faction or coalition able to control a majority. The perks of legislative leadership would raise the stakes of forming and maintaining that majority. They would foster the consolidation of a coherent legislative majority and prevent the split-personality condition of the individual legislator by fusing the separate faction and committee identities into a more integrated identity. Factions in a coalition partnership would have to work together, to coordinate their actions, to maintain their control over the legislative leadership. This would occur at the leadership level and at the level of rank-and-file members throughout the legislature. Being a member of one or another faction would then mean something: either access to leadership posts and the privileges of majority status or relegation to opposition status.

In each of these methods of promoting linkage, the increased links would bring immediate benefits to the legislature. First, they would obviate the need for duplication of committees, as the jealous competition between all factions expecting committee chair posts would be removed. The result would be fewer committees with larger memberships. Second, those memberships would more accurately represent on those committees their respective factions. With each faction having greater numbers on each committee, their respective members would be better able to carry their committee's decisions within their factions. Five members would find it much easier to persuade a faction of their committee's decision than would one, as five are more likely to accurately represent that faction's line in the committee than would one. Third, work between the committees would be more coordinated and consistent, for if all committee chairs were from the same faction or coalition of factions they would presumably meet with each other regularly in the meetings of their faction or coalition. Fourth, one might expect that the effort to put together such a majority to elect the leadership would also work to control majorities on the committees as well. Indeed, even this could be made a rule. In all respects, rather than having split identities, one's position would be intricately intertwined with one's partisan affiliation. From the leadership down to the rank-and-file member, the faction identities and committee identities of the members would be linked and complementary rather than autonomous and competing.

Several other design features to foster linkage spring from the perspective of the committees, in addition to those elaborated above that focus on how to integrate the partisan organizations into the legislature. Again, these prescriptions are by no means mutually exclusive. The Duma, for example, could take a lesson from Ukraine and include the committee chairs in the leadership body. In any legislature that adopted one of the options above while still allowing all faction leaders access to the legislative leadership body, to include the committee chairs would in effect weight that leadership in favor of the majority. Again, this would work only in instances where the legislative design had already made all committee chairs representative of the same faction or majority coalition. In the Duma, therefore, this would have to be combined with one or more of the changes already discussed above. Such a design feature would have the politically appealing effect of securing the majority's dominance in the legislative leadership without excluding any factions from that leadership.

However, including committee chairs in the leadership is beneficial in its own right. Even if none of the design features that aim at creating partisan majority were adopted, including committee chairs in the leadership improves links between factions and committees and improves intercommittee ties. First, it ensures the committees a direct and consistent voice in setting the legislative agenda. Their legislative issues do not as easily fall victim to extra-legislative issues of most immediate concern to the faction leaders, and their presence helps prevent bills from coming to the floor that are not ready for action. More generally, it means the committee chairs and the faction leaders sit together in an institutional forum where they discuss, coordinate, and negotiate to build consensus on legislative and procedural issues rather than the current Duma norm of rampant, often debilitating competition and conflict over both.

Perhaps most significant, including committee chairs in the leadership fosters intercommittee coordination. If a partisan coalition controlled all committee chairs, those chairs would presumably meet in coalition leadership meetings. Without such partisan control, including the committee chairs in a leadership or coordinating forum is the only way to bring about cross-committee coordination. Therefore, if no partisan majority exists in a legislature, a separate institutional body for the committee leaders would go a long way toward preventing the chronic confrontation and jealousy that tears at Duma committees. A committee on committees, whether made part of the overall legislative leadership or a separate institutional body, would foster communication between committee chairs and their staffs and prevent duplication and destructive competition. In such a body the various committee leaders would learn of each other's overlapping interests where these occur; and they would arrange joint committee work to collaborate and reach consensual positions rather than pursuing independent, competing positions as is currently the norm in the Duma. This is precisely what including the committee chairs in Ukraine's legislative leadership has done, and it is why Ukraine's legislative committees are better able to cooperate than are the Duma's.

If the leadership is to span all factions, with no institution-wide partisan majority, providing a forum for committee leaders to meet will by definition also be a forum for factions to meet. It is thus an important element in linking factions to committees and to each together. Where a partisan majority is created, such an intercommittee forum enhances the links and ensures cross-committee linkage as well.

Another design feature from the perspective of committees that would improve linkage would be to limit their number. The disadvantages of many committees with overlapping profiles has been alluded to throughout this book, as have the advantages of limiting the number of committees. And as already discussed, creating a stable partisan majority and other means of selecting committee chairs and delegating committee assignments can go a long way toward preventing the proliferation of committees. However, the number and type of committees could also be established in the rules or in the constitution. Ideally, committees would be roughly equal in size with enough members on each to enable significant representation from all factions on each committee. If there are a large number of very small factions, this goal can be further achieved by allowing individual members multiple committee assignments. This latter step can also help foster intercommittee coordination.

Each of these design features would serve, severally and collectively, to strengthen the links between partisan organizations and committees and thus to avoid or minimize the duality of identities for individual legislators currently suffered in unlinked, dual-channel designs such as the Duma. By limiting or removing the incentives for legislators to play the two channels off each other, or to arbitrarily play either the faction or the committee "game," legislative processes would be more stable than in an unlinked design. Consensus building and conflict management could become the norm rather than the exception, and the legislature would better be able to act and to make policy on major decisions as a result.

Such changes could be effected in the Duma to improve links in that legislature. They may be incorporated in part or in whole. There may be degrees of linkage, and any legislature seeking to improve its conflict-management capacity may do so by strengthening linkage in one or more of the ways suggested here. The effects would be similar. In other words, a legislature with some of the features sketched here would be expected to be more effective in its internal conflict management on legislative issues compared to the present-day Duma. Adding still more of these features could be expected to improve those capabilities further. The benefits for conflict management and legislative efficiency will be substantial. However, it is now time to turn to the question of whether one would want to improve those capabilities.

DIFFERENT DESIGNS FOR DIFFERENT PURPOSES

This conclusion has focused on the prescriptive value of comparative institutional theory, and it has suggested means to create strong links between parties and committees with an eye to improving the conflict-management capacity of legislatures. It is perhaps worthwhile to remind ourselves of Packenham's comments cited in the introduction. It may not be wise to be an unconditional cheerleader for strengthening legislatures. The comparative institutional framework advanced here is neutral with regard to this normative question. Its strength is its flexibility to explain variations in the performance of different types of legislatures and to explain how different designs can lead to effective or ineffective institutions. As such it is flexible enough to provide prescriptive lessons to those wishing to create legislatures of weak internal capacity as well as strong. It is best to specify these lessons as well rather than leaving them implied.

In the wake of the violent conflict with the Supreme Soviet, the designers of the new State Duma wanted a legislature more constrained in its internal activities and more pliable in its relations with the executive. They certainly got both in the Russian State Duma, although they "got it right" for the wrong reasons. Neither those designers nor the President for whom they worked paid much heed to institutional design and its effects when considering the future legislature's behavior. This is hardly surprising, for they had no blueprint on how different legislative designs function with which to operate. They believed that a combination of constitutional rules giving the executive more powers and an intended design of few legislative committees would leave the legislature weak. However, constitutional provisions on paper are too frequently ignored, skirted, or changed in a state such as Russia with no history of the rule of law. As for few, large committees, such a design should strengthen rather than weaken the internal capacity of a legislature. From that perspective, the designers were lucky that their efforts in this regard failed.

Be that as it may, the unlinked, dual-channel design they wound up with has built-in structures for partisan political cooperation and conflict management internally and, most important, in relations with the executive branch. On extra-legislative issues in particular, the Duma has a higher capacity for managing conflict with the executive branch. A dual-channel legislature is not able to run uncontrolled against the policy direction of a determined executive. At the same time, an unlinked, dual-channel legislature is largely unable to establish the routine internal legislative processes necessary to be able to take decisive action on legislation. Again, the executive will be in a favored position.

A legislature that finds it difficult to maintain internal order and to institutionalize procedural fluidity may be just the legislature that Russia needs for its social, political, and economic development. Or it may not be.[10] The point is that if one wants a legislature that is consistently negotiating and collaborating with the executive branch while unable to take control of important policy on its own, the unlinked dual-channel design seems to be a compelling design.

Russia has already learned quite painfully that excluding the multitude of partisan orientations from the legislature is highly undesirable. Now, having included them, it would be extremely hard to imagine how they could be excluded again even if it were decided that they ought to be excluded. However, the lessons the Supreme Soviet provides would seem to suggest that that design would only be appropriate to a system in which the legislature itself runs policy, in essence a system in which the legislature is the executive, as in many city governments, for example. However, such a design will not be conducive to consensus building between the legislature and an autonomous executive, and it may be downright destructive to such relations.

Similarly, more or less effective legislatures may be created by lessening or increasing the links between the partisan and the committee channels. The weaker the links, the more the legislature will look like the Duma; the stronger the links, the more it will look like the Estonian Riigikogu in a parliamentary system or the U.S. Congress in a presidential system. The more one wishes a legislature to be an active player in legislative and political processes, the more desirable is strong linkage between the organizational channels. The less one wishes a legislature to have such a capacity, the more compelling would be an unlinked design.

Perhaps most important, these designs need not be permanent. Just as congressional parties have gained more autonomy, even if one believes that Russia is better off with an internally weak Duma today, it is conceivable and indeed hopeful that a future incarnation of political leaders or legal scholars will find themselves in a different sociopolitical environment, one that calls for a more effective Duma. The result can be achieved with internal institutional changes that need not wrack the entire political system, as suggested in the passages above. Those changes would bring a more effective legislature internally without sacrificing or jeopardizing its conflict-management capacity with the executive branch.

Comparative institutionalism certainly does take us beyond an "ability to say something comparative" or merely to note that legislatures "evolve and develop." It recognizes that people design legislatures and make choices in designing them that carry real consequences, both for the performance of that institution of government and for the stability of government more generally. It holds promise both for legislative designers, for guiding them to create appropriate and efficient legislatures, and for scholars wishing to understand and to explain variations in legislative performance within and across states.

NOTES

Introduction

1. I have settled on using the term "legislature" to refer to all elected assemblies, be they in presidential, parliamentary, or mixed political systems. I avoid use of the term "parliament," as it refers to a specific institutional form. While other authors have made good arguments for using other terms like "representative assemblies" and "elected assemblies," I find the gains in precision are outweighed by the increase in convolution.

2. Polsby (1975).

3. Blondel (1973), pp. 2–3. Blondel's sweeping survey contains interesting data on the survival rates of legislatures in dozens of countries across history.

4. See Kornberg and Musolf (1970), p. 28.

5. March and Olsen (1995), pp. 60–61.

6. Ibid.

7. Shugart and Carey (1992), p. 166.

8. Students of legislatures identify "system maintenance" and "conflict resolution" among the functions legislatures perform. See Blondel (1973); Loewenberg (1971); Packenham (1970); Kornberg and Musolf (1970); and Mezey (1979).

9. Although I do not propound a path dependence theory, it nevertheless seems clear that the choices I discuss here do carry long-term consequences for the legislatures and the states more generally. Still, consequences do not mean dependence on an institutional form, for those forms can be changed as evidenced by Russia's elimination of the Supreme Soviet. For a nice elaboration of path dependence theory, see Stark (1992).

10. March and Olsen (1984), p. 738.

11. Shugart and Carey (1992), p. 56.

12. Wilson (1913), p. 78.

13. Peabody and Polsby (1992), p. viii. Among those who focus on committees are Fenno (1966; 1978); Shepsle and Weingast (1984; 1987); Dodd and Oppenheimer (1985); Price (1985); McCubbins and Sullivan (1987); Krehbiel (1991); Krehbiel, Shepsle, and Weingast (1987). See also earlier editions of Peabody and Polsby (1963; 1969; 1992).

14. See Cox and McCubbins (1993), pp. 277–78; also Cox (1987); and Kiewiet and McCubbins (1991).

15. See, for example, Loewenberg (1971); Blondel (1973); Mezey (1979); Olson

and Mezey (1991); and Cox (1987). For a comprehensive review of research on committees and parties in legislatures, see Loewenberg, Patterson, and Jewel, eds. (1985). They, too, clearly recognize the role of both channels in a legislature and attempt to show the symbiotic relationship between the two. However, most of the essays in the volume do treat the two entities as primarily separate — a general symptom, as argued here, of legislative research to date. The divide between those focusing on committees and those focusing on parties goes beyond students of Congress and reflects a division between those who study the British Parliament and/or parliamentary legislatures on the one hand and those who study Congress and/or legislatures in presidential systems on the other. The point implicit in the works of the comparative legislative studies cited here is that both channels must be accounted for in designing legislatures regardless of the type of constitution.

16. The comparative legislative studies literature virtually without exception does not probe beyond this assertion. For two of the most recent volumes that follow this pattern see Olson (1994a); Olson and Mezey (1991).

17. See, for example, Simon (1996); Olson (1994).

18. See Olson (1994a), although in the comparative legislative studies literature one could point to almost any author for such universal statements.

19. See, for example, Krehbiel (1991); Krehbiel, Shepsle, and Weingast (1987).

20. Much of the comparative legislative studies literature takes a large number of committees as sufficient evidence of an active, efficient, institutionalized legislature, taking a flawed leap of faith from the literature on Congress cited above. For two recent examples, see Olson and Norton (1996); and Olson and Mezey (1991).

21. See, for example, Chambers (1963); Cox and McCubbins (1993); Dodd and Oppenheimer (1985); Olson and Mezey (1991); Ostrogorski (1964); Sartori (1976).

22. See, for example, Cox and McCubbins (1993), esp. chap. 5, for a recent discussion of the role of legislative parties in the U.S. Congress.

23. Edward Shils quoted in Putnam (1971).

24. Ibid. However, I would hasten to add that the findings in Putnam's article, that partisanship did not appear to affect attitudes toward compromise in Britain, do not apply to the cases in this study. It is not only how one thinks about politics that is important; the institutions within which one acts and the nature of constraints on action those institutions impose also matter.

25. On the representative role of parties, see Pitkin (1967), pp. 83–84, 219–21.

26. These are some questions implicit in Mezey's call to emphasize the importance of parties and party development for the legislature. See Mezey (1996).

27. Cox and McCubbins (1993), pp. 11–12; Fenno (1966); and Olson and Mezey (1991).

28. See, for example, Polsby (1975); and Olson and Mezey (1991).

29. Loewenberg (1971), p. 13.

30. The best work on the trials and tribulations of fledgling parties in post-Soviet Russia is Moser (1995; 1997). See also Colton (1994); Olson (1994a; 1994b);

Olson and Norton (1996); Norton and Olson (1996); Shevtsova (1993); Dallin (1993).

31. President Yeltsin vociferously and consistently avoided any direct association with any political organization whatsoever from the beginning of his 1991 presidential campaign through his entire first term of office. He maintained that nonpartisan posture to win reelection in 1996.

32. See Sartori (1976), pp. 3–13; Shevtsova (1993); Dallin (1993); and Moser (1995). Perhaps the most vivid example of the point is the faction in the Russian State Duma called "Yabloko," Russian for "apple." The name was coined by Moscow newspapers during the 1993 parliamentary campaigns for the electoral bloc officially called the "Yavlinskiy-Boldyrev-Lukin Bloc." These three leaders didn't even bother to present a facade of a party title, highlighting instead the familiarity of their names. An example of the general antipathy against parties is the acceptance even by members of the Russia's Choice faction of the name "vybros," a fusion of the Russian name "Vybor Rossiiya." *Vybros* means refuse, as in trash.

33. Olson (1994b), pp. 104–105; Reschova and Syllova (1996), p. 100.

34. Ágh (1996), pp. 20–21.

35. Simon (1996), p. 70.

36. Kask (1996), p. 195.

37. Chambers (1963), pp. 45–50. For these reasons, I refer to factions instead of parties. For the purposes of the theoretical framework I develop, however, the two are interchangeable. I should also note that I translate the Russian *fraktsiya* as "faction," never having understood why some in the West continue to insist on "fraction."

38. Polsby (1975). Because of the dominance of committees in the U.S. Congress, many studies have considered the implications of their relative weakness in other legislatures. Fewer studies, however, consider the effects of varying institutional roles for legislative parties, much less to simultaneously consider the implications of the roles of both committees and parties.

39. Although in recent years standing committees have been introduced in the British Parliament, a recent study suggests that they remain tangential to the overall rules and workings of the institution as a whole. Although not a pure arena, the British Parliament still approximates this model more than any other. See Jogerst (1993). Also see Mackintosh (1971); Pollard (1920); and Polsby (1975).

40. See Pfeffer and Salancik (1978), esp. pp. 143–46.

41. Simmel (1950).

42. Evans (1975).

43. Olson and Mezey (1991); Olson and Norton (1996).

44. Hahn (1996a); Remington (1994); Olson (1994a).

45. For a nice discussion of the same point, see Schick (1980), pp. 18–48.

46. White (1995).

47. Caiden and Wildavsky (1980), pp. vii–viii.

48. Blondel (1973); Bryce (1971); Close (1995a); Grumm (1970); Jewell (1970); Loewenberg (1971); Mackintosh (1971); Packenham (1970); Robinson (1970).

49. Mezey (1979); Olson and Mezey (1991); Olson and Norton (1996); Polsby (1975).

50. Blondel (1973); Crick (1970); Kornberg and Musolf (1970); Olson (1994a).

51. Cox (1987); Krehbiel (1991).

52. Norton and Olson (1996).

53. Close (1995b).

54. March and Olsen (1995).

55. Hahn (1996b), p. 5; also Close (1995b), p. 4.

56. Close (1995b), p. 9, holds the former view.

57. Remington (1994a); Mezey (1996).

58. My focus on how institutional design affects individual strategies for behavior is greatly influenced by the work of Thomas Koelble. See Koelble (1991).

59. Hall (1987).

60. A surprising, but vivid and telling example of this property of dual channels of organization may be found in Leach's 1954 study of politics in Highland Burma. He found a single ethnic group that exhibited two very different modes of organization within one contiguous geographic area. Both were unstable, with individuals essentially having a choice of moving back and forth between the two to serve their personal and political ends. When an individual became disillusioned with the one, he could refer to the other. Similarly for legislatures, there are dual channels of parties and committees. With no hierarchy between or links connecting the two, members may demonstrate the same tendency to jump back and forth between these modes of association and to play one off against the other, thereby undermining the internal stability of the legislature as a whole. My chapters on the State Duma demonstrate this effect. I am deeply indebted to Chris Ansell, both for the citation and for his insights into the sometimes paradoxical consequences of what he calls "dual hierarchies."

61. See, for example, the argument of Selznick (1952) applied to the strategies of the Bolsheviks.

62. Evans (1975).

63. March and Olsen (1995).

64. This is because a law on patents, for example, may be adopted and not arise in the legislature again for years, while a law on the budget must be passed every year.

65. Putnam (1993), pp. 58–60.

66. Packenham (1970), pp. 523, 578–79.

67. Mezey (1996), pp. 225–27.

68. The most important works in comparative legislative studies came in a flurry of studies in the 1970s and early 1980s. See, for example, Blondel (1973); Boynton and Kim (1975); Eldridge (1977); Kornberg (1973); Kornberg and Musolf (1970);

Loewenberg (1971); Mezey (1979); Olson and Mezey (1991); Patterson and Wahlke (1972); Smith and Musolf (1979).

69. Several recent volumes on postcommunist legislatures don't even try; their authors are explicitly descriptive and do not try to explain successes and failures in any consistent theoretical fashion. See Remington (1994); Hahn (1996a); Olson and Norton (1996).

70. For a persuasive argument calling for studies such as this one, see Mainwaring (1992).

71. The lack of a consistent framework, by contrast, prevents achieving such answers regardless of how many cases are studied. Recent volumes by Remington (1994); Hahn (1996a); and Olson and Norton (1996) are testimony to that fact, and repeat the limitations of earlier volumes in comparative legislative studies of the 1970s and 1980s.

72. Hahn (1996c), p. 242, is only the most recent to issue such a call.

73. My citations focus on those offering institutionalist arguments. The entire literature on legislatures would make up a bibliography simply too vast to reproduce here.

74. Although their titles and introductory chapters frequently speak of "legislatures," their "theories" are limited to the House. See, for example, Cox and McCubbins (1993); Kiewiet and McCubbins (1991); Krehbiel (1991); McCubbins and Sullivan (1987); Shepsle and Weingast (1984; 1987).

75. See Moe (1990) for one highly persuasive critique of this literature.

76. See Krehbiel (1991); Shepsle and Weingast (1987).

77. See, for example, Krehbiel (1991), pp. 28–29; and Shepsle (1987); for a critique, see Cox and McCubbins (1993).

78. One recent work promises to demonstrate how institutional rules affect "legislative influence" but reneges on that promise, examining instead only the electoral system and constitutional balance with the executive branch, erroneously and inexplicably labeling these indices of "consolidation." Remington (1994a), pp. 12–14.

79. I make no attempt to summarize the differences and debates between the political, economic, and sociological strands of institutionalism. Such reviews are capably provided and widely available in Pfeffer and Salancik (1978); Powell and DiMaggio (1991); Moe (1990); and March and Olsen (1984; 1989).

80. Recent studies on this question are Shugart and Carey (1992); Lijphart (1992).

81. March and Olsen (1984), p. 738.

82. Ibid., pp. 741–42.

83. See Moe (1990; 1991) and Barnett and Carroll (1993), pp. 98–99, who call for such studies.

84. Krehbiel (1991), p. 14. See also Jepperson (1991), p. 153.

85. See Schick (1980; 1990); Ellwood (1985); Wildavsky (1992).

86. Schick (1980; 1990); Wildavsky (1992); Ellwood (1985).

87. Fenno (1966) wrote the classic work on the pre-1974 House appropriations process. Wildavsky (1979) provides a broader view of the overall pre-1974 budget process.

88. Schick (1990); Wildavsky (1992).

89. Schick (1990), pp. 170–80.

90. See Cox and McCubbins (1993); Schick (1990); and Wildavsky (1992).

91. Wildavsky (1992), pp. 229–30. Also Schick (1980; 1990); Ellwood (1985).

92. See Fenno (1966; 1978).

93. Indeed, on several occasions Committee members asked me what time a Committee session was scheduled for, what room it was in, where I got copies of documents they had not yet seen, if I knew what was on the agenda. Fenno suggested his "soaking and poking" was more amenable to research of congressional members in their districts, rather than in Washington. I did not observe Russian deputies in their districts. However, my research was far from limited to formal, strictly timed office interviews. Most of my information was gleaned from continual personal observation, informal discussions over so-called coffee in the *bufety* and casual encounters in the corridors during breaks in committee and plenary session proceedings.

94. Given that the interviews were conducted in my second language and the respondents' first, use of a Dictaphone significantly sped up the interviews. It became less important to get bogged down in the meaning of unfamiliar words, as I could look them up when transcribing the interviews later. Taking notes in Russian would significantly have slowed the process. By pointing out that using the Dictaphone would significantly save time for the respondent and allow for a freer discussion, the respondents became more comfortable with its presence.

95. Fenno (1978), pp. 249–95.

96. In order to protect the anonymity of those who so desired and those who so required, I have necessarily left all interview responses anonymous. Where information comes directly from interviews, they are identified in footnotes simply as "Interviews."

97. Unfortunately, access to the Supreme Soviet archives continues to be extremely difficult, even for current members of the Duma.

98. The database is produced by INDEM (Informatics for Democracy), and I am personally grateful to INDEM for a long and continuing relationship. The database on the Supreme Soviet is incomplete in some key aspects, and I have found the data in it to be somewhat less reliable.

Part 1

1. The conventional wisdom I refer to is expressed in daily Western newspapers such as the *New York Times*, in current events journals such as the various

incarnations of Radio Free Europe/Radio Liberty's *Research Report*, and as espoused by various television news analysts from late 1991 through late 1993, most clearly from late September through the end of 1993 at the culmination of the battle between the Supreme Soviet and the Russian President. These sources largely mirror the standard line in their Russian media counterparts — *Izvestia, Nezavisimaya gazeta, Komsomolskaya pravda*, and Russian television.

2. My discussion of the Supreme Soviet considers the period from the failed 1991 August Coup that marked the end of the USSR and marked the beginning of Russia's existence as an independent state through the October 1993 Uprising that ended with the Supreme Soviet being bombed out of existence. For analysis of the Communist-era Supreme Soviet, the standard is still Vanneman (1977). Although he analyzed the USSR Supreme Soviet, in the Soviet period all the legislatures in the constituent republics, including in Russia, mimicked the operations of the central body.

3. Formally, the Committee on the Budget, Plan, Taxes and Prices.

4. Remington (1994).

5. Hahn (1996b), p. xvii; Clark (1997).

6. The quotations are from Remington (1996), p. 107.

7. Clark (1997) seems misguided in suggesting that these are contradictory goals.

8. Mezey (1996).

Chapter 1

1. Interviews.

2. A curiosity of the Supreme Soviet is that, although it was formally divided into two houses, the Council of the Republic and the Council of Nationalities, the Supreme Soviet was not a bicameral legislature. Indeed, the basis for the division was never even clear to the deputies themselves, and in fact the Supreme Soviet acted as a unicameral legislature in almost all respects. The one exception was the larger Congress of People's Deputies, the formally higher body from which the Supreme Soviet sprang, which was technically responsible for broader constitutional and political matters as discussed later in this and subsequent chapters. Interviews. See also *Byulleten* SZ5.14, November 5, 1992, pp. 4–48; *Byulleten* SR. 6.1, January 13, 1993, pp. 4–18; *Byulleten* SR. 6.7, March 3, 1993, pp. 7–25.

3. Formally, there were commissions of the two councils and committees of the full Supreme Soviet. As I treat the Supreme Soviet as a unicameral legislature, and to avoid unnecessary confusion, I refer to them all as committees.

4. *Byulleten* SZ4.30, January 23, 1992, p. 3. Emphasis added.

5. See, for example, *Byulleten* SZ5.14, November 5, 1992, pp. 46–48.

6. *Byulleten* SR. 6.7, March 3, 1993, pp. 7–25.

7. Sobyanin (1994).

8. Colton (1994), p. 60.

9. In the same volume in which Sobyanin offered his observations and Colton his survey findings, Remington et al. (1994), p. 165, are blinded by these artificial and fundamentally flawed categorizations.

10. Kolomiyets (1994), p. 32. See also Parlamentskiy Tsentr (nd), pp. 10–11. The factions of the Russian legislature and of the USSR Congress of People's Deputies before it formed much as factions formed in the early U.S. Congress as described by Young (1966). Non-Moscow deputies living on the same floor of the Hotel Moskva or eating at the same tables in the cafeteria also tended to sit together at legislative sessions, much as those living in the same boardinghouses and eating at the same dining clubs in early Washington, D.C., did in Congress. The fluidity of the factions in both cases is attributable to the simple fact that roommates and dinner buddies may change or may discover that they have wildly divergent political views.

11. Kolomiyets (1994).

12. Interviews. Unfortunately, neither Kolomiyets (1994) nor Sobyanin (1994), who makes the same point, provide concrete statistics for how many deputies were in more than one faction in the Supreme Soviet. Kolomiyets's estimate of thirty must be an underestimate. My interview evidence suggests that as many as one in four deputies may have had multiple faction affiliations. But it is the fact that this was possible, not the precise figure, that is most telling.

13. See, for example, the Supreme Soviet's own debate on its internal organization at the halfway point of its term, *Byulleten* SZ5.14, November 5, 1992. pp. 4–48. See especially Khasbulatov's comments on pp. 10–17.

14. Olson (1994b), pp. 104–5; and Olson and Norton (1996), pp. 3–4.

15. Hough (1996), p. 99.

16. The initial Regulations allowed deputies to sit on two committees, but this was soon changed in the Law on Committees. See "Reglament Verkhovnogo Soveta RSFSR" (hereafter Supreme Soviet Regulations; and Parlamentskiy Tsentr (nd).

17. Parlamentskiy Tsentr (nd); interviews.

18. Interviews.

19. Fenno (1966), esp. pp. 138–44) filled his study of the House Appropriations Committee with examples of members who came to the committee with no prior experience either in budget work or in the issues of the appropriations subcommittees to which they were assigned. The one major difference, of course, is that few bus drivers and physicists become members of the U.S. Congress. This was not always the case, however, and in this respect, too, Russia's post-Soviet legislatures compare in interesting ways with the first years of the U.S. Congress. Young (1966) discusses the varied backgrounds of the first members of the U.S. Congress.

20. Formally, the committees selected their new chair; the Supreme Soviet ratified the selection. I could find no instances in which the full Supreme Soviet rejected a committee's choice, nor were any former deputies I interviewed aware of such instances.

21. Hough (1996), p. 99, confirms this point.

22. On the old USSR Supreme Soviet, see, for example, Hazard (1980); Fainsod (1963), esp. chaps. 11–12; and Hough and Fainsod (1979), esp. chap. 10.

23. CPD members could still work in committees, although only a handful worked on a full-time basis. Twenty of the Budget Committee's forty-seven members were CPD deputies, but not Supreme Soviet members. Most worked on specific pieces of legislation or issues of particular personal interest to them on a voluntary basis. I was frustrated in my attempts to compile reliable data on exactly who did and who did not work full-time. My estimates are based on data derived from interviews and evidenced throughout the stenographic records.

24. Full-time or part-time, the deputy received his full Supreme Soviet salary. See, for example, *Byulleten* SR4.12, December 4, 1991, pp. 20–27; and *Byulleten* SZ4.72, July 1, 1992, pp. 6–48.

25. *Byulleten* SR6.16, June 23, 1993, pp. 24–32, contains the transcript of the "accounts" of the chairs of several committees. *Byulleten* SR6.15, June 21, 1993, pp. 35–45, contains the "account" of the Budget Committee Chair. Also *Byulleten* SZ6.48, July 8, 1993, pp. 15–16, 26–27, and interviews.

26. Interviews.

27. Actually, there was a first deputy chair and two deputy chairs, the latter being the heads of the two councils.

28. Interviews.

29. Interviews. Except where noted, this discussion is taken from "Supreme Soviet Regulations," chaps. 2 and 4.

30. Interviews.

31. Two chairs explicitly viewed themselves, viewed each other, and were viewed by others as "dictators." This attitude is evident throughout the stenographic record of the entire period.

32. *Byulleten* SZ5.18, November 13, 1992, pp. 14–16. For some of the many exchanges between Deputy G. P. Dorofeyev and Khasbulatov, see *Byulleten* SZ4.18, December 7, 1991, pp. 2–3; *Byulleten* SR4.16, February 5, 1992, pp. 56–64; *Byulleten* SZ5.14, November 5, 1992, pp. 45–47; *Byulleten* SZ6.19, March 24, 1993, pp. 3–16.

33. Supreme Soviet Regulations.

34. Those who call it an "electoral college," however, miss the essence of the Congress altogether. See, for example, Roeder (1994).

35. See Sergeyev and Biryukov (1993), pp. 115–48, for a fascinating discussion of the USSR Congress of People's Deputies. Much, though not all, of what they say is transferable to the Russian Congress of People's Deputies.

36. Kolomiyets (1994), pp. 12–20.

37. Parlamentskiy Tsentr (nd), pp. 1–2.

38. See, for example, Krasnow (1979).

39. Armstrong (1986); White (1985); Tucker (1973); and Inkeles and Bauer (1959).

40. Interviews.

41. Interviews. See also, for example, *Byulleten* SR4.8., November 13, 1991, p. 38.

42. See the accounts of the committees before the Supreme Soviet that took place throughout the spring 1993 session. For example, see *Byulleten* SR6.16, June 23, 1993; *Byulleten* SZ6.41, pt. 2, June 24, 1993. Two committee chairs in interviews revealed the same attitudes regarding professionalism and partisanship:

> In the Supreme Soviet, the committees were formed and worked on a professional basis, and the chair of the committee was elected internally, by the committee membership. This allowed us to concentrate professionals who were able to work seriously.

> Our committee worked professionally. We had a professional attitude. . . . Always, always the authority of the committee, the authority of the professionals, influenced the whole Supreme Soviet.

43. Colton (1994), pp. 68–70.

44. *Rossiya*, September 15–21, 1993, p. 1.

45. *Byulleten*, SZ6.41, pt. 2, June 24, 1993, pp. 46–50.

46. Interviews.

47. *Byulleten* SR6.15, June (n/a), 1993, p. 37.

48. Ibid., pp. 42–43.

49. Interviews.

50. Interviews. It is worth noting that there was certainly wariness of the legislature among government officials. Indeed, this same official claimed he had lobbied hard at the time of the drafting of the Budget Process Law and later of the new constitution for denying the legislature the ability to amend the budget at all. He wanted the legislature only to have the ability to vote on the budget up or down, as received from the government, without the right to budgetary initiatives.

51. Some respondents remember nine or ten full-timers, while others say there were eleven or twelve. My guess, given the answers of different respondents, is that the number varied over time, with ten being the average. Interviews.

52. Interviews; *Byulleten* SZ6.48, July 8, 1993, pp. 26–27. Another one or two committee members worked somewhat less diligently on the budget.

Chapter 2

1. Interviews.

2. Interviews.

3. Interviews. Such comments were present in virtually every news account of and Supreme Soviet debate on the budget between 1991 and 1993 and in the State Duma debates on the 1994 budget.

4. It passed a 1991 budget as well, but the USSR was still in existence, and as such it was a republican budget within the broader Union budget. Budget policy only became significant with the demise of the Soviet Union and Russia's emergence as an independent federal state. The revised budgets were indexations, recalculations of figures to account for the high inflation after price liberalization in January 1992.

5. Interviews. See also the Budget Committee Chair's remarks before the Supreme Soviet, *Byulleten* SR6.15, June (n/a), 1993, p. 35.

6. Krehbiel, Shepsle, and Weingast (1987); Shepsle and Weingast (1987). See also earlier works by Fenno (1966); Wildavsky (1979); Wilson (1913).

7. "Zakon RSFSR Ob osnovakh byudzhetnogo ustroystva i byudzhetnogo protsessa v RSFSR." Hereafter cited as Law on the Budget Process.

8. Law on the Budget Process, arts. 21–22.

9. Law on the Budget Process, arts. 22–23.

10. Law on the Budget Process, arts. 16, 23.

11. Law on the Budget Process; interviews.

12. The right to legislative initiative belonged to: individual deputies; the committees; the Presidium; the Supreme Soviet Chair; the President; the government; the Constitutional, Supreme, and Arbitrational Courts; the General Prosecutor; the republics and regions within the Federation; the cities of Moscow and St. Petersburg; "and also societal organizations active across the whole territory of the Russian Federation." RSFSR Constitution.

13. Supreme Soviet Regulations, arts. 74–82.

14. The others devoted their time to banking, planning, and the other issues under the Committee's purview. Interviews.

15. Different respondents used different terms. Some referred to a "subcommittee," others to "informal professional discussions with government officials," others to "hearings with the government," and others to a "working group" or "conciliation commission." I will refer to it as the Budget Working Group, which is technically speaking the most accurate. The Committee did have subcommittees, including one on the budget, and reconciliation commissions were specifically provided for in the Regulations to work out differences on multiple drafts of laws between various committees and the government. While the terms for the Working Group were different, a piecing together of the stories of participants from a variety of committees and government ministries reveals the picture described in the text. Unless otherwise noted, all information and quotations in this section are from interviews.

16. It is not clear who decided which committees would have a full member on the Working Group. My best guess is that this was uncontroversial, most likely an agreement between the Chair of the Budget Committee and the Finance Ministry representative, tacitly approved by the committee chairs in the Presidium. If one committee were left out and its chair strongly wanted to be represented in the Group, all evidence suggests he would have been granted his request.

17. Interviews.

18. Interviews.

19. See Fenno (1966); Wildavsky (1979).

20. *Byulleten* SZ4.72, July 1, 1992, pp. 6–48.

21. *Byulleten* SZ6.12, February 25, 1993. pp. 16–17. The minimum wage was and remains one of the most contentious issues in the budget, as it is the basis on which all state sector salaries and all pensions are computed.

22. Interviews.

23. Interviews.

24. *Byulleten* SZ4.81, July (n/a) 1992, pp. 24–25.

25. *Byulleten* SZ6.5, January 28, 1993, pp. 11–58.

26. *Byulleten* SZ6.12, February 25, 1993, pp. 6–34; *Byulleten* SZ6.20, March 25, 1993, pp. 16–78; and *Byulleten* SZ6.57, July 22, 1993, pp. 19–23.

27. Interviews.

28. It is possible, indeed I rather suspect, that these appearances were actually before the Budget Working Group and not before a session of the Budget Committee proper. It is simply impossible to determine with certainty which was the case. The evidence of extensive interview data and from the stenographic record refers to the Committee and to the Working Group, often using the two interchangeably. Therein lies the clue. It may have been before the Working Group, because nearly all respondents note the presence of officials from the Finance Ministry and from the sectoral ministries. But such officials would also have been present had the appearances been at Budget Committee sessions. It is understandable why the boundary between Working Group and Budget Committee was blurry for virtually all concerned, including for Budget Committee members themselves. In a sense, the Working Group *was* the Committee when it came to analysis of the budget. I refer here to the Committee, in the interests of (I hope) clarity.

29. Interviews.

30. *Byulleten* SZ6.15, March 6, 1993, pp. 24–30. The reference to hearings is somewhat confusing in this context but relates to the sectoral committees' appearance before the Budget Committee, not the open hearings described above. There was no argument that the latter type of hearings took place.

31. *Byulleten* SZ6.20, March 25, 1993, pp. 16–78. The reference to this committee chair's foreign travel touched a particularly sensitive nerve in the Supreme Soviet, foreign travel being one of the most highly prized perks doled out by and taken advantage of by committee chairs.

32. *Byulleten* SZ6.80, July (n/a), 1992, pp. 15–48.

33. Interviews.

34. Interviews.

35. Interviews. See also the readings of the budgets at plenary sessions in *Byulleten* SZ4.72, July 1, 1992, pp. 6–48; *Byulleten* SZ4.80, July (n/a), 1992, pp. 15–48; *Byulleten* SZ5.27, December 16, 1992, pp. 3–25; *Byulleten* SZ 5.29, December 18,

1992, pp. 35–45; *Byulleten* SZ6.5, January 28, 1993, pp. 11–58; *Byulleten* SZ6.12, February 25, 1993, pp. 6–34; *Byulleten* SZ6.20, March 25, 1993, pp. 16–78; *Byulleten* SZ6.52, July 16, 1993, pp. 39–51; *Byulleten* SZ6.53, July 17, 1993; *Byulleten* SZ6.54, July 19, 1993.

36. I chose to exclude the double votes and repeat votes from my analysis to minimize repetition or exaggeration. I also chose to exclude from the figures votes on the resolutions that accompanied the laws, on which the Committee's recommendations carried almost without exception. The total number of votes was therefore probably closer to 550. If anything, these exclusions mean I actually *underestimate* the Committee's authority.

37. Again, if anything, this understates the Committee's authority. At the outset of voting on amendments, the Committee proposed adoption of blocs of several dozen amendments on which they proposed adoption or rejection. That is, with a single vote over one hundred amendments submitted by the government, other committees, individual deputies, and others were summarily adopted or rejected on the recommendation of the Budget Committee. Such "package votes" I count as a single vote, even though they pertained to several dozen separate amendments each.

38. I include here votes on the ten post-veto amendments submitted by the President.

39. I regret that I failed to code these instances, although I estimate that it breaks down to roughly one-third in opposition to the Committee, two-thirds in support. I searched the records for something different—for instances in which Khasbulatov's position differed from the Committee's and on which Khasbulatov's position won out. As stated in the text, I found not a single such instance on the budget.

40. Remington et al. (1994), pp. 162–63; also see Remington (1996), p. 131.

41. See Fenno (1966); Wildavsky (1979); and Schick (1980).

42. Again, the time period covered is from after the August 1991 Coup through July 1993. For both the Budget Committee and for other committees, I chose bills on which there were at least fifteen votes.

43. Interviews.

44. Pfeffer and Salancik (1978), pp. 143–44.

45. Ibid.

46. See, for example, Price (1985), pp. 162–63.

47. Wildavsky (1979), pp. 47–51; (1992), pp. 101–5.

48. Shepsle and Weingast (1987), pp. 85–87, 100–1.

49. Shepsle and Weingast (1987), p. 938.

50. Krehbiel (1991). See also Fenno (1966); Kingdon (1981).

51. Krehbiel (1991), pp. 80–82, 99.

52. Ibid., p. 78.

53. Ibid., pp. 28–29; Shepsle (1987).

54. *Byulleten* SZ5.14, November 5, 1992, pp. 4–48

55. Interviews.
56. Interviews.

Chapter 3

1. *Rossiya,* April 29, 1993.
2. See, in particular, Remington (1994a; 1996); Remington et al. (1994); and Hahn (1996a).
3. One Russian account of this variety is Shevtsova (1996).
4. Mezey (1996) forcefully makes these points in a concluding chapter of a recent edited volume.
5. One such account focusing on the Supreme Soviet is Hough (1996).
6. See, for example, *New York Times,* September 22-October 4, 1993.
7. *Byulleten* SZ6.53, July 17, 1993; and *Byulleten* SZ6.54, July 19, 1993.
8. Interviews.
9. The notation "RnT" indicates n trillion rubles.
10. *Byulleten* SZ4.80, July (n/a) 1992, pp. 15–48, and pt. 2, pp. 2–24; *Byulleten* SZ4.81, July (n/a) 1992, pp. 24–25.
11. On another two amendments totaling R100 billion, or 0.5 percent of total spending, I could not find an expressed opinion of the government. So the total Supreme Soviet increase over government objections could actually have been equal to 0.6 percent of the total spending side of the budget, still a fairly low figure.
12. *Byulleten* SZ6.20, March 25, 1993, pp. 16–78.
13. Interviews.
14. Interviews.
15. Interviews.
16. Interviews.
17. Pochinok (1992).
18. *Byulleten* SR6.7, March 3, 1993, pp. 7–25.
19. Interviews.
20. *Byulleten* SZ6.45, July 1, 1993, pp. 37–44.
21. *Byulleten* SZ4.80, July (n/a), pp. 15–48, and pt. 2, pp. 2–24.
22. "Zakon O byudzhetnoy sisteme Rossiyskoy Federatsii na 1992 god." Hereafter, Law on the 1992 Budget. The draft debated contained 300 pages, of which fewer than 5 were the budget law; the remainder, explanation. Interviews.
23. *Byulleten* SZ6.5, January 28, 1993, pp. 27–31; "Zakon O respublikanskom byudzhete Rossiyskoy Federatsii na 1993 god." Hereafter, Law on the 1993 Budget.
24. Interviews; *Byulleten* SZ4.31, January 24, 1992, pp. 2–34.
25. For two references to this issue in the stenographic record, see *Byulleten* SZ4.72, July 1, 1992, pp. 6–48; and *Byulleten* SZ4.49, March 27, 1992, pp. 21–48.
26. *Byulleten* SZ5.33, December 25, 1992, pp. 4–12.
27. *Byulleten* SZ6.5, January 28, 1993, pp. 27–31.

28. Interviews.

29. Interviews.

30. Interviews.

31. *Byulleten* SZ6.5, January 28, 1993, pp. 27–31.

32. Interviews.

33. See, for example, *Byulleten* SZ6.12, February 25, 1993, pp. 28–29.

34. See, in particular, Remington (1994a); Remington et al. (1994); and Hahn (1996a).

35. Interviews.

36. See, for example, *Byulleten* SR6.15, June (n/a), 1993, pp. 24–37.

37. See, for example, Remington et al. (1994); Hough (1996); and Shevtsova (1996).

38. *Byulleten* SZ4.1, September 19, 1991.

39. *Byulleten* SZ4.49, March 27, 1992.

40. Interviews.

41. *Byulleten* SZ4.59, May 22, 1992. pp. 10–16, 38–40.

42. Ibid.

43. *Byulleten* SZ4.27, December 27, 1991.

44. Interviews; *Byulleten* SZ4.72, July 1, 1992; *Byulleten* SZ5.24, November 26, 1992; *Byulleten* SZ5.27, December 16, 1992; *Byulleten* SZ5.33, December 25, 1992.

45. Interviews.

46. Remington et al. (1994), p. 177.

47. See the stenographic record of virtually any Supreme Soviet session. Four representative samples are *Byulleten* SZ4.39, March 5, 1992, pp. 1–12; *Byulleten* SZ4.50, April 1, 1992, pp. 1–10; *Byulleten* SZ5.1, September 22, 1992, pp. 1–22; and *Byulleten* SZ6.23, April 2, 1993, pp. 3–10.

48. The citations in the previous note provide evidence for this argument, although such evidence is again to be found in the stenographic record of most sessions.

49. Remington (1996).

50. Interviews.

51. Interviews.

52. Interviews.

53. Interviews. It is interesting to note that this situation is not much different than that for the committees. Since the committees were not created on partisan lines, if the committee chair was confrontational by ideology or nature, he could isolate the committee's work from the executive branch and pursue a confrontational line, as discussed above. Some did precisely that and tended to produce radical legislation, which neither the government nor different-minded deputies had much means of influencing.

54. Interviews.

55. RSFSR Constitution, arts. 87 and 104.

56. See the first and last items in the stenographic record for each seasonal session of the Supreme Soviet. These speeches are also available in Yeltsin and Khasbulatov (1994).

57. *Byulleten* SZ4.73, July 2, 1992, 4–35.

58. *Izvestia*, September 22, 1992.

59. See, for example, *Byulleten* SZ5.14, November 5, 1992, pp. 4–48; *Izvestia*, April 3, 1992; July 8, 1992; June 11, 1992; July 15, 1992; July 16, 1992; July 20, 1992; July 29, 1992; October 22, 1992; December 28, 1992.

60. *Izvestia*, June 2, 1992.

61. Interviews.

62. *Byulleten* SZ4.7, October 11, 1991, p. 41. The Committee on Legislation was responsible for overseeing the constitutionality of bills in the Supreme Soviet, and therefore presumably expert on the constitution itself.

63. *Byulleten* SZ5.5, October 6, 1992, pp. 28–31.

64. Yeltsin and Khasbulatov (1994), pp. 98–99, 126–28.

65. Interviews.

66. *Byulleten* SZ4.51, April 2, 1992, pp. 6–17.

67. *Byulleten* SZ4.4, October 4, 1991, *Byulleten* SZ4.73, July 2, 1992, pp. 4–35. Also *Izvestia*, April 14, 1992; April 15, 1992; *Los Angeles Times*, April 14 and 15, 1992.

68. Interviews.

69. *Rossiya*, April 29, 1993.

70. Kolomiyets (1994), p. 20.

71. Interviews.

72. *New York Times*, December 11, 1992; March 12, 1993.

73. *Byulleten* SZ. 6.58, July 23, 1993, pp. 19–24.

74. Interviews.

75. Remington (1994a; 1996); Remington et al. (1994); Hahn (1996b; 1996c); Shevtsova (1996); Hough (1996).

76. Bach (1996).

77. While Belarus's President Lukashenko turned out to be a ruthless dictator, the writing was on the wall for the Belarus Supreme Soviet even before his election. It is doubtful that legislature could have coexisted with a presidency, for the same reasons as in Russia.

Part 2

1. For a comprehensive account of the campaign and elections for the constitution and the Duma, see Colton and Hough (1998).

2. On the triangular relations, see Huskey (1996; 1999).

Chapter 4

1. Several deputies independently use this term, and it is more than a little humorous that *bardak* literally means "brothel." This eyewitness can confirm that

for the Duma the proper translation is "complete chaos" (although the hotel across the street which houses a large percentage of the deputies is another matter!).

2. Interviews.

3. The Duma elected in 1993 referred to itself as the Fifth Russian State Duma, in recognition of the first four Dumas that sat between Russia's revolutions of 1905 and 1917.

4. Interviews; *Izvestia*, October 11, 1994.

5. See Moser (1995; 1997; 1998a; 1998b).

6. For a comprehensive report on the 1993 campaign and the elections themselves, see Colton and Hough (1998).

7. Moser (1997; 1998a) explains the strange dynamics of party proliferation in the plurality elections.

8. White, Rose and McAllister (1997), p. 135.

9. Moser (1997; 1998b).

10. See also Colton and Hough (1998).

11. The Duma Regulations refers to "factions" as those that formed on the basis of the PR election and to "deputy groups" as groups of deputies that formed later, mostly from among those elected from the territorial districts. The latter had to number thirty-five to gain "registration," and only one formed in time to participate in the allocation of committee chair positions. To avoid confusion, I refer to them all as factions, and the only distinction I make is between those that are registered and those that are not. See *Reglament Gosudarstvennoy Dumy*, art. 28.

12. On the electoral side, see Moser (1997; 1998a; 1998b).

13. Remington and Smith (1996), p. 169.

14. These sessions actually began before the elections, and representatives of all thirteen electoral blocs participated. See *Segodnya*, November 16, 1993; December 2, 1993; and *Izvestia*, December 24, 1993. Comparing the early agreements, as reported by these sources, with the eventual design and rules of the Duma demonstrates that the leaders of the eight factions that gained representation ultimately decided the organizational framework of the new legislature.

15. Although the official title is Chair of the State Duma, I use the titles Chair and Speaker interchangeably to avoid redundancy.

16. See Moser (1998a); also Ostrow (1998b).

17. Interviews.

18. This was true except for those factions elected directly in the PR campaign, whose size was determined by the percentage of the vote that they received plus any independents who happened to join. In the Fifth Duma, four of the original eight had fewer than thirty-five members, and they set the barrier so high precisely to guarantee their own continuing influence.

19. *Nezavisimaya gazeta*, March 19, 1994, and personal observations.

20. Minus committee leadership posts, which were all distributed in the first days of the Duma before the Decembrists had enough members for official recognition.

21. Notes from the joint press conference of Russia's Choice and the December 12 Union, December 7, 1994.

22. Interviews.

23. Interviews.

24. Olson (1994a), p. 124. Also see Olson and Norton (1996).

25. Interviews. Because one can run in both the PR and plurality elections, the dominant strategy was to form a bogus electoral bloc to gain national exposure in the PR campaign, which projected one as a political leader with clout in a local plurality election. See Moser (1996; 1998a).

26. See Moser (1997); Hough (1998).

27. Moser (1998b) offers a nice comparison of postcommunist states in this regard.

28. See the *OMRI Daily Digest* reports for a chronological tracking of the amoebic alignments among the legislators and factions from July through November 1995. Moser (1998b) analyzes the continued weakness of Russia's parties. Hough (1998) describes the "peculiarities" that have inhibited party formation in Russia since 1993. See also Ostrow (1998b).

29. For a similar discussion in the context of the campaign, see Ostrow (1998b).

30. Interviews.

31. Comments of Ivan Rybkin at July 26, 1994, press conference.

32. Interviews.

33. See, for example, Jogerst (1993), p. 113–18, for a restatement of the standard view that adding standing committees makes legislative work a full-time enterprise.

34. This account is based on the author's personal observations. For another description of this process, see Remington and Smith (1996).

35. While this was something of an exaggeration, it demonstrates the point well. See *Segodnya*, January 26, 1994.

36. Interviews.

37. See the excellent reporting on this process in *Segodnya*, January 5, 1994; January 13, 1994; January 18, 1994; *Nezavisimaya gazeta*, January 6, 1994; January 18, 1994; January 20, 1994.

38. See the comparative legislative studies literature, notably Blondel (1973); Mezey (1979); Olson and Mezey (1991), p. 209; Norton and Olson (1996), p. 238. For a similar theme in the literature on Congress, see Krehbiel (1991).

39. Price (1985), pp. 165–70.

40. The Committee on Health Care had eight members, and the Committees on Natural Resources and on Nationalities had ten each. The Budget Committee had forty-three members.

41. Interviews.

42. Interviews.

43. Interviews.

44. The Duma Regulations state that the Chair and deputy chairs may not be from the same faction, a principle that was extended to committee chairs and deputy chairs. *Reglament Gosudarstvennoy Dumy.*

45. Interviews.

46. Jogerst (1993), esp. pp. 90–92.

47. See Wildavsky (1992); and Schick (1990).

48. Interviews.

49. Selznick (1952); Evans (1975); Simmel (1950).

50. Pfeffer and Salancik (1978), esp. pp.144–45. See also Evans (1975).

51. See Simmel (1950); Selznick (1952); and Evans (1975).

52. Pfeffer and Salancik (1978), pp. 144–46, describe in more general terms these various ways of linking dual organizational structures.

53. A rather macabre cover story on the eve of the elections about Russia's eighteen "Speakers" in history served as a warning to the new legislators. The article noted the "many criminals" among the group, from Lukyanov and Khasbulatov to two pre-Revolution Duma Speakers, who were also imprisoned for crimes against the state. *Komsomolskaya pravda*, December 2, 1993.

54. Interviews.

55. Selznick (1952), p. 257.

56. Simmel (1950), pp. 154–62.

57. Interviews.

58. See Simmel (1950), pp. 145–47. Also see Spykman (1925), esp. pp. 97–98, 132–35.

59. Pfeffer and Salancik (1978), p. 144.

60. Evans (1975), pp. 250–55.

61. Pfeffer and Salancik (1978), p. 145.

62. See Remington and Smith (1996) for an account of the inability of the factions of the Fifth Duma to coalesce.

63. *Izvestia*, April 2, 1994.

64. *Byulleten* 5GD N.60, October 27, 1994, pp. 49–50.

65. Cox and McCubbins (1993), p. 160.

66. Ibid., pp. 232, 270.

67. Kiewiet and McCubbins (1991); Cox (1987).

68. For an excellent elaboration of this idea, see Mainwaring (1992).

69. *Konstitutsiya.* Hereafter cited as Russian Constitution.

70. For a thorough account of the design of the Russian executive branch, see Huskey (1996; 1999).

71. Russian Constitution, art. 90. Emphasis added.

72. A wonderful analysis of the situation may be found in an article by Moscow State University law professor Suren Avakyan, published in *Nezavisimaya gazeta*, January 20, 1994. The article is titled "Law or Decree: Which is More Important? A Country May Only Have One Law-Maker."

73. See *Nezavisimaya gazeta*, August 5, 1994, for one article discussing the problems of the nomadic Duma.

74. The Chair was absent at this meeting, and it was only the failure of any Committee member to agree to be the one to notify him of the decision that prevented passage of this decision and the carrying out of what would truly have been a hysterical event.

75. Personal observations and interviews; *Zayavleniye Komiteta po byudzhetu, nalogam, bankam i financam*, May 18, 1994.

76. See, for example, *Izvestia*, October 11, 1994.

77. On the threat of dissolution, see, for example, *Nezavisimaya gazeta*, November 17, 1993; December 23, 1993.

78. *Segodnya*, October 26, 1994.

79. Interviews.

80. PRES press conference, October 28, 1994.

81. Huskey (1996) offers one early attempt to disentangle this puzzle. Also see Ostrow (1999) for a comparison of Russia's legislative and executive dual channels.

82. Interview.

83. Interviews. Unfortunately, the figures that I was able to compile are not reliable enough to warrant reporting. But leaders of all factions agree that while not necessarily the most popular in their own faction, the Budget Committee was most requested for assignment among all Duma deputies.

84. Even the rather suspect practice of counting Russia's Choice, PRES, Yabloko, and Decembrist deputies as a "democratic" camp in the Duma yields only twenty-one members, short of a majority. The consistent oppositionist factions — LDPR, the Communists, the Agrarians, and DPR number eleven.

85. Interviews.

86. Interviews.

87. Tape of Budget Committee session, April 4, 1994.

88. Unfortunately, the position at this closed session of Committee Chair Mikhail Zadornov, a Yabloko member, could not be determined with certainty either from the tape, which expired, or from subsequent interviews. But given the dynamics of the relations between the Chair and the deputy in question, the fact that Zadornov had himself worked on the Supreme Soviet Committee staff, the outcome of the argument, and Zadornov's relations with the Committee staff, it is safe to say that he defended the staff.

89. Threats to dock the pay of members absent from plenary sessions continue, and the Budget Committee distributed an attendance record sheet at one session after repeated failure to gather a quorum prevented the Committee from passing official decisions even on the budget. Personal observations, Budget Committee session, June 6, 1994. The Committee failed on at least two occasions to gather a quorum when discussing the first reading of the 1994 budget, and an embarrassed Committee Chair was compelled to report this to the Duma. See *Byulleten*

5GD N.31, May 11, 1994. For an article on absenteeism, see *Komsomolskaya pravda*, April 21, 1994.

90. Interviews.

91. Interviews.

92. Remington and Smith (1996), pp. 177–78.

93. Ibid.

Chapter 5

1. In 1994 and 1995 these were called the Resolution on the 1994 Budget Process, the Law on the 1995 Budget Process, and the Resolution on the 1995 Budget Process. See *Postanovleniye Gosudarstvennoy Dumy* (1994a; 1994b).

2. For the Duma Budget Committee's explanation, see Komitet GD po Byudzhetu (1994), *Poyasnitelnaya zapiska*.

3. This first reading was fused with the second reading for reasons of time in the rules for the 1994 budget.

4. The 1994 Draft Budget had fifteen such sections: state support for the economy, foreign economic activities, social-cultural activities, basic research and fundamental science, defense, realization of arms reduction treaties, law enforcement and security forces, federal judicial system and prosecutors, state administration, reserve funds, state reserves, warning and response to emergency situations, internal and external debt servicing, financial support to Federation subjects and local governments, and other state spending. From *Proyekt: Zakon Rossiyskoy Federatsii o Federalnom Byudzhete na 1994 God.* Hereafter and in text cited as Draft Law on the 1994 Budget. The 1995 Budget had nineteen sections: state administration; international activities; defense; law enforcement and state security; basic research and fundamental science; industry, energy and construction; agriculture and fishing; environmental protection; transportation; development of market infrastructure; warning and response to emergency situations; education; culture and art; mass media; health care; social policy; debt servicing; state reserves; and other spending. From *Proyekt: Zakon Federalniy Byudzhet Rossiyskoy Federatsii na 1995 God.* Hereafter and in text cited as Draft Law on the 1995 Budget.

5. And, in 1994, no change to the totals for each section were to be permitted either.

6. Interviews.

7. Personal observations, Duma Budget Committee sessions, February 25, 1994; March 21, 1994; March 24, 1994; *Byulleten* 5GD N.20, March 23, 1994; *Nezavisimaya gazeta*, March 22, 1994; March 24, 1994.

8. Caiden and Wildavsky (1980), pp. 115–17.

9. Again, in 1994 the first and second readings were fused — approval of the conception and prognosis and of the basic characteristics were joined in the interests of saving time.

10. See the 1994 and 1995 Budget Process Resolutions, and the 1995 Budget Process Law cited above.

11. Interviews.

12. Interviews.

13. See, for example, Remington and Smith (1996), pp. 182–86.

14. Personal observations and interviews.

15. Personal observations, Budget Committee sessions, May 23, 1994; May 24, 1994.

16. Interviews.

17. Personal observations, Budget Committee sessions, May 23, 1994; May 24, 1994.

18. Interviews.

19. Interviews.

20. Personal observations, Budget Committee sessions, April 27, 1994; May 10, 1994. The Duma's Regulations require half of a committee's members be present for it to have a quorum for decisions.

21. Interviews. The Committee on Economic Policy had on at least one occasion met and voted with only eight of its twenty-three members present.

22. Personal observation, Budget Committee session, July 7, 1994.

23. Personal observations, Budget Committee session, November 22, 1994.

24. Personal observations, Budget Committee session, November 22, 1994.

25. Interviews.

26. *Byulleten* 5GD N.68, November 25, 1994.

27. Interviews.

28. Personal observations, Budget Committee session, November 22, 1994.

29. Interviews.

30. Interviews.

31. Because large hearings take place in the legislative chamber, only those on the list of approved participants may enter.

32. Personal observations and interviews.

33. Fifteen of the twenty-two other committees submitted an evaluation to the Budget Committee by the deadline for the first reading. Personal observations, Budget Committee session, November 22, 1994.

34. *Byulleten* 5GD N.68, November 25, 1994.

35. See Komitet GD po Ekonomicheskoy Politiki (1995a; 1995b). Also see *Delovoy Mir*, June 29, 1994; *Nezavisimaya gazeta*, June 21, 1994. These sources identify only a few of the press conferences and public release of detailed challenges to both the government and the Budget Committee by the Committee on Economic Policy. There were several other such instances by this committee alone in 1994–1995.

36. See *Nezavisimaya gazeta*, December 3, 1994. This article's vicious attack on the secretary to the Budget Committee Chair, however, was entirely unjustified and unfounded.

37. Interviews.
38. Interviews.
39. Krehbiel (1991).
40. Shepsle and Weingast (1984; 1987).
41. Remington (1996), p. 135.
42. Personal observations, Budget Committee session, May 10, 1994.
43. Interviews.
44. See *Nezavisimaya gazeta*, April 16, 1994; and *Segodnya*, April 16, 1994.
45. Interviews. Committee unanimity among those who attended, of course.
46. *Byulleten* 5GD N.35, May 25, 1994.
47. Interviews.
48. In the end, the Committee was unable to even print the table of amendments by May 27, and without the necessary documents the budget this time had to be removed from the agenda anyway. See also *Segodnya*, May 28, 1994.
49. Because the first and second readings had been fused to accelerate the process, the second reading in 1994 corresponded to what is normally the third reading — ratification of the individual articles and line items.
50. *Byulleten* 5GD N.38, June 8, 1994.
51. Personal observations, Duma Plenary Session, June 8, 1994; interviews.
52. *Byulleten* 5GD N.42, June 22, 1994.
53. Interviews.
54. Interviews. See also *Segodnya*, June 9, 1994, and *Nezavisimaya gazeta*, June 9, 1994.
55. Interviews.
56. Interviews.
57. *Byulleten* 5GD N.88, February 22, 1995.
58. Cox and McCubbins (1993); Cox (1987).
59. Kiewiet and McCubbins (1991), pp. 43–44; Cox (1987), pp. 75–79; Cox and McCubbins (1993), pp. 160–61, 270; and Olson and Norton (1996). This is by no means a complete listing — the tendency is virtually universal to legislative and comparative legislative studies.
60. *Byulleten* 5GD N.88, February 22, 1995.
61. See *Byulleten* 5GD N.31, May 11, 1994; *Byulleten.* 5GD N.42, June 22, 1994.
62. *Byulleten* 5GD N.88, February 22, 1995.
63. Interviews.
64. *Byulleten* 5GD N.82, January 25, 1995.
65. Personal observations, Budget Committee session, March 17, 1994.
66. *Byulleten* 5GD N.89, February 24, 1995.
67. Ibid.
68. Dodd and Oppenheimer (1985), pp. 38–39.
69. See Schick (1990; 1980).
70. Schick (1980), esp. pp. 159–60, 174–76.

71. Schick (1980), pp. 189–93.

72. Wildavsky (1992), pp. 241–45.

73. The quotation is from Lindsay (1988), pp. 62–64. See also Dodd and Oppenheimer (1985), pp. 49–51.

74. Budget Committee press conferences, November 25, 1994, and May 27, 1994.

75. *Byulleten* 5GD N.38, June 8, 1994.

76. *Segodnya*, April 2, 1994.

77. See, for example, *Byulleten* 5GD N.38, June 8, 1994; *Byulleten* 5GD N.42, June 22, 1994; *Byulleten* 5GD N.81, January 20, 1995.

78. Interviews.

79. Interviews.

80. Interviews.

81. *Segodnya*, April 2, 1994.

82. *Byulleten* 5GD N.42, June 22, 1994.

83. The first reading was held twice in 1994.

84. See *Byulleten* 5GD N.42, June 22, 1994; *Segodnya*, June 23, 1994; *Nezavisimaya gazeta*, June 23, 1994.

85. Hall (1987).

86. Interviews.

87. Interviews.

88. The data is from a representative sample of 100 deputies. The author thanks Roper Starch Worldwide, Inc., for their kind permission to include this data. The survey was conducted in July 1995. A similar survey in 1996 yielded similar results. A superb if at times cumbersome database compiled by the Moscow-based INDEM organization provides statistical and graphical confirmation of these same results.

89. See Remington and Smith (1996), pp. 177–78. Also Norton and Olson (1996), p. 236.

90. Zhirinovskiy's LDPR had fought hard to allow for such strict internal control over faction members but failed during adoption of the Regulations to carry this provision. PRES at one point removed one of its members from the faction and appealed for this person to be stripped of his committee chair post, claiming that the post belonged to the faction as a result of the initial bargain for leadership posts, and not to the individual deputy. The appeal failed. Personal observations.

91. Because the new electoral law prevented electoral blocs from having an overabundance of members from any one region, several had to drop Moscow-based members from their lists. Among the Moscow deputies Yabloko dropped was Budget Committee Chair Mikhail Zadornov, who was left to fight for a seat from a single-member district in the Far East.

92. *Izvestia*, July 7, 1994.

93. Interviews.

94. See *Byulleten* 5GD N.43, June 24, 1994.

95. "Itogi" news program, NTV, June 26, 1994; and personal observations.

96. *Krasnaya zvezda*, June 7, 1994.

97. Defense Committee press conference, May 19, 1994; interviews. Also *Segodnya*, May 20, 1994.

98. *Byulleten* 5GD N.68, November 25, 1994.

99. *Byulleten* 5GD N.68, November 25, 1994.

100. *Byulleten* 5GD N.68, November 25, 1994.

101. Interviews.

102. See Taylor (1994) for a discussion of the political weakness of the Russian military.

103. *Segodnya*, March 10, 1994; and personal observations, Defense Committee press conference, May 19, 1994.

104. Interviews.

105. *Byulleten* 5GD N.31, May 11, 1994.

106. *Byulleten* 5GD N.68, November 25, 1994.

107. Personal observations, Duma Budget Committee sessions, May 23, 1994; May 24, 1994.

108. Personal observations and interviews.

109. This Russian TV report of February 8, 1994, was quoted in the *Moscow Times*, February 9, 1994. I thank Brian Taylor for this citation.

110. Personal observations and interviews.

111. Interviews.

112. Personal observations, Budget Committee session, July 21, 1994.

113. This analysis is based on interviews with and observations of both of these individuals and their staffs.

114. See *Stenogramma soveshchaniya u Prezidenta Rossiyskoy Federatsii.*

115. Interviews.

116. Interviews

117. *Izvestia*, February 18, 1994.

118. Personal observations.

119. Interviews.

120. Interviews. See also *Segodnya*, July 22, 1994.

121. *Byulleten* 5GD N.47, July 13, 1994.

122. *Byulleten* 5GD N.45, July 7, 1994; *Byulleten* 5GD N.48, July 14, 1994; *Byulleten* 5GD N.51, July 21, 1994; *Izvestia*, July 15, 1994; *Segodnya*, July 22, 1994; July 29, 1994; August 2, 1994.

123. *Byulleten* 5GD N.43, June 24, 1994.

124. *Byulleten* 5GD N.59, October 26, 1994.

125. Personal observations, Duma plenary session, December 9, 1994.

126. *Byulleten* 5GD N.63, November 10, 1994.

127. *Stenogramma soveshchaniya u Prezidenta.*

128. Both of the Supreme Soviet's Chairs, Boris Yeltsin and Ruslan Khasbulatov

after him, endured multiple failed votes in their struggle to be elected. Indeed, Khasbulatov for a long period was "acting" Chair because a majority of votes could not be found to elect him. See *Delovoy Mir,* May 20, 1994.

129. *Segodnya,* January 5, 1994, and January 26, 1994.

130. Press conference of Duma Speaker Ivan P. Rybkin, July 26, 1994.

131. Interviews. Also *Izvestia,* February 18, 1994; *Nezavisimaya gazeta,* February 18, 1994; *Segodnya,* April 28, 1994; and *Nezavisimaya gazeta,* April 28, 1994.

132. Personal observations and interviews.

133. See *Segodnya,* October 6, 1994. Also see *Byulleten* 5GD N.53, October 5, 1994. What I call the "legislative plan" is officially the *Primernaya programma zakonoproyektnoy raboty Gosudarstvennoy Dumy Federalnogo Sobraniya Rossiyskoy Federatsii na # sessiyu # goda.* The "legislative calendar" is the *Kalendar rossmotreniya voprosov Gosudarstvennoy Dumoy v # goda.*

134. Interviews.

135. Interviews.

136. *Izvestia,* April 21, 1994.

137. Interviews

138. On three occasions, twice when sessions immediately closed to mourn the death of a colleague, once at the opening of the fall session, there was no agenda to debate at all. My data come from *Byulleten* 5GD N.17–68, 1994.

139. *Byulleten* 5GD N.54, October 7, 1994.

140. I define a change as an addition of an item to or removal of an item from that day's agenda. Initiatives frequently pass ordering distribution of documents, instructing committees to look into one or another matter, demanding the appearance before the Duma at some point of a member of government, or including an item on an unspecified future agenda. None of these concern the current day's agenda and could easily have been raised in the Duma Soviet rather than wasting the legislature's time.

141. See virtually any issue of the stenographic record for wasted time on the agenda debate. These come from *Byulleten* 5GD N.66, November 18, 1994; and *Byulleten* 5GD N.68, November 25, 1994.

142. *Byulleten* 5GD N.60, October 27, 1994.

143. *Trud,* May 11, 1994.

144. Interviews.

145. See *Byulleten* 5GD N.51, July 21, 1994; Tumanov (1994), pp. 28–29.

146. RTV television show at the end of the Duma's first session, interviews with Duma leaders, July 22, 1994.

147. Press conference, Duma Speaker Ivan P. Rybkin, July 26, 1994.

148. Personal observations. Also, press conference, Duma Speaker Ivan P. Rybkin, October 5, 1994.

149. *Finansovyye Izvestiya,* January 13–19, 1994.

150. The barbs thrown back and forth between Russia's Choice and the Decembrists on the one hand and Zhirinovskiy's LDPR on the other are evidenced in

almost the entire stenographic record of the first Duma's plenary sessions. The quotations come from press conferences all three held on December 7, 1994.

151. Pfeffer and Salancik (1978), pp. 144–46.

152. Ágh (1996); and Soltesz (1995).

153. Ukraine changed its electoral system to mirror Russia's in 1998.

154. See Bach (1996).

155. Ibid., pp. 32–35.

156. Interviews.

157. *RFE/RL Newsline*, vol. 2, no. 221, pt. 2. November 16, 1998.

Chapter 6

1. See Hall (1987).

2. Remington (1996), p. 135.

3. See Huskey (1998), p. 68, and chap. 6.

4. This is even more true of the Sixth Duma, as the 1995 elections allowed those who were banned from the 1993 elections to compete. Among them were a number of ultra-nationalist and neo-fascist groups some of whom were responsible for the October 1993 violence.

5. Quotations are from the Minister of Finance, *Byulleten* 5GD N.31, May 11, 1994; and *Byulleten* 5GD N.42, June 22, 1994.

6. Caiden and Wildavsky (1980), pp. 116–17.

7. Interviews.

8. *Byulleten* 5GD N.25, April 15, 1994; *Rossiyskiye Vesti*, June 1, 1994.

9. Personal observations, Budget Committee session, May 23, 1994.

10. Interviews.

11. *Perechen materiyalov k proyektu federalnogo byudzheta na 1995 god* (1994); *Svodnoye zaklyucheniye komitetov Gosudarstvennoy Dumy* (1994). The programs were ratified in art. 19 of the final 1995 Budget.

12. Caiden and Wildavsky (1980), p. 102.

13. Personal observations, Budget Committee session, March 21, 1994.

14. Interviews.

15. Personal observations, Budget Committee session, April 4, 1994. The government document, *Izmeneniye v osnovnyye pokazateli . . .* , April 26, 1994, also mentioned the government's presentation of this material.

16. *Spravka O vnesenii Pravitelstvom RF izmeneniye i dopolneniye. . . .* That the breakdowns were not provided in the revised draft was made clear on May 10, 1994, at the Budget Committee session. As far as I am aware, the information was never provided even informally after this date.

17. Interviews.

18. *Prognoz dokhodov i raskhodov federalnogo byudzheta na 1995 god . . .* , November 4, 1994.

19. Personal observations, Budget Committee session, April 4, 1994.

20. Art. 15 in the Draft 1994 Budget, in which all spending items are listed.

21. *Finansovaya izvestiya*, April 21, 1994.

22. Interviews.

23. Personal observations and interviews.

24. *Byulleten* 5GD N.68, November 25, 1994.

25. Interviews.

26. Press conference, Ivan P. Rybkin, July 26, 1994.

27. *Rossiyskiye vesti*, June 1, 1994.

28. Personal observations, Budget Committee session, April 4, 1994.

29. Personal observations, Budget Committee session, November 22, 1994. See also *Byulleten* 5GD N.68, November 25, 1994.

30. Budget Committee press conference, November 25, 1994.

31. I was unable to determine just how many government representatives were included.

32. See *Resheniye Komiteta po byudzhetu, nalogam, bankam i finansam* (1994).

33. Personal observations.

34. Interviews.

35. *Utochneniya v proyekt federalnogo Zakona "O federalnom byudzhete na 1995 god"...*, January 9, 1995 (1995).

36. Interviews.

37. The figures come, respectively, from the Draft Law on the 1994 Budget, Draft Law on the 1995 Budget, and Law on the 1995 Budget.

38. See *Byulleten 5GD N.31*, May 11, 1994.

39. See *Utochneniya v proyekt federalnogo Zakona "O federalnom byudzhete na 1995 god"...*, January 9, 1995. Also *Byulleten* 5GD. N.81, January 20, 1995; and *Byulleten* 5GD N.82, January 25, 1995.

40. Interviews.

41. Caiden and Wildavsky (1980), pp. 114–17.

42. Interviews.

43. Personal observations, Budget Committee session, May 23, 1994; and interviews.

44. *Byulleten* 5GD. N.38, June 8, 1994.

45. Personal observations, Budget Committee press conference on the 1995 Federal Budget, November 25, 1994.

46. Personal observations, Budget Committee hearings on the 1995 Draft Budget, November 17, 1994. See also the comments of the Committee Chair in *Byulleten* 5GD N.68, November 25, 1994.

47. *Byulleten* 5GD. N.81, January 20, 1995.

48. See *Byulleten* 5GD N.82, January 25, 1995.

49. See *Segodnya*, May 17, 1994; *Izvestia*, November 18, 1994.

50. *Byulleten* 5GD N.68, November 25, 1994.

51. Huskey (1998), pp. 270–78.

52. *Izvestia,* January 14, 1994.

53. These quotations are from personal notes of plenary sessions between February 1994 and June 1994. Again, they may be found in any session's stenographic record.

54. See *Byulleten* 5GD N.45, July 7, 1994.

55. See *Nezavisimaya gazeta,* July 8, 1994; *Segodnya,* July 8, 1994.

56. *Segodnya,* August 2, 1994.

57. Huskey (1998), p. 281.

58. Budget Committee press conference, March 18, 1994.

59. State Duma document SGD/71, January 26, 1994.

60. State Duma document ISKh N.71, March 15, 1994.

61. *Sovmestnoye zayavleniye* (1994).

62. Interviews.

63. *Byulleten* 5GD N.25, April 15, 1994.

64. See *Byulleten* 5GD N.31, May 11, 1994, for the Finance Minister's continued acceptance of the September deadline.

65. Personal observations, Budget Committee session, July 7, 1994.

66. Personal observations, Budget Committee session, July 11, 1994.

67. *Byulleten* 5GD N.50, July 20, 1994.

68. The override vote was October 12, 1994. See *Byulleten* 5GD N.55. The budget was submitted October 27, 1994.

69. Interviews with Budget Committee members and Finance Ministry representatives alike suggest that had there been no veto, the budget could have been ready the first week of October. See *Segodnya,* October 11, 1994, for the idea that the Finance Ministry was simply trying to gain time. Oddly enough, the report in this issue ignored an article in the same newspaper from September 16, 1994, confirming my own interpretation of the events.

70. See *Kommersant Dayly.* September 6, 1995.

71. See State Duma document SGD/71, January 26, 1994, and *Rekomendatsii prinyatyye na parlamentskikh slushaniyakh (1994).*

72. Personal observations, Budget Committee session, April 4, 1994.

73. Ibid.

74. Interviews.

75. Personal observations, Budget Committee session, April 4, 1994.

76. *Spravka o vnesenii Pravitelstvom* (1994).

77. Personal observations, Budget Committee session, October 6, 1994.

78. *Byulleten* 5GD N.55, October 12, 1994.

79. I am not aware of a consolidated budget having been provided in 1995 or of any further Committee demands for one. If the Duma ever received this "after the fact" consolidated budget for 1995, it did so well after the federal budget had been adopted.

80. *Byulleten* 5GD N.31, May 11, 1994.

81. Personal observations.

82. Interviews.

83. Interviews.

84. Personal observations, Budget Committee session, November 22, 1994.

85. *Proyekt Postanovleniye Gosudarstvennoy Dumy* (1995). Also Gosudarstvennaya Duma, KN1.1–516. (1995).

86. Interviews.

87. Interviews.

88. Interviews.

89. Huskey (1998), pp. 270–71.

90. Interviews and personal observations.

91. Interviews.

92. See Huskey (1998); *New York Times*, April 24, 1998.

93. See *RFE/RL Newsline*, February 21–25, 1994.

94. The order to not implement the amnesty led to the General Prosecutor's resignation, for in spite of the political controversy the decision aroused, it was nevertheless an entirely legal decision. That is, the Duma had clear, unambiguous authority to issue the amnesty.

95. Although not regularly scheduled, beginning in March 1994, the President each week met with a different faction head. These gradually tapered down to every other week. But the point is that the President met regularly with the faction heads.

96. *Segodnya*, May 25, 1994. Two weeks later, he added the Chair of the Federation Council.

97. See "O polnomochnykh predstaviteliyakh Prezidenta RF v palatakh Federalnogo Sobraniya RF," *Sobraniye zakonodatelstva*, No. 11 (1996), St. 1034.

98. *Izvestia*, February 11, 1994.

99. *Stenogramma soveshchaniya u Prezidenta (1994)*.

100. Interviews.

101. *Izvestia*, May 12, 1994.

102. *Byulleten* 5GD N.33, May 18, 1994; *Izvestia*, May 12, 1994.

103. *Dogovor ob Obshchestvennom Soglasii* (1994).

104. *Nezavisimaya gazeta*, April 21, 1994; April 22, 1994; April 27, 1994; *Izvestia*, April 23, 1994; *Segodnya*, April 21, 1994; April 22, 1994; April 27, 1994; April 29, 1994.

105. *Nezavisimaya gazeta*, April 29, 1994; *Segodnya*, April 29, 1994. The leaders of the Communist, Agrarian, and Yabloko factions were the three who did not sign. According to these reports, the Agrarians had little reason not to sign, as all of their demands had been met. The leaders of the Communist Party and Yabloko, Gennadiy Zyuganov and Grigoriy Yavlinskiy, respectively, abstained purely owing to their personal presidential ambitions, which they saw as precluding them from sharing any public forum with President Yeltsin.

106. *Dogovor ob Obshchestvennom Soglasii* (1994).

107. *Byulleten* 5GD N.66, November 18, 1994.

108. Personal observations, Budget Committee sessions, May 10, 1994, and November 22, 1994. Also *Segodnya*, May 12, 1994; *Nezavisimaya gazeta*, July 26, 1994; July 27, 1994.

109. See Lijphart (1992), p. 19.

110. Mainwaring (1992), pp. 113–14.

111. On October 27, 1994, the vote failed by some two dozen votes. No confidence passed on July 21, 1995.

112. See arts. 111 and 117.

113. Interviews.

114. Lijphart (1992); Mainwaring (1992).

Chapter 7

1. *Financial Times*, July 13, 1993.

2. A brief initial Soviet occupation of the Baltic States in 1940 was soon displaced by the Nazi occupation of 1941–44.

3. Radio Liberty Archive Document FF0123, May 19, 1992. Also see the article by Budget Committee MP Heido Vitsur in *Postimees*, June 4, 1994.

4. The interwar period of the Estonian Republic was only briefly democratic, quickly succumbing to dictatorship under the regime of President Pats and his 1932 Constitution.

5. Lijphart (1996a; 1997b); Linz (1992a; 1992b).

6. The Estonian President is elected by the legislature, guaranteeing he will be of the same party or coalition as the legislative majority.

7. For an overview of Estonia's constitution and the battles over its provisions, as well as a description of the modified d'Hondt electoral system for the legislature, see *RFE/RL Research Report*, November 20, 1992, pp. 6–11; Pettai (1993).

8. See Olson and Norton (1996) for a recent survey on the lack of party systems in the region.

9. Later, two independent deputies joined the coalition.

10. See *RFE/RL Research Report*, November 20, 1992, pp. 6–11. Unlike Westminster systems, although the government emerges from the legislature, government members do not retain seats in the legislature. An alternate from their party fills the seat if and until the minister resigns or is removed from office, at which point he or she reclaims the legislative seat. See *Baltic Observer*, November 12, 1992; *Republic of Estonia Constitution*, art. 64.

11. *Eesti Ringvaade Internet Edition*, April 9–15, 1995; *Estonia Today*, April 12, 1995.

12. See Lijphart (1992); Linz (1992a; 1992b).

13. For recent expressions of this assumption, see Kiewiet and McCubbins (1991); Cox and McCubbins (1993).

14. The quotations are from Cox and McCubbins (1993), pp. 189, 270.

15. See the *RFE/RL Newsline*, vol. 2, no. 37, February 24, 1998.

16. Kask (1996).

17. Olson and Norton (1996).

18. See Moser (1998b); and Hough (1998).

19. *Baltic Observer.* June 23–29, 1994; July 7–13, 1994.

20. Ibid., September 15–21, 1994.

21. Ágh (1996).

22. Ibid.

23. Interviews.

24. *Law on the Riigikogu By-Laws*, chap. 2.

25. Interviews. See also *Estonia Today*, June 5, 1995; *Law on the Riigikogu By-Laws*, November 23, 1993.

26. The ten Estonian standing committees are Finance (formerly Budget and Taxation), Economics, Constitutional Law, Foreign Affairs, Defense, Cultural Affairs, Social Affairs, Rural Affairs and Agriculture, Environment, and Legal Affairs (formerly Civil Rights).

27. Interviews.

28. For an account of the travails of the new committees in the world's oldest parliament, see Jogerst (1993). His account of the British Parliament echoes the findings in the earlier comparative legislative studies literature. See, for example, Loewenberg (1971); Mezey (1979); or Olson and Mezey (1991).

29. Interviews.

30. Personal observations and interviews.

31. Polsby (1975); also see, for example, Robinson (1970); Mackintosh (1971).

32. Interviews.

33. Cox (1987); Linz (1992a; 1992b).

34. *Estonia Today*, April 12, 1995.

35. *Baltic Observer,* October 20–26, 1994.

36. Ibid.

37. Interviews.

38. Interviews. See also *RFE/RL Daily Report*, no. 112, June 15, 1994.

39. Interviews. *Baltic Independent*, September 9–15, 1994; *Baltic Observer,* September 15–21, 1994; September 29-October 5, 1994.

40. Estonian Ministry of Foreign Affairs, press release, no. 95.10.11, October 11, 1995; no. 95.10.17, October 17, 1995; *Eesti Ringvaade Internet Edition*, October 22–28, 1995.

41. The Estonian legislature sits in three-week cycles, separated by a week for work in districts and parties.

42. Personal observations, September 12 and October 24, 1994; and *Law on the Riigikogu By-Laws*, chap. 13.

43. See, for example, *Hommikuleht*, November 15, 1993. Also *Pravda*, November 17, 1993; and *Nezavisimaya Gazeta*, November 16, 1993.

44. Ágh (1996).

45. "Zakon o gosudarstvennom byudzhete." Hereafter and in text cited as Law on the Estonian Budget (1993). This is Estonia's budget process law.

46. Interviews.

47. Interviews.

48. Interviews.

49. Interviews.

50. Interviews. See also the remarks of the Finance Ministry representative in the stenographic record of the first debate on the 1995 Budget, October 12, 1994. While the Estonian legislature does not publish its stenographic record, printouts are available from the Riigikogu archives on request.

51. Interviews.

52. Interviews.

53. Interviews.

54. Cox (1987); Linz (1992a; 1992b).

55. Interviews.

56. Interviews.

57. Interviews.

58. Interviews.

59. *Baltic Observer,* July 9, 1993.

60. Interviews.

61. Wildavsky (1992), p. 34.

62. Interviews.

63. Interviews.

64. Interviews.

65. Interviews.

66. Interviews.

67. Stenographic record, November 10, 1993.

68. Interviews.

69. Institute of Economics (1994); and interviews.

70. Interviews.

71. Interviews.

72. Interviews.

73. Interviews.

74. Institute of Economics (1994).

75. Law on the 1994 Estonian Budget.

76. 1995 Estonian Budget, translated for the author by Tarvo Tamm; and interviews.

77. Interviews.

78. Interviews.

79. Interviews.

80. Interviews.

81. Interviews.

82. Interviews.

83. Interviews.

84. Interviews.

85. Interviews.

86. See, for example, the stenographic record of the second reading of the 1994 Budget, November 10, 1993.

87. Interviews.

88. See Law on the Estonian Budget (1993), art. 43; and the stenographic record of June 8, 1994.

89. Interviews.

90. Interviews.

91. Interviews.

92. Polsby (1974).

93. Quoted in Lijphart (1992), p. 68.

94. Cox (1987); Jogerst (1993).

95. Interviews.

96. Interviews.

97. Interviews.

98. Interviews.

99. Interviews.

100. *Republic of Estonia Constitution*, art. 104.

101. Law on the Estonian Budget (1993), arts. 16–19.

102. Interviews.

103. Jogerst (1993), p. 139.

104. See, in particular, the stenographic record of November 8, 1994, the second reading of the 1995 Budget.

105. Interviews.

106. Interviews.

107. Interviews.

108. Jogerst (1993), pp. 44–45.

109. Interviews.

110. Interviews.

111. Stenographic notes of October 21, 1993, first reading of the 1994 Budget.

112. Stenographic notes of November 10, 1993, second reading of the 1994 Budget.

113. Interviews. See also the Budget Committee Chair's comments at the first reading of the 1995 Budget, stenographic notes of October 12, 1994.

114. Interviews.

115. Interviews.

116. Interviews.

117. See Lijphart (1996a); Linz (1992b).

118. Cox and McCubbins (1993), pp. 232–40.

119. All statistics have been compiled from the stenographic records of the budget readings, as cited throughout the chapter. Unfortunately, for the 1994 Budget, I have breakdowns only for the second reading.

120. The factions were even more active on the supplementary budgets, submitting forty of the fifty-two amendments on the Second Supplementary 1994 Budget, for example.

121. Interviews.

122. Interviews.

123. Interviews.

124. Interviews.

125. Interviews.

126. Interviews.

127. Interviews.

128. Interviews.

129. See *Republic of Estonia Constitution.* To the best of my knowledge, through 1995 no issue has been tied to confidence in the government.

130. The conviction has also been expressed on the floor. See, for example, the stenographic record of the second reading of the 1994 Budget, November 19, 1993.

131. Jogerst (1993), p. 35.

132. Personal observations and interviews.

133. Interviews.

134. Interviews.

135. Interviews and stenographic record, readings of the 1994 Budget, October 21, 1993; November 10, 1993; December 8, 1993; December 15, 1993. Also *Hommikuleht,* November 19, 1993.

136. Stenographic record, readings of the 1994 Budget, October 21, 1993; November 10, 1993; and December 8, 1993.

137. Interviews.

138. See the stenographic record, second reading of the 1995 Budget, November 8, 1994.

139. Interviews and stenographic record, readings of the 1995 Budget.

140. See the stenographic record, November 8 and 23, and December 7 and 14, 1994. Interestingly, the 1994 Budget featured nearly identical figures. The budget adopted was smaller, balanced at EEK 5.8 billion. This reflected a EEK 100 million increase, again as a result of changes in the tax revenue situation. A new income tax law had been passed during consideration of the budget, accounting for the additional sum. Eventually, two supplementary budgets hiked the total 1994 Budget to nearly EEK 7 billion. The increases to the base budget were again heavily in the areas of education and culture. See the stenographic records of October 21, 1993, and December 15, 1993, and Law on the 1994 Estonian Budget.

141. Interviews.

142. Interviews.

143. Wildavsky (1992), p. 194.

144. The total of the 1994 supplementary budgets exceeded 25 percent of the total of the base budget. Personal observations and interviews.

145. The sources are, respectively, *Baltic Observer,* February 12, 1993; stenographic record of the Riigikogu session, December 15, 1993; stenographic record of the Riigikogu session, December 14, 1994; and *Eesti Ringvaade Internet Edition,* December 17–23, 1995.

146. Unfortunately, on the main 1994 and 1995 Budgets, I am lacking information on how many amendments were actually voted on. My research assistant counted amendments rejected by the Committee and withdrawn by the initiator as having been rejected. Also, I am lacking data on amendment votes for part of the second and the entire third reading of the 1994 Budget. For these reasons, I have found it necessary to temporarily exclude the data I do have on these votes in the Estonian legislature from the text. However, of the 237 votes I do have information on, the legislature followed 209 recommendations of the Committee, recommendations supported by the government and the coalition. This is a rate of over 88 percent. Interview data and my personal impressions indicate that the complete data on these budget votes would parallel the results reported in the text for the 1994 Supplementary Budget.

147. Interviews.

148. Stenographic record, second reading of the 1995 Budget, November 23, 1994.

149. See Lijphart (1992; 1996a; 1996b); Linz (1992a; 1992b); Riggs (1992); Shugart (1993).

150. Mainwaring (1992), pp. 114–16.

151. Horowitz (1992), pp. 205–6.

152. *Baltic Observer,* July 9, 1993.

153. Jogerst (1993), pp. 113–18.

154. Krehbiel (1991); Shepsle and Weingast (1987).

155. See, for example, Simon (1996).

Conclusion

1. The book is called *Do Institutions Matter?*, edited by Weaver and Rockman (1993).

2. Clark (1997); Remington (1994a); Colton (1994); Olson (1994a); Remington et al. (1994); Sobyanin (1994); Remington (1994b); Hahn (1996a); Shevtsova (1996); Colton (1994); Hough (1996); Remington (1996); Mezey (1996); Hahn (1996b); Olson and Norton (1996); Ágh (1996); Karasimeonov (1996); Simon (1996); Reschova and Syllova (1996); Crowther and Roper (1996); Remington and Smith (1996); Kask (1996); Bach (1996); Norton and Olson (1996); Olson (1994); Ágh and Kurtan (1995); Soltesz (1995); Szarvas (1995).

3. The quotation is from Simon (1996), p. 78, but see the other contributions to the volume edited by Olson and Norton (1996); and volumes edited by Remington (1994); Hahn (1996a); and Ágh and Kurtan (1995).

4. Hahn (1996b), p. 242.

5. Ibid.

6. Mezey (1996), pp. 224, 227.

7. March and Olsen (1995), pp. 60–61.

8. Simmel (1950), pp. 145–47; Pfeffer and Salancik (1978), pp. 144–45. While this study considers dual-channels only, from the perspective of institutional theory it would seem logical that the same conclusion would apply to multichannel institutions, although the more channels that exist the more linkage would begin to take the appearance of a spider web.

9. Fish (1995).

10. On the perceived virtues, or lack thereof, of presidential versus parliamentary systems, see Lijphart (1992) and Diamond and Plattner (1996).

BIBLIOGRAPHY

English-Language Books and Articles

Ágh, Attila (1996). "Democratic Parliamentarism in Hungary: The First Parliament (1990–94) and the Entry of the Second Parliament." In Olson and Norton, eds. (1996).

Ágh, Attila, and Sandor Kurtan, eds. (1995). *Democratization and Europeanization in Hungary: The First Parliament (1990–1994)*. Budapest: Centre for Democracy Studies.

Ansell, Christopher, Keith Darden, and Craig Parsons (1994). "The European Union as Dual Hierarchy: A Network-Theoretic Approach to International Integration." Unpublished manuscript.

Armstrong, John A. (1986). *Ideology, Politics and Government in the Soviet Union*. 4th ed. New York: Praeger.

Bach, Stanley (1996). "From Soviet to Parliament in Ukraine: The Verkhovna Rada during 1992–1994." In Olson and Norton, eds. (1996).

Barnett, William P., and Glenn R. Carroll (1993). "How Institutional Constraints Affected the Organization of Early U.S. Telephony." *Journal of Law, Economics, and Organizations* 9, no. 1: 98–126.

Blondel, Jean (1973). *Comparative Legislatures*. Englewood Cliffs, N.J.: Prentice-Hall.

Boynton, G. R., and Chong Lim Kim, eds. (1975). *Legislative Systems in Developing Countries*. Durham, N.C.: Duke University Press.

Bryce, James (1971). "The Decline of Legislatures." In Loewenberg, ed. (1971).

Caiden, Naomi, and Joseph White, eds. (1995). *Budgeting, Policy, Politics: An Appreciation of Aaron Wildavsky*. New Brunswick, N.J.: Transaction Books.

Caiden, Naomi, and Aaron Wildavsky (1980). *Planning and Budgeting in Poor Countries*. New Brunswick, N.J.: Transaction Books.

Chambers, William Nisbet (1963). *Political Parties in a New Nation*. Oxford: Oxford University Press.

Clark, Terry (1997). "Comparative Politics — Democratization in Russia: The Development of Legislative Institutions." *American Political Science Review* 91, no. 1: 213–14.

Close, David, ed. (1995a). *Legislatures and the New Democracies in Latin America*. Boulder, Colo.: Lynne Rienner.

——— (1995b). "Introduction: Consolidating Democracy in Latin America: What Role for Legislatures?" In Close, ed. (1995a).

Colton, Timothy J. (1994). "Professional Engagement and Role Definition among Post-Soviet Legislators." In Remington, ed. (1994).

Colton, Timothy J., and Jerry F. Hough, eds. (1998). *Growing Pains: Russian Democracy and the Election of 1993*. Washington, D.C.: The Brookings Institution.

Cox, Gary W. (1987). *The Efficient Secret: The Cabinet and the Development of Political Parties in Victorian England*. Cambridge: Cambridge University Press.

Cox, Gary W., and Matthew D. McCubbins (1993). *Legislative Leviathan: Party Government in the House*. Berkeley: University of California Press.

Crick, Bernard (1970). "Parliament in the British Political System." In Kornberg and Musolf, eds. (1970).

Crowther, William, and Steven D. Roper (1996). "A Comparative Analysis of Institutional Development in the Romanian and Moldovan Legislatures." In Olson and Norton, eds. (1996).

Curry, Landon (1990). *The Politics of Fiscal Stress: Organizational Management of Budget Cutbacks*. Berkeley, Calif.: Institute of Governmental Studies Press.

Dallin, Alexander, ed. (1993). *Political Parties in Russia*. Berkeley: University of California, International and Area Studies.

Diamond, Larry, and Marc F. Plattner, eds. (1996). *The Global Resurgence of Democracy*. 2d ed. Baltimore, Md.: Johns Hopkins University Press.

Dodd, Lawrence C., and Bruce I. Oppenheimer, eds. (1985). *Congress Reconsidered*. 3d ed. Washington, D.C.: CQ Press.

Eldridge, Albert F., ed. (1977). *Legislatures in Plural Societies: The Search for Cohesion in National Development*. Durham, N.C.: Duke University Press.

Ellwood, John W. (1985). "The Great Exception: The Congressional Budget Process in an Age of Decentralization." In Dodd and Oppenheimer, eds. (1985).

Evans, Peter (1975). "Multiple Hierarchies and Organizational Control." *Administrative Sciences Quarterly* 20, no. 2: 250–59.

Fainsod, Merle (1963). *How Russia Is Ruled*. Cambridge: Harvard University Press.

Fenno, Richard F., Jr. (1966). *The Power of the Purse: Appropriations Politics in Congress*. Boston: Little, Brown.

———— (1978). *Home Style: House Members in Their Districts*. Boston: Little, Brown.

Fish, M. Steven (1995). *Democracy from Scratch: Opposition and Regime in the New Russian Revolution*. Princeton, N.J.: Princeton University Press.

Grumm, John G. (1970). "Structural Determinants of Legislative Output." In Kornberg and Musolf, eds. (1970).

Hahn, Jeffrey W., ed. (1996a). *Democratization in Russia: The Development of Legislative Institutions*. Armonk, N.Y.: M. E. Sharpe.

———— (1996b). "Analyzing Parliamentary Development in Russia." In Hahn, ed. (1996).

———— (1996c). "Studying the Russian Experience: Lessons for Legislative Studies (and for Russia)." In Hahn, ed. (1996).

Hall, Richard L. (1987). "Participation and Purpose in Committee Decision-Making." *American Political Science Review* 81, no. 1: 105–28.

Hazard, John N. (1980). *The Soviet System of Government.* 5th ed. Chicago: University of Chicago Press.

Horowitz, Donald L. (1992). "Comparing Democratic Systems." In Lijphart, ed. (1992).

Hough, Jerry F. (1996). "The Structure of the Russian Legislature and Its Impact on Party Development." In Hahn, ed. (1996).

———— (1998). "The Failure of Party Formation and the Future of Russian Democracy." In Colton and Hough, eds. (1998).

Hough, Jerry F., and Merle Fainsod (1979). *How the Soviet Union Is Governed.* Cambridge: Harvard University Press.

Huskey, Eugene (1996). "Democracy and Institutional Design in Russia." *Demokratizatiya: The Journal of Post-Soviet Democratization* 4:453–73.

———— (1999). *Presidential Power in Russia.* Armonk, N.Y.: M. E. Sharpe. Forthcoming. (Citations from unpublished manuscript.)

Inkeles, Alex, and Raymond A. Bauer (1959). *The Soviet Citizen: Daily Life in a Totalitarian Society.* Cambridge: Harvard University Press.

Institute of Economics (1994). *Budget Reform in Estonia.* Reform Round Table Working Paper No. 7. Estonian Academy of Science. February.

Jepperson, Ronald L. (1991). "Institutions, Institutional Effects, and Institutionalism." In Powell and DiMaggio (1991).

Jewell, Malcolm E. (1970). "Attitudinal Determinants of Legislative Behavior: The Utility of Role Analysis." In Kornberg and Musolf, eds. (1970).

Jogerst, Michael (1993). *Reform in the House of Commons.* Lexington: University Press of Kentucky.

Karasimeonov, Georgi (1996). "The Legislature in Post-Communist Bulgaria." In Olson and Norton, eds. (1996).

Kask, Peet (1996). "Institutional Development of the Parliament of Estonia." In Olson and Norton, eds. (1996).

Kiewiet, D. Roderick, and Matthew D. McCubbins (1991). *The Logic of Delegation: Congressional Parties and the Appropriations Process.* Chicago: University of Chicago Press.

Kingdon, John W. (1981). *Congressmen's Voting Decisions.* 2d ed. New York: Harper and Row.

Koelble, Thomas A. (1991). *The Left Unraveled: Social Democracy and the New Left Challenge in Britain and West Germany.* Durham, N.C.: Duke University Press.

Kornberg, Allan, ed. (1973). *Legislatures in Comparative Perspective.* New York: David McKay.

Kornberg, Allan, and Lloyd D. Musolf, eds. (1970). *Legislatures in Developmental Perspective.* Durham, N.C.: Duke University Press.

Krasnow, Wadislaw G. (1979). "Richard Pipes's Foreign Strategy: Anti-Soviet or Anti-Russian?" *Russian Review* 38, no. 2: 180–91.

Krehbiel, Keith (1991). *Information and Legislative Organization.* Ann Arbor: University of Michigan Press.

Krehbiel, Keith, Kenneth A. Shepsle, and Barry R. Weingast (1987). "Why Are Congressional Committees Powerful?" *American Political Science Review* 81, no. 3: 929–35.

Law on the Riigikogu By-Laws. Riigikogu Kodukorra. Seadus. *Seadus voeti Riigikogu poolt vastu.* November 23, 1993. Translated by Liis Metusala.

Leach, E. R. (1954). *Political Systems of Highland Burma: A Study of Kachin Social Structure.* Cambridge: Harvard University Press.

Lijphart, Arend, ed. (1992). *Parliamentary versus Presidential Government.* Oxford: Oxford University Press.

——— (1996a). "Constitutional Choices for New Democracies." In Diamond and Plattner, eds. (1996).

——— (1996b). "Double-Checking the Evidence." In Diamond and Plattner, eds. (1996).

Lindsay, James M. (1988). "Congress and the Defense Budget." *Washington Quarterly* 11 (Winter): 57–74.

Linz, Juan J. (1992a). "The Perils of Presidentialism." In Lijphart, ed. (1992).

——— (1992b). "The Virtues of Parliamentarism." In Lijphart, ed. (1992).

Loewenberg, Gerhard, ed. (1971). *Modern Parliaments: Change or Decline?* Chicago: Aldine-Atherton.

Loewenberg, Gerhard, Samuel C. Patterson, and Malcolm E. Jewell, eds. (1985). *Handbook of Legislative Research.* Cambridge: Harvard University Press.

Mackintosh, John P. (1971). "Reform of the House of Commons: The Case for Specialization." In Loewenberg, ed. (1971).

Mainwaring, Scott (1992). "Presidentialism in Latin America." In Lijphart (1992).

March, James G., and Johan P. Olsen (1984). "The New Institutionalism: Organizational Factors in Political Life." *American Political Science Review* 78, no. 3: 734–49.

——— (1989). *Rediscovering Institutions: The Organizational Basis of Politics.* New York: Free Press.

——— (1995). *Democratic Governance.* New York: Free Press.

McCubbins, Matthew D., and Terry Sullivan, eds. (1987). *Congress: Structure and Policy.* Cambridge: Cambridge University Press.

Mezey, Michael L. (1979). *Comparative Legislatures.* Durham, N.C.: Duke University Press.

——— (1996). "Studying Legislatures: Lessons for Comparing the Russian Experience" In Hahn, ed. (1996).

Moe, Terry M. (1990). "Political Institutions: The Neglected Side of the Story." *Journal of Law, Economics, and Organization* 6 (special issue): 213–53.

————. (1991). "Politics and the Theory of Organization." *Journal of Law, Economics, and Organizations* 7, no. 2 (Spring): 106–29.

Moser, Robert G. (1995). "The Emergence of Political Parties in Post-Soviet Russia." Ph.D. diss., University of Wisconsin.

———— (1997). "The Impact of Electoral Systems in Russia." *Post-Soviet Affairs* 13:284–302.

———— (1998a). "Independents and Party Formation: Elite Partisanship as an Intervening Variable in Russian Politics." *Comparative Politics* 31, no. 2 (January): 147–65.

———— (1998b). "Electoral Systems and the Number of Parties in Post-Communist States." Paper presented at the Annual Meeting of the American Political Science Association. *World Politics*, forthcoming.

North, Douglass C. (1990). *Institutions, Institutional Change, and Economic Performance.* New York: Cambridge University Press.

Norton, Philip, and David M. Olson (1996). "Parliaments in Adolescence." In Olson and Norton, eds. (1996).

Olson, David M. (1994a). *Democratic Legislative Institutions: A Comparative View.* Armonk, N.Y.: M. E. Sharpe.

———— (1994b). "The Sundered State: Federalism and Parliament in Czechoslovakia." In Remington, ed. (1994).

Olson, David M., and Michael L. Mezey (1991). *Legislatures in the Policy Process: The Dilemmas of Economic Policy.* Cambridge: Cambridge University Press.

Olson, David M., and Philip Norton, eds. (1996). *The New Parliaments of Central and Eastern Europe.* London: Frank Cass.

Olson, David M., and Philip Norton, eds. (1996). "Legislatures in Democratic Transition." In Olson and Norton, eds (1996).

Ostrogorski, Mosei. (1964). *Democracy and the Organization of Political Parties.* Ed. Seymour Martin Lipset. Chicago: Quadrangle Books.

Ostrow, Joel M. (1996). "Institutional Design and Legislative Behavior: The Russian Supreme Soviet—A Well-Oiled Machine, Out of Control." *Communist and Post-Communist Studies* 29, no. 4: 413–33.

———— (1998a). "Procedural Breakdown and Deadlock in the Russian State Duma: The Problems of an Unlinked Dual-Channel Institutional Design." *Europe-Asia Studies* 50, no. 5: 793–816.

———— (1998b). "The Press and the Campaign: Comprehensive but Fragmented Coverage." In Colton and Hough, eds. (1998).

———— (1999). "How Institutions Impede Rational Budgeting: Unlinked Dual-Channels in Russia." *Journal of Public Budgeting and Financial Management.* Forthcoming.

Packenham, Robert A. (1970). "Legislatures and Political Development." In Kornberg and Musolf (1970).

Patterson, Samuel C., and John C. Wahlke, eds. (1972). *Comparative Legislative Behavior: Frontiers of Research.* New York: John Wiley & Sons.

Peabody, Robert L., and Nelson W. Polsby, eds. (1992). *New Perspectives on the House of Representatives.* 4th ed. Baltimore, Md.: Johns Hopkins University Press.

Pettai, Vello A. (1993). "Estonia: Old Maps and New Roads." *Journal of Democracy* 4, no. 1: 117–25.

Pfeffer, Jeffrey, and Gerald R. Salancik (1978). *The External Control of Organizations: A Resource Dependence Perspective.* New York: Harper & Row.

Pitkin, Hanna Fenichel (1967). *The Concept of Representation.* Berkeley: University of California Press.

Pollard, A. F. (1920). *The Evolution of Parliament.* London: Longmans, Green.

Polsby, Nelson W. (1975). "Legislatures." In *Handbook of Political Science.* Vol. 5. Ed. Fred I. Greenstein and Nelson W. Polsby. Reading, Mass.: Addison Wesley.

———— (1968). "The Institutionalization of the U.S. House of Representatives." *American Political Science Review* 62, no. 1: 144–68.

Powell, Walter W., and Paul J. DiMaggio, eds. (1991). *The New Institutionalism in Organizational Analysis.* Chicago: University of Chicago Press.

Price, David E. (1985). "Congressional Committees in the Policy Process." In Dodd and Oppenheimer, eds. (1985).

Putnam, Robert D. (1993). *Making Democracy Work: Civic Traditions in Modern Italy.* Princeton, N.J.: Princeton University Press.

———— (1971). "Studying Elite Political Culture: The Case of 'Ideology.' " *American Political Science Review* 65, no. 3: 651–81.

Ray, Larry, ed. (1991). *Formal Sociology: The Sociology of Georg Simmel.* Brookfield, Vt.: Edward Elgar.

Radio Liberty Archives. Document FF0123. May 19, 1992.

Remington, Thomas F., ed. (1994). *Parliaments in Transition: The New Legislative Politics in the Former USSR and Eastern Europe.* Boulder, Colo.: Westview Press.

———— (1994a). "Parliamentary Elections and the Transition from Communism." In Remington, ed. (1994).

———— (1994b). "Conclusion: Partisan Competition and Democratic Stability." In Remington, ed. (1994).

———— (1996). "Ménage à Trois: The End of Soviet Parliamentarism." In Hahn, ed. (1996).

Remington, Thomas F., et al. (1994). "Transitional Institutions and Parliamentary Alignments in Russia: 1990–1993." In Remington, ed. (1994).

Remington, Thomas F., and Steven S. Smith (1996). "The Early Legislative Process in the Russian Federal Assembly." In Olson and Norton, eds. (1996).

Republic of Estonia Constitution (nd). Ministry of Foreign Affairs Unofficial Translation.

Reschova, Janica, and Jindriska Syllova (1996). "The Legislature of the Czech Republic." In Olson and Norton, eds. (1996).

Riggs, Fred W. (1992). "Presidentialism: A Problematic Regime Type." In Lijphart, ed. (1992).

Robinson, James A. (1970). "Staffing the Legislature." In Kornberg and Musolf, eds. (1970).

Roeder, Philip. G. (1994). "Varieties of Post-Soviet Authoritarian Regimes." *Post-Soviet Affairs* 10, no. 1: 61–101.

Sartori, Giovanni (1976). *Parties and Party Systems*. Vol. 1. Cambridge: Cambridge University Press.

Schick, Allen (1980). *Congress and Money: Budgeting, Spending and Taxing*. Washington, D.C.: Urban Institute Press.

——— (1990). *The Capacity to Budget*. Washington, D.C.: Urban Institute Press.

Schurmann, Franz (1966). *Ideology and Organization in Communist China*. Berkeley: University of California Press.

Selznick, Philip (1952). *The Organizational Weapon: A Study of Bolshevik Strategy and Tactics*. New York: McGraw-Hill.

Sergeyev, Viktor, and Nikolai Biryukov (1993). *Russia's Road to Democracy: Parliament, Communism, and Traditional Culture*. London: Edward Elgar.

Shepsle, Kenneth A., and Barry R. Weingast (1984). "When Do Rules of Procedure Matter?" *Journal of Politics* 46, no. 1: 206–21.

——— (1987). "The Institutional Foundations of Committee Power." *American Political Science Review* 81, no. 1: 85–104.

Shevtsova, Lilia (1993). "Political Pluralism in Post-Communist Russia." In Dallin, ed. (1993).

——— (1996). "Parliament and the Political Crisis in Russia, 1991–1993." In Hahn, ed. (1996).

Shugart, Matthew Soberg, and John M. Carey (1992). *Presidents and Assemblies: Constitutional Design and Electoral Dynamics*. New York: Cambridge University Press.

Simmel, Georg (1950). *The Sociology of Georg Simmel*. Edited and translated by Kurt H. Wolf. New York: Free Press.

Simon, Maurice D. (1996). "Institutional Development of Poland's Post-Communist Sejm: A Comparative Analysis." In Olson and Norton, eds. (1996).

Sisson, Richard (1973). "Comparative Legislative Institutionalization: A Theoretical Exploration." In Kornberg, ed. (1973).

Smith, Joel, and Lloyd D. Musolf, eds. (1979). *Legislatures in Development: Dynamics of Change in New and Old States*. Durham, N.C.: Duke University Press.

Sobyanin, Alexander (1994). "Political Cleavages among the Russian Deputies." In Remington, ed. (1994).

Soltesz, Istvan (1995). "The Committee System of the First Parliament: Functioning of the Committees and Their Role in Legislation, 1990–1994." In Ágh and Kurtan, eds. (1995).

Spykman, Nicholas J. (1925). *The Social Theory of Georg Simmel*. Chicago: University of Chicago Press.

Stark, David (1992). "Path Dependency and Privatization Strategies in East-Central Europe." *East European Politics and Societies* 6, no. 1 (Winter): 17–51.

Szarvas, Laszlo (1995). "Personnel and Structural Changes in the First Hungarian Parliament." In Ágh and Kurtan, eds. (1995).

Taylor, Brian D. (1994). "Russian Civil-Military Relations after the October Uprising." *Survival* 36, no. 1 (Spring): 3–29.

Tucker, Robert C. (1973). *Stalin as Revolutionary, 1879–1929: A Study in History and Personality.* New York: W. W. Norton.

Vanneman, Peter (1977). *The Supreme Soviet: Politics and the Legislative Process in the Soviet Political System.* Durham, N.C.: Duke University Press.

Weaver, R. Kent, and Bert A. Rockman, eds. (1993). *Do Institutions Matter? Government Capabilities in the United States and Abroad.* Washington, D.C.: Brookings Institution.

White, Joseph (1995). "(Almost) Nothing New under the Sun: Why the Work of Budgeting Remains Incremental." In Caiden and White, eds. (1995).

White, Stephen (1985). "Soviet Political Culture Reassessed." In *Political Culture in Communist Studies,* ed. Archie Brown. New York: M. E. Sharpe.

White, Stephen, Richard Rose, and Ian Mcallister (1997). *How Russia Votes.* Chatham, NJ: Chatham House.

Wildavsky, Aaron (1979). *The Politics of the Budgetary Process.* 3d ed. Boston: Little, Brown.

———— (1992). *The New Politics of the Budgetary Process.* 2d ed. New York: HarperCollins.

Wilson, Woodrow (1913). *Congressional Government: A Study in American Politics.* New York: Houghton Mifflin.

Young, James Sterling (1966). *The Washington Community, 1800–1828.* New York: Columbia University Press.

Russian-Language Articles, Books, and Documents

Byulleten 5GD N.#. Date. This notation refers to stenographic records of the Fifth Russian State Duma, the issue number, and the date.

Byulleten SN/SR/SZ. #.N This notation refers to the stenographic records of the Russian Supreme Soviet. SN refers to sessions of the Nationalities Council, SR to the Council of the Republic, and SZ to joint sessions. # indicates the session number (fourth, fifth or sixth), while N refers to the issue number for that session. Thus, *"Byulleten* SZ5.5. October 6, 1992" refers to joint session stenographic record number 5 of the fifth session of the Supreme Soviet, which met on October 6, 1992. Dates and page numbers are given where available, which is true for all but a very few.

Dogovor ob Obshchestvennom Soglasii (1994). Rossiyskaya Federatsiya. Moscow: Yuridicheskaya Literatura.

Gosudarstvennaya Duma. SGD/71. January 26, 1994.

Gosudarstvennaya Duma. ISKh N.71. March 15, 1994.

Gosudarstvennaya Duma. KN1.1–516. January 18, 1995.

Izmeneniye v osnovnyye pokazateli proyekta Zakona RF "O federalnom byudzhete na 1994 god." April 26, 1994.

Kolomiyets, V. P. (1994). "Predstavitel'naya vlast' rossii (mezhdu sovetskoy sistemoy i parlamentskoy)." *MIR Rossii,* no. 1: 3–35.

Komitet GD po Byudzhetu, Nalogam, Bankam i Financam (1994). *Poyasnitelnaya zapiska k proyektu postanovleniya Gosudarstvennoy Dumy Federalnogo Sobraniya: O poryadke rassmotreniya i utverzhdeniya zakona "O federalnom byudzhete i vzaimootnosheniyakh s byudzhetami subyektov federatsii v 1994 godu" i kontrole za ego ispolneniyem.*

Komitet GD po Ekonomicheskoy Politiki (1995a). *K rassmotreniyu proyekta federalnogo byudzheta na 1995 god vo vtorom chtenii (analiticheskaya zapiska).* January 17.

——— (1995b). *Zayavleniye o rassmotrenii v Gosudarstvennoy Dume proyekta federalnogo byudzheta 1995 god vo vtorom chtenii.* January 18.

Konstitutsiya (osnovnoy zakon) Rossiyskoy Federatsii — Rossii (1993). Moscow: Izvestia. Cited as RSFSR Constitution.

Konstitutsiya Rossiyskoy Federatsii (1993). Moscow: Yuridicheskaya Literatura. Cited as Russian Constitution.

Law on the Budget Process (1991). "Zakon RSFSR Ob osnovakh byudzhetnogo ustroystva i byudzhetnogo protsessa v RSFSR." *Vedemosti Syezda narodnykh deputatov RSFSR i Verkhovnogo Soveta RSFSR,* no. 46. November 14. Moscow: Verkhovnogo Soveta RSFSR. St. 1543, art. 20.

Law on the 1992 Budget (1992). "Zakon O byudzhetnoy sisteme Rossiyskoy Federatsii na 1992 god." *Vedemosti Syezd narodnykh deputatov Rossiyskoy Federatsii i Verkhovnogo Soveta Rossiyskoy Federatsii.* Moscow: Verkhovniy Sovet Rossiyskoya Federatsiya No. 34. St. 1979.

Law on the 1993 Budget (1993). "Zakon O respublikanskom byudzhete Rossiyskoy Federatsii na 1993 god." *Vedemosti Syezd narodnykh deputatov Rossiskoy Federatsii i Verkhovnogo Soveta Rossiyskoy Federatsii.* Moscow: Verkhovniy Sovet. No. 22. St. 794.

Law on the 1994 Budget (1994). Federalnyy Zakon o Federalnom Byudzhete na 1994 god.

Law on the 1995 Budget (1995). Federalnyy Zakon o Federalnom Byudzhete na 1995 god.

Law on the 1994 Budget Process (1994). Federalnyy Zakon "O proyadke rassmotreniya i utverzhdeniya federalnogo byudzheta na 1994 god."

Law on the 1995 Budget Process (1994). Federalnyy Zakon "O proyadke rassmotreniya i utverzhdeniya federalnogo byudzheta na 1995 god."

Law on the Estonian Budget (1993). "Zakon o gosudarstvennom byudzhete." *Pra-*

vovyye akty Estonii: Perevod s izdaniya "Riigi Teataja." St. 614. No. 36. September, pp. 1203–14.

Law on the 1994 Estonian Budget (1994). "Zakon o gosudarstvennom byudzhete na 1994 god." *Pravovyye akty Estonii: Perevod s izdaniya "Riigi Teataja."* St. 47. No. 12. March 2.

Law on the 1995 Estonian Budget. Riigikogu documents translated for the author by Tarvo Tamm.

Parlamentskiy Tsentr (nd). "Kak Rabotayet Rossiyskiy Parlament." Typescript of the Parliamentary Center of the Russian Congress of People's Deputies.

Perechen materiyalov k proyektu federalnogo byudzheta na 1995 god. November 4, 1994.

Pochinok, A. P. (1992). "Rossiyskiy byudzhet na novom etape (intervyu s predsedatelyem Kommissii Soveta Respubliki VS RF po byudzhetu, planam, nalogam, i tsenam A.P. Pochinkom)." *Financy,* no. 9 (September): 3–10.

Postanovleniye Gosudarstvennoy Dumy Federalnogo Sobraniya Rossiyskoy Federatsii: O poryadke rassmotreniya proyekta federalnogo zakona "O federalnom byudzhete na 1994 god" i ego prinyatiya Gosudarstvennoy Dumoy. (1994a).

Postanovleniye Gosudarstvennoy Dumy Federalnogo Sobraniya Rossiyskoy Federatsii: O poryadke rassmotreniya proyekta federalnogo zakona "O federalnom byudzhete na 1995 god" i ego prinyatiya Gosudarstvennoy Dumoy. (1994b).

Prognoz dokhodov i raskhodov federalnogo byudzheta na 1995 god v pokvartalnom raspredelenii. November 4, 1994.

Proyekt Postanovleniye Gosudarstvennoy Dumy o proyekte federalnogo zakona "O federalnom byudzhete na 1995 god." January 16, 1995.

Proyekt: Zakon Rossiyskoy Federatsii o Federalnom Byudzhete na 1994 God. Cited in text as Draft Law on the 1994 Budget.

Proyekt: Zakon Federalniy Byudzhet Rossiyskoy Federatsii na 1995 God. Cited in text as Draft Law on the 1995 Budget.

Reglament Gosudarstvennoy Dumy Federalnogo Sobraniya—parlamenta Rossiyskoy Federatsii (1994). Moscow: Gosudarstvennaya Duma.

Reglament Verkhovnogo Soveta RSFSR (1990). *Vedomosti Syezda narodnykh deputatov RSFSR i Verkhovnogo Soveta RSFSR.* No. 26. November 29. Moscow: Izdaniye Verkhovnogo Soveta RSFSR. St. 320. Cited in text as Supreme Soviet Regulations.

Rekomendatsii prinyatyye na parlamentskikh slushaniyakh po rassmotreniyu proyekta federalnogo zakona "O federalnom byudzhete na 1994 god." April 5, 1994.

Resheniye Komiteta po byudzhetu, nalogam, bankam i finansam o proyekte federalnogo zakona "O federalnom byudzhete na 1995 god" (nd).

Sovmestnoye zayavleniye komiteta Soveta Federatsii po byudzhetu, finansovomu, valyutnomu i kreditnomu regulirovaniyu, denezhnoy emissii, nalogovoy politike, tamozhennomu regulirovaniyu, i komiteta Gosudarstvennoy Dumy po byudzhetu, nalogom, bankam i finansam. March 17, 1994.

Spravka O vnesenii Pravitelstvom Rossiyskoy Federatsii izmeneniye i dopolneniye v mate-

riyaly k proyektu Federalnogo byudzheta na 1994 god v sootvetstvii s postanovleniyem GD "O federalnom byudzhete na 1994 god" i Svodnym zaklyucheniyem Komitetov GD po federalnomu byudzhetu na 1994 god i proyektu federalnogo zakona "O federalnom byudzhete na 1994 god" (nd).

Stenogramma soveshchaniya u Prezidenta Rossiyskoy Federatsii po vsaimodeystviyu v zakonoproyektnoy deyatelnosti Prezidenta Rossiyskoy Federatsii, Pravitelstva Rossiyskoy Federatsii i Federalnogo Sobraniya Rossiyskoy Federatsii. November 17, 1994.

Svodnoye zaklyucheniye komitetov Gosudarstvennoy Dumy Federalnogo Sobraniya Rossiyskoy Federatsii po prognozu sotsiyalno-ekonomicheskogo razvitiya Rossiyskoy Federatsii na 1995 god i proyektu Federalnogo zakona "O federalnom byudzhete na 1995 god" (1994).

Tumanov, Vladimir. (1994). "'Troyechka' po zakonodatelstvu." *Novoye Vremya*, no. 31 (August).

Utochneniya v proyekt federalnogo Zakona "O federalnom byudzhete na 1995 god" v sootvetstvii s postanovleniyem GDFSRF ot 23.12.94 N.431–1-GD. January 9, 1995.

Yeltsin, B. N., and R. I. Khasbulatov (1994). *Yeltsin — Khasbulatov: Yedinstvo, kompromis, borba.* Moscow: Terra-Terra.

"Zakon o gosudarstvennom byudzhete" (1993). *Pravovyye akty Estonii: Perevod s izdaniya "Riigi Teataja."* St. 614. No. 36. September, pp. 1203–14.

Zayavleniye Komiteta Gosudarstvennoy Dumy po byudzhetu, nalogam, bankam i finansam. May 18, 1994.

English-Language News Sources

Baltic Independent.
Baltic Observer.
Financial Times.
Los Angeles Times.
Moscow Times.
New York Times.
RFE/RL Research Report.
RFE/RL Newsline.
Transitions.

Russian-Language News Sources

Delovoy Mir.
Finansovyye Izvestia.
Izvestia.
Kommersant dayly.
Komsomolskaya pravda.
Krasnaya zvezda.

Nezavisimaya gazeta.
Rossiya.
Rossiyskiye Vesti.
Segodnya.
Trud.

Estonian News Sources

Hommikuleht.
Postimees.

World Wide Web and Internet Resources

Eesti Ringvaade Internet Edition.
Estonia Today.
Estonian Ministry of Foreign Affairs Press Releases.
OMRI Daily Report.
RFE/RL Daily Report.

INDEX

Adviser for Cooperation with the Federal Assembly, 186
agenda debate: in Duma, 9, 154–55; in Supreme Soviet, 84–86
Ágh, Attila, on Hungarian legislature, 157, 199–200, 205
Agrarian faction, in Duma, 103–4, 105, 132, 173, 184, 280n105
Agrarian Party of Russia (APR), 106, 115, 147–48
Agreement on Social Accord, in Duma, 184, 187–88
Agriculture Committee: of Duma, 122; of Supreme Soviet, 50
Albania, 102
APR. *See* Agrarian Party of Russia
Atomic Energy Ministry, 79–80

Bach, Stanley, 91; on Ukrainian legislature, 157
Bagehot, Walter, on British Parliament, 214–15
Belarus, 73, 91–92, 196, 233, 266n77
British Parliament, 237; Bagehot on, 214–15; Jogerst on committees in, 221–22; Westminster model of, 7–8
Budget Committee, 13
of Duma, 93–191; hearings, 125–27
of Riigikogu, 208, 210–25 passim
success rate of, 65–66
of Supreme Soviet, 31–32, 37–39, 42–45, 46–71 passim, 74–80, 82–83, 90; authority of, 56–65; hearings, 53–54
Budget Committee Chair:
of Duma, 114–15. *See also* Zadornov, Mikhail
of Supreme Soviet, 43, 49, 73, 75–80, 90; authority of, 44, 50–51; use of public attacks, 82–83
budget content: in Duma, 160–74; in Supreme Soviet, 74–81

budget process, 10–11, 17–18
in Duma, 118–58 passim
of Supreme Soviet, 48–51, 77; collaboration in, 49–50, 73; sectoral committees and, 52–55
in U.S. Congress, 21–22
Budget Process Law, 260n50
Budget Working Group, of Supreme Soviet, 49–50, 51–52, 76, 78–79, 123, 261nn15, 16, 262n28
Bulgaria, 196

Caiden, Naomi, 120, 162, 171, 173
Central Election Commission, support for Law on Voting Rights, 151
Centre Party, of Estonia, 198
Chechnya, 182
Chernomyrdin, Viktor, 184
Chubais, Anatoliy, 151, 175–76
CIS (Commonwealth of Independent States), 164
Coalition Party, of Estonia, 198
collaboration in budget process, Supreme Soviet, 49–50, 73
Colton, Timothy J., 36, 43, 47
committee assignments: in Duma, 9, 103–4; in Supreme Soviet, 38–39
committee-centered institutional design, of Supreme Soviet, 35–45
committee-centered legislature, defined, 8
Committee on Agriculture, of Duma, 105, 106, 122
Committee on Defense, 79
Committee on Ecology, of Duma, 105
Committee on Economic Policy, of Duma, 105, 131, 151, 173
Committee on Education, of Duma, 121
Committee on Federation Policy, of Duma, 121
Committee on Foreign Affairs: of Duma, 105; of Supreme Soviet, 70

301

Committee on Geopolitics, of Duma, 105
Committee on Industry, 79; of Duma, 121
Committee on Legislation, of Supreme
Soviet, 38, 70, 88
Committee on Legislation and Judicial
Reform, of Duma, 149, 152
Committee on Natural Resources and the
Environment, of Duma, 105, 152
Committee on Property, of Duma, 151
Committee on Science and Education, of
Supreme Soviet, 81
Committee on Science and Technology, of
Duma, 121
Committee on Security, of Duma, 152
Committee on Social Policy, 38, 52, 81,
91, 149
Committee on the Budget, Taxation,
Banking, and Finance. *See* Budget Com-
mittee: of Duma
committees: combined with parties, 17;
coordination between, 68–71; in Duma,
9, 95, 99, 103–7, 111; vs. parties, 4–6,
12; in Riigikogu, 200–201; sectoral, 52–
55; selection of chairs, 38; in Supreme
Soviet, 37–41; in Supreme Soviet, reciprocity between, 50, 51–56, 59, 68; in
Ukrainian Rada, 246–47
Commonwealth of Independent States
(CIS), 164
communication, in Duma, 15–16
Communist Party, 37, 102, 136–37,
280n105; Central Committee, 38, 56;
and Estonia, 196
Communist Party of the Russian Federation, 106
comparative institutionalism, 19–23, 80–
81, 197
conciliation commissions, in Duma, 124–
25, 174–75
conflict management, 11–19, 15; in Duma,
153–56, 160–77 passim, 187, 190; linkage and, 195–228 passim; in Riigikogu,
202–15 passim; in Supreme Soviet, 47,
68, 81–90
confrontation, on Duma floor, 129
Congressional Budget Act (U.S., 1974), 22
Congress of People's Deputies (CPD), 84,
86, 89, 257n2, 258n10, 259n23; role in
elections, 41
consensus building: between committees,
51–52; in Duma, 177–89; in Riigikogu,

199, 202–25 passim; in Supreme Soviet,
in budget process, 47, 49–52, 72, 76–91,
95, 123
Consultative Council, of Duma, 175
coordination, intercommittee, Supreme
Soviet, 68–71
Cox, Gary W., 130, 134, 135, 203, 208,
215
CPD. *See* Congress of People's Deputies
Criminal Code, 66
Czech Republic, 7

deadlock: in Duma, 96, 118–58 passim; in
Supreme Soviet, 44–45, 47, 86, 87, 90, 91
December 12 Union. *See* Decembrists
Decembrists, 101–2, 106
Decree No. 1400, 31, 74
defense budget, in Duma, 164–66
Defense Committee: of Duma, 131; of
Supreme Soviet, 50
democracy, requirements of, 2–3
Democratic Party of Russia (DPR), 105,
106, 176
deputies, Duma, lack of constraints on, 135
deputies, Supreme Soviet: committees
and, 37–38, 91; factions and, 35–36; as
full-time positions, 38–39, 80
DPR. *See* Democratic Party of Russia
dual-channel institutions: creating links,
108–11, 232, 237–48; defined, 8–10;
linked, 8–10, 16–17, 197–202;
unlinked, 8–10, 99–117, 190–92
dual-channel legislatures, 233–37, 254n60;
defined, 8–10; evaluation of Duma's,
156–58
Duma, 2, 3, 93–191 passim, 249–50;
authority of, 112, 159–60; author's
access to, 23–24; budget content in,
160–74; budget process in, 118–58 passim; committees in, 95, 99, 103–7, 111;
conciliation commissions in, 124–25,
174–75; conflict management in, 153–
56, 160–77, 187, 190; consensus building in, 177–89; Consultative Council,
175; deadlock in, 118–58 passim; defense budget in, 164–66; Defense vs.
Agriculture, 144–48; evaluation of, 156–
58; independent deputies, 101; institutional design of, 96–97, 99–117 passim;
intercommittee relations in, 125, 127–
29; lack of linkage in, 125–29; legislative

design of, 9, 15–16; privatization in, 173, 175–76; procedural breakdown in, 118–58 passim; professionalism of deputies, 116–17; proportional representation in, 100; sectoral committees in, 125–26; veto override in, 179; Water Code debates in, 151–52. *See also* Budget Committee: of Duma; factions: in Duma; *and names of individual committees*

Duma Chair, constrained authority of, 108–9, 243–44

Duma Regulations, 118, 123, 134; and agenda debate, 154–55; "factions" under, 267n11; passage of, 153; violation of, 131–32

Duma Soviet, 100–101; and committee assignments, 103–4; interfaction coordination in, 153–54; as linking mechanism, 110, 180, 183; Speaker, 101, 103, 109, 130, 166, 183, 185

Economics Ministry, 79
electoral design, 100
Ellwood, John W., 23
ENIP (Estonian National Independence Party), 198
Estonia, 7, 16–17, 193–228 passim; Riigikogu (*see* Riigikogu); Supreme Soviet of, 218
Estonian National Independence Party (ENIP), 198
Estonian Riigikogu. *See* Riigikogu
European Union, 195
Evans, Peter, 108, 110

factions, 7, 12, 13, 232–37; coordination in Duma Soviet, 153–54; in Duma, 9, 95, 96, 99–103, 107, 111; linkage with committees, 108–11, 197–200, 237–48; in Riigikogu, 197–98, 200–201, 207–8, 219–21; in Supreme Soviet, 35–37, 73
Fenno, Richard F., Jr., 4, 23–24, 65; and House Appropriations Committee, 38, 139, 258n19
Finnish Ministry of Finance, advice from, 211
Foreign Counter-Intelligence Service, 152

Gaidar, Yegor, 143, 144
GKI. *See* State Property Commission
Glazyev, Sergey, 173

Hahn, Jeffrey W., 230
Hall, Richard L., 14, 141
Horowitz, Donald L., 226–27
Hough, Jerry F., 37, 47, 102
Hungary, 6, 196; legislature of, 157, 199–200, 238–39, 242
Huskey, Eugene, 159–60, 188; on conciliation commissions, 174–75

ideological purity, vs. technical expertise, 6–7
independence, of Duma deputies, 101
institutional design: conclusions on, 229–50 passim; of Duma, 99–117 passim; as independent variable, 4–10; nonpartisan, 35–37; of Riigikogu, 197–202; of Supreme Soviet, 35–45 passim
intercommittee relations: in Duma, 125, 127–29; in Riigikogu, 218; in Supreme Soviet, 50–56, 59
Isamaa (Estonia), 198

Jogerst, Michael, 215, 217, 218; on committees in British Parliament, 221–22, 227

Kallas, Siim, 203
Kask, Peet, 199
Khasbulatov, Ruslan, 39, 56, 57, 73, 108–9, 235, 236; freed from prison, 185; violation of rules by, 40–41, 64–65, 82, 83–90 passim
Kiewiet, D. Roderick, 135
Kiriyenko, Sergei, 184
Krehbiel, Keith, 47, 69, 129, 130, 227

Laar, Mart, 198, 225; and financial scandal, 204
Land Law, 66; drafts of, 151
Law on Budget Classifications, 78–79
Law on Fighting Organized Crime, debate in Duma, 152
Law on Indexation of Pensions, 149
Law on Military Service, 66
Law on the 1995 Budget Process, of Duma, 162–63, 179, 181
Law on the Bank of Estonia, 223
Law on the Budget Process: of Duma, 118; of Supreme Soviet, 48, 49, 119; violation of, 168
Law on the Estonian Budget, 206, 221, 226

Law on the Status of Deputies, 186
Law on Voting Rights, 151
LDPR. *See* Liberal-Democratic Party of
    Russia
"legislature," 251n1
Liberal-Democratic Party of Russia
    (LDPR), 105, 106, 143, 152, 156, 176,
    274n90
Liberal-Democratic Union of December
    12, 106
Lijphart, Arend, 188, 189, 196, 198, 226
linkage: benefits of, 108, 180, 237–41;
    conflict management and, 195–228 pas-
    sim; of factions, 108–11; lack of, in
    Duma, 125–29; mechanisms for effect-
    ing, 241–48; in Riigikogu, 197–202; in
    Ukraine's Supreme Rada, 158
Linz, Juan J., 196, 198, 208, 226
List of Federal Programs, in Duma, 162
Loewenberg, Gerhard, 7
logrolling, 65, 69

Mainwaring, Scott, 188, 189, 226
March, James G., 17
McCubbins, Matthew D., 134, 135
Mezey, Michael L., 33, 230
Ministry of Agriculture, of Supreme
    Soviet, 78–79
Ministry of Internal Affairs, of Duma, 152
Moderate faction (Estonia), 198
Moser, Robert G., 100, 102

New Regional Policy, 106
1991 August Coup, 82, 185, 257n2
nonpartisan institutional design, in
    Supreme Soviet, 8, 35–37, 69–71, 232–
    37
Norton, Philip, 199

"October Events," 32
Olsen, Johan P., 17
Olson, David M., 102, 135, 199, 230

Packenham, Robert A., 19, 248
"parliament," 251n1
"Parliamentary Guard," 86
parties: benefits of inclusion, 232–37;
    combined with committees, 17; vs. com-
    mittees, 4–6, 12
partisan factions. *See* factions
partisan legislature, defined, 7–8

Party of Russian Unity and Accord, 106
Pfeffer, Jeffrey, 110, 157
Pipes, Richard, 42
Pochinok, Aleksander, 40, 49, 76, 163, 184
Poland, 6, 102
polarization, in Supreme Soviet, 72–73, 83
political factions. *See* factions
Polsby, Nelson W., 2, 7, 201, 214
pork-barrel politics, 65
PRES, 106, 274n90
Presidium: as committee of committees,
    51–52; of CPD, 41; role of, 39–40; of
    Supreme Soviet, 35, 48, 50, 51, 70, 84–
    92 passim; violation of rules by, 40
Price, David E., 104
privatization, in Duma, 173, 175–76, 182
procedural breakdown, in Duma, 96–97,
    118–58 passim
professionalism: defined, 6–7, 42–43; of
    Duma deputies, 116–17; in Supreme
    Soviet, 38–39, 42–45, 68
proportional representation (PR): in
    Duma elections, 100, 102; in Ukrainian
    elections, 157–58
Putnam, Robert D., 6, 18

reciprocity, in Supreme Soviet, 50, 51–56,
    59, 68
Remington, Thomas F., 47, 83, 117, 121,
    130; on Duma factions, 100; on Khas-
    bulatov's power, 85
Resolution on the Examination and
    Ratification of the 1994 Budget, 133
Riggs, Fred W., 226
Riigikogu, 3, 193–228 passim, 239–40,
    250; author's access to, 25; Budget Com-
    mittee of, 208, 210–25 passim; budget
    implementation, 213–15; conflict man-
    agement in, 202–15 passim; consensus
    building in, 199, 202–25 passim; con-
    trasted with Duma, 9, 26; formal budget
    process, 216; institutional design of, 16–
    17, 197–202; Speaker, 200, 208, 227. *See
    also* factions: in Riigikogu
Rules Committee, of Supreme Soviet, 40
Russian Constitution, 112
Russian State Duma. *See* Duma
Russian Supreme Soviet. *See* Supreme
    Soviet
Russia's Choice, 106, 115, 144, 176,
    253n32

Rutskoi, Aleksandr, 185
Rybkin, Ivan, 109

Salancik, Gerald R., 110, 157
Schick, Allen, 22, 23, 65, 107
sectoral committees: and budget process, 52–55; in Duma, 125–26
Security Ministry, 79
Seleznev, Gennadiy, 109
Selznick, Philip, 108, 109
Shepsle, Kenneth A., 47, 69, 129–30, 227
Shugart, Matthew, 226
Simmel, Georg, 8, 109–10; on "dyads," 108, 232
single-channel legislatures: defined, 7–8; Supreme Soviet as, 35–41
Smith, Steven S., 100, 117, 121
Sobyanin, Alexander, 36
"Social Relief of the Population," 86
Soltesz, Istvan, on Hungarian legislature, 157
Soviet Union, 37; demise of, 3; pre-*perestroika*, 38
State Duma. *See* Duma
State Property Commission (GKI), 151, 175–76, 184
State Security Committee (KGB), and Estonia, 196
Supreme Soviet, 29–92 passim; author's access to, 24–25; budget process, 48–51; committees in, 37–41; compared to U.S. Congress, 69–70; conflict management in, 47, 68, 81–90; demise of, 2–3, 31–32, 72, 80–91, 95; division of, 257n2; of Estonia, 218; factions in, 35–37; institutional design of, 8, 15, 31, 35–45; Presidium, 35, 39–40, 84–92 passim, 91, 261n16; reciprocity in, 50, 51–56, 59, 68; Regulations, 40, 48–49, 89; similarities of Duma to, 95. *See also* Budget Committee: of Supreme Soviet; Budget Committee Chair: of Supreme Soviet; Budget Working Group; *and names of individual committees*
Supreme Soviet Chair, 32; absence of constraints on, 73, 74; and CPD, 41; violation of rules by, 40–41, 56–57, 82, 83–92 passim
Sweden, 211

Tax Service, of Duma, 184
technical expertise, vs. ideological purity, 6–7
Transportation Committee, of Supreme Soviet, 52

Ukraine, 73, 233; Supreme Rada, 91–92, 157–58, 231, 238, 246–47
Union of Soviet Socialist Republics. *See* Soviet Union
U.S. Congress, 4, 20, 22, 107, 237, 250, 258nn10, 19; breakdown in, 137; budget process in, 21–22; committee members in, 38; resources of, 201; role of committees in, 233–34; Supreme Soviet compared to, 69–70
U.S. House of Representatives, 20, 22, 47; Appropriations Committee, 4, 38, 139, 258n19; Speaker, 244
USSR. *See* Soviet Union

Vahi, Tiit, 198, 204
value-added tax (VAT), 172
veto override, in Duma, 179

Water Code debates, in Duma, 151–52
Weingast, Barry R., 47, 129–30, 227
Westminster model, 7–8, 218
Wildavsky, Aaron, 23, 65, 69, 107, 120, 137, 162, 171, 173, 209; and House Appropriations Committee, 139
Wilson, Woodrow, 4
Women of Russia, 106
World Trade Organization, 195

Yabloko, 104–5, 106, 115, 116, 144, 176, 280n105; and Law on Voting Rights, 152; origin of name, 253n32; Zadornov dropped from, 143, 274n91
Yavlinskiy, Grigoriy, 144, 280n105
Yeltsin, Boris, 2, 184–85, 236, 280n105; Decree No. 1400, 31, 74; Khasbulatov and, 89

Zadornov, Mikhail, 130, 138–39, 143, 171, 182, 184, 270n88; dropped from Yabloko, 143, 274n91
Zaveryukha, Aleksander Kh., 147
Zhirinovskiy, Vladimir, 156, 274n90
Zyuganov, Gennadiy, 280n105

OTHER BOOKS IN THE SERIES

Citizens as Legislators: Direct Democracy in the United States
Shaun Bowler, Todd Donovan, and Caroline J. Tolbert, eds.

Party Discipline and Parliamentary Government
Shaun Bowler, David M. Farrell, and Richard S. Katz, eds.

Cheap Seats: The Democratic Party's Advantage in U.S. House Elections
James E. Campbell

Coalition Government, Subnational Style: Multiparty Politics in Europe's Regional Parliaments
William M. Downs

Beyond Westminster and Congress: The Nordic Experience
Peter Esaiasson and Knut Heidar, eds.

Parliamentary Representation: The Case of the Norwegian Storting
Donald R. Matthews and Henry Valen

Creating Parliamentary Government: The Transition to Democracy in Bulgaria
Albert P. Melone

Senates: Bicameralism in the Contemporary World
Samuel C. Patterson and Anthony Mughan, eds.

Politics, Parties, and Parliaments: Political Change in Norway
William R. Shaffer

DATE DUE